Dan Smyer Yü
Mindscaping the Landscape of Tibet

Religion and Society

Edited by
Gustavo Benavides, Kocku von Stuckrad and
Winnifred Fallers Sullivan

Volume 60

Dan Smyer Yü

Mindscaping the Landscape of Tibet

—

Place, Memorability, Ecoaesthetics

DE GRUYTER

ISBN 978-1-61451-562-3
e-ISBN (PDF) 978-1-61451-423-7
e-ISBN (EPUB) 978-1-61451-980-5
ISSN 1437-5370

Library of Congress Cataloging-in-Publication Data
A CIP catalog record for this book has been applied for at the Library of Congress.

Bibliographic information published by the Deutsche Nationalbibliothek
The Deutsche Nationalbibliothek lists this publication on the Deutsche Nationalbibliografie;
detailed bibliographic data are available on the Internet at http://dnb.dnb.de.

© 2015 Walter de Gruyter, Inc., Boston/Berlin
Printing and binding: CPI books GmbH, Leck
♾ Printed on acid-free paper
Printed in Germany

www.degruyter.com

To my father, a dreamer of a better tomorrow
With love, always

Acknowledgements

This book would merely be expecting completion in the "indefinite future" without the unsurpassed dedication and systemic support to social scientific research from the New Millennium Scholar Fund of Minzu University of China, the Max Planck Institute for the Study of Religious and Ethnic Diversity, and the Center for Tibetan Studies at Yunnan Minzu University. Therefore I would like to give my foremost thankfulness to these globally engaged institutions for making my research possible for the book. Their kind support recurrently convinces me that doing social scientific work in the twenty-first century is an orb-weaving process for the ever-widening global web of interdisciplinary scholarship and collaborative sharing of wisdoms and resources.

For the ethnographic research and the writing up of this book, I am deeply indebted to the support from many friends and colleagues in the fields of modern Tibetan studies, China studies, anthropology, geography, religion and ecology, development studies, and film studies. Among them I would like to express my profound gratitude to Joseph Adler, Martin Baumann, Nancy Chen, Philip Clart, Ding Hong, Banbal Dorje, Georgina Drew, John Grim, Ashok Gurung, Gasang Gyal, Chris Hann, Mette Halskov Hansen, Hu Xiaojiang, Jin Ze, Liu Mingxin, David MacMahan, James Miller, David Palmer, Qi Jinyu, James Robson, Geoffrey Samuel, Sara Shneiderman, Tsering Shakya, Axel Schneider, Shen Weirong, Deborah Sommer, Su Faxiang, Ronpa Tashi, Bron Taylor, Tsering Thar, Mark Turin, Tu Weiming, Mary Evelyn Tucker, Peter van der Veer, Cameron David Warner, Robert Weller, Wu Yinghui, Fenggang Yang, Yang Shengmin, Emily Yeh, Zhang Haiyang, Li Zhang, and Zheng Xiaoyun. There have been too many occasions to recount, during which I receive invaluable comments, suggestions, and innovative theoretical perspectives from these marvelous minds of social sciences and humanities. In particular, Mary Evelyn Tucker and John Grim's opening talk "Environmental Ethics for a Chinese Context" at Religious Diversity and Ecological Sustainability in China Book Workshop in 2012 afforded me an astronautic appreciation of the Planet Earth on which all life forms and their habitats are ethically bound to each other for mutual flourishing; Bron Taylor's keynote speech "What is Nature?" at the 2011 annual meeting of International Society for the Study of Religion, Nature and Culture at Vatican Ethnological Museum prompted me to rethink the meanings of eco-hapticity and eco-aesthetics. "Everyday Religion and Sustainable Environments in the Himalaya Conference" organized by Ashok Gurung and Georgina Drew at The New School for Social Research in March 2013 inspired me to sustain a global perspective in my book.

I extend my heartfelt thanks also to Dan Olds, Director of Asia Pacific Program of Council on International Educational Exchange (CIEE), for lending resources to my designing and leading field-based, cross-institutional courses and U.S. faculty seminars on religion, ecology, and identity. The integration of teaching and field research activities proved to be innovatively successful for both students and faculty members as well as contributed to ethnographic data for the chapters on non-Tibetans' affective bond with the Tibetan landscape.

As always, I am indebted to Tibetan communities in both rural Tibet and urban China for every success in my anthropological career. I feel exceptionally fortunate to have sustained our bonds over the last decade. It is they who always illuminate the path of my anthropological work for the study of religion, ecology, and sentient flourishing in both regional and global contexts. At the mid-point of my writing in summer 2012, I was privileged to spend two days with Khenpo Sodargye of Sertar Buddhist Academy discussing how potency of Tibet manifests itself globally. He, as a Tibetan leading public intellectual in China, is truly an embodiment of Tibet as a power place. From his global vision I see the inseparability of landscape and mindscape, and the oneness of everything within the same sentient enclosure of Planet Earth. I am also extremely fortunate that my visual ethnographic research of Tibetan mountain/mountain deities is often nurtured by the luminaries of New Tibetan Cinema – a community of Tibetan indie filmmakers such as Pema Tseden, Sonthar Gyal, Dukar Tserang, Tserang Dondrub, Sangye Gyatso, Tsewang Norbu, Dekyid, Pema Tashi, Hwador Gyal, Zom kyid Drolma, Gensang Drolma, and Angchu Bem. I want to thank them for their cinematic and cultural insights that nourish my critical perspective in this book.

Writing is like hiking, periodically without pre-made trails; thus path breaking is commonplace but exceedingly challenging when obstacles are encountered. I alternated between my computer and my Pelikan fountain pen and particularly give more credit to my fountain pen as an obstacle removing instrument. Ms. Abigail (Abi) Weeks at Chartpak, Inc. based in Leeds, MA quickly revived a dead nib and I would like to thank her for rescuing my pathbreaking instrument which was well used as a critical medium of my thoughts during the entire process of my writing this book.

Those whom I have saved to last express my thankfulness and affection are my family members who are always lending their courage to my intellectual pursuits. From my parents and my sisters, I have learned to sustain hopes and dreams for a better future and to see the most precious things of life always within reach. With the companionship of my wife Wendy and our daughters Devin and Merlin, writing becomes the creative rather than the dull task of my profession. Besides being the most committed deep reader of my writings, Wendy lends her insight to my theoretical buildup on place and eco-aesthetics by sharing with me her collected titles on landscape studies, permaculture, and eco-poetics from her bookshelves. Without her corrections, comments, and suggestions this book would not stand. Both Devin and Merlin always give me a clearer sense of life whenever I encounter stressful moments and self-defeating thoughts. While I thank them for their gifted kindred spirits, I also seek pardon from them for my many hours of work – but I believe it won't be too long before we set out to our dreamplaces together, maybe filming the northern lights in Finland or Iceland or learning from the mountain gods of the Andes.

Dan Smyer Yu						Center for Trans-Himalayan Studies
								Yunnan Minzu University

Contents

Chapter One Introduction: Placiality of Tibet —— 1
1.1 Contextualizing Tibet as a "Hot Spot" and a "Power Place" —— 8
1.2 Mindscaping the Tibetan landscape —— 16
1.2.1 Mindscape —— 20
1.2.2 Landscape, place, and placiality —— 21
1.2.3 Eco-aesthetics —— 24
1.2.4 Affordances —— 26
1.3 A geographic navigation of my fieldwork —— 28
1.3.1 Beijing —— 29
1.3.2 Qinghai —— 32
1.3.3 Lhasa and Shangrila —— 35
1.4 Mapping the book —— 38

Chapter Two Geopoetics of place, gods, and people in Sambha (སམ་བྷ) —— 43
2.1 Eco-aesthetics of an outsider looking in —— 43
2.2 Geopoetic affordances of the Tibetan landscape —— 47
2.3 Sambha mandalized —— 52
2.4 Inter-dwelling with gods and spirits —— 58
2.5 Ancestral rootedness of Sambha and beyond —— 63
2.6 "Place has its own being…" —— 68

Chapter Three Confessions of an Inner Liberation —— 71
3.1 The second Long March —— 75
3.2 Elation and desolation in the eco-sublime Tibetan landscape —— 79
3.3 Communist "liberation theology" —— 83
3.4 Puzzling statistics and the social scene of Old Lhasa —— 87
3.5 Searching for serfs in the midst of the "black bones" and the "white bones" —— 88
3.6 The clash of Marxist class struggle and Buddhist fate —— 92
3.7 Reminiscing about Old Tibet's enchantments —— 93

Chapter Four Memorability of place among anti-traditionalists —— 98
4.1 "Pulling one hair moves the entire body" —— 99
4.2 Forgetting as Remembering —— 105
4.3 Subalternity of radical modernism —— 113
4.4 Pathogenic force of modernity —— 117
4.5 Placial antecedence of the Subaltern —— 123

Chapter Five Touching the skin of modern Tibet in the New Tibetan Cinema —— 128
5.1 Initiating cinematic landscape of a Buddhist Tibet —— 129
5.1.1 Repairing Buddhist moral fabric in *The Grassland* —— 129
5.1.2 Landscaping Buddhism in *The Silent Holy Stone* —— 134
5.2 Touching the Skin of the Modern Tibetan Landscape —— 137
5.2.1 Rescuing the Buddhist "soul" of the nation in *The Search* —— 139
5.2.2 A modern Tibet in *Old Dog* —— 143
5.3 After-effects and affordances of the New Tibetan Cinema —— 149

Chapter Six Ensouling the Mountain —— 156
6.1 "Wherever I travel I can't wait to rush home!" —— 157
6.2 "You know the origin of my ancestors" —— 163
6.3 "*Machen Bomra* [རྨ་ཆེན་སྤོམ་ར] is a living being" —— 168
6.4 "Bury them here…" —— 174
6.5 "Eco-aesthetics of Touching and Being Touched" —— 178

Chapter Seven Drifting in the Mirages of the Tibetan Landscape —— 183
7.1 Tibet, branding a mindscape of utopia —— 185
7.1.1 An American experience —— 185
7.1.2 A Chinese experience —— 189
7.2 Tibet, branded as a dreamworld —— 191
7.3 Seeking material empowerments in the dreamworld —— 195
7.4 Drifting in the Mirages of the Tibetan Landscape —— 200
7.4.1 Geo-poetic affordance —— 200
7.4.2 Utopian attributes of Tibet —— 203
7.4.3 Escape, self-exile and metamorphosis in "magical Tibet" —— 204

Chapter Eight Conclusion – Mindscaping Tibetophilia —— 212
8.1 The missing Orient in Post-Orientalism —— 214
8.2 Tibet as a geopsychic terrain —— 218
8.3 Tibetophilia, topophilia, and eco-aesthetics revisited —— 222
8.4 An anthropological mindscape of Tibet —— 225

References —— 231

Index —— 246

Chapter One Introduction: Placiality of Tibet

In early July 2012, with a crew of eight, I was filming a documentary about pilgrimage at Mt. Amne Machen (ཨ་མྱེས་རྨ་ཆེན་) in Golok, Qinghai. It was a late afternoon when we began to walk up to a ridge separating us from Queen's Peak (ཨ་ཡུམ་རྫོ་རྗེའི་དགའ་ཚལ་) at an altitude of 5,600 meters. Since a little before 6:00 we had attempted to film predawn landscape scenes at a lower altitude but had been thwarted by rain and snow. About an hour later the sun briefly showed its morning face but for the next nine hours, fog, rain, sporadic snow, and windy air enveloped us. Now, as we approached the ridge, the gusty wind began to clear away the thick clouds to reveal the sun tilting westward in the blue sky. The colors and the shapes and figures of the mountains surrounding us overwhelmed my senses. Before reaching the ridge, I requested that the crew position the camera on the ridgeline to film a few long takes of the breathtaking landscape cast in the setting sun. However, upon reaching the top, every single one of us dashed down the other side toward a glacier that covered a wide slope descending from the snow-capped Queen's Peak. The Tibetan crewmembers shouted, "Lha gyalo" (ལྷ་རྒྱལ་ལོ། Gods win!). After a long, singled-breathed holler one of the crewmembers ran out of oxygen and passed out for some seconds. Regaining consciousness he continued to run to the glacier. Each of us felt moved to touch the surface of the glacier with our bare hands and some rolled on top of it while from within its crevices many of us hugged the icy precipices. In the crevices I saw treasure vases (གཏེར་པ་), coral earrings, ivory prayer beads, and silver rings, the offerings from past pilgrims, frozen in the ice. We were not the only visitors to show affection to the glacier which is embedded with human touches and material offerings. The next day, the two lamas who were our documentary subjects, buried precious minerals, rare medicinal herbs, soil collected from Bodh Gaya, and pieces of cloth torn from their late masters' winter coats, all neatly enclosed in several cloth tubes, as offerings to Amne Machen.

Like the items I saw in the frozen ice, the offerings packed in the cloth tubes are called *ter* (གཏེར་) or treasures. The lexical meaning of *ter* generally refers to rare minerals or precious metals. Its use in Tibetan Buddhism and the indigenous Bon religion is often associated with *terma* (གཏེར་མ་) and *terton* (གཏེར་སྟོན་). The former refers to hidden religious treasures in the forms of texts, ritual objects, and intangible teachings that are buried in the earth and stored in the "mind streams" (སེམས་རྒྱུད་ *sems rgyud*) of masters. The masters who can access knowledge of *terma* whereabouts are visionaries, able to discover past treasures hidden in the earth as well as the hidden spiritual consciousness of their masters (Fremantle 2001, 17). As seen in the act performed on Mt. Amne Machen, the hiding of a *terma* is not always intended for the preservation of a given lineage but serves to strengthen the bond of people with their sacred places. Offering items of value to the land invests human affection and subjectivity to it. Such a bond, as expressed in our pilgrimage case, monumentally reminds people that their homeland, animated with earthly gods and spirits, is a critical source of blessings and empowerments for their worldly wellbeing. In a mutual saturation, the place is the people, the people are the place, and the place is simultaneously the earthly gods who inextricably reside in the "mind streams" of the people.

Due to heavy rain prior to reaching the glacier at the foot of Queen's Peak, we missed filming what contemporary photographers would label "epic landscape scenes." In landscape photography and motion pictures, violent weather can metaphorically express emotions, temporalize the mind's transitioning from one state to another, and initiate moments of awe, contemplation, and nostalgia. "Epic" in this case does not necessarily pertain to the local story of a given landscape but rather to the grand scale of its appearance in terms of unusually striking panoramic views, rich saturation of different shades of light, and the depthless horizon. It is a moment of positive aesthetics, with a nod toward the Kantian idea of the sublime, framed in the photographer's gaze.

Limiting my gaze or that of the camera to the frontal view makes the filmed experience of Amne Machen's landscape incomplete. Considering meteorological influences alone, when enveloped in the changing weather of an actual "epic" landscape, the relationship of a photographer and his subject is not merely optical. The photographer's gaze is physically environed in the landscape's totality coming from all directions rather than the commonly held notion that the gaze encompasses all. The pleasing look of the landscape is saturated with environmental conditions that our camera is mostly unable to convey – high elevation, sparse oxygen, strong wind, and low temperatures. When adding the human sentiments, the religiosity and spirituality embedded and deposited in the landscape of Amne Machen, our cameras simply fail to capture, in entirety, such a range of intangible human-place engagements. For the rest of our time at Amne Machen it was in mythological, imaginative, and affective terms that the two lamas and my Tibetan colleagues narrated their felt connection with Amne Machen – the mountain and the mountain god –and the dreamworld in which the mountain is personified as a gigantic bodhisattva warrior-god, with the wavy glacier a camp site of his celestial soldiers' thousands of white tents pitched across the field. It requires imagination and visualization to express such an emotional and spiritual bond between a place and people.

* * *

In modern Tibetan studies, an increasing number of scholars look upon non-Tibetans' perceptions of Tibet as what is known as "the imagined Tibet" – a projection of a collective fantasy that is not Tibet itself. Such critique has mostly been centered upon how Tibet is imagined in the West and is shown in the works of Donald Lopez (1998), Peter Bishop (1993), and Dibyesh Anand (2008). In these works, Tibet is Orientalized and imagination is frequently equated with fantasy; thus what is imagined is associated with the socio-psychological issues of the West rather than with Tibet itself. Tibet then is an object of transference in the psychological sense. Such a critical trend has also been growing in China since the turn of the twentieth century; however, how Tibet is imagined among Tibetans and Chinese in contemporary China is given little attention by most scholars.

Since the publication of Lopez's *Prisoners of Shangrila* in 1998 and its subsequent introduction to the fields of anthropology, ethnology, sociology, and Tibetology in China, the discourse on imagined Tibet among Chinese academics has culminated in the public lectures, discussions, and publications of Shen Weirong (2010) and Wang Hui (2011), two contemporaries of Lopez in China and leading critics of the Western Orientalist image of Tibet from their Chinese standpoints. The global connectivity of Chinese academics with their North American counterparts is obvious in the case of modern Tibetan studies. The talks and publications of Wang and Shen continue Lopez's critique of the Orientalism inherent in how Tibet is imagined in the West. Building upon Lopez's critical perspective, both Shen and Wang criticize the Western imagination of Tibet as an eroticization of tantric Buddhism and a mystification of Tibet by travelers, colonialists, spiritual seekers, and the Nazis of the fallen Third Reich. This scholarly critique has revealed a significant, far-reaching effect of the Western tendency to imagine Tibet as an ideal: by juxtaposing Tibet and China, as though they are antithetical, the pro-Tibet cause assumes a position whereby "Tibet embodies the spiritual and the ancient, China the material, the modern, and the destructive. Tibetans are superhuman, Chinese are subhuman" (Lopez 1998, 7). In the scholarship of Wang, Shen, Lopez, and other like-minded scholars, the West is given full credit for the birth of the idealized version of imagined Tibet.

A careful reading of the texts of Lopez, Shen, and Wang shows that their critiques are built upon the writings of "the great mystifiers" of Tibet (Lopez 2001, 183), namely Lama Anagarika Govinda (born Ernst Lothar Hoffmann), Alexandra David-Neel, Losang Rampa (born Cyril Henry Hoskin), and James Hilton. Writing in the first half of the 1900s, these four "great mystifiers" were looked to as "experts" on Tibet. However, the credibility of two of these writers is questionable. Rampa, according to Lopez, never set foot in Tibet, while Hilton, who likewise may not have visited, was a novelist credited with the literary creation of Shangrila, whose intention was to tell a story, not to invent knowledge regarding traditional Tibet. The imagined Tibets of both Rampa and Hilton can be seen as fantasy worlds; however, both had access to secondary sources from travelers, missionaries, explorers, and seekers who had been to Tibet. In the cases of David-Neel and Lama Govinda, regardless of allegations that they did not read Tibetan (Lopez 2001, 183), their descriptions of Tibet cannot be solely looked upon as a result of their imagination or fantasies because they travelled and lived there.

Returning to Lopez and his Chinese contemporaries, the difference between their works is that Wang and Shen contextualize their critiques in the Chinese state's framework of the Tibet Question – its alleged slave-owning past and the territorial claim that it has belonged to China since the Mongols' conquest in the thirteenth century. Although the critical motives of Lopez, Shen, and Wang differ, these three scholars' critiques nevertheless seem to coincide – rendering the globally popular, positive encounter of Tibetan Buddhism and Tibet's magnificent landscape into a collective mental chimera or a fantasy that has little corresponding reality. In a colloquial sense they appear to be the "joy killers" of a global fascination with Tibet.

In November of 2009, shortly after Wang Hui gave a talk titled "Tibet between the East and the West" at Minzu University of China, I was invited, as a visiting scholar, to give a talk on Tibet as imagined in the West. Utilizing my fieldnotes on contemporary Sino-Tibetan Buddhist encounters and my reading notes on the works of Lopez, Shen, and Wang, I emphasized the current state of this "imagined Tibet" not merely as a product of Western Tibetophilia. Instead, I suggested, it is a complex vehicle conveying a plurality of perceptions and psychological responses, feelings of guilt, utopianism and spiritual aspirations, aesthetics and desires for transcendence, originating from different cultural and ideological origins, including those of modern China.

In the first half of my talk I shared with the audience how Tibet and Tibetans have been imagined in China since the 1950s in order to compare how Tibet is perceived and represented outside China. It was not particularly comfortable for a few of my Chinese colleagues to hear the suggestion that China's notions of Old Tibet and New Tibet are a product of socialist modernity and not unbiased "fact." In the second half, rather than repeating the perspectives of Lopez, Bishop, Wang, and Shen, given that many in the audience had attended Wang's lecture, I showed slides of how Tibetan Buddhism is practiced by North Americans at Shambhala Centers, Odiyan Retreat Center, the Center for Wisdom and Compassion, the Tibetan Nyingma Institute, and Naropa University. These slides became the center of the discussion session after my talk when both Han and Tibetan students expressed particular interest in my former anthropology professor's conversion to Tibetan Buddhism and his becoming an active meditation instructor at a Dharma center. It is important to note that religion and science, in contemporary China, are still viewed as being diametrical opposites; thus when a scientist embraces a religion, it is seen as his or her betrayal to science. From their queries I saw that the subject of Tibet possessed some kind of power drawing forth inquisitiveness, emotional engagement, and contemplative comments from a group of diverse young students of different ethnic backgrounds in contemporary China.

The captivating power of Tibet is not waning in popularity in either the West or China. In his critique of the popular imagination of Tibet, Lopez makes the distinction between Tibetophiliacs and those who belong to what he calls "the cult of Tibetology" (Lopez 2001, 184) with the latter referring to the academic studies of Tibet. From my own disciplinary perspective as an anthropologist I do not see how relevant it is to draw this distinction, as ultimately many Tibetologists are also integrally related to global Tibetophilia. This distinction simply does not explain why the popular trend of "imagining Tibet" is not declining but is rather spreading across the world and entering the psyches of individuals who wish to know more about all aspects of Tibet. The "romance" of Tibet in China and the West continues regardless of these scholars and public intellectuals' relentless effort to quell it. The epistemic ballast of this global trend cannot be possibly strung on the narratives of a few historical "imposters" and "mystifiers." The global public is not that uninformed, ignorant, or, therefore, gullible. Tibet is accessible to many, with the exception of the times when the Chinese state limits tourism in an attempt to curb Tibetan civil disobedience against its rules and regulations.

Parallel to the on-going scholarly critiques of imagined Tibet, the publications of contemporary travelers, nature photographers, mountain climbers, pilgrims and seekers continue to meet public demand with their awe-inspired tone and affection toward Tibet. If one flips through the pages of *A Plumber's Progress* (O'Connell 2003), *The Heart of the World* (Baker 2004), and *To a Mountain in Tibet* (Thubron 2011), for instance, one can see these contemporary travelers to Tibet write with great similarity to the "mystifiers" such as David-Neel and Lama Govinda.

How do we make sense out of this on-going popular enchantment with Tibet? Based on my own fieldwork and travel in Tibetan regions I see the *place* of Tibet in both geographic and imaginative terms as antecedent to all our public debates and contentions, and even to moments of our private contemplations and emotional responses to anything Tibetan. In other words, to both Tibetans and non-Tibetans the landscape of Tibet itself possesses an imaginative, mythological, and eco-psychological quality that is scarcely taken into account when the subject of "imagined Tibet" is evoked.

I write this book as a sequel to my first book *The Spread of Tibetan Buddhism in China: Charisma, Money, Enlightenment* (Smyer Yu 2011), in order to continue the discussion on "mindscaping eco-Buddhist Tibet" (Smyer Yu 2011, 173–196). In drawing the conclusion of my first book, I could see the need for further thought on place, imagination, and the fate of Tibet. Before I address what I hope to accomplish in this book, I wish to tell my readers what this book does not do: it does not continue the polemical tendency of the existing debates between Tibetologists and Tibetophiles since that boundary is thin and porous; it does not dwell on the legacy of Orientalism and Western colonial ventures in Asia as the sole cornerstone of the currently popular imagination of Tibet; it does not treat the imagined Tibet only as a Western cultural phenomenon; it does not take a side between pro-Tibet and pro-China positions; it does not treat modernity and tradition as two mutually exclusive ideas and social realities; it does not see Tibet only as a geographic location; it does not look upon the popular trend of "imagining Tibet" merely as an activity of non-Tibetans; it does not fixate on representing Chinese, Tibetans, Westerners, or anybody involved in this matter as a people with a singular collective subjectivity; it does not equate imagination with fantasy; and finally it does not find intellectual comfort in treating issues of imagined Tibet only as affairs of human-to-human perceptions, relations, and contentions.

With these negations out of the way, I envision my book as an anthropological work with a trans-disciplinary orientation. It narrates and interprets a unique place-people interaction. I wish to inform my readers that the anthropology evoked in this book has a reflexive-phenomenological orientation. The reflexive part refers to my methodological preference toward reflexive anthropology (Marcus 1994, 45–46) as a result of the "interpretive turn" (Rabinow and Sullivan 1987) in the history of anthropology. The core of this anthropological reflexivity or interpretivity "replaces the observational objective 'eye' of the ethnographer with his or her personal 'I'" (Marcus 1994, 45). By freeing the anthropologist from "the natural scientist's documentary, observational stance" (Clifford 1988, 28) or from the "iron cage" of positivism (Rabinow and Sullivan 1987, 2), reflexive anthropology aims at writing the collaborative text ethnographically woven together by the anthropologist and his or her interlocutors. In this regard, the "I" in this book is the engaged subjectivity of the anthropologist as a person with multifarious personal, cultural, and institutional backgrounds. This "I" then threads together the piecemeal ethnographic data accumulated daily over a span of time in the buildup of "a common, meaningful world, drawing on intuitive styles of feeling, perception, and guesswork" (Clifford 1988, 36). In other words it weaves together a web of meanings (Geertz 1973, 5; Rabinow and Sullivan 1987:6) for the sake of the anthropologically and publicly shared interpretations of the issues concerned. The subjective engagement of this "I" with its ethnographic constituencies and the broader public arena of Tibet-related concerns is not meant to pursue a flawless, impartial understanding of Tibet, but to acknowledge upfront the partiality of the anthropological making of cultural meanings. To battle this inherent limitation of the discipline, the most effective and honorable approach is to accept the fact that "we are fundamentally self-interpreting, self-defining, living always in a cultural environment" (Rabinow and Sullivan 1987:7). The seemingly self-referential narratives in this book are therefore intended to make transparent the social scientifically conditioned but intersubjectively engaged narrating "I."

This leads to the phenomenological aspect of my anthropological undertaking to illustrate the relationship between the "I" and the world in my landscape-mindscape study. While the "I" is embodied and grounded in the living body absorbing, responding to, and adapting itself to the *lebenswelt* or lifeworld (Husserl 1970:108; Paci 1972:43), its embodied sensing consciousness is itself enveloped in its cultural-natural environment. In the phenomenological study of landscape, the intersubjective engagement of the "I" with its living world rests upon "the relationship between Being and Being-in-the-world" established "through perception (seeing, hearing, touch), bodily actions and movements, and intentionality, emotion and awareness residing in systems of belief and decision-making, remembrance and evaluation" (Tilley 1994, 12). The immateriality of the perceptual consciousness moves with its physical body in the lifeworld, and thus "cannot be an absolute interiority, a pure presence to itself" (Tilley 2004, 3). In this sense, because of the obvious dependency of the perceptual consciousness on the physical world, human subjectivity enveloped in the physical environment is physical to start with; thus the causal relationship is: "subjectivity arises from objectivity" (Tilley 2004:3–4). In the landscape studies of Christopher Tilley, Tim Ingold, Barbara Bender, Edward Casey, and other phenomenologically grounded scholars, this "objectivity" is simultaneously the human subjectivity invested in the given place and the natural-supernatural power of the place affording human dwelling and social nesting as a gregarious species (Ingold 2011, 78). In this sense, "Places, like persons, have biographies inasmuch as they are formed, used and transformed in relation to practice" (Tilley 1994:33). "Place has its own being" (Casey 1997, 90) is a critical mantra in this book for my illustrations of the intersubjective relationship between Tibet as a unique place and humans situated in divergent contexts and circumstances. In this case, my phenomenological intentionality is geared toward an ethnographic empathy for the native Tibetan vision of their mountainous landscape as a place animated with a pantheon of gods and supernatural beings that are deemed sentient and therefore conscious. Besides humans, such a uniquely animated landscape is also my ethnographic interlocutor. As a Native American proverb goes, "Never judge a person till you have walked a mile in his moccasins" (Smart 2009, 7). In the same manner, an empathetic understanding is only fulfilled when an intersubjective engagement takes place.

To elaborate further, in my case study of the landscape-mindscape nexus concerning Tibet, "intersubjectivity" signifies the respective subjectivities of place and people, and their reciprocity through religious, mythological, and spiritual expressions. In particular I emphasize that place communicates with people with its own being as an embodiment of a specific geological history and human social activities. Grounded in this intersubjective connection or bonding between place and people, I bring in narratives from my cross-regional and cross-ethnic fieldwork concerning how Tibet, beyond its geography, has a different life of its own in the minds of Tibetans and Chinese in China. The sense of Tibet as a unique place on earth occurs not only with its natives but also with outsiders who are attracted to what Denis Cosgrove and Veronica Della Dora call "high places" (2009, 3). Bonding, in the interpersonal sense, takes place when affinity and mutuality exist. While people may choose their dwelling place, place may also choose its dwellers and, in its own way, communicate with visitors. Thus the primary message of this book is: place has a voice of its own and it speaks to the people who dwell in it and who are in contact with it. In articulating this message, I emphasize the aesthetic, religious, ecological, and creative dimensions place provides to humans.

1.1 Contextualizing Tibet as a "Hot Spot" and a "Power Place"

Tibet, undoubtedly, as the "third pole" of the earth in the view of the global public, is the highest and largest "water tower" in the world, feeding the aquatic arteries of East Asia, Southeast Asia, and South Asia. If we overlook the political boundaries, ethnic differences, and strategic interests of nations bordering it, the environmental and ecological value of the Tibetan plateau is simply not limited to its own people but benefits billions outside its physical geography. To put it plainly Tibet's water sustains nearly a quarter of the world's population. The public vision of Tibet as the third pole, with more water in the form of snow and ice than anywhere outside the north and south poles (Chellaney 2011, 95), does not stop at its geological and environmental height but continues with a set of place-human dialogues regarding the fate of humanity and the Earth. Cosgrove and Della Dora remark, "Physically or imaginatively, high places mark the ends of the earth" (2009, 8). Hereto I add that these ends are the beginnings of our realization of the fragility of the earth as they are the barometers informing us of the results of environmental degradation including deforestation, melting glaciers, species loss, and soil erosion.

Furthermore, unlike the north and south poles (the two latitudinally "high" places without history of sustained human settlement), Tibet, being the symbolic third pole, is home to a unique civilization that has proved itself a "power culture," a term I derive from Adrian Ivakhiv's "power place" to which people are drawn because they respond to such notions as "energy shift," "higher self," or "voice of spirit" (Ivakhiv 2001, 228). Much like the waters flowing from its mountain heights to feed the lowland rivers, Tibet's cultural treasures stream into the rest of the world. In particular, Tibet's Buddhist traditions and the state of its awe-inspiring landscape have set off a new set of global discourses on humanitarian and environmental concerns since the Dalai Lama went into exile in 1959. The unique civilization of Tibet grips public attention as does its ecosphere, an exemplary environment imbued with a strong sense of magnificence and fragility.

Tibet is a thermally cold place but it's also a hot spot as seen from humanitarian, spiritual, and ecological angles. Since the mid-twentieth century, communists, hippies, development professionals, statesmen, rock singers, and movie stars have chanted the slogans of "Free Tibet" and "Save Tibet." In the midst of non-Tibetans' passionate outcries, Tibet has been regarded both as a victim of its own heritage or of external oppression. The latest humanitarian "heat" coming from this hot spot is the self-immolation of ninety-five Tibetans since 2009 (ICT 2012) in Central Tibet, Kham and Amdo. These events have rocked the Chinese state's "stability" in the regions, triggering another round of global outcry and social activism concerning the human rights and collective wellbeing of Tibetans under the rule of China. Besides the public uproar, social scientists in the West are becoming ever more socially engaged in this matter. For instance, the Hot Spots Forum of the *Journal of Cultural Anthropology* has designated a special issue to publishing concerned scholars' commentaries on the humanitarian crisis in Tibet (McGranahan and Litzinger 2012). Herein it is noteworthy to point out that this global moral outcry is occurring mostly outside China. As the editors of the issue note, the Chinese state locks down the areas where self-immolation take place and in more than one case "the Chinese media was noticeably silent" (McGranahan and Litzinger 2012). What is the Chinese media doing then? Where does it direct the attention of the Chinese public in terms of Tibet?

The Chinese media also considered Tibet a humanitarian hot spot in 2008 but the framing of media reports was set on allegations that the Tibetan uprisings were an act of sabotage to the Olympic Games hosted in Beijing and a violent subversion to the "unity of nationalities" or *minzu tuanjie* (民族团结) in Chinese. The Chinese media quickly moved on to present Tibet to the public as a different hot spot – one that is attracting millions of tourists annually since the Qinghai-Lhasa railway began to transport passengers in 2006 (Smyer Yu 2011, 178):

> In 2006, after the completion of the Beijing-Lhasa railway, the overwhelming number of tourists heading to Lhasa was described in Chinese media as *jingpen* (井喷) or "blowout," meaning that the number of tourists had surpassed the carrying capacity of Lhasa's tourist facilities, i.e. hotels, restaurants, and transportation. According to Xinhua Net, in 2007, Lhasa received over four million tourists, a record-breaking number. Although this number decreased by 44 % in March 2008 due to Tibetan demonstrations, it quickly rose again in 2009. For the first six months of 2009, over 1.5 million tourists poured into Lhasa and brought ¥113 million (RMB) in revenue to the city (Niu, Tu and Hu 2009).

Tibet is China's "cash crop." In 2007 when Xinhua News interviewed Hao Peng, the Deputy Party Secretary of TAR, about the rapid growth of tourism in Tibet, he responded, "Up until the end of National Day [October 1], the number of tourists to Tibet has reached 3.5 million. But, last year Yunnan received over 50 million tourists. The size of Tibet [TAR] is 1.2 million square meters, far bigger than Yunnan. So I say Tibet is not having too many tourists but too few" (Quan and Wang 2007). Tourism numbers collected since 2007 show that Hao has gotten his wish. By the end of 2010, the total number of tourists to Tibet reached six million, a twenty-two percent increase from the previous year. Tourist revenue was seven billion Yuan (Xinhua News 2010). In the month of July 2011 alone, 1.3 million tourists and 1.2 billion Yuan poured into Tibet. When the year ended, Tibet had seen a total 8.6 million tourists (PD 2012), a number exceeding the entire Tibetan population. The People's Daily calls this unprecedented growth "a colossal business opportunity" (PD 2012).

Scratching at the surface of Chinese tourism as a profit venture, I ask, "What exactly is the "hotness" of Tibet which attracts millions of tourists every year? For tour companies, profit is the obvious incentive, but what are they selling to attract so many tourists? "It is the high, snowy mountains, the sunshine, and Tibetan culture that tourism in Tibet relies on," says the Chinese state news agency (Xinhua News 2010). In other words the landscape and the materiality of Tibetan traditional culture are the products in this expanding tourist market. Tibet, whether as an idea or as a geographic reality, is obviously an object of desire. However, it is unlike conventional consumer products. For example, Tibet is not a Bentley Diamond Jubilee that one can drive out of the dealership in Canton after putting down a million Yuan – a not uncommon impulsive consumption product among the *nouveau riche* of contemporary China.

Tibet is physically immobile but something about it is moving millions of people annually to see it. Bracketing our moral judgment on money and consumerism, I see two-way traffic between object and desire. The object, being in this case a unique place, is most certainly magnetizing and overwhelming a growing number of people with its geography, geology, and culture. In my work with Tibetophiles in China I find their desire to visit or to be in Tibet originates more from repugnant environmental conditions in Chinese cities, their frustration over existential issues and general pressures of life rather than from their desire to "possess" the object. The desired "object" or place, as the case may be, seems to function as a multidimensional reference or a sign pointing to alternative ways and means for people to engage existentially or spiritually with their current state of being. While visitors to Tibet cannot possibly return home with Tibet in their suitcases, they do return with a range of photographic and imaginative images, affective reflections, and transformative realizations as a result of what I call an "appreciative consumption pattern." In this regard, the "hot-topic" status of Tibet enters the minds and psyches of those who enter its physical domain.

While Western Tibetophiles have a longer tradition of imaginative appreciation toward Tibet, called by many "inner peace" (Schuyler 2012) or "a journey of the heart" (Mathiessen 1978) or, conversely, "New Age Orientalism" (Lopez 1994) or "a collective hallucination" (Bishop 1993, 16), in comparison, Chinese Tibetophilia is a rather recent occurrence. In the history of the People's Republic of China (hereafter PRC), the image of traditional Tibet has been depreciated as a morally dark place, one portrayed in black and white photos of beggars and prisoners whose bodies are maimed. Before the early 1990s, only a little over twenty years ago, being sent to work in Tibet was taken as going to a place of hardship and desolation (Miao 2007, 29). Credit for the sudden rise of Chinese positive appreciation of Tibet has to be given to contemporary Western backpackers roaming through Tibetan villages and expansive landscapes, and Chinese Buddhists taking refuge in the monasteries of their Tibetan masters (Smyer Yu 2011). The message they brought to the rest of China was clear: Tibet is a jewel on earth and one from which many successful artists and writers have benefitted.

Chai Chunya, author of *A Vagabond in Tibet* (2009), *The Seventh Treasure Book of Grandma Ayima* (2010), and *The Silent Mani-Song* (2011), is known as a "Dharma vagabond" (达磨浪人 *damo langren*) among Chinese Tibetophiles. He began his career as a photojournalist for Southern Weekly based in Guangzhou. At the turn of the century he left his job and took residence in Dege, Kham, currently Sichuan Province, where he converted to Tibetan Buddhism. In *A Vagabond in Tibet*, his narratives reflecting his perception of Tibet appear to be influenced by his own existential anxiety as a photojournalist. After a substantial revision, *A Vagabond in Tibet* reappeared in the book markets of China and Taiwan as *The Silent Mani-Song* (2011). He retains his poetic prose while building his literary bond with Tibet, starting the book with the dichotomy of his discontent in urban China and his hopeful dreams in Tibet in these imaginative utterances:

> ...The most outstanding poets and photographers are sinking deep into a craze. Between the West and the Southwest [of China] they have lost their way. Because this path is a secret, it demands a youthful commitment...The grassland expands thousands of miles into the horizon. Here, there are ancient monasteries built with wooden structures. I'll soon live in the attic of the monastery. Through the wooden window frames the brilliance of the sunlight will descend on the flower petals of a potted wild rose on the windowsill and on my peaceful face when I'm asleep. Soon sounds of sutra recitation and ringing bells will wake me up...Sick and tired of city life, determined to be a vagabond, this was my simple wish (Chai 2011, 1).

In mid June 2012, I attended the opening ceremony for the preview of Chen Yalian's paintings at Beijing's Fuyou Monastery, which had once housed the office of the 10th Panchen Lama. Chen, a Tibet-inspired celebrity artist, spent over ten years traveling in Tibet before she became famous. The price tag on each of her works of art is at least one million Yuan. This preview was a preparatory exhibit for her art tour to France, Germany, Italy, and Switzerland. Critics of celebrity artists, such as Chen Zui and Wang Yong, congratulated her at the preview praising her as "a lotus in the snow." Chen spoke to her audience, "Someone once asked me what I make my art with. I said, 'it is made from my life!'" This sentimentality was also expressed in her art book *My Ten Years in Tibet:*

> On an early summer morning in July I returned to Lhasa where my dream had begun. The airplane landed at Gonga Airport where the fog still lingered above it. I was falling in love with this morning full of dew and vapor. I realized it was the hour of day foretelling the birth of a world enveloped with hope. It was a moment pregnant with power and illumination before the sunrise...At this moment while walking down the airplane's stairs I felt my blood surging and rushing out of my heart chamber reaching all ends of my body, up to my face. Lhasa River was flowing peacefully as usual. Different kinds of vehicles were shuttling back and forth on the newly built highway. Potala, I'm back to where I feel at home – my Tibet (Chen 2005, 49).

Other Tibetophiles who, unlike Chai and Chen, do not have the same literary drive and creative skill for traditional publication, often utilize blogs to broadcast their affective reflections resulting from their travels to Tibet. One blogger writes:

> An insignificant, tiny person stands in front of an immensely magnificent architectural structure. Between them, it is an event taking place with two asymmetrical meanings.

I'm unable to explain why I feel elated when I'm "looking at" it. I'm even not certain what exactly I'm "looking at." The details of Potala Palace present themselves much more [in person] than in the images from the Internet, the TV, and films. Perhaps I should ask myself: Shall I make a hypothesized premise? Shall I prove my predetermined outcome with my enthusiasm and passion accompanying me along the way? I'm not a religious person but I feel the primary function of religion bestows us with the right to imagine. This fundamental right is being encroached upon by the materialism we so cherish. Who can say the materialistic lifestyle we're seeking isn't a hypothesis? How many people can prove that all happiness has already been embodied in the life of our "materialism"? Potala Palace, a palace of religion and the state, is not merely a kind of visual miracle, but also opens a heavenly window to our depressingly worldly life (Desert Bell 2008).

In many ways, each travel experience to Tibet is different; however, the most visible commonality among Chinese Tibet travel writings is manifested in the fantastical claims of the travelers' elemental touch or re-connectedness with the earth and of an experience of rebirth in a paradise on earth. The blue sky, white clouds, crystal clear waters, the white snow on the mountains, and the mesmerizing colors of mountain ridges, valleys, and open grassland are absorbed, first, as the physical characteristics of Tibet but they are soon elevated to the domain of the transcendent and the celestial. One dedicated Tibetophile recounted the fantastical moment on a bus ride to Lake Yamdrok Yumtso (ཡར་འབྲོག་གཡུ་མཚོ) in his blog, "…Yamdrok Yumtso is a goddess descending from heaven. She seductively wraps herself around the snow covered mountains and glaciers, looking like the long sleeves of an opera princess' silk dress. She resembles a long blue rainbow. Her water, after bathing in the sunlight, becomes a lake of rainbows. I can't help but reach out to touch her magnificent beauty, filled with awe by how naturally beautiful she is" (Tukeba 2012).

The imaginative, contemplative, and critical modes of these narratives are commonplace among those published writers and bloggers who have traveled to Tibet. They fit into a "Tibetophiliac narrative genre" sustained with a range of exclamations, phrases, and single words that personify and ensoul the physical place and culture of Tibet: "Tibet is a dream," "Tibet is intoxicating," "Tibet is a pure memory," "Tibet is an earthquake in the soul," "simplicity of infinite magic," "pureland," "sacred," and "heavenly." This list is but a sample of the phrases used by Chinese travelers to Tibet and is noticeably similar to their Western contemporaries, indicating that a traveler's Tibet journey, regardless of the traveler's place of origin, is a rite of passage. For many it marks a threshold crossed in the paths of their lives, or a breakthrough bringing a revolutionary awareness of their current states of being. Patrick French, author of *Tibet, Tibet* (2004) summarizes succinctly that what drew him to Tibet was "the place and the spirit" (2004, 19). To him Tibet is "a place of dreams," "a place of serenity," and "a place to feel at home" (2004, 19). The difference between the Chinese Tibetophiles and their Western counterparts like French, is that the former are critical of all of China's rapid urbanization, the loss of community fabric, the state's materialist ideology and its corresponding materialistic consumerism, while the latter express outrage over what the Chinese state has done in Tibet since the mid-twentieth century.

What many critics often aren't aware of is that Tibet influenced and challenged and inspired many Chinese PLA soldiers and state aid workers who were stationed there in the 1950s and 60s in the exact same ways. With their diaries, journals, and memoirs being published since the late 1990s, it's now possible to read of former officers', soldiers', and administrators' recognition of Tibet's magnificent landscape. Some of them even narrate their witness of Tibet's international connectivity with Nepal, India, and Europe (Ling 2000, 50). The witness and expression of the brilliance of Tibet provokes a transcendental sentiment from these former soldiers and they present a Tibetan landscape drastically different from a place labeled "the darkest place on earth" (Lin 1997, 28) in the Chinese state's creative propaganda works such as *The Serf* (PLA 1963) and *The Past of Tibet* (CCTV 2009). In the meantime some of these veterans' publications inadvertently sketch out the social world of Tibetans in Lhasa during that era as a place with relatively fair distribution of wealth (Ling 2000, 52). These belated but emerging publications are subverting the Chinese Communist Party's Tibetophobia, the aim of which was to topple traditional Tibetan society.

Both the current popular Tibetophilia and the past Communist Tibetophobia all show that the public image of Tibet in China has been inextricably caught in deep entanglement with the perceptions and representations of the state. This once-uniform image is, however, encountering a diverse body of images and discourses from the popular realm. In the midst of this, many participants of the Chinese Communist "liberation project" of the 1950s and the 1960s are starting to make public their opinion that Tibet has its own "saving power" in terms of environmental health and human flourishing.

Now, in Lhasa and other places of Tibet, one finds a new class of Tibetophiles, popularly known as *zangpiao* (藏漂) or "Tibet-drifters," from urban China. They are seeking new existential meanings and creative opportunities just as Chai Chunya and Chen Yalian have done. The phrase "Tibet-drifters" was derived from *beipiao* (北漂) or "Beijing-drifters" referring to those college graduates and young professionals who come to Beijing to explore "the sky's limit" in their dreamed-of professions and trades. While Chinese "Dharma vagabonds" and "Tibet-drifters" continue to head to Tibetan regions, an increasing number of Tibetans are also becoming "Beijing drifters" as they find themselves taking deeper roots in this megacity for their creative ventures in the fields of art, film, and entertainment. Successful artists and filmmakers, such as Garma Dorje Tserang, Pema Tseden, and Sonthar Gyal, are telling their stories of Tibet through painting and film. In their creative works Tibet is again revealed as a place of inspiration with its immensely breathtaking landscape, Buddhist spirituality, kinship bonds, and communal intimacy. Many of their artworks and films also show a different face of modern Tibet – one that is endangered by the physical transformation and moral destabilization brought in by the advancing modernization and consumerism of urban China. To be noted, the creative works of these Tibetan "Beijing-drifters" are often intended not for their Tibetan compatriots, but for international film festivals, and for an urban Chinese audience who possess what many sophisticated entertainment reviewers call *xizang qingjie* (西藏情结) or "Tibet sentimentality." The productions of this group of Tibetans in Beijing are adding more heat and complexity to Tibet as a "hot" place and a power culture.

Undoubtedly Tibet stands as a hot spot to Chinese, Westerners, and Tibetan writers, intellectuals, and artists as well. In my observation, I see that the initiatives of the Chinese Communists' "liberating Tibet" and of Westerners' "saving Tibet" are fundamentally reversed in the course of the global popular enchantment with Tibet: Tibet is saving those who come with what might be termed a "rescue complex" that treats Tibetans as a subject of "liberation" and "freedom." The narratives of Chinese and Western Tibetophiles all seem to reach the limits of their native languages in their attempt to express what Tibet means to them. The "saving power" of Tibet starts with its physical place, its unique geological formation and a unique eco-sublime quality (Smyer Yu 2011, 73). If it is not a spirit, as Patrick French sees it, it is spiritualized on-site as well as beyond the bounds of its geography. Those who spiritualize it often admit, as though confessionally, to having experienced inner transformation and they express that transformation, as seen above, through imaginative, poetic, metaphoric, and philosophical prose.

The place of Tibet is the antecedent, the source, linking itself with those who desire to reach it, to be in it, and to return home with a story to tell. Thus, eventually, it is not the desire of these travelers, tourists, artists, writers, and activists to possess Tibet like an object of acquisition or a consumer product; instead Tibet possesses the individuals it is in contact with by giving fresh existential perspectives, intellectual contemplations, sudden spiritual realizations, creative inspirations, and even new livelihoods built upon Tibet, the place.

1.2 Mindscaping the Tibetan landscape

The images of Tibet in the popular realm of China are inextricably part and parcel of the ongoing global popular fascination of Tibet. The critics of this popular trend in China heavily rely on Lopez's critical view of Westerners' enthrallment toward Tibet and Tibetan Buddhism as "New Age Orientalism;" however, the critical intention of the Chinese has a geopolitical angle. As China is rising as an economic superpower, its academic world is increasingly receiving a financial boost for global connectivity and the importation of Western critical theories deemed relevant for strengthening the disciplines of the social sciences and humanities as well as for increasing China's visibility in various global public discourses (Chen 2012, 79). Lopez's critique is hailed as the authoritative text among these Chinese critics. His invocation of Said's *Orientalism* is particularly appealing to them. The wide influence of both Lopez and Said on Chinese academics and cultural critics is an example of the global connectivity of the Chinese public to the Western imagination of Tibet in the geopolitical context of Tibet Question.

Before I address the public impact of Lopez's work in China, it is necessary to sketch out the contour of Said's Orientalism discourse in Chinese academic circles. Said's works and associated publications such as *Orientalism: Concepts in the Social Sciences* (Sarder 1999) and *China and Orientalism: Western Knowledge Production of the PRC* (Vukovich 2011), are widely read representatives of postcolonial literature. At the same time, these works are inevitably being used in support of Chinese popular nationalism and an associated antipathy toward the derogatory image of China as a colossus of "despotism" and "totalitarianism" (Zhong 2013) and as "a barbaric Other" and "a cultural Other" (Zhou 2005, 86). This scholarly and popular adoption of Said's critical perspective in China is telling of Said's polemical legacy of treating the West and the Orient as two monoliths (Clifford 1988, 262). On one hand, Chinese scholars and public intellectuals fully inherit Said's polemical legacy by revitalizing a historical discourse begun by their predecessors in the Republic era concerning China's Westernizing path, as expressed in Hu Shi's "Whole-Hearted Westernization" (1936) and Chen Xujing's *The Way Out for Chinese Culture* (1934). On the other hand they fling criticisms from Said's post-colonial perspective at the "West-centric biases and misreading of China," and consider the West "the invasive master of modernity" (Wang 2010).

As Said's texts become more widely read in China, more nuanced understandings are emerging, especially among those who analyze the representation of China and the Chinese in the contemporary motion picture industries of Hollywood and China in the midst of the interactive globalization between geopolitical and geo-economic powers. Tianpan Zhang, a sociologist and a cultural critic, points out that Orientalism, in the multi-directional traffic of motion pictures going between China and the West, can be characterized as "a special catering" (Zhang 2013) with variations presented to different audiences in China and the West. When a Western audience desires to see exotic images of China, Chinese directors oblige in their films. For instance, the story in Zhang Yimou's *Raise the Red Lantern* (1991) takes place in rural Shanxi Province, which had no foot binding custom; however Zhang's addition of the practice to the film affords him more melodrama. The film was a success in the West but received heavy domestic criticism. Hollywood producers no longer make Fu Manchu-type of images of Chinese (Yang 2010, 62), especially under the circumstances that Chinese production companies are also pouring multi-million dollar investments into Hollywood. American producers and directors are becoming more and more flexible in engineering their cinematic images of China which best serves their market interest as long as "the Orientals see the ideal images of the Orient in the theater and as long as they happily walk into the theater and contribute to the box office earnings" (Zhang 2013). This "special catering" is a trait of what Tianpan Zhang calls "neo-Orientalism," in which both Westerners and Chinese make stereotypical images of the Chinese; however, fundamentally "The Orient is a sheer fabrication of the West. It is an epistemic system that permits the invention of 'Oriental cultures' and prejudices toward Asian cultures" (Zhang 2013).

Though his critique is intended in a North American context, Lopez's characterization of the Western romance of Tibet as a New Age Orientalism is swiftly made use of in the Chinese State's debate with the global public concerning the past of Tibet. Tibetologists and cultural critics like Du Yongbin, Shen Weirong, and Wang Hui readily cite from Lopez's *Prisoners of Shangrila* (1998) to emphasize the alleged hallucinatory nature of Westerners' appreciation of Tibet's Buddhist civilization. In this regard, celebrating Tibet's past as a Buddhist nation is taken as a challenge to the Chinese state's socialist modern Tibet – the New Tibet "liberated" from its oppressive past. Lopez's text is often referenced as an admission of the West that the positive, spiritual, often inspiring images of Tibet are sheer fantasy. In his search for the pattern of the West's fascination with Tibet, Lopez shares his historical view that Tibet oscillates between resistance to "the colonial ambitions of a European power" and submission to "the colonial ambitions of an Asian power" (Lopez 1998, 3). As Lopez continues his critique, these two extremes between which Tibet oscillates lie in the imagination of the West, within the same enclosure of the West's construct of the Occident and the Orient; thus both are "a historical rather than a geographic construct" (Lopez 1998, 4). Lopez's adoption of Said's polemical approach inadvertently lends favor to China's interest in the global debates of the Tibet Question. In this sense, I insist that how Tibet appears in the mindscapes of the Chinese and Tibetans in China has to be examined in the global context.

To further elaborate my point, I see Lopez's dichotomization of the Occident and the Orient (or the West and Tibet) is not unique in the critical pursuits of scholarly understanding of the West's encounter with different peoples of the world. This dichotomy is synonymous with other sets of the West-East or the West-South dichotomies e.g. modernity versus tradition, the progressive versus the backward, and the dominant versus the dominated, to name a few. These critical dichotomies once rippled through nearly all disciplines of the social sciences and humanities and engendered a series of perspectival revolutions among scholars whose works involve interpretation, translation, and representation of non-Western peoples and their social realities. The West and the East, and the North and the South are all interlocked in moralizing critiques of all kinds. In this environment the West has become an easy target to which responsibility for a pandemic of human vices across the globe is ascribed. Yet at the same time, many Western countries are havens for refugees, political dissidents, and immigrants fleeing war, persecution, and unequal distribution of economic and social resources in their home countries. People are on the move, traveling in and out of one another's geographic domains and affecting each other's national interests. In the context of the global movements of peoples and ideas, fixed cultural perspectives, such as those of Orientalists and of their antagonists, are becoming intellectually stale and therefore less viable in their ability to help us understand the dynamics and complexities of human encounters.

In this book I prefer to take a post-Orientalist position. Herein, "post-" indicates a sense of moving beyond a cultural consciousness initiated in the last century and giving birth to a collective scholarly awareness of the colonialism-colored gaze on non-Western peoples and places. This temporally understood "post-" is not meant to advocate an intentional forgetting of physically destructive and morally lethal acts of oppression in human history but pushes for a deeper view of locally expressed human universals in past and present conditions of human conflicts, one-sided curiosities, and mutual interactions on a global scale. As we are literally situated in the "super-diversity" (Vertovec 2007, 9) of the world thanks to transnational migration and the global visibility of human cultures, religions, and intellectual thoughts in the twenty-first century, the totalizing effect of Orientalist discourses, such as those of Said, Lopez, and Sardar, is obviously counterproductive to our understanding of multi-faceted issues such as why and how Tibet continues to spark imaginations, attract visitors, and induce eco-spiritual and geopoetic depictions of Tibet from both Tibetans and non-Tibetans.

In the context of contemporary Tibetan studies, I feel compelled to repeat Georges Dreyfus's question – "Are we prisoners of Shangrila?" (Dreyfus 2005, 1) – in response to Lopez's claim that "We are all prisoners of Shangrila" (Lopez 1998, 13). My post-Orientalist approach in this book is intended to pluralize and contextualize "we" as concerned scholars, public intellectuals, Tibetans, and non-Tibetans, and to re-examine "Shangrila" or the imagined Tibet as a locus of diverse human affects, emotions, perceptions, lived experiences, and public discourses instead of continuing to ossify the Orientalist divisions of "us" and "them" or of the defining and the defined. James Clifford lucidly points out, "Said's work frequently relapses into the essentializing modes it attacks and is ambivalently enmeshed in the totalizing habits of Western humanism" (Clifford 1988, 33). Heavily dependent on Said's totalizing discourse, Lopez's critique produces the same effect in Tibetan studies beyond North America.

My re-examination of this "we" and "Shangrila" in post-Orientalist terms thus has to go beyond such splits and dichotomizations in order to highlight the interactive modes of human living in the contemporary world in which human ideas and practices of different origins have found new roots and fruits beyond their native lands. While the most widely spread forms of humanism come from Western Europe – anarchism, communism, socialism, and idealism being among those that have changed lifestyles and governing systems in most parts of the world, non-Western thought systems and religious practices are entering deeper into the core of Western cultural consciousness. Tibetan Buddhism is one of the many non-Western belief systems growing roots in the West (Paine 2004, 115), and also finding new soil in which to grow among Chinese in China (Smyer Yu 2011). Its perceived eco-spirituality (Ivakhiv 2001, 8) plays a critical role in non-Tibetans' conversion to or deep interest in Tibetan Buddhism and Tibet. In this case, place-human bonding occurs not only between Tibetans and their homeland, but also between non-Tibetans and Tibet. "The West," "the East," "Tibet," and "China" in this book are thus conceptualized with my experienced diversity of cultural, ecological, religious, spiritual, aesthetic, and political perspectives and modes of being.

A fixed perspective would not serve the purpose of our understanding of place-based human universals in the forms of home making, dwelling experience, nostalgia, and pilgrimage. Thus, in this segment of the chapter I delineate my key conceptual terms and methodological approach to making sense out of how Tibet is being perceived, imagined, and represented among both Chinese and Tibetans in contemporary China.

1.2.1 Mindscape

"Imagination" and "fantasy," two familiar words in the texts of contemporary critics of imagined Tibet, continue to be useful in my discussion of the same topic in the context of China. However, it is noticeable that in the course of their alleged intellectual association with the Orientalist mindset, they are more often considered a value judgment only. In my pursuit of a multifaceted understanding of place-human bonding, imagination and fantasy are a part of but not the only human mental activities that occur in response to the external physical environment – namely, place. I'll discuss how I use the word "place" shortly, however, in working with physical place and human responses to and imprints on it, I see that the juxtaposed use of mindscape and landscape by such scholars as R.J. Zwi Werblowksy (1998, 9) and Allan Grapard (1989, 162) are rather much more ontologically and intellectually generative than "imagination" and "fantasy."

With this said, the meaning of mindscape in this book refers to a range of reflexes, intellectual reflections, emotional responses, memories, moving images, and mental data storage of scents, colors, sounds, temperatures, and meteorological patterns, all of which originate from human lived experiences enveloped in the external physical environment, namely, landscape, which I will also define. Mindscape in this regard mirrors landscape itself and the social acts and events taking place in it. It can be seen metaphorically as the "inner landscape" (Bunkse 2007, 219) of mountains, rivers, forests, oceans, villages, towns, and cities but it is immersed in one's depthless and shapeless thoughts, affections, feelings, fears, hopes, and dreams. Like flora and fauna rooted in the external landscape, the "flora" and "fauna" rooted in the mindscape are also animated, not with nutrients from the biosphere but with one's intellectual faculty and emotionality. In other words, a mindscape consists of one's intellectuality and emotionality with both a spatial and a temporal structure of its own.

This leads to another critical aspect of mindscape germane to this book, that is, the temporality of mindscape in relation to what Tim Ingold calls "the temporality of landscape," which "...inheres in the pattern of dwelling activities" (Ingold 1993, 153). Such a pattern is not only materialized as the human built environment and other markings on the landscape but is also inscribed on one's mindscape as memories, daily routines, and cultural consciousness. To go a bit further, unlike the physical nature of landscape, the temporality of mindscape is what I would call "place in time" meaning that what one has seen and experienced in a landscape does not only become memory in the mindscape but also takes on another active mode of being as a remembered place that continues to speak to the person. This aspect of mindscape is particularly important to my discussion of how Tibet, as a place, speaks to Tibetans when they are away from Tibet and to non-Tibetans after returning from their travel to Tibet. Geographic distance in this respect is overcome in one's remembered place taking root in the mindscape. Such place in time is the animating force that triggers creative aspirations, existential reflection, spiritual revolution, or nostalgia at a later date.

1.2.2 Landscape, place, and placiality

In anthropology, my own discipline, the works of active scholars of landscape studies such as Tim Ingold, Christopher Tilley, and Barbara Bender have manifested intertextual relations with the works of geographers, philosophers, psychologists, and critical theorists such as Denis Cosgrove, Edward Casey, James Gibson, Edward Relph, and James Ferguson. In this book I continue this line of transdisciplinary practices affirming the inherent mutual saturation and bonding between landscape and mindscape in the case of Tibet. The characteristic approach of the abovementioned scholars does not treat landscape as a distanced object that is soundless, scentless, senseless, and upon which one gazes. Instead, landscape pertains to "spatial experience" (Tilley 1994, 11), "dwelling perspective" (Ingold 1993, 152), "cultural image" (Daniels and Cosgrove 1988, 1), and "the materiality of the world" (Bender 2001, 4). Landscape is what Husserl calls "lifeworld" or *Lebenswelt* (Husserl 1970, 137), that which embraces all forms of life, their biospheres and cultural domains. In this regard, landscape in this book does not conform to the meaning of its Dutch influenced English heritage (*landschap-landscape*) referring to the pictorial quality of a given piece of land serving to frame natural scenes for artistic purposes.

As the lifeworld itself, landscape environs us, invades and permeates our body and mindscape with its air, water, nutrients, and its solid surface supporting our bipedal locomotion. It is what Ingold calls the "weather world" (Ingold 2011, 126) and is what Tilley characterizes as a world entering each of us through "a visionscape, a touchscape, a soundscape, a smellscape, and a tastescape" (Tilley 2011, 27–28) before it becomes a memory, an unforgettable image, a sense of nostalgia, or a collective sentiment in one's mindscape. Therein the emphasis on the sensorial and ecological dimensions of landscape is critical, as all cases of imagined Tibet in the narratives in this book are not fantasies arising out of the mind as though it were unrelated to physical reality, but come from the actual bodily experiences of individuals in the landscape of Tibet whether they are natives or outsiders. These individuals may not have been to every corner of Tibet but every one of them was either born or has set his or her foot in particular places of Tibet. They feel drawn to these places, e. g. villages, nomadic seasonal camps, towns, or sacred mountains and lakes, which share the common geographical location and geological features of the Tibetan plateau. This is what I mean by "place-based human universals" that prompt Tibetophiles' imaginative relationships with Tibet after they return from their travels.

Throughout this book the ideas of landscape and place overlap one another and therefore are synonymously used in different cases; however, the slight difference between the terms is that landscape is broadly understood as lifeworld while place refers to a particular region, location, site, or community as an integral part of the larger lifeworld. It is therefore a relationship between the whole and the part. Quantitatively the whole and the part are different only in scale. Particularities of place are determined by geology, ecology, or the human built environment. What is crucial is that there is always a give-and-take relationship between place and those lives enveloped by it. In the recollection of his pilgrimage to Mt. Kailas, Lama Govinda narrates, "They [mountains] attract and collect invisible energies from their surroundings: the forces of the air, of the water, of electricity and magnetism; they create winds, clouds, thunderstorms, rains, waterfalls, and rivers. They fill their surroundings with active life and give shelter and food to innumerable beings. Such is the greatness of mighty mountains" (2005, 272). This observation did not require Tibetan language competency but was based on his bodily experience in the mountains. It was precisely his being-there that allowed him to speak of Tibet as a power place on earth.

Like landscape, place can be both naturally and human constructed; however it is essential to reiterate that its physical presence is antecedent to human social and emotional investments in it. Oftentimes among scholars, the humanization of place is understood merely as the result of human initiatives, thus permitting us to perceive place as a passive container or simply a social construct (Greider and Garkovich 1994, 2). In this book, on the contrary, the humanization of place is also understood the other way around: it is a process of place taking root in the human mindscape. This is the "potency" of place (Casey 2000, 184) at work, which, besides sustaining us as a biological species, imbues us with the senses of rootedness (Relph 1976, 38) and memorability (Casey 2000, 200). Once again, such rootedness is a mutual connectedness between place and mindscape. As mentioned earlier, in this intercourse between physical but humanized place and human mindscape, place becomes placeless-place in human consciousness and is akin to remembered place.

Casey opens *The Fate of Place* with this thetic assertion, "...we are implaced beings to begin with, that place is an a priori of our existence on earth" (1997, x). I wish to add that place is also imprinted in our mindscape as memory, sentiment, or simply a state of the mind. To address the empirical experiences of

1.2 Mindscaping the Tibetan landscape — 23

place and placeless-place in the case of Tibet and its imagined incarnations, I find Casey's phrase "placiality" (1997, 266) best links the materiality and immateriality of place. While reflecting the physical presence of place, placiality also signifies "nonsensible forms of place" or "psychic place" in the Aristotelian sense, which affirms "the soul as a place or set of places" (Casey 1997, 288). Thus, the employment of placiality as a conceptual vehicle is crucial in my discussion of a variety of manifestations of place beyond geography to include poetic narratives, works of art, cinematic images, memoirs, and public discourses concerning topophilia toward Tibet as a high place.

On one hand, my use of placiality is deliberately employed to avoid reaching quick conclusions about non-Tibetans' poetic and imaginative recollections and reflections of their travels to Tibet as "fantasies" or "hallucinations" as the perspective of existing critiques and criticisms suggest. This is because in my work I find the alleged "fantasies" and "hallucinations" often become more acute, intense, and concentrated during the post-Tibet phase of many non-Tibetan travelers. This could be seen as the rootedness of Tibet in the mindscapes of the travelers or as the place of Tibet establishing itself as a placeless-place in the mindscape of the non-Tibetan. On the other hand, as in other cultural systems, the manifestations of placiality, in both material and immaterial senses, are found in Tibetans' own terminology, grasping the mutual rootedness between their living place and their mindscape, revealed in the language with terms such as *sagzhi-rinpoche* (ས་གཞི་རིན་པོ་ཆེ།, earth as treasure), *sagyang* (ས་གཡང་། the potency or power of place), *sa zangngan je degtsan* (ས་བཟང་ངན་གྱི་རྒྱགས་མཚན། geomancy), *sa-ur-ur* (ས་འུར་འུར། roar of the earth), and *sa'og rempagu* (ས་འོག་རིམ་པ་དགུ the nine supernatural beings below the earth). The list goes on but shows that native Tibetans' understanding of their homeland also involves their reflexive, reflective, utilitarian, and transcendental absorbing of their living place as "the perceptual unity" (Relph 1976, 4) formed and solidified with lived experiences of place and the knowledge therefrom. The immaterial place of Tibet equally lives in the mindscapes of different individual Tibetans as a property of *sem* (སེམས།), or the mind naturally filled with the presence of imagination (བསམ་པའི་འཆར་སྣང་།) and fantasy (འཆར་སྣང་།).

Thus the combined materiality of landscape, place, and placiality finds its immaterial counterpart in the mindscape. Through the dialectics, contradictions, and synergies of both, my book is intended as a visit to different dimensions of Tibet's placiality.

1.2.3 Eco-aesthetics

In my earlier study of Chinese Buddhist pilgrimage to Tibet, I discussed the eco-sublime experience as a pattern of interaction between the pilgrim and the Tibetan landscape. It is a process of an engagement between landscape and mindscape centering upon a shared sense of greatness that is immediate in place but latent in mind. It is the greatness of the place that activates the latent greatness of the mind. Both eventually become inseparably one and the same (Smyer Yu 2011, 194–195). I see this eco-sublime pattern of non-Tibetans' pilgrimage to Tibet as a unique experience of crossing a territorial passage whose spiritual impact on the pilgrim is no less than a ritual-oriented rite of passage. The initial emphasis of my discussion is on how "the territorial charisma" (Smyer Yu 2011, 51) of the Tibetan landscape empowers Chinese pilgrims in addition to the religious empowerment they receive from their Tibetan teachers. In this engagement of landscape and mindscape I viewed Tibet as an "eco-Buddhist Tibet" (Smyer Yu 2011, 173).

In this book, I continue to discuss the dynamics of pilgrimage but do not limit it to what, in the earlier stage of my research, I saw as only a "Buddhist" experience. After working with pilgrims, tourists, and Tibetan writers and artists in their post-pilgrimage state, and re-reading the writings of "the great mystifiers," Tibetans in diaspora, and contemporary travelers, I recognize the antecedent role of place in the popular recognition of Tibet as a hot spot and a power place. In this context the appreciation of Tibetan landscape in the language of positive aesthetics is a common theme of Tibetans' and non-Tibetans' experiences of Tibet. It is precisely because of the imaginative and poetic expressions of the positive aesthetics that critics of imagined Tibet often separate the cultural subjectivities of non-Tibetans from geographic Tibet or look upon the non-Tibetan subjectivities as a projection of a fantasy world onto Tibet; thus the "real" and the "imagined" Tibets are distinguished from each other and dichotomized; however, such dichotomization needs to be contextualized case by case.

From the perspective of my anthropological study of landscape, the "real" and the "imagined" are both antecedently conditioned upon Tibet as a concrete place. Because of this concrete place, seekers, travelers, or Tibetans in diaspora begin their imagination; likewise the critics initiate their critiques from the perspectives of their own trained subjectivities. Tibet deserves its own place not only in geographic and historical terms but also in the varied experiences of those who have been to and enveloped by its topography, meteorological fluxes, and cultural ethos.

In this context I propose an eco-aesthetic understanding of why and how Tibet is a potent place generative of cultural, spiritual, and environmental perceptions and critiques. In Western scholarship the original meaning of "aesthetics" based on its Greek etymon pertains to sense-based perceptions; however, its currently popular use is generally associated with the idea of beauty objectively and artistically defined (Berleant 2010, xii) or with the "formal qualities of an object" (Carlson 1979, 100). The sensorial base appears to recede into its etymological background. By adding the prefix "eco-" I hope to re-emphasize the sensoriality and environmentality of aesthetic experiences centered upon what Tilley calls "the lived body" or "the body-subject" as "a mind physically embodied, a body and a mind which always encounters the world from a particular point of view in a particular context at a particular time and in a particular place, a physical subject in space-time" (Tilley 2004, 2). In this regard, aesthetic activities yield particular experiences and knowledge with all senses involved, namely, a synaesthesia (Howes 2006, 161) or a "fusion of the senses" (Tilley 2004, 14). This is the case with most writers and critics concerning Tibet in the twenty-first century and whose claims are often based on their physical travel to Tibet in addition to their historical reading of literature about Tibet.

My eco-aesthetic approach aims to produce two interpretive results from my study of the potency of Tibetan landscape. First, I see that non-Tibetans' visual articulation of the Tibetan landscape, including mine, reflect our reflexive appreciation of it as a collage of "earthworks" or earth art with the caveat that the magnificent mountains and expansive grasslands in Tibet are the works of the earth's geological and ecological forces, not of human artistic creativity. For instance, the stunning images of Mt. Kailesh and Lake Namtso possess enough aesthetically suggestive power to prompt an increasing number of people to travel to Tibet. In this respect my eco-aesthetic approach is centered upon the potency of the Tibetan landscape as environmental art with a unique aesthetic force generating "feelings of uplift" (Berleant 2010, 22).

While acknowledging the formal aesthetic qualities of the Tibetan landscape, the critical point of my eco-aesthetic discourse in this book is placed on recognizing the felt empowerment of many pilgrims, writers, and artists from the Tibetan landscape as a result of their immersion in the physical environment of Tibet which sets the premise of their later imaginative recollections and descriptions of their experiences in Tibet. In this context, if a Tibet (or Tibets) is imagined, it is the body of the pilgrim or the traveler that is the medium linking Tibet with his or her mind. In this imaginative process one's subjectivity is physical and one's perception is filled with ambient activities (Tilley 2004, 4). Eco-aesthetics in this regard is what Tilley calls "dehiscence" or "an opening of my body to things, a reversible relationship between touching and being touched, myself and other, the effect of myself on things and those things on me" (Tilley 2004, 30). Thus, the imaginative language of Tibet-related writings is not a pure mental creation of the writer but is a dehiscent entwinement of place, body, and mind, of landscape and mindscape.

The second aspect of my eco-aesthetic approach is to exercise what Ingold calls "a sentient ecology" (Ingold 2000, 24) in which the scenic, artistic, and wholistic qualities of landscape are recognized with a deeper and thicker understanding rather than only the formal qualities assessed in terms of variety, unity, and balance as the keywords of aesthetic appraisal of a given landscape as environmental art (Carlson 1979, 100). By "sentient" I mean that the aesthetic potency of the Tibetan landscape resides in the crisscrossed lineages of humans and earthly deities embodied in mountains and lakes. The shared sentience of people, gods, and the earth deeply moves many pilgrims and visitors who sense the enspirited landscape of Tibet. Landscape in the Tibetan context is seen as "a sphere of nurture" (Ingold 2000, 144) with entwined genealogies of humans and gods, both of which are intertwined in "a rhizomatic world" (Ingold 2004, 140) and are amalgamated into a massive complex of interconnected roots. To emphasize, the sentient ecology embedded in my eco-aesthetic approach pertains to the eco-religious practices and eco-spiritual sentiment embodied in the landscape (Smyer Yu 2011, 59), in which the ancestries of humans and earthly gods are interlocked in a mutually nurturing relationship or an interdwelling relationship.

1.2.4 Affordances

Tibet, as a "hot" spot and a power place, affords Tibetans as well as non-Tibetans the ability to perceive, to imagine, to envision, to engage, to critique, and to transform whatever personal or collective conditions we encounter in or outside Tibet. Engagements *between* Tibetophiles and Tibet are multitudinal and multifarious. My emphasis is meant to discern an intersubjective relationship between a place and people who are either native or outsiders with deep topophiliac commitment to Tibet. Recognizing the subjectivity of place is the starting point before I move further to affirm the materiality of placial potency as what James Gibson calls "affordances" of place in *The Ecological Approach to Visual Perception* (1986). This long lasting theoretical model continues to find its vitality in different disciplines working at the intersection of place, ecology, perception, and information. An affordance, according to Gibson, is innate in an environment but becomes perceptible when an organism finds utility from it, as he says in this frequently cited quote, "The affordances of the environment are what it offers the animal, what it provides or furnishes, either for good or ill...It implies the *complementarity* of the animals and the environment" (1986, 127). The emphasis is mine and indicates that both the environment and the organism enter a relationship which affords the organism values and meanings, be they biological or utilitarian.

Such a relationship is, in fact, a niche for the organism, which "refers more to how an animal lives than to where it lives" (1986, 128). An affordance, as a relationship, is present in both the environment and the organism. As a gift of the environment it is latent to start with. The organism is prompted to identify the affordance in the environment. The materialization of this relationship involves invitation, demand, and identification. Random objects in the environment are thus not affordances until they have entered this complementary relationship. A cave would not be a wolf's den until the wolf takes residence in it. It appears that the relationship between the cave and the wolf are that of an object and a subject, but I prefer to see it from Gibson's perspective – "An affordance cuts across the dichotomy of subjective-objective and helps to understand its inadequacy. It is equally a fact of the environment and a fact of behavior. It is both physical and psychical, yet neither. An affordance points both ways, to the environment and to the observer" (1986, 129). This perspectival emphasis is meant to highlight affordance as a form of interlocution between the environment and the organism, in which each speaks to the other, and each is a subject rather than an object to the other.

In my interpretation of how Tibet's placiality speaks to both Tibetans and non-Tibetans, Gibson's concept of affordance is employed to help me build the case of how landscape engenders internal "tipping points" when one is enveloped in it and when one savors an in-it-experience in a private moment away from it. The phrase "tipping point" is often used in the political and environmental arenas to highlight the imminence of crises or systemic collapses (Shen, Downing and Hamza 2010, 1). Politically, as discussed earlier, Tibet is at a tipping point as indicated in the high number of self-immolation cases. Environmentally the vulnerability of Tibet's ecosystems is self-evident although it is not at a tipping point leading to a total collapse. Here I am referring to "internal tipping points" to mean that the landscape of Tibet affords multiple inner changes to those outsiders who have physical encounters and to those natives who are in diaspora or who live bilocally between Tibet and elsewhere. Such changes mostly signify intellectual and epistemic insurrection in the Foucaultian sense (Foucault 1980, 81) or in the sense of *rigpa* (རིག་པ། unhindered vision or realization) in Tibetan Buddhist philosophy, which subverts or revolutionizes existing worldviews and established values. The word "tip," as either a noun or a verb, suggests overbalance, imminent fall, or turning over on a high point.

From my fieldwork I see the tipping points that Tibet affords its visitors and natives range from the emotional, the aesthetic, and the intellectual to the environmental, the sublime, and the humanitarian. The height and expansiveness of the Tibetan landscape communicates with the human mindscape in myriad ways.

In their study of high places, Cosgrove and Della Dora find, "The human connection with high places is a two-way physical and imaginative dialogue in which geographical knowledge is continuously built and destabilized, shaped, and reshaped" (Cosgrove and Della Dora 2009, 4). Such imaginative dialogue often leads to moments of what they call "purification, eschatology and transcendence" (Cosgrove and Della Dora 2009, 5). So, it isn't we who exercise a gaze of some sort, e. g. the colonial, Orientalist, or aesthetic gaze, over the landscape; instead, it is the other way around: the landscape gazes at us or through us and makes us self-conscious of our own state of being when we are fully in the embrace of a lifeworld with its mediums, substances, and surfaces in both geological and meteorological senses (Gibson 1986, 19–22; Ingold 2011, 22) and when our mindscape is overpowered by its continuing presence outside its geographic domain.

Historically it was not merely those seekers like Lama Govinda who experienced an internal tipping point in the Tibetan landscape. Military officers like Francis Younghusband (1863–1942) and Li Guozhu (1938 –) also felt "a deep inner-soul satisfaction" (Younghusband cited by Matless 1991, 273) and "the soul is purified" (Li 2010, 199) in their post-military assignments. In the current transnational spaces where I work and live, many of my Tibetan friends in Beijing feel their homeland becomes bigger when they are away from it. In other words the geographic distance does not diminish but rather increases the size of the Tibetan landscape in their mindscape. This common feature of Tibetans and non-Tibetans' experience with the Tibetan landscape is at the core of my writing.

1.3 A geographic navigation of my fieldwork

Scholarly works of contemporary Tibetan studies are characteristically cross-regional. Contributors to such volumes as *Amdo Tibetans in Transition* (Huber 2002), *Contemporary Tibet* (Sautman and Dreyer 2006), and *Tibetan Modernities* (Barnett and Schwartz 2008) have all visited or are regular travelers between the highlands of Tibet and the lowlands of China. It is precisely their cross-regional awareness of Tibet in the context of contemporary China that generates their critical scholarship. Not all scholars of contemporary Tibetan studies are geographers and anthropologists; however, I notice fieldwork or travel experience is a core foundation of their writings. This book is also the result of cross-regional fieldwork involving not only my living and working in urban China and rural Tibetan areas, but also my participating in a variety of activities and events as well as reading archival materials and literary works of Tibetans and Han Chinese, which are, to me, emblematic of the topophiliac engagements between landscape and mindscape.

Geographically this book covers the Amdo region of Qinghai, Beijing, Shanghai, Yunnan's Shangrila, and the Tibet Autonomous Region (TAR). Temporally it is set between 2008 and 2013. The fieldwork was conducted in Chinese and Tibetan Amdo dialect. What committed me to writing this book was my working and living on a university campus with the largest body of Tibetan students and faculty members in Beijing. This unique urban community of Tibetans exerts a gravitational pull to Tibetan scholars, writers, artists, musicians, and filmmakers scattered in different institutions and residential districts of Beijing. Precisely because of the physical distance between Beijing and Tibetan regions, I see the varied engagements of Tibetan landscape and human mindscape taking place among both Tibetans and Chinese Tibet fans. Resembling its imperial era, contemporary Beijing still draws China's ethnic minorities to its centrality and to an engagement in the popular realms of literature, art, and entertainment.

1.3.1 Beijing

In Beijing, along with my interaction with Tibetan scholars and students, I also spent time with Tibetan "Beijing-drifters" many of whom are actors, artists, writers, and filmmakers. As mentioned in the earlier discussion on "Tibet-drifters" and "Beijing-drifters," the latter are independent career seekers and professionals, not formal employees of any institutions or companies. They often start out as freelancers in their chosen fields and their livelihoods in Beijing depend upon paid projects of different kinds, e. g. voice dubbing for a TV show, stage performances, recording assignments for film preproduction, or textual translation. They may have residential permits but not official household registration cards issued by the city of Beijing. Their living space is often shared with several other "Beijing-drifters" since housing in this city is prohibitively expensive to newcomers and to those whose creative works are still in the making. Many established Tibetan artists combine living space with work space. In 2009 I visited the apartment of a well-known popular singer. He was taking a year-long intensive film course at Beijing Film Academy. The monthly rent for his 1,600 square foot apartment was 11,000 RMB (approximately US$1,700), expensive even by North American standards. Six other artists from his home region shared the rent.

In late 2008 I started a film co-op whereby I converted my apartment near the university into a studio, because I wanted to have a space for creative collaboration with my Tibetan friends. The film co-op was initiated in order to share resources, talents, and skills among Tibetan "Beijing-drifters" and students drawn to filmmaking and literary creativity. In less than eighteen months it evolved into a fully functional studio that could handle both preproduction and postproduction work. In the meantime it became a live-work space for me, a recent graduate from Beijing Film Academy, and a screenwriter, both of whom were from Amdo. The small communal space proved to be imbued with critical openness among ourselves and our friends. By "critical openness" I mean mutuality, confidence, ease, and trust not only on a daily basis but also on social occasions. Besides the three of us every other participant in the co-op was simultaneously a learner, an inquirer, and an expert. My anthropological work-mode was both participant observation and observant participation, in which my co-working and co-living experiences with my Tibetan friends prompted me to engage a new study of landscape and mindscape concerning how images and imaginations of Tibet are woven together and reproduced with both personal and collective sentiments in contemporary China.

The height of Tibet is not lessened when it is represented in Beijing. Aside from the state policies of the Tibet Question that continue to make Tibet a global hot spot, the images of Tibet in the popular realm have diversified in travel writings, pilgrimage narratives, photo exhibits, art galleries, film shows, and tourism commercials. What has not changed in this growing range of images is the landscape itself. No matter how a writer, an artist or a photographer wishes to romanticize Tibet and project his or her ethnocentric aesthetic sentiment onto it (as some scholarly opinion suggests), he or she cannot do away with the geological, ecological, and meteorological elements of the Tibetan plateau, all of which contribute to the positive aesthetics or the sublime perception of Tibet. To engage the subjectivities of writers and artists in this midst, my film co-op and visual anthropology class often hosted guest speakers to consider such topics.

Both the Tibetan and Han Chinese visitors had professions or personal interests that reproduced images of Tibet in the forms of fiction and non-fiction writing, painting, and film. Among the Han Chinese guests many of them often emphasized the altitude of their travel routes in Tibet as one of their critical experiences. Being in Tibet, to them, meant both absorbing an exotic culture and its sublime landscape with a mixture of inspiration and fear. The conclusive statements of their talks were identical: the sentiment that Tibet is "the last pureland" (*zuihoude jingtu* 最后的净土) on earth was consistently made in contrast to the rapid urbanization of China.

In fall 2009, a senior faculty member of Beijing Film Academy displayed his photos of Tibetan cities, towns, and mountains taken in fifteen days of travel in TAR. While expressing his marvel at Tibet's natural landscape he was pessimistic in suggesting that Tibet would end up like urban China. To him, modernization will eventually and inevitably transform Tibetan villages, towns, and even the natural landscape into something urbanites of China are all too familiar with. In an attempt to collect or record what he feels is threatened, he spent the summer of 2012 with a Tibetan family in southern Gansu as part of his fieldwork in order to write a script based on contemporary Tibetan families' stories.

In fall 2010, with a group of Tibetan indie filmmakers I attended the premiere of *Once upon a Time in Tibet* (2010), a fiction film directed by Dai Wei from CCTV. Said to be a 50-million RMB production, it tells a love story between a young Tibetan woman and an American pilot whose fighter plane is shot down by the Japanese in the 1930s, and is based on Tashi Dawa's unpublished Chinese language novel *Shambhala's Cat*. The film was given mostly negative reviews by my Tibetan friends who thought Dai Wei made too great of an effort to tie China and the U.S. together with Tibet against a common enemy while the love story had too many narrative mistakes. From the angle of my landscape-mindscape studies, I noticed Dai Wei spent much of her preproduction budget on landscape filming including aerial shots. The landscape cinematography was more impressive than the love story. At the premiere I could not help but suspect that a tourism commercial was embedded in the film. Whether or not Dai Wei intentionally embedded this "tourist tease" in her film could not be ascertained, but I did see the landscape of Tibet as a marketable commodity of tourism.

From Tibetan artists and filmmakers whom I know in Beijing I see two ongoing debates. On one side the Chinese image of Tibet is similar to its counterpart in the popular realm of the West. This image sustains Tibet as a nation of Buddhism and a paradise on earth. It noticeably frames the emerald summer grasslands, the blue sky, idyllic villages, and high mountains, while simultaneously excluding non-traditional elements as much as possible. On the other side, a growing number of Tibetans advocate verisimilitude in their creative reproductions of contemporary Tibetan social life, religious practices, and natural landscape. This group of Tibetan artists in Beijing describes their approach as "desymbolizing" or *qufuhaohua* (去符号化) in Chinese, which might be best translated as "destereotyping." Many of them feel Buddhist symbols and natural elements of the Tibetan plateau are presented *ad nauseum*. This symbolic overkill in many contemporary creative works either make Tibet look like a thangka painting with an overabundance of Buddhist elements, or overshadow the current modern realities of Tibet. *The Sun Beaten Path* (2010) by Sonthar Gyal and *Old Dog* (2010) by Pema Tseden are prime examples of this growing effort to de-symbolize representations of Tibet.

This is the context of my fieldwork in Beijing, in which I work with both Han Chinese and Tibetans. The mediums of my ethnographic work are our shared photographic equipment, film gear, and editing stations. The spaces of our interactions occur in the studio, classrooms, film review sessions, art galleries, restaurants, cafes, private homes, and en route from Beijing to Tibetan regions for ethnographic assignments, film projects, and pilgrimages.

1.3.2 Qinghai

Toward the tail end of my 2006 fieldwork in which I explored the dynamics of an increasing number of Chinese being attracted to Tibetan Buddhism, I suspected that it must be more than the charismatic lamas and their lineages that draw so many Chinese Buddhists from urban China to Tibet. The gravity of my fieldwork was placed on the interactions between Tibetans and Han Chinese, between Tibetan and Chinese monasteries, and between Tibetan lamas and the Chinese state; so it was a people- and institution-oriented work in which I emphasized the politics of Sino-Tibetan religious encounters rather than what could be called the "place-human interaction." However, during the revision of my first book, I designated textual space in two chapters to the view that Chinese Buddhists are also attracted to Tibet's "territorial charisma" (Smyer Yu 2011, 51), a phrase coined from van Gennep's "territorial passage" (1960, 19) for the purpose of emphasizing that Tibet, to many Chinese pilgrims, is a charismatic place.

My ethnographic work on place-human interaction and bonding began in late 2008. Since then, Qinghai has been the primary site where I work with rural Amdo Tibetans, joining them in their dwelling places and surrounding landscape and in relation to their sacred mountains. Both built and natural environments have been the focus of my research. My participatory fieldwork activities with Amdo Tibetans include co-designing a meditation retreat house, helping to build two solar powered school libraries, volunteering as an assistant to Tibetan lamas' and yogis' cave-based retreats, and filming two documentaries concerning place-human bonding among Amdo Tibetans. These hands-on (and feet-on-the-ground) activities in different places in Qinghai have led to many of the textual themes of this book.

In fall 2008 I helped Akhu Norbu, a *ngapa* (སྔགས་པ། yogi), raise funds in Beijing to build a house for meditation retreats in his village, I was invited by him to contribute my ideas to the design of the house. His reasoning was that because this intended meditation house would receive his students from urban China, he was looking for some "modern conveniences" that his Chinese students would be accustomed to. Having lived in northern California for over twenty years I thought of the architecture at Green Gulch Zen Center in Mill Valley, Spirit Rock Meditation Center in Woodacre, and a former hippie commune in Albion. These places host fine architecture which blends in with the surrounding hills and the idyllic rural scenery of northern California, while also giving enough familiar functionality to urban visitors. My Californian references were too costly for Qinghai as the price of lumber was rising quickly, but the idea of exchanging a pit toilet for a seated toilet and septic system was approved. During the installation, Akhu Norbu made sure the tank and the pipes had no leaks and the liquid waste would be directed only to the wheat field next to the house site. His careful planning of the waste treatment qualified him as a good environmentalist; however, according to him, the primary importance of his precision and meticulousness was to ensure none of the untreated human waste would offend a *kle* (ཀླུ a waterborne, dragon-like supernatural being) living beneath the wheat field where the house would be built.

From Akhu Norbu I began to see a dwelling place as a living space shared with many other beings. In his eyes the seemingly silent *sa* (ས earth; dirt; place) is not merely a physical thing. It comes into human perception in the forms of sand (བྱེ་མ hsima), surface (ས་ཁ sa-kha), rock (རྡོ rdo), field (ཞིང་ས hsangsa), place (ས་ཆ sa-cha), region (ས་ཁུལ sa-khul), domain (ས་རྒྱ sa-rgya), and topography (ས་ཁྱད sa-khyad). What is important is that various forms of *sa* are animated with beings other than humans as shown in Akhu Norbu's case. This aspect of place-people relationship is also identified by other scholars such as Toni Huber and Poul Pedersen (1997) and Axel Michaels (2003). Landscape, for Akhu Norbu and his ancestors, is *sasum* (ས་གསུམ) or "the three domains of the earth," namely *sabla* (ས་བླ the celestial sphere above the earth), *sadang* (ས་སྟེང the surface of the earth), and *sa'og* (ས་འོག the underworld of the earth).

The realms above, on and beneath the earth are residences of a variety of gods, semi-gods, spirits, and demons. No single corner of the earth or its underworld and celestial firmament is unoccupied. To add to Ingold's landscape-as-weather-world, I say landscape is also a multidimensional spirit world as well as "a storied world" (Ingold 2011, 141) with not only tales of humankind but also tales of other beings and their encounters with humans. The question of whether or not these beings exist or whether or not they are imaginative products of the human mind is not relevant to this book since their believed or felt existence to human perception is already an integral part of the eco-spiritual worldview and practices of Tibetans with whom I work. To them the place on earth in which they live speaks as well as listens to them.

On an early May morning in 2010 a small film crew and I walked from a meditation cave up to the ridgeline before dawn to film a scene of "cloud herding" by Akhu Norbu as day broke. This long ridgeline is also a "weather-line" over which rain and hail clouds pour from the east into the village's valley. Dawn broke but no herd-able dark rain clouds converged on us; instead a thick, silvery fog covered the rising sun and blanketed the mountains in front of us. The viewfinder of the camera showed only the small dense droplets of vapor moving in the wind and obscuring the topographic references that indicated the high elevation and the mountainous terrain we were in. My minimum hope from the ridgeline was to capture a few scenes of the sunrise, but even slightly after 6:00 this didn't seem likely. The sun was rising but was hidden behind the dense fog. However, Akhu Norbu, our documentary subject, was rather optimistic. Upon telling us he was going to break the fog he proposed to have the camera follow him. He began to walk along the spine of the ridge with his ritual recitation. Within fifteen minutes the fog thinned. The mountain tops around us began to appear, like small islands in a retreating silvery sea. Akhu Norbu performed a recitation of *sang-chod* (བསང་མཆོད་), verses written to eulogize local deities. To him, the physical contents of fog are indeed tiny water droplets in the air; however fog is more than a meteorological event. It is the work of earth deities, especially those who reside in the celestial domain and on the surface of the earth. By pleasing or sometimes threatening the deities it is possible to work the weather in one's favor. From this filming occasion I learned again that natural events are not seen as neutral happenings among rural Tibetans. They are willed and manipulated by both supernatural beings and humans.

It has been over a decade since I began my Tibet-related career and most of my fieldwork assignments have been completed in Amdo regions of Qinghai, Gansu, and Sichuan. I am not native to Tibet and neither have I gone native. However, what should be said about my working in Tibet is that I recognize my empathetic understanding of place-human relationship among Tibetans. I make this statement because my building activities, participation in my Tibetan friends' pilgrimages to sacred lakes and mountains, and volunteering as an assistant to lamas' and yogis' cave retreats has led the state of my mind into an "empathetic insideness" referring to the willingness of an outsider "to be open to significances of a place, to feel it, to know and respect its symbols;" therefore, "to be inside a place empathetically is to understand that place as rich in meaning…" (Relph 1976, 54).

As an empathetically engaged anthropologist, I regard the Amdo region of Qinghai as my primary geographic reference when I evoke the Tibetan landscape in this book. To be noted, Amdo does not represent the entirety of Tibet but its mountain ranges, linguistic identity, and eco-cultural practices are an inherent part of Tibetan civilizational fabric. Works of R.A. Stein (1962), René de Nebesky-Wojkowitz (1956), John Vincent Bellezza (2005), and Toni Huber (1999a) among others, point to the common eco-spiritual dimension of the Tibetan landscape. Relph once remarked, "The world is peopled with place-spirits and ties to places are spiritual rather than physical" and "...people are their place and a place is its people" (1976, 65, 34). Tibet is such a case. Thus in this book the understanding of the imaginative dialogues between people and high places like Tibet rests upon these inter-braided scholarships of anthropology, geography, religious studies, and Tibetology. In this regard my work in Amdo is a case, not a representation, of such commonality among Tibetans and their native lands.

1.3.3 Lhasa and Shangrila

Between 2008 and 2011 I led U.S. students and faculty members to Lhasa, TAR, and Shangrila, Yunnan Province for field-based courses and faculty seminars on religion and ecology in Tibet. My own fieldwork objective in these two popular tourist destinations was to examine the intersections of tourism as pilgrimage and pilgrimage as tourism. I look upon both as forms of landscape consumption in the commercial and spiritual senses. Lhasa and Shangrila are in two different regions of Tibet and yet they are intimately connected in the current development of China's tourism in Tibet. The emphasis of my work in these two global tourist destinations is not merely on tourism as a commercial industry. Like my other fieldwork locations, I have focused on the connectivity of mindscape and landscape among tour companies, urban landscape masterminds, the regional economic development drive, and consumer desires for natural landscapes.

"I'm going to Lhasa" or "I just returned from Lhasa" are often uttered with an exclamation among tourists, Buddhists, and artists whom I met. The display of pride in this exclamation draws attentive curiosity from friends, colleagues, and acquaintances and makes many of them envious of going to the high place too.

Lhasa is often the first stop of tourists and pilgrims in TAR via aerial or land routes. Since 2006 when the Qinghai–Lhasa railway was completed, riding the train has been the most desirable means to reach the city. The pop singer Xu Qianya's song "Riding the Train to Lhasa" was among China's hottest pop hits since 2007. Its Tibetan versions sung by Tibetan singers like Sho'er Dawa (ཟོར་ཟླ་བ།), Dechan Wangmo (བདེ་ཆེན་དབང་མོ།), Amuna (ཨ་སྨུ་ན།) often fill the audial space of the train from Beijing to Lhasa and are found in the music collections of Chinese tourists and pilgrims on board. The utterance of "Lhasa," like this pop song, oftentimes possesses imaginative qualities and the anticipation of tourists and travelers. The representation of Lhasa in this regard is not limited to the city itself but to its role as a gateway opening up to the entirety of Tibet. Both the inner drama and the travel-pilgrimage drama of the traveler begin before he or she boards the train or the plane. In other words the mindscape of the traveler has already been in contact with Tibet through stock images, travel writings, TV programs, and peer stories. The place of Tibet has what I would call a "mirage effect," a concept I will explore later, but simply explained it is an effect that enables an image to be bounced to far places through the "atmosphere" of mindscape.

Before drafting up my travel course and seminar itineraries I often started with soliciting wish lists from both student and faculty participants about what places they wanted to see in Tibet. The first timers' lists mostly matched the popular and familiar images of Tibet – Potala Palace, Sera Monastery, Johkang Temple, Barkor Street, Namtso Lake and so on. For more sophisticated participants, those who had read about Tibetan Buddhism and the current state of Tibet, there were requests to visit places like Ani Tsangkong Convent (ཨ་ནི་གཙང་ཁང་བཙུན་དགོན་པ།), Tibet Museum, Tibet Revolutionary Exhibit Hall, and other places which are informative of the modern history of Tibet.

In actually touring Lhasa with North American or Chinese scholars and students, I noticed that the ancient architecture of Lhasa amazed them. At the same time the natural landscapes at Namtso Lake, Drak Yerpa Cave Meditation Site, and Mt. Yarlha Shampo excite tourists and pilgrims alike with a different set of aesthetics and inner responses than those elicited by the city of Lhasa. Often the sublime quality of the Tibetan landscape draws emotional currents besides intellectual, philosophical, and environmental reflections from travelers. I would not hesitate to qualify the landscape as what Giuliana Bruno calls an "atlas of emotion" (2002, 6) involving the motion of emotion in both landscape and mindscape in terms of visual-audial stimuli, atmospheric sensations, haptic desires, and imaginative dialogues. The mindscape moves along with the changing terrain. Both are kinesthetic. Each year between 2008 and 2011 at least two or three participants in my field classes and seminars expressed their deep emotional connection with Tibetan landscape in the manner of crying and/or requesting extended private time to "soak up the energy" of the landscape.

In this age of simultaneously occurring late-capitalism and late-socialism in China, the market economy, whether centralized or in a laissez faire state, is always keen on identifying popular desires, aspirations, and trends as potential and actual opportunities for profit. Once a popular desire is amassed around an object, this object, whether a brand name product or a geographic place or a charismatic person, is instantly given commercial value and thus is turned into a commodity.

Åshild Kolås' *Tourism and Tibetan Culture in Transition: A Place Called Shangrila* offers a representative look of this perspective: because Shangrila is "a space of dream" (2008, 104) it is transformed into a tourist commodity as well as a site of place-making, nation-building, and identity contestation. In this regard, as Kolås remarks, Shangrila is an arena for a "representational game" geared toward the contested "authenticity" of Tibetan culture from multiple angles (2008, 120, 124). I also see this aspect of Shangrila in the nexus of tourism and pilgrimage. While touching on this important aspect of the expansion of tourism in Shangrila I steer the emphasis of my work toward what scholars of landscape studies commonly refer to as the "energy" (Ivakhiv 2001, 228) or "potency" of place (Casey 2000, 184). With this said, when a place is turned into a hot commodity of tourism, the "energy" of the place, likewise, also enters this externally discerned "commodity" which becomes a vessel of its mobility beyond its home environment. Shangrila in Yunnan Province is such a vessel of Tibetan landscape in both physical and symbolic terms.

The name "Shangrila" is not native to Kham in Yunnan. Its placial association is fantastically found in *Lost Horizon*, the 1933 novel by James Hilton. Mr. Hugh Conway, the main character, describes it as a serene world with which he "felt the invasion of a deep spiritual emotions, as if Shangrila were indeed a living essence, distilled from the magic of ages and miraculously preserved against time and death" (Hilton 2006, 261). Shangrila of Yunnan was formerly called Zhongdian (中甸) in Chinese and Gyaltang (རྒྱལ་ཐང་) in Tibetan. In 2001, its name was officially changed to Shangrila with approval from the Chinese State. The state explicitly describes Shangrila landscape's resemblance to Hilton's original utopian version (ebeijing.gov.cn). Hilton's fantasy world was thus "discovered" in Western Yunnan Province sixty-eight years after its "creation."

Shangrila, known as "Little Lhasa" in tourist brochures and travel writings, is split into "new" and "old" sections. It is no secret that the "old" section is also new, meaning that most of it was recently (re)built to resemble Shuhe, another "old town" adjacent to Lijiang, 200 kilometers away from Shangrila. In my work, I find that when asked to choose between the "old" and the "new," backpackers and tour groups predominantly choose the "old" as the destination of their lodging, sightseeing, and shopping in spite of the fact that these "old" locations are reproductions. Because of the evidenced newness of Old Town Shangrila, I prefer to see its "oldness" as the materialization of a modern popular mindscape desiring a return to a past placiality in which communal intimacy, organic lifestyle, and accessibility to the natural landscape are readily available. The present place is thus made to represent a time of the past. The selling point is definitively the reconstructed "oldness" in the new space of the city.

Both tourism and pilgrimage possess a shared quality of treating Tibet as a sacred site as well as a site of what Yifu Tuan calls "escapism" (1998, 79), a distinct sense of alienation and disconnectedness resulting from the overhumanized living and working environments of modern cities. In this regard Lhasa and Shangrila ("Little Lhasa") are the travel destinations of tourists and pilgrims and, simultaneously, they are both concrete and symbolic places full of varied affordances connecting landscape and mindscape and interlocking both in an intersubjective relationship.

1.4 Mapping the book

The chapters of this book are strung together with the theme of the intertwinement of landscape and mindscape, or of place and people as I have discussed thus far. What needs to be emphasized is that the meanings of landscape, mindscape, place, and people in different local contexts are all conveyed in a plural and/or relational sense. Tibet, in this book, is recognized as a unique high place that affords a variety of sentiments, perceptions, emotions, imaginations, reflections, thoughts, and social actions to a variety of people in China.

By "variety" I also mean the varied personal, social, cultural, and geographic conditions of different individuals including Tibetans and Westerners traveling or working in China as well as Chinese traveling in Tibet. For instance, among the Tibetans with whom I work, there are rural and urban Tibetans. Among urban Tibetans, there are those who have lost their native tongue but strongly express their sense of belonging to traditional Tibet. Among those who read, write, and speak Tibetan, there are those who are committed to sustaining the Buddhist orientation of Tibetan culture as well as those who have developed antithetical sentiment toward their Buddhist counterparts. All are situated in the context of the growing popular fascination of Tibet and emerging Tibetan self-perceived and self-claimed modern destinies in the political domain of China.

Thus both people and the materiality of their expressed perceptions of Tibet, in the form of publications, film, and artwork, are the center of my anthropological engagement. In this regard, the chapters of this book are interconnected through shifting geographic locations of Chinese and Tibetans moving in and out of tourist-pilgrimage routes, and between the urban and the rural, recognizing the past that is repressed, escaping collective discontentment with modernity, and searching for both existential and spiritual meanings. However, the one thing that does not physically translocate is the place of Tibet. It is the concrete presence of such a place that is truly powerful and takes root in the mindscapes of different individuals.

Chapter Two is the entry point of my inquiry into how the Tibetan landscape (re)enchants its visitors and its natives in diaspora and migration with its eco-aesthetic, eco-sublime, and eco-religious affordances. In this inquiry I treat myself as an outsider but with what Edward Relph calls "empathetic insideness" resulting from my sustained ethnographic rapport with rural communities of Amdo for the last decade. The ethnographic case of this chapter is a Tibetan farming village in Amdo, through which I attempt to show how, in non-Tibetans' positive aesthetics, the Tibetan landscape is often seen as a massive "earthwork" in the geological, topographic, and artistic senses. In the meantime, "earthwork" is also understood as a gerund – that is, "earthworking" stressing intentions and actions embodied in the affective bond between place and people. In my ethnographic study, earthworking among rural Tibetans is regarded as the material manifestation of a synergetic relationship between place and human needs for health and the fertility of people and the fecundity of the land. Eco-religious practices mediate this unique place-human relationship. In this regard, the potency of the earth is animated through demons, ghosts, gods, and spirits in both celestial and terrestrial realms. The highlight of the chapter is what I call the "inter-dwelling mode of being" referring to the mutual saturation of landscape and mindscape, place and memory, and divinity and humanity.

To situate my work in the context of China, Chapter Three addresses how Old Tibet and New Tibet were constructed as complementary products of socialist China. The diachronic shift from contemporary Amdo in Chapter Two to the transitional phase of Tibet over half a century ago is not meant for a sudden temporal return to the past so as to repeat the same macro-political discourses as works by other scholars (Goldstein 1999; Dawa Norbu 2001); instead, it is intended as an anthropological reading of history on the level of the individuals who participated in the Communist transformation of Tibet as military personnel. Based on my archival research and review of recently published journals, diaries, and memoirs by former PLA officers and soldiers I attempt to address two parallel occurrences among former Chinese soldiers stationed in Tibet in the middle of the last century. On one side, in reading their publications, I see the ideologically-ecstatic young PLA soldiers and officers as "missionaries" of Chinese Communism in their long march from Kham into Central Tibet. Seen from the perspective of utopian studies, this historical enactment of Chinese communism in Tibet was a de facto utopianism locked in a negative dependency with dystopia as its dialectical "twin." Such negative dependency permits what I call the "hyper-temporalization" of traditional Tibet and modern socialist Tibet. On the other side, while the PLA brought socialist modernity into Tibet, many of its officers and soldiers felt a sense of "newness" from the lifeworld of Tibetans. The immersion of many PLA personnel in the spectacular landscape of Tibet in the

1950s, in fact, is now yielding a belated eco-aesthetic and even transcendental realization that Tibet was (is) a place of brilliancy with both outer sublime qualities and inner transformative force. If the Chinese troops overpowered Tibetans with their tactical superiority, Tibetan natural and built environments profoundly overpowered many of them on a different scale – a delayed inner transformation.

Chapter Four discusses how many contemporary Tibetan cultural critics reclaim a series of socialist neologisms introduced to Tibetans half a century ago in an attempt to re-envision and redefine what a new modern Tibet will be in their direct referencing of modern political practices of the West in the twenty-first century. In the meantime taking the works of Shogdong, a contemporary Tibetan writer and cultural critic based in Xining, Qinghai, as a case study, chapter four also serves as a pathology of modern practices among urban Tibetans. Shogdong and like-minded Tibetans appear to be anti-traditionalists when they imagine a modern Tibet, not as a replica of socialist China, but as a new Tibet of their own with a true sense of equality. What I see in this intra-Tibetan discourse is that their negative evocation of traditional Tibet is a remembering process that is inversed in the manner of intentional subversion, rejection, and forgetting. The argument I intend to make is that intentional forgetting is unconscious remembering in the nexus of place and memory. In this case, many urban Tibetans' seemingly dismissive attitude toward traditional Tibet is an exercise of a place-based power-discourse in a subaltern sense.

Chapter Five turns to pro-traditionalist Tibetans' affective bond with their homeland in a case study of what I call "a New Tibetan Cinema" spearheaded by Pema Tseden. This emerging indie filmmaking trend among Tibetan artists only began in the twenty-first century; however their productions are already being premiered and are winning awards at international film festivals. The intent of many Tibetan filmmakers is set on contributing their cinematic productions to the ongoing reconstruction and revitalization of their native culture, often with a Buddhist orientation. In my fieldwork with Tibetan filmmakers in Beijing and Qinghai I find their path is marked with their own genre of creativity and verisimilitude as well as with changing approaches in portraying Buddhist and other social practices of their compatriots at home. The cinematic screen obviously becomes the public medium of the interplay between their native landscape and mindscape. Ethnographically Chapter Five is concerned with how Buddhism, in the films of Pema Tseden, the leading figure in the making of the New Tibetan Cinema, is deployed to connect the mindscape of the spectator with both the cultural and the physical landscapes of Tibet. By revisiting critical scenes in these films I argue that the cinematic Buddhist landscape of Tibet is simultaneously home, a remedy for easing nostalgia and felt social marginality, and a potent source of creative empowerment. And yet at the same time, the emerging Tibetan indie films reflect a social reality in which Buddhism-based cultural and communal fabric is encountering destabilizing forces of globalization, modernization, and the market economy.

Chapter Six documents my filming and pilgrimage experience at Mt. Amne Machen (ཨ་མྱེས་རྨ་ཆེན།) in Golok with two Tibetan lamas and a small film crew of Tibetan writers and graduate students, and Han Chinese filmmakers. My ethnographic focus is on our emotional currents and eco-aesthetics in the mountains. Pilgrimage, in this case, entails physical and emotional touches that produce profuse meanings regarding how Amne Machen, as one of the prominent mountain deities of Tibet, symbolizes home, belonging, and the humanization of the native landscape to the Tibetan crew members, and how its environmental conditions present a set of challenges to a few Han Chinese crew members suffering altitude sickness. The leading ethnographic subject in this chapter is Amne Machen as both a mountain deity and the awe-inspiring mountainous landscape in Amdo. In examining how he/it induces emotional responses from us, the pilgrims, I extensively discuss how the two lamas and Tibetan writers and students culturally, spiritually, and emotionally connect themselves with the multiple identities of Amne Machen as a soul mountain (བླ་རི། *bla-ri*), a Tenth Stage Bodhisattva, a wealth god, a warrior god, a fertility god, and a rainmaker according to local folklore. Among all these identities, I find Amne Machen as a soul mountain is the primary source of the emotionality of my Tibetan colleagues' placed-based cultural identity with ancestral memories and religious significance.

In Chapter Seven I shift my ethnographic focal point to a post-Orientalist reading of what I call "the mirage effect" of Tibetan landscape in tourism development and in the creative works of writers and artists whom I call "the mirage-makers." On one hand my findings concur with a scholarly consensus that Tibet is a tourist commodity for both domestic and international tourist consumption. On the other hand I take a step further to argue that the potency of the Tibetan landscape brands a mindscape of utopia in popular China, which is simultaneously real and illusory like a mirage – a trick of refracting light but with the image of an actual object. With a reasonable supposition of Tibet as a topographical utopia as the a priori condition of the mirage effect, I illustrate how the mirage-makers conflate their personal fantasies and dreams with Tibet and how they re-possess Tibet as the space of their own nostalgia, dreams, and visions – the illusory components reflective of their personal and social conditions. While the landscape of Tibet affords contagious geo-poetics and sublime inspiration to, and provokes spiritual responses from those who come into contact with it, the self of the mirage-maker, whether a writer or a filmmaker or a mastermind of tourist design, often recreates itself in the otherness of Tibet. In this process a topographical utopia is turned into a fantastical utopia of the mindscape.

I draw an open-ended ending to this book in Chapter Eight by re-encapsulating my primary point: the lifeworld of Tibet touches us before the outpouring of our sentiments, emotions, perceived realities, moralizing critiques, and reflexive Orientalism disguised as a pilgrim's revelation, humanitarian concerns, or euphoric expressions of felt self-realization. In the meantime, the chapter serves as my postscript regarding where my own subjectivity stands in my critical narratives throughout the book, how I respond to the growing body of critiques of Western imaginations of Tibet among scholars in China, and how I see my geo-anthropological perspective as a contribution to the transdisciplinary studies of modern/contemporary Tibet and landscape-mindscape of high places in the senses of topophilia, eco-aesthetics, eco-spirituality, and eco-entheogeneity. In summarizing the main points of my ethnographic findings and theoretical perspectives, I re-emphasize that I write this book not only as a social scientist but also as a subject of my own research as I am equally entangled in the web of varied symbolic, material, political, religious, and spiritual affordances between landscape and mindscape, between place and memory, and between geological but monumental sites and human emotionality. Topophilia or rather, Tibetophilia in this case, never one-sidedly originates from human perceptions but is a communion of landscape and mindscape, open-endedly undergoing challenges, shocks, sublime depression, ecstasy, narcissism, realization, self-reassurance, renewal, restoration, regression, or what have you.

Chapter Two Geopoetics of place, gods, and people in Sambha (སེ་བྲ)

2.1 Eco-aesthetics of an outsider looking in

I first went to Sambha Village in Amdo (northeastern Qinghai Province) in the summer of 2005, having heard of it while doing fieldwork in a nearby village. I accompanied Akhu Norbu, the ngapa (སྔགས་པ། tantric yogi) from Rachekyi (ར་ཆག་སྐྱི) mentioned in the introduction, to visit his cousin's family in Sambha. The distance between Rachekyi and Sambha is less than twenty kilometers but because it is tucked in a valley surrounded by mountains it feels less accessible. The county bus goes there only once a day in the late afternoon. Once the bus leaves the provincial highway, the narrow dirt road winds eastward between cliffs and Machu (རྨ་ཆུ།) which feeds the Yellow River, into Sambha. On our late afternoon ride, the sun gradually set behind us and the blue waters of Machu steadily but forcefully headed in the same direction as our bus. The mountainous landscape along Machu was both the object of my distanced aesthetic appreciation of the Earth and an encompassing, moving subjectivity that included the motion of the bus and my mind as well as the smell of the diesel exhaust and the mixed sounds of the engine, the tires pressing the gravel road, and the passengers' conversations. The landscape kept moving eastward, new terrain unfolding while my mind tracked its own conflicting desires: one part wanted the bus to continue so as to unfold new, aesthetically pleasing scenes to my view and another wished to freeze or frame segments of the moving landscape as if I were a living camera. These parallel states of the moving landscape and my mindscape continued until the driver honked, signaling the bus's approach to a sharp turn. As the echoes of the horn bounced back from the mountains on both shores of Machu, the bus slowly made a ninety-degree turn. This turning point is not just the gateway into Sambha but is also a vista overlooking the entirety of the village. From that point we saw its wheat fields, the surrounding mountains and the moving river caressing the south edge of the village like a giant blue serpent slowly fading into a narrow gorge toward where Machu eventually becomes the Yellow River.

Looking at the panorama of Sambha through the bus window as the sun set, I was awed, not because I had not seen awe-inspiring landscapes in Tibet before but because I was enthralled by the wholeness of this small human settlement in the embrace of the large mountains and the moving water and it seemed as if it were a place enclosed by itself in a way only possible in fairytales – with nothing lacking and with everything abundant and harmonious. This sudden opening of the vista undoubtedly gave my mindscape a subliminal kick, awakening dormant images of fantasy worlds. My aesthetic and photographic desire was fulfilled later, after I had a contemplative moment at the vista point: I measured the light and clicked the shutter of my panoramic camera, feeling as if, by imprinting the eternity of Sambha through my lens onto the film, my camera had been consecrated by it. In retrospect, during the few minutes in which I framed the landscape of Sambha with my camera, I admittedly treated the totality of this small village and its ambient environment as an earthwork, and as an outsider looking in.

The landscape of Sambha is not as spectacular as that of Amne Machen or Gang Rinpoche (Mt. Kailas) experienced by countless travelers, pilgrims, and professional photographers. My eco-aesthetic sensing of the Sambha landscape stirred up images of the myths of Arcadia and the Shire of the Lord of the Rings, in which self-sustainability, abundance, and harmony are the essence of their ecosystems inclusive of not just humans but also plentiful species of flora and fauna. Furthermore because of humans' care of and stewardship over both the built and natural landscapes, the Earth in these mythic realms appears especially delightful as it radiates a heightened sense of enchantment to those who encounter it. My first encounter with the Sambha landscape could be said to be an experience of the positive aesthetics of nature (Carlson 1984, 6). My aesthetic experience is centered on an "order appreciation," which, as Malcolm Budd explains, means "ordered pattern – a pattern ordered by and revelatory of the forces of creation or selection responsible for it" (Budd 2000, 146–47). These creative forces are the geological, biological, and meteorological forces by which all natural objects in a given landscape are formed with "equal positive aesthetic value" (Budd 2000, 147). From this perspective, I see the Sambha landscape as an order of its own in an aesthetically pleasing enclosure of both natural elements and human creativity.

I have walked up to the mountains around Sambha in all cardinal directions except where it is precipitous on its north edge. My earlier aesthetic sensing of the Sambha landscape automatically and reflexively contrasted with the urban landscape of Beijing where I had been working and living for the last four years. In such a cross-cultural and cross-ethnic contrast, I qualify Sambha's landscape as pleasingly balanced in direct contradiction to the urban landscape of Beijing which, in my mindscape, appears too humanized, thus having lost the aesthetic and ecological balance initially intended by the imperial architects of the Ming and Qing Dynasties. By "too humanized" I mean, in Edward Relph's words, "...the paradox of modern landscapes is that they are dehumanizing because they are excessively humanized...there is almost nothing in them that can happen spontaneously, autonomously or accidentally, or which expresses human emotions and feelings" (Relph 1981, 104). In contrast, the village, though appearing insignificant in size in comparison to Beijing, is comfortably nestled in the embrace of the surrounding mountains and the moving water of Machu. In addition to this horizontal embrace of the village by the natural environment, it is enveloped by the earth below and the sky above. The earth below is fertile enough for farming and stable enough for dwelling, while the sky above brings the villagers profuse sunlight and the starry firmament as well as moisture precipitated from thick, fantastically-shaped clouds. Sambha is in union with the moving sky and the Earth.

Since the first visit, I have returned annually to Sambha for more fieldwork. Each time I look at Sambha's physical appearance or its formal structure, my mindscape brings forth the aforementioned idyllic, scenic, and self-sustaining images. I am not sure whether the subjectivity of the Sambha landscape speaks to me or if my mindscape converses with the landscape. From Tilley's phenomenological perspective, I can at least claim that my experiencing Sambha's different earth formations allows me to gain insights through a "subject-observer's immersion" (Tilley 2010, 26). Like Tilley, I also sense that "landscapes have agency in relation to persons" (Tilley 2010, 26).

The landscape of Sambha, whether seen from the positive aesthetics of nature or from a phenomenological angle, is an earthwork of both the Earth and humans, but it is most definitely not an earthwork created by hands of professional artists. Robert Smithson's *Spiral Jetty* in the Great Salt Lake was a pioneering earthwork in 1969 which brought forth "a new artwork, a new world for art," as Edward Casey commented, "Far from being a mere shadow projected somewhere outside mind and body, in creating such a work Smithson was in a very particular place, Utah, and he was there body and mind in an experience that was nothing other than an *ecstasis*" (Casey 2005, 192). The uniqueness of an earthwork lies in its intimacy with its artists and viewers in both aesthetic and physical manners, both of whom place themselves in the earthwork when creating, appreciating, sensing, feeling, and letting themselves be enveloped by it and the surrounding landscape. Viewing, or rather experiencing, an earthwork requires sensibility from the participant. In fact it is not merely a viewing process but a self-implacing, moving, process as Casey remarks "...the body's action on earth, and this action is that of journeying amid matter, making its way in the material world, mapping not only materially but kinetically" (Casey 2005, 104).

Whether sitting on a mountain for hours in the evening or gazing at the night sky from the mouth of a cave, I see the kinesis of the Sambha landscape as an earthwork always in motion with the weather and gradients of light. It does not stop its engagement with my subjectivity; likewise my mindscape, while absorbing the landscape as though its contours, colors, and textures are spread on a canvas, moves with its own speed and on its own intellectual-spiritual terrain and yet utterly grounds itself in the landscape. Like Tilley's walk in the environs of Stonehenge (Tilley 2010, 63–98), my experience in the mountains around Sambha and along the bank of Machu resonates with Tilley's reflection, "To understand landscapes phenomenologically requires the art of walking in and through them, to touch and be touched by them" (Tilley, 27). Although my camera could frame a particular moment and a particular view of the landscape, the landscape itself is not static, it encompasses the shifting position of the sun, incoming storm clouds, falling raindrops, loose rocks pushed downhill by high winds, and the entrance of a twittering eagle into the aerial space of the village. The landscape is never the same – it moves and is moved, although its physical structure retains its position on the Earth.

My affective bond with the Sambha landscape is strengthened each time my body and mind move across it, and each time I scan the panoramic photos of Sambha I keep in my office far from the region. My peripatetic movements, both circumambient and vertical, on the high and low edges of Sambha, have also been the movements of my mindscape as I enter an absorptive mode, derived from Casey's idea of "absorptive mapping," "that is done from the lived body's standpoint…from its concrete experience of existing and moving on the Earth, being extended in traction there, tracing out its trajectory, thus literally choro-graphic and topo-graphic; rather than detachment and view…" (2005, 170). In this absorptive mode of sensing Sambha's landscape with my walking, touching, smelling, and feeling it, I see why and how I reflexively qualify it as an earthwork of unity, wholeness, and delightfulness. In the interactions between my mindscape and the landscape, the idea of nature and being natural keeps emerging, affirming the same affective and reverential mood of many other non-Tibetans' absorptive experiences with the Tibetan landscape, which I elaborate later. "Nature" in this case is not understood necessarily as an opposite of culture as in the classic debate of anthropology and other social sciences but is that which is seen, smelled, and touched by our moving, sensing body situated in it. In other words, "nature" here consists of what Budd calls "natural *substances* (gold, water), natural *species* (animals, insects, trees, shrubs, plants), natural *objects* (icebergs, mountains, volcanoes, planets, moons), natural *forces*, (gravity, magnetism), natural *appearances* (the sky, sunrise and sunset, a rainbow, shadows)…" (Budd 1996, 208). With both the substances of nature and its natural appearance, the Sambha landscape, as an aesthetically balanced earthwork in contrast to over-humanized urban landscapes, contains elemental components of the Earth as well as humans' willingness to apply these natural elements to building their settlement. Thus, this unique earthwork is a totality of natural elements and powerful but idyllic geological formations in which the ancestors of Sambha's residents chose to build their homes.

In this regard, Sambha is also a work of environmental art that bears relational dynamics between itself and its settings (Bender, Hamilton and Tilley 2007, 317). The Earth is the fundamental source for the creation of this art. In the case of Sambha, it was not a deliberate act of its original dwellers to "build" the pleasing geological formations as such. Rather, they were persuaded to live there by the natural place of Sambha itself. It was a pre-existing work of the Earth where a large body of water flows from the glaciers and snowy mountains and is self-contained within the natural bounds of the mountains and the river. In other words, Sambha, or the place which was named Sambha by its first dwellers, was an earthwork prior to the current human settlement. Thus, the landscape itself was an existing-in-potential work of art until humans moved into it and built a symbiotic relationship with it. Eventually the mutual absorption between the Earth and people became a union – the current Sambha. So the place is art, and the art is the place, interchangeably: the landscape then is an artwork of the Earth with living beings and natural objects, i.e. mountain tops, caves, rocks, trees, insects, birds, and mountain goats.

The sense of the beautiful I perceive toward Sambha in my mindscape is not a concept or an ephemeral mental phenomenon that could be effortlessly deconstructed or dismissed solely as an "imagination" induced by the "global fetish" of Tibet. Instead this sense of the beautiful evokes images of positive ecological soundness and communal wholesomeness. It touches or springs from something archetypal and universal, and yet relies on our culturally-conditioned aesthetic terms and images to articulate.

2.2 Geopoetic affordances of the Tibetan landscape

Before stunning landscape photos and cinematic productions about Tibet saturated the global mediascape, only a handful of exceptional individuals had traveled to and lived in Tibet in the capacities of seeker, explorer, and imperial officer. Many of them shared with their compatriots their memories and reflections by writing books about their travels. Their narratives are most revealing about their first physical, intellectual, and spiritual contact with the Tibetan landscape. A sense of awe and contemplative ecstasy is present in their narratives. For instance, Lama Anagarika Govinda (1898–1985, born Ernst Lothar Hoffmann) recollected his memory of the Tibetan landscape in the late 1940s when he was crossing an 18,000-foot mountain pass:

> Nowhere have I experienced this deeper than under the open skies of Tibet, in the vastness of its solitudes, the clarity of its atmosphere, the luminosity of its colours and the plastic,

almost abstract, purity of its mountain forms...the landscape itself appears like the organic expression of primeval forces. Bare mountains expose in far-swinging lines the fundamental laws of gravitation, modified only by the continuous action of wind and weather, revealing their geological structure and the nature of their material, which shines forth in pure and vivid colours (Govinda 2005, 101–102).

I see Lama Govinda's pilgrimage experience in Tibet as a confession of his affective bonding with the landscape with a transcendental overtone. Many of Lama Govinda's contemporaries such as Alexandra David-Neel (1868–1969) and Walter Evans-Wentz (1878–1965) had similar poetic exaltations toward Tibet.

Besides this group of Western seekers' memories that show their spiritual reflections of the Tibetan landscape, British imperial officers like Francis Younghusband (1863–1942), also expressed their affection toward the land after returning from Tibet. Regardless of the post-colonial characterization of Younghusband, the imperial officer leading the British mission to Lhasa in 1905, as a "gentleman" and a "thief" (Carrington 2003), he, the youngest member of the Royal Geographical Society, did not lack spiritual retrospection of his Tibet experience. In David Matless' study of nature-mysticism in the early twentieth century Younghusband is referenced as a mystic of nature. Matless notes, "Alone in the hills above Lhasa, the mission having brought him to the 'highest pitch' of his existence, Younghusband felt 'a deep inner-soul satisfaction', which remained with him for many years after, a sense of the world as fundamentally good..." (Matless 1991, 273).

This stream of early, non-native, spiritual responses to Tibet did not recede into the historical background; instead it continues, manifesting itself in the current contexts of Tibet's humanitarian issues and religious revitalizations. An increasing amount of knowledge available about Tibet does not "demystify" it; instead it contributes to contemporary Tibetophiles' and spiritual seekers' ventures for "unlocking the secrets of the Land of the Snows" (Lee 1996) and seeking spiritual "know-how" in Tibet.

Chen Xiaodong, a freelance Buddhist writer based in Shanghai, shares his first experience with an online audience in China, "I was sitting on a hilltop looking at the endlessly expanding horizon under the blue sky...A bliss began to permeate my body and mind. I didn't know that my eyes welled up with tears. I bent down to kiss this earth. This is a magic land, a sacred pureland..." (Chen 2002, 5).

After discovering a 108-foot-high waterfall in eastern Tibet, Ian Baker, a mountain climber and a Buddhist practitioner sponsored by the National Geographic in the 1990s, shared his reflection, "With the chrome taps opened wide, and the wild thundering of the waterfall still within me, I could only hope those radiant waters, hidden in our deepest collective being, would never be dammed or diverted but – like the dream of unknown places – carry us beyond all divisions into the currents of the unbound heart" (Baker 2004, 416).

Whether in the colonial era or in the contemporary world, many of these personal narratives about Tibet found in books or on the Internet share a similar aesthetic and spiritual experience which van Gennep called "the territorial passage" (van Gennep 1960, 19), a rite of passage that pilgrims on rough but magnificent terrain might experience. The landscape of Tibet itself then becomes a medium of the person's spiritual transformation resembling a hero's journey in the ancient Greek sense (Campbell 1968). Publishers readily provide venues for this niche of personal narratives about Tibet as shown in the blurbs on the back covers of their publications: *Adventure Magazine* gives accolades to Baker's book, "Reading the book is itself a big, almost a transcendent, experience" (2004); *National Geographic Magazine* congratulates Sorrel Wilby, author of *Journey across Tibet*, as "one of the most talented, courageous, and irresistibly delightful explorers on the face of the earth" (1988); and *Booklist* promotes Russell Johnson and Kerry Moran's photo book *Tibet's Sacred Mountain*, "Both the vivid description and the awe-inspiring color photographs help to capture the mystical experience of this region and its religious significance" (1999).

In the global marketplace, the Tibetan landscape, in its entirety, is often perceived as a tectonic work of the Earth's natural forces with the addition of human cultural and spiritual touches. The attributes described by many experiencing their first contact are aesthetically positive and contain such words and phrases: divinely radiant, primeval forces, self-renewing, immaculate, holistic, sublime, magnificent, and splendid. This list can go on and on but it is recognizable that the list characteristically pushes the limits of our lexicon to express appreciation of the Earth as well as the experiencer's perceived experience of transcendence in Tibet. These indications of non-Tibetans' aesthetics, over the course of time, cannot be simplistically dismissed as an idealization and/or Orientalization of Tibet; instead it rather deserves to be treated as a unique landscape subjectivity, inextricable from Tibet itself.

Tibet is a gift to those who enter it. I make this statement not to be deliberately poetic as I write up this ethnographic and interpretive text but because it is a recognizable pattern: the traveler or pilgrim usually returns home with poetically-articulated statements of having been initiated by travel in Tibet. It is a unique bond, an affordance, between the traveler and the Tibetan landscape that deserves sympathetic understanding not moral judgment from social scientists.

From the perspective of James Gibson's ecological psychology, Tibet presents a set of affordances to its natives as well as to its visitors. To reiterate the idea, an affordance is a gift from the environment to an organism (Gibson 1986, 127);

however, it is not a pre-made gift waiting for the organism to pick up; instead it requires the organism's participation in the environment before the gift is identified. This required participation of the organism builds its intimate relationship with the environment. Before a rock is reshaped into a hand axe, it is only one of many random rocks in the environment. It is the toolmaker who recognizes its instrumental potential and subsequently transforms it into a tool called a hand axe. The environment makes the rock available while the toolmaker embodies his or her utilitarian vision into the rock. The complete formation of the hand axe out of the rock signifies the identified affordance from the environment to the toolmaker and thus, the environment and the toolmaker enter a relationship characterized by Gibson as the complementarity of the environment and the organism (Gibson 1986, 127).

Likewise the poetic narratives of the abovementioned non-Tibetan pilgrims and travelers are a result of a complementarity between human consciousness and a unique landscape. Such complementarity builds itself upon the physical environment of Tibet but finalizes itself as an intangible earth-inspired spirituality (Smyer Yu 2011, 191) or a unique state of mind in which the luminosity of the Tibetan landscape overpowers the visitor who, sooner or later, enters a state of ecstasy. By "luminosity" I mean the solar light in its maximum brilliancy and diverse manifestations over the landscape of Tibet in both radiant and ambient senses. No mental imagination can produce such luminosity. No imaginative mind can produce the spectrum of rich colors. The luminous landscape of Tibet does inevitably induce metaphoric, poetic, and imaginative descriptions from pilgrims and travelers when they write up their experiences after their time in Tibet. Take Lama Govinda again as an example, he writes, "The roles of heaven and earth are reversed...while the landscape stands out against it in radiating colors, as if it were the source of light. Red and yellow rocks rise like flames against the dark blue velvet curtain of the sky" (Govinda 2005, 101). In this way as well, my aesthetic response to Sambha was enacted as I stood on the immense, colorful earth that holds the tiny village.

To re-emphasize, the case I attempt to build here is premised upon the condition that all poetic expressions in this book concerning the Tibetan landscape come from individuals who have had a physical immersion experience in the landscape of Tibet. They were physically surrounded by the solid earth, the air, the flux of the weather, the cultural ethos – simply, both the natural and built environments of Tibet. The environed body is irresistibly included in the luminous profusion of light which stimulates the vision of the person and subsequently his or her intellect and spirituality. The luminosity is an inherent part of the sublime quality of the Tibetan landscape. Taking Gibson's ecological approach to visual perception, we can refer to the light as being two different types, namely radiant and ambient. The former refers to the direct light from the sun in the sky, while the latter is understood as indirectly sourced light resulting from the radiant light "reverberating between the earth and the sky, and between surfaces that face one another" (Gibson 1986, 50).

The ambient light is particularly worthy of attention for my ecological understanding of how Tibet is generative of the earth-inspired spirituality expressed in poetic terms. The mountainous landscape of Tibet permits a spectrum of ambient light to bounce off countless mountains. The environment is saturated with different shades of light reflected in different colors. In a way, the solid, uneven surface of the earth is at once "soaked" in light and reproduces the vision-inspiring radiant energy by reflecting the direct sunlight. Furthermore, the air is also a medium of light. Water vapor in the form of fog and clouds produces its own shades of ambient light. The sublime greatness of the landscape is already unarguably magnificent and when the ambient light pervades the "skin" of the landscape, it generates a luminosity that envelops everything and everyone in the environment. Like the mountains, the pilgrim or the traveler is equally immersed in such a luminous environment and also produces ambient light through absorbing and reflecting the incoming light from the sky and the surrounding earth.

In this regard, the geopoetics shown in Tibet-related writings is not solely the mental invention of the writers but is a response to the light saturating the landscape of Tibet. The radiant energy of the light from the solar source above and countless ambient sources in the landscape are the primary stimulus that fire off intellectual and spiritual responses from the person enveloped in the light-saturated, color-vibrant environment. The energy is embodied in the perceiving person and environed in the perceived environment. Perception, as Gibson remarks, is "an act of information pickup" (Gibson 1986, 57) with external stimuli and internal receptors. In such a process, Gibson continues, "The observer, being an organism, exchanges energy with the environment by respiration, food consumption, and behavior" (Gibson 1986, 57). In this sense, Tibet "enters" both biological and psychic receptors of the perceiver. Thus, the body and the mind of the perceiver are both marked and penetrated by the Tibetan landscape. The geopoetics found in Tibet-related narratives are one of the many affordances or offerings from Tibet as a unique high place. I will continue to address non-Tibetans' eco-aesthetics and geopoetics later in the chapter, but for now it is crucial to recognize how native Tibetans bond with their homeland.

2.3 Sambha mandalized

My fieldwork has involved both my physical experience of the landscape and life in a home in Sambha, so I am not building a case of Tibet-as-imagination. On the ground level, Sambha is not the Tibetan cousin of Arcadia or the Shire as my image-association spurred by the view from the surrounding mountains suggested. Although it is less affected by China's advancing modernization project in comparison with larger Tibetan communities in Amdo (Makley 2007; Fischer 2005; Yeh and Henderson 2008), like other parts of cultural Tibet, Sambha has undergone a series of socialist changes brought about by the Chinese state since the late 1950s prior to its encounter of the current modernization project specifically targeting western China. Recent changes are almost all economically induced.

On the first day, after getting off the bus, Akhu Norbu and I walked toward his cousin's house and saw elders sitting at the roadside and children playing outside their homes. For the next twenty days of my stay I did not meet a single young adult. This demographic dynamic has stayed the same and the village has become quieter each time I return. Tserang, Akhu Norbu's cousin and a history professor at a provincial university in Qinghai Province, told me that residents above eighteen and below forty-five had gone to other places to work as *sa-lee-wa* (ས་ལས་བ། construction workers) and *gu-wa* (雇娃 contracted workers who are specifically assigned to dig caterpillar fungi, wild mushrooms, and other tonic herbs). This economically-driven social change is also documented by the scholarly works by Toni Huber (2002), Andreas Gruschke (2008), Daniel Winkler (2008), and Emily Yeh (2004), among others. Tserang's younger brother left Sambha for Xining where he has a small shop selling Tibetan crafts; Tserang himself lives in Xining as he is tied to his university job. For most of the year, then, only children and their grandparents are in the village. The human gravity of the village centers on the kindred bonding between grandparents and grandchildren. The village school was the communal center. However, in the last three years, more changes have come to the village. All school children are now required by the state to attend larger boarding schools in the county. They return to their homes for short visits once a month. Two kilometers away along the upper stream of Machu, another bridge is being built connecting the provincial highway to a large tract of land across the river where a golf course and a five-star tourist resort are under construction. Directives have already come from the county informing residents that Sambha will also be developed as a tourist resort soon.

In this setting my ethnographic rapport has been established mostly with the older population of Sambha who are above forty-five years of age. Through their narratives and memories I see how the landscape of Sambha has its own cosmology, subjectivity, and sublimity. The interior being of the Sambha landscape resides not only within its aesthetically pleasing geological formations but also in the mindscapes of the elders of Sambha.

* * *

The origin of the village name has two contradictory stories. The official name that the county uses is Semba (སུམ་པ།) which literally means "three" but geographically is understood as "the intersection of the three" referring to Sambha as being in the location of two neighboring villages, respectively in the north and the west, with Machu in the south. Semba is widely known to outsiders. Topographically the two "neighboring villages" are separated from Sambha by several mountains; thus the topographic distance is significantly greater than the official cartographic distance that doesn't consider the varied elevations and gradients of the mountainous terrain. The name Semba became known after the socialist system was established during the latter half of the last century when the originally tribe-based human settlements were placed on the administrative map of Qinghai Province. Many original Tibetan names of locations were replaced by or transliterated into Chinese. For instance, Guide County's Tibetan name was Chekha (ཁྲི་ཀ) but this is no longer officially used and is fading from use among the younger generation of local Tibetans.

In the second story, told by elders and yogis of Sambha and other villages in the area, the spelling of the village's name is *Sambha* (སེམ་བྲ།). The difference between *Semba* and *Sambha* is not just in its spelling and lexical meanings, but rather in the religious, spiritual, and historical connotations. Sambha is, in every way, concentrated with the history and religiosity of the village in terms of how the initial dwellers decided to build their homes there. The village's oral tradition says the name of Sambha started in the thirteenth century when a tantric lama named Hsichan Namkhapa (ཞི་ཆེན་ནམ་མཁའ་པ) came into the valley from Kham where he discovered a rock-inlaid face print and meditation site of Padmasambhava (པདྨ་སམ་བྷ་ཝ), the Indian tantric master responsible for Tibet's Buddhist conversion. Tserang's father, an elder yogi, told me that Hsichan Namkhapa also found a rock on which Yeshe Tsogyal, Padmasambhava's consort, meditated and performed ritual dances. Similar stories from other villages in the area corroborate Sambha elders' claims.

The dominant form of Buddhism in the area is not monastic-based but rather lay-based. Tantric practitioners call themselves *ngapa* (སྔགས་པ། yogi), and *ngama* (སྔགས་མ། yogini). Yogis of other villages all know the cave meditation site of Padmasambhava. To the Buddhist yogis and yoginis in the area, the village in the valley is Sambha not Semba, which is clearly derived from the name of Padmasambhava: *pedma* (པདྨ) means lotus while *sambhava* (སྦྲ་བ) means "truthfully revealing from" or "truthfully emerging from." Yogis in the area have traditionally held periodic solitary retreats at the cave site that Hsichan Namkhapa found in Sambha. When county administration renamed the village as *Semba*, local yogis did not overtly resist it but gave justified the change by fully aligning it with their ancient Buddhist association with Padmasambhava. *Semba*, with its emphasis on the number three, is explained as referring to the three Dharma names of the Indian tantric master: Guru Padmasambhava (གུ་རུ་པདྨ་སཾ་བྷ་ཝ), Guru Padmajungne (གུ་རུ་པད་མ་འབྱུང་གནས), and Guru Tsokye Dorje (གུ་རུ་མཚོ་སྐྱེས་རྡོ་རྗེ་གསུམ). Regardless of this understanding, the yogis insist that the spelling of the village's name has to be Sambha not Semba.

The first dwellers of Sambha clearly consecrated the valley with the name and legacy of Padmasambhava. The mountain standing on the east of the village, where the face print and meditation cave are found, was named by Sambha's ancestors as *Sambhadrubgne* (སཾ་བྷའི་སྒྲུབ་གནས). *Drub* (སྒྲུབ) means expedient accomplishment and *gne/gnas* (གནས) refers to geographic locations that are marked with sacred sites and supernatural power of deities. Thus, *drubgne* (སྒྲུབ་གནས) means a place of expedient accomplishment. In the Buddhist context, it implies spiritual achievement in a given location. In this regard, the spiritual gravity of Sambha is Sambhadrubgne. When one enters the village from the west side on bus or on foot, the spectacular scene of the village with Sambhadrubgne towering behind arrests one's vision. Proportionally the residential domain and most of the wheat fields of the village extend from the foothill of Sambhadrubgne westward. The closer the distance a house is to the mountain, the older its age is or the longer its resident family can trace their historical connection to Sambha, and vice versa. The construction of the initial homes corresponds to the oral history of village that states that the foot of the mountain, recognized as sacred site, was the starting point of human dwelling in Sambha.

The village is mandalized or consecrated. In his study of Japanese sacred mountains, Allan Grapard points out two significances of mandalas in the context of Buddhism. One pertains to the "representation of the residence of the Buddha...a metaphysical space which provided an insight into what Buddhism called the Realm of Essence" (Grapard 1982, 209). Another spiritual significance represented by mandalas is "the original nature of our heart-mind, free of illusions and passions" (Grapard, 1982, 209).

The Buddhist mandalization of dwelling space or the natural environment is commonplace in Tibet. It is not an exaggeration to state that nearly all Tibetan human settlements are mandalized as sacred space. In comparison, in Grapard's Japanese case, mandalization appears as almost purely a Buddhist activity in terms of its representations of Buddhist spirituality and cosmology. The Tibetan case of mandalas (དཀྱིལ་འཁོར་ *kyilkhor*) and mandalization signifies not simply humans' recognition of a given place as a hierophany of the Buddha-field but involves a type of nested hierarchy in which multiple relationships of humans, spirits, deities, indigenous beliefs, and Buddhist practices are interwoven. These relationships mutually saturate each other regardless of the symbolic fact that everything is subordinated to the spiritual authority of the Buddha Dharma (Smyer Yu 2011, 70). The religious map of the Tibetan landscape shows that a Buddhist mandala, in the sense of an underlying metaphorical structure or view of the land itself, has been laid over Tibet. The historical Buddhist conversion of Tibet is not only an indication of the mindwork of humans, but is also a conversion process for the entire landscape of Tibet which embodied/embodies indigenous earthly deities.

Many scholars have found evidence in Tibetan folk history of a common belief that prior to the entrance of Buddhism, Tibet was the home of what Buddhists call the supine demoness (སྲིན་མོ་གན་རྒྱལ་ *shenmo Gangyal*) (Miller 1991). This somewhat pejorative term has been filtered through the Buddhist lens to view the pre-Buddhist pantheon of Tibet. The word *shenmo* (སྲིན་མོ་) is the translation of the Sanskrit word rākṣasa, referring to demonic humanoid beings popularly known as human-eaters among Buddhists. This pre-Buddhist goddess lies within the landscape of Tibet stretching out to all directions of the historical Tibetan empire. The eventual Buddhist consecration of Tibet was a project that sought to pacify the demonness and subjugate her dominion. Early Buddhist conversion in Tibet was not simply a spreading of Buddha Dharma into the mindscape of Tibetans; instead it initiated a long and complex relationship with the Tibetan landscape that was subsequently also subject to Buddhist conversion. More precisely the deities residing in the landscape were subject to this massive Buddhist conversion project.

In this sense, although the landscape remains the same in terms of its topographical and geological formation, the pre-Buddhist human relationship with earthly deities has nevertheless been transformed, re-ordered, and re-hierarchized. The absolute superiority of the deities over humans and other life forms has been transformed into subordination to Buddha Dharma and to those humans who possess mastery of Buddhist ritual techniques to counter or appropriate the deities' supernatural power. Fundamentally, Buddhism ideologically and spiritually demoted the earthly deities to the level of sentient beings who are subject to the same cycle of birth and death; thus they are, like all sentient beings, equally situated in existential suffering. In this way the pre-Buddhist pantheon is re-moralized in the Buddhist spiritual hierarchy (Huber and Pedersen 1997, 584). Alliances, gift exchanges, and reciprocity regularly occur between humans and Tibet's earth-based deities within the sentient realm yet all parties are now oriented toward the Buddha Dharma. In this respect, mindscape and landscape, and humans and deities are interlocked.

Sambha's Buddhist mandalization is identical to the historical Buddhist conversion of Tibet but on a much smaller scale. Its landscape was re-cosmologized as a Buddhist sacred place centered on the legend of Padmasambhava. The surface of Sambhadrubgne retains the natural formation it had centuries ago; however human markings and inscriptions on it are all monumental and commemorative to Padmasambhava. They are daily reminders to the residents of Sambha of this Indian Guru's spiritual prowess and of the inherent Buddhist-ness of the landscape. Meditation caves on Sambhadrubgne, like many others in Tibet, are modified with human touches. Their entrances and interiors resemble small cabins rather than natural caves, with wooden structures and masonry having been added to them. Prayer flags fly over the temple on the mountain in honor of Padmasambhava. Khata (ཁ་བཏགས་), scarves used for honorary purposes, and piles of white pebbles from Machu are laid over the rock where Yeshe Tsogyal, Padmasambhava's spiritual companion, performed tantric ritual dances. These markings of Buddhist spirituality function as monuments in relation to the landscape on which they stand.

Herein I particularly see the relevance of Tilley's points on the relationship between a monument and the place where it is situated. Padmasambhava's cave sites and the yogis' temple are not visually imposing but are visible from distance. They imbue the landscape of Sambha with "a symbolic reference point" or "a new sense of place" (Tilley 2010, 50) in contrast to its pre-Buddhist natural state of being. Sambhadrubgne, in this sense, reminds the residents in the valley of their Buddhist identity and their moral orientation follows accordingly. Tilley points out, "As a shared set of socially mediated conventional understandings, landscapes can be claimed to be an extension of the social self, providing a series of principles and norms for living, relating to others, and the past" (Tilley 2010, 40).

According to Tserang's father, the temple on the mountain used to be bigger and hosted numerous annual Dharma events and rituals performed by yogis from the area and afar. In 1966, the year that marked the start of the Cultural Revolution, the temple was completely demolished. In 1980 when the Chinese state became more open to religious practices, villagers raised the funds to reconstruct the temple though it is significantly smaller than the original. Although there are not as many Dharma events as were held in the past, the caves of Sambhadrubgne have been frequented by yogis from the village and other places since the 1980s. Akhu Norbu and his father, who both come from another village, are among the yogis who have made solitary retreats in Sambha's caves. In this way the surrounding landscape has been re-mandalized through the reconstructed temple and renewed Buddhist activities on the mountain.

It is noteworthy that the resident-initiated surface markings are on the side of the mountain overlooking the village while the mountain's other side remains natural and without such modifications and inscriptions. In this respect the human settlement of Sambha implaces itself in a sanctuary marked off from other places. Its geological formation has pre-determined the human spiritual association with the pristine realm of enlightened beings. This corresponds to the same pattern of sacralization of human dwellings elsewhere in the world, especially in those communities with distinct geological forms that allow them to establish both physical and symbolic boundaries. In their study of sacred sites and their relation with the Earth, J. Donald Hughes and Jim Swan notice, "The places chosen were almost always distinguished by some natural feature: an impressive grove of large old trees, a spring, a lake, a fissure in the earth, or a mountain peak. These were often landscapes of great natural beauty" (Hughes and Swan 1986, 248). From this angle, the mandalization of Sambha resembles the ancient Greek idea of *temenos* (Latin *templum*) referring to "a part cut off" or "a space marked out" (Hughes and Swan 1986, 248). Such places are sanctuaries or temple grounds, for, as Hughes and Swan continue, "What we call a temple is such a structure, but for the ancients the enclosure itself, and everything within it, served as the temple. There the god lived and became manifest. And there a fugitive could seek sanctuary, a sick person could ask for healing, and anyone seeking wisdom…could sleep overnight in expectation of a meaningful dream. There were hundreds of those places in the ancient world." (Hughes and Swan 1986, 248–49).

As Tserang's father told me, Sambha, in the time of his great grandfathers, was briefly a sanctuary for outlaws. During that time, according to stories passed on to him, Sambha was once called *kyamashetoka* (རྒྱ་མ་ཤི་ཐོག). Its literal meaning is "the mountain where the Han did not die." The story held that a group of outlaws attempted to bury a Han-Chinese man alive but he did not die. However, this was only a very brief period when the Buddhist sacredness of Sambha was compromised.

From this story, I learned that the human mindscape is not separated from the very landscape with which it is always in sensorial, emotional, memorial, and spiritual contact. The nodes of mindscape and landscape are not only the surficial connections of our senses but also the deeply entwined memories of the past, regardless of how we re-shape our memories for our present needs. Herein I reemphasize that landscape is place-based and almost synonymous to place as a vessel or a container in the Aristotelian sense (Casey 2000, 184) though it is not devoid of its own subjectivity.

In the case of Sambha, both human mindscapes and place-landscape are not separate from each other but are inter-subjectively enmeshed. The potency of such place is concentrated with intertwined human memories, surficial monument markings, and positive aesthetics radiating out of the geological formation. The intangibility of the human mind has never ceased being surrounded, enveloped, and saturated by the tangibility of the place where it exercises its cognitive activities and inner reflections on phenomena of the outer world. Thus the *bio*-graphy of a place lives in and through the human mindscape, beyond its physical, objective, anonymous presence in the world. Those who have no conscious knowledge of it simply call it "nature." The potency of the place of Sambha thus lies in its memorability that is actualized through a passage of time and space in the human mindscape eidetic to its corresponding landscape. What Casey says about place and memorability is most elucidating, "Thanks to its 'distinct potencies,' a place is at once internally diversified – full of protuberant features and forceful vectors – and distinct externally from other places. Both kinds of differentiations, internal and external, augment memorability" (Casey 2000, 186).

Sambha is such a place that interweaves the human mindscape and the natural landscape. Its *bio*-graphy sustains itself in both. I call this human-Earth relation "inter-dwelling" meaning that landscape is an inherent part of human consciousness and that both mindscape and landscape are merged and mediated by symbolic and physical mediums. In Sambha, the pattern of inter-dwelling is multilayered and multidimensional. What stands out in this pattern is that the collective memory of human history and the myths and stories of the spirit-world are stored in both the human mindscape and the natural, albeit humanized landscape.

2.4 Inter-dwelling with gods and spirits

Sambha's mandalization was undertaken in ancient times but continues to present its embedded sanctity to both current residents and visitors alike. Its sanctity is not always vertically or hierarchically linked to the sacredness of Buddhism and saints like Padmasambhava, but also horizontally saturates the landscape through the connection with earthly deities, animals, and people – the immediate sentient residents of Sambha. On a few occasions I volunteered to be Akhu Norbu's caretaker when he entered solitary cave retreats on Sambhadrubgne. I cooked for him and fetched water from the stream. The privilege of a cave-meditator's caretaker is that he or she has full access to the cave and is permitted to speak with the meditator, usually after eight o'clock at night. The first thing Akhu Norbu did in the morning was recite prayers for the mountain deities and that was the last thing he did at night before we could speak to each other with the addition of an offering of liquor to the deities. The opening and close of day were marked by his invocations to local deities, whom he calls Dharma protectors. As he explained to me, it is essential that a Buddhist cave dweller maintain a reverential attitude toward mountain or other local deities. The offerings help prevent unpleasant or even dangerous occurrences such as sickness or the sudden departure of his caretaker during his time in the cave.

According to Akhu Norbu, *sa* (ས་), which means "earth" or "landscape," is not merely the inorganic mass always beneath one's feet; instead it is seen as *sasum* (ས་གསུམ་) – a three-component world – consisting of the celestial realm (ས་བླ་ *sabla*) above, the surface of the earth (ས་སྟེང་ *sadang*) in the middle, and the world beneath the earth's surface (ས་འོག་ *sa'og*). These three realms are not merely a spatial division of the world. Each is a lifeworld of its own, inhabited by beings many of which would not be found in a modern scientific taxonomy of organisms. They are the formless beings often regarded as deities and spirits with supernatural power. In local folk culture they include *yul-lhas* (ཡུལ་ལྷ་ country gods), *zhedek* (གཞི་བདག་ local deities), and *sadek* (ས་བདག་ soil deities), to name a few. As Akhu Norbu told me, they are supernatural beings who, like human beings, have a strong sense of home. Their power lies in their ability to make destructive weather and inflict illnesses on humans and livestock; however, when these gods and spirits are pleased, their power is also shown in their life-giving, healing, and hindrance-removing abilities. The lifeworlds of these deities and humans often intersect and overlap with each other. Thus, it is considered natural that by offering them prayers and incense, Akhu Norbu keeps a congenial rapport with these formless yet powerful beings who share their dwelling place with humans.

In the valley of Sambha, many families have similar offering routines though they may not be as ritually elaborate as those of a yogi in a cave. Burning juniper incense in the morning is a common offering to the deities and the Buddha Dharma. Both Akhu Norbu and villagers direct their prayers specifically to Ami Megbon (ཨ་མྱེས་དམག་དཔོན་), the mountain god of Sambhadrubgne, whose name is another appellation of the mountain itself.

In Tibet, the name of a mountain deity and the name of the mountain are often the same. This non-differentiation of the deities and the landscape they occupy perceptively makes it easier for people to see the Earth as animated and spirited with these deities (Smyer Yu 2011, 62). Among farmers of Sambha, while they maintain a clearly vertical, reverential, relationship with the Buddha Dharma, in the annual cycles of their farming and other worldly affairs they invoke their local deities to ensure the success of their needs and desires. They both fear and revere Ami Megbon, as he is a fearful warrior god (དགྲ་ལྷ་ *dgra-*

lha). All the trees and the wildlife on the mountain are said to be his subjects and family members.

For instance, villagers are protective of the few trees that survived the twentieth century's deforestation. Tserang's father told me a story of how a person from another village died of a festering skin rash all over his body soon after he peeled a large piece of bark off from one of the few trees left on the mountain. Everyone believed he had angered Ami Megbon. The intimacy between the village and Ami Megbon does not rest merely on fear of his punishment but is mostly built upon an exchange of gifts between people and the warrior god. Along with the routine offerings of incense, grain, milk, and liquor, the entire village holds an annual festival called *denbe dgra-lha* (འདུན་པའི་དགྲ་ལྷ། festival of warrior gods), specifically designated to Ami Megbon and other warrior gods in the area. The climax of the festival is the ending moments when the ritual-performing yogis insert the names of illness-causing demons and ghosts, and names of some villagers' personal enemies, into a yak horn. The attendees are instructed as to where the horn, containing undesirable elements, should be buried in the Earth. One's potential misfortune, hindrances, and illnesses for the coming year then all disappear with the buried horn deeply pressed down into the Earth with the power of the invoked warrior gods. People's general fear of Ami Megbon is, in fact, an act of reciprocity or repayment to his protection, and this reciprocal relationship is sustained through their caretaking of the body of Ami Megbon – the mountain which also once hosted Padmasambhava and his spiritual companion, and now is home to the village's temple and yogis' meditation caves.

The reciprocity between humans and deities does not only happen at higher elevations. The most fertile wheat fields of the village are at the foothill of Sambhadrubgne and the fertility of the Earth in this part of the village is attributed to the presence of the earthly deities, particularly the ones known as *klu* (ཀླུ། serpent-like deities). *Klu* are a type of waterborne deity in charge of underground water, springs, streams, and rivers. Any waterborne plants and animals are said to be *klu*'s family members and belongings. In this part of Sambha, two small springs flow out from underground. The streams are thin but consistent. These two springs are called "klu-chu" (ཀླུ་ཆུ།) or water secreted from *klu*. Their water is cool in the summer and warm enough in the winter that they are free of snow and ice. They flow into a small reservoir as a source of drinking water and irrigation, but all water from the mountains and underground enter Machu.

In spite of the impact of modern infrastructural activities, Machu's symbolic significance is retained by the village: it is seen as a floating, giant turquoise earing signifying wealth and prosperity. All homes in the village face this giant earing, hoping it will bring them fortunes. On that first visit to Sambha, when I took landscape photos from the vista at the entry point of the village, I assumed that villagers irrigated their fields with water from Machu. Later I found out water from Machu was only responsible for a very few family plots because it requires an electricity-consuming pump. The large amount of water flowing in Machu visually dominates the scene of the village; however, it has little practical benefit to the village. In the past before the river was damned downstream for a hydraulic power station, the river was very rapid. The gorge at the east side of the village was called *Kebkygga* (ཁབ་བཅག་ག) which means "needle-breaking point." *Kebkygga* was also a word used for cursing at one's personal enemies as if to imply that the person deserved being tossed into the rapids at the gorge where even a needle would not make it through whole. In the past, the bodies of those who died in accidents or feuds underwent a "water burial" at the gorge because the corpse was easily "tenderized" by the rough currents making it easier for fish to feed. Now water burial has become rare as the currents are inadequate for sweeping away a corpse.

The fields near the spring are obviously more moist and fertile than those plots further away, but according to Tserang's father, they once had a much greater flow of water coming from below ground between four large trees. During the Cultural Revolution, these special trees were identified as objects of superstition because they were wrapped in layers of prayer flags. On a summer day some villagers, led by the Party Secretary, tested the power of gods and nature by chopping down all four of them. The spring dried up. Even after several months, the water still did not return. As this water had been the primary irrigation source of the village's crops, a group of people quietly planted new trees at the same place. A month later the water resumed though it was drastically less than before. The following year a pond was dug to hold the water and it still serves as a small reservoir. The decreased flow of the water also meant a reduction in the arable plots near the springs. In Tserang's father's explanation, the destructive acts toward the Earth are not simply the physical dissolution or alteration of natural objects but, more critically, are offenses to the deities and spirits who reside in them.

A landscape involving the inter-dwelling of people, spirits, and deities is much more complex than that understood by an outsider who looks in with an aesthetic eye only. All residents, whether humans or gods, live in each other's physical, mental, and symbolic spaces. The subjectivity of each speaks to the other. This is not unique to Tibet and is a way of understanding relationship to place found among many indigenous people throughout the world. Indigenous Andeans, for instance, make ritual offerings to their mountain deities who are believed to be in control of meteorological occurrences and the fertility of land and people (Reinhard 1985, 307). Australian Aboriginals' dream-tracks are their ancestral trails of migration for both symbolic empowerment and physical sustenance (Morphy 2003).

The Tibetan case is sophisticated, too, in its own context. It is commonly recognized by many Tibet scholars that the eco-religious worldview of Tibetans shows that "the phenomenal world is held to be inhabited by a host of spirit powers and deities who are organized into a single ritual cosmos and must be ritually acknowledged" (Huber and Pedersen 1997, 584). Although many human and natural places in Tibet, including Sambha, are mandalized or consecrated in the framework of Buddhism, their residents nevertheless guard their worldly interests very seriously in terms of health, wealth, and the protection of various species within their landscape. On the folk level, I notice that often it is not the doctrine of Buddhism that many people are afraid of violating, such as the Buddhist injunction to refrain from killing, but they worry about potential harm to their day-to-day worldly life caused by the invisible world of gods, spirits, demons, ghosts, and inter-personal feuds. For those whose livelihood is at the mercy of the meteorological forces manipulated by such an array of supernatural beings, preventing loss and suffering is then not a matter of the Dharma explicated in rational language but requires that people be alert for actual and potential harm. At the same time, they regularly harness both merit and power from their supernatural counterparts by establishing reciprocity through participating in routine performances of rituals, especially offering-making. In their study of native Tibetan meteorological practices Toni Huber and Poul Pedersen point out that to sustain such reciprocity with non-human residents of the same piece of land "ensures a stable environment which yields its bounty" (Huber and Pedersen 1997, 585) and thus minimizes unfavorable natural conditions for crops and unwanted illnesses.

Tibetans in Sambha do not passively defend themselves from the harm of supernatural forces. Armed with ritual techniques, yogis who specialize in weather control can allegedly counter their local deities' mischievous meteorological acts toward humans and their livelihoods. In this regard, the supernatural power of the deities is not always absolute. Yogis' ritual weaponry includes slingshots, bows and arrows, and other paraphernalia. All these instruments have a common goal: to maintain favorable living conditions by defeating any actual or potential meteorological violence or causes of illness and inter-personal hindrances. For farmers in Sambha, stopping advancing hail clouds or redirecting the course of a devastating storm are essential tasks of the yogis who are weather-making specialists. According to Akhu Norbu and other yogis, the most effective weapon is made of buckwheat seeds. They are small but prickly and, when ritually empowered as "pellets of secret teachings" (སྒྲུབ་བརྒྱུད་པའི་ཡུངས་ཀར་སྔགས།), they are loaded into slingshots or onto the tips of arrows and used as "bullets". When on weather patrol, yogis who encounter approaching hail clouds shoot these "bullets" into them, targeting the trouble-making deities hiding in the clouds. Instead of seeing the "bullets" reach the clouds, I have seen them all fall back to the Earth. The symbolic act and ritual meaning of the "bullets" is obviously more important than the observable physical trajectory. I find the locally-cherished legend of Yutog Yontan Gonpo (གཡུ་ཐོག་ཡོན་ཏན་མགོན་པོ), the ninth century Tibetan medicine man, is telling in its revelation of how the mindscapes of both humans and gods are so entwined with the landscape:

> Once when Yontan Gonpo was crossing a bridge on the way to treat a patient, a beautiful young girl walked toward him requesting his help to heal her father. He asked, "Who's your father? Where is he?" The girl pointed at the sky. The medicine man then understood the place the girl referred to was the realm of the Eight Legions of Devas and Demigods (ལྷ་སྲིན་སྡེ་བརྒྱད། *lhashendegyid*). As soon as Yontan Gonpo agreed to treat her father, the girl requested him to close his eyes and hold her right arm. In a split second, they were in the palace of the Eight Legions. The king of the Eight Legions was lying on his golden bed in obvious agony. The girl then said to the famous medicine man, "When my father was releasing turbulent weather into the human realm, a skilled yogi shot him with buckwheat seeds." Yontan Gonpo then examined his wounds. The king's body was covered with the thorny seeds and he was in unbearable pain. Yontan Gonpu carefully pulled every single seed out of the king's skin and he soon recovered. The girl escorted the medicine man back to the bridge. Before parting, she said, "Please come here at this time next year to receive your reward." A year later, Yontan Gonpu returned to the bridge as instructed. Not long after his arrival, he saw a girl covered in turquoise stones being washed down the river toward him. He quickly lifted her out of the water and found it was the king's daughter who bore the turquoise stones as the king's gift in reward for his healing. Upon returning home, the medicine man planted the stones in his yard and more turquoise grew from them. Since then, he was given another name, Yutog (གཡུ་ཐོག) meaning "turquoise."

2.5 Ancestral rootedness of Sambha and beyond

The mythopoetic aspect of landscape shown in the above folk story is common elsewhere in Tibet. Humans and earthly deities always appear in some kind of union in both the physical landscape and intangible mindscape, so that a particular place is associated with a story and its appropriate deities. In contemporary landscape studies, the subjectivity of a given landscape is a theoretical focal point for discussion and debate on the question: is there a subjectivity of the landscape itself or is this a projection of human subjectivity onto it? In my reading of theoretical works by leading scholars like Bender, Ingold, and Tilley, I see that such a subjectivity is attached to the landscape but is not entirely the landscape's own subjectivity. It is mostly the activities of humans that have given birth to this landscape subjectivity. Landscape, as Ingold puts it, is not land, not space, and not nature but dwelling place; therefore "...through living in it, the landscape becomes a part of us, just as we are a part of it" (Ingold 1993, 154). The subjectivity of landscape comes to being through what he calls "taskscape" or "the pattern of dwelling activities" (Ingold 1993, 153). To emphasize a bit more, Ingold continues, "the taskscape exists only so long as people are actually engaged in the activities of dwelling" (Ingold 1993, 161). In this sense, the subjectivity of landscape then depends upon what Bender calls the "materiality of social relationships" (Bender 2002, 104). Such subjectivity is the result of the "interactivity" (Ingold 1993, 163) between people and the piece of the Earth that they choose as their dwelling place. From this perspective, the subjectivity of landscape is heavily contingent upon human activities on the land as "a physical context" (Bender 2002, 104), as a "contoured and textured surface" (Ingold 1993, 154), and as a "ground for all thought and social interaction" (Tilley 2010, 26).

As I see the interconnectedness between people and their place from both ethnographic and theoretical viewpoints, I prefer "intersubjectivity" to "subjectivity" in this context in response to many scholars' claim of landscape subjectivity based on human activities. To be specific, this intersubjectivity can also be understood as an earth-people subjectivity in which human subjectivity has more weight since the landscape has passively been worked on by humans in both material and symbolic terms. This human trail is well articulated with Ingold's idea of "temporality of landscape" (1993), Tilley's "lived body" (2010, 26), and Casey's "passage of time" (2000, 196), which all point to the inter-relatedness between humans and landscape, and the rootedness of humans in place. In this sense, the materiality of human memories of the past and present activities clearly grow roots downward into and surficially across the landscape in the forms of architecture, agriculture, monuments, and burial grounds.

In the case of Sambha the roots of people and their place-based consciousness started with the initial pre-Buddhist state of being and subsequent Buddhist mandalization of the valley as a site sacred in its connection to Padmasambhava. The first residents also brought in their historical and cultural roots from Ü-Tsang or Central Tibet. These roots from elsewhere are Sambha ancestors' collective memory and its preservation. The nomenclatural and perceptual interchangeability between the names of mountains and of mountain deities is one noticeable way of preserving the cultural origin of Sambha residents. Besides its positive ecological significance, the perceptual conflation of a mountain with the deity residing in it also preserves the village's memory of their ancestors.

Ami Megbon is one of the offspring of Ami Machen in Amdo, one of the nine original deity-mountains (སྲིད་པ་ཆགས་པའི་ལྷ་དགུ་ *srid pa chags pa'i lha dge*) in Tibet, who resides seven hundred kilometers away in Qinghai's Golok Prefecture. Ami Megbon and Amne Machen, are considered to have either "blood relations" (Smyer Yu 2011, 55) or a social alliance with their human counterparts in Tibet. For instance, Ode Gungyel (ཨོ་དེ་གུང་རྒྱལ), the patriarch of the mountain deities, is also recognized by Tibetans as Mutri Tsenpo (མུ་ཁྲི་བཙན་པོ), the second king of ancient Tibet (345 B.C. – 272 B.C.). Yarlha Shompo, another original mountain deity and a son of Ode Gungyel, was enthroned as King Chatri Tsenpo (68 B.C. – 31 B.C.) according to Tibetan folklore (Smyer Yu 2011, 54). These nine mountain deities populated Tibet. Ami Megbon in Sambha is one of their many descendants. His nomad-warrior appearance resembles that of his nine ancestors. The geographic distribution of the descendants of the nine original mountain deities shows the migration pattern of Tibetans since ancient times.

In this regard Sambha residents have two levels of collective memories embedded in their landscape. The actual Buddhist inscriptions on the surface of the landscape recollect their Buddhist ancestor Hsichan Namkhapa (ཞི་ཆེན་ནམ་མཁའ་པ) and the saint, Padmasambhava, while Ami Megbon reminds them of where their cultural and ethnic origin is. This people-earth subjectivity in the landscape clearly indicates a passage of a place through time and of time through a place. In other words the landscape embodies time; it allows spaces of past times to be preserved. Such complex preservation of myths, histories, religious sacredness, and ancestral origins occurs simultaneously in both the landscape and mindscape. Through this passage of time-space the landscape has become "a living process" or "a process of incorporation" (Ingold 1993, 162). Undoubtedly the temporality of landscape is social and filled with human activities (Ingold 1993, 159), and it is in this way that the human mindscape is rooted there.

This rootedness can be understood as "place-memory" or the state of being in which the content of human mindscapes is incorporated into particular places and thus become the content of the place itself (Casey 2000, 184). A *bio*-graphy of a place thus constitutes its geographical evolution as well as its intimate and almost kindred relationship with the humans who live in it. This idea of place-memory helps us understand the nation and identity of Tibetans. Nation in this sense retains most of its etymological meaning as birthplace. It is particularly relevant for us to understand place-based identity, whether it is land-specific or on the move. In current nationalism studies, Benedict Anderson's idea of nation as an imagined community (Anderson 1991) is widely applied in various human constituencies and national contexts. Its perspective weight is more on the ideology of nationhood as a production of modernity and its modern mediums than on the place of nation. This theoretical vantage point is an eye-opener for us to see that the origin of the fundamental structure of the modern nation-state lies in the ideology and religiosity of the Enlightenment idea of liberty, equality, and democracy. Nation in this sense is idea-based, or "a state of the mind, an act of consciousness" (Kohn 1944, 10). In the overall trend of nationalism studies the role of place/landscape in shaping a nation and its identity is often relegated to the past tense, and is overlooked or under-researched.

Everything is on the move in this era of globalization but within context-specific places and landscapes. The place/landscape of Tibet plays a vital role in shaping the sense of home and nation among Tibetans both inside and outside Tibet. Tibetan farmers and nomads are constantly reminded of their ancestral and spiritual origins when deity mountains or mountain deities enter their vision and other sense-scapes. Tibetans who are in diaspora or exile also express their place-based sense through nostalgia. In his autobiography, the 14th Dalai Lama begins his narrative with his birthplace, Taktser, in Amdo. The first topographic element of Takster in the description of his home is a mountain of significance:

> ...there was a mountain which was higher than the rest. Its name was Ami-chiri, but the local people also called it The Mountain which Pierces the Sky, and it was regarded as the abode of the guardian deity of the place. Its lower slopes were covered by forests; above them a rich growth of grass could be seen; higher still, the rock was bare; and on the summit was a patch of snow which never melted... Clear springs of water fell in cascades, and the birds and the wild animals—deer, wild asses, monkeys, and a few leopards, bears and foxes—all wandered unafraid of man; for our people were Buddhists who would never willingly harm a living creature (Dalai Lama 1997, 1).

This childhood experience of Tibet's ultimate spiritual teacher is identical to that of Sambha's residents where Ami Megbon, as a mountain god, is the protective deity of the village. Like common Tibetan folks, the Dalai Lama's Buddhist national identity is deeply embedded in the landscape of Tibet. His mother's memoir confirms the idyllic scene of their homeland, as she writes in *Dalai Lama, My Son*, "My earliest memories are of a land that nature had made a plentiful paradise. It was a wealth of forests, lakes, hills, mountains, and fertile soil. This is how I remember the village of Churkha, in the district of Tsongkha, where I was born" (Diki Tsering 2000, 18).

Deity-mountains and scenes of nature are commonplace in human settlements throughout Tibet. When the place-ness of home is invoked, especially in a nostalgic mood far from home, this leitmotif of deified and personified place occurs frequently. The late Chögyam Trungpa Rinpoche also begins the recollection of his home place with its topography rather than with his kinsmen. In *Born in Tibet*, the natural awesomeness of Pagö-pünsum, the highest mountain in his home region, monumentally ushers readers into the home of this legendary tantric master, "Centuries before Buddhism was brought to Tibet, the followers of the Bon religion believed that Pagö-pünsum was the home of the king of spirits, and the surrounding lesser peaks were the abodes of his ministers. Myths linger on among the country folk, and these mountains have continued to be held in awe and veneration in the district" (Chögyam Trungpa 1995, 23).

In this interplay and interlocking of place and memory, the lived body is a place of its own which implaces everything encountered and lived, into its mindscape. The *bio*-graphy of a geological and humanized place has its own physical evolution since place is always in a process of its own making and being made (Tilley 1994, 33); however, its perceived counterpart residing in the lived body via its mindscape undergoes a different path of evolution especially when the lived body has moved away from its physical place. This evolution of place-memory in human mindscapes takes root in emotional currents, existential circumstances, and nostalgic recollections of the past. The elements of place, whether natural or religious or cultural, are deposited into the mindscape of the lived body. The sediments of the mindscape are reproductions of the physical counterparts but are ordered according to the current lifeworld and circumstances. The difference between the sediments of physical landscape with both geological and human elements, and of human mindscape lies in the malleability, plasticity, and agility of the lived body. In a geological order of place, the deeper a sediment resides in the Earth the older it is. However, the order of the mindscape's sediments is not definitively set as pure records of the past; instead they comply with the current situatedness of the lived body. This is how place and memory interact with each other and finally unite with each other. Memory grows roots in place and vice versa, but both place and memory grow roots in the lived body as a mobile place. In this regard, past events and scenes of place in memory return to the present, as if they were eternally framed in time, and yet present themselves as if they had never changed. One's earthly paradise could be lost to human destruction but it is invoked time again into the present and thus its past life relives in the mindscape.

The physical surface of the Dalai Lama's birthplace has been transformed into another site of China's urbanization; however his and his mother's published memories have become what I call "a memorial place" for Tibetans in diaspora, where memory sustains place and national identity. Thus this memorial place is undoubtedly a national place in Tibet except that it is globalized. Because it is physically detached from geographic Tibet, it could be seen as a placeless "imagined community;" however, it does not rest itself on the Enlightenment-based, modern idea of nation; instead its rootedness is found in the place of Tibet in both symbolic and geographic terms. This is what Casey refers to as the paradox of body and place: "…the power of place is most fully manifested at the very moment when place and body fused and lose their separate identities" (Casey 2000, 200). In the case of the Tibetan diaspora, the emotionality of this united identity of body and place further increases the memorability of the Tibetan landscape in a nostalgic fashion appearing as a severe state of homesickness which "admits no remedy other than a return to the homeland" (Casey 2000, 201).

In this case, rootedness to a place does not start unidirectionally from the person to the place. It is rather overwhelmingly the other way around, that is, from the place to the person. The antecedent here is the immersion of the person in the place in which he or she does not just "occupy" a space but is fully engaged with and environed by all elements of his or her lifeworld (Ingold 2000, 135). The "dwelt-in world" (Ingold 2000, 42) never stops filling the body and the mind of the person with nutrients, cultural ethos, and social events. Herein, physical landscape and intangible mindscape could be visualized as a combined placiality in which one finds the past present and the dead very much alive. Such placiality permits us to see place as moving between the dwelt-in world and the world of memory. It is a mobile "rhizomic world" (Ingold 2000, 140) whose complex roots intertwine place and memory, and landscape and mindscape. In his studies, Ingold sees place-based identity formation as resting on these five key phrases – ancestry, generation, substance, memory, and land (Ingold 2000, 132). I would also add the earthly gods and spirits as an integral part of such placiality in the Tibetan case. If landscape is "storied" with human history (Ingold 2011, 141), mindscape can be "storied" with the presence of earthly deities and human memories as shown in the cases of Sambha, the Dalai Lama, and the late Chogyam Trungpa Rinpoche. The lived place and the remembered life, in both tangible and intangible terms, are a sentient realm in which the land nurtures the body, the gods nourish the psyches of the people, and the mind becomes an inner field of roots grown from both the land and the gods.

2.6 "Place has its own being…"

To understand landscape/place as more than merely background or as recipient of human actions, it is essential that we recognize that it has its own subjectivity, that this subjectivity is intangible in nature but manifests itself in tangible geological and topographic forms. Likewise, this intangible Earth-subjectivity can be seen as an independent being. The materiality of this independent being is not defined by the human taskscape to start with, but is expressed through its physical forms in geological and topographical terms with latent eco-aesthetic and eco-spiritual affordances.

In *The Fate of Place*, Casey writes, "…place has its own being, on the basis of which it is a 'cause' (*aita*) and not something merely inert or passive (*argos*, *adranēs*) – something caused by something else in turn" (Casey 1997, 90). Likewise I see the place of Sambha as having its own being, too, as its relationship with humans has manifested differently with different residents in history and current non-Tibetan visitors through the affordances it offers. The history of how Sambha was named indicates that the a priori being of its landscape spoke to Sambha residents' ancestors through those affordances at different times. Both their Buddhist and outlaw ancestors recognized the landscape as a sanctuary but with two different moral orientations. To the Buddhist ancestors, the landscape was a Buddha-field because of the alleged marks left by Padmasambhava and his consort; to the outlaw ancestors, the landscape was a perfect haven for a hideout. In those different times, both groups of ancestors farmed the same land protected by the high mountains and the rapid river. Both groups regarded the valley as their home environment. Settling there was not an accident. What the place speaks through the form of what it can give to the humans, its affordances, plays a pivotal role in people's decision to settle there. Dwelling is not one-sided and place is antecedent to the creative directionality of human activities. Place is the mythical and historical prerequisite to dwelling.

Sambha is one of countless cases of rural human settlements in Tibet with the pattern of inter-dwelling with gods and spirits who share the same ecosphere with humans. Humans, gods, and other beings dwell in each other's midst with only a porous boundary between them. In the Tibetan worldview, whether they are humans or gods, the fact of sentience connects everyone (Smyer Yu 2011, 70). There is no clear-cut dichotomy separating humans from gods, as occurs in the relationship between humanity and divinity found in Semitic religious traditions. Furthermore, the natural environment in the case of Tibet is not necessarily a separate domain without human presence. Nature in this sense is not cognized as "wilderness" or "wild nature" (Fisher 2003, 667) with a clear modern civilizational bias. This is where I would like to differentiate my eco-aesthetic approach from what is known as "environmental aesthetics" based upon a view that sees the natural environment as an object of artistic appreciation (Fisher 2003, 667). Environmental aestheticians often express their positive aesthetics toward this humanless nature, holding that "all virgin nature is beautiful" (Carlson 1984, 10) and that anything "…untouched by man has mainly positive aesthetic qualities" (Fisher 2003, 671). This man-nature relationship apparently requires that the only human involvement be a distant gaze on pristine, untouched nature.

Tibet is a critical reference for worldwide environmental activism and many parts of its physical landscape contain no human dwelling; however, its sustained sublime quality, besides its geological force and topographic immensity, is saturated with human eco-religious perceptions, ancestral memories, daily prayers intended to please earthly deities, and seasonal renewal of human bonds with sacred sites. When the physical presence of humans is not found in a place, the presence of human consciousness is still most likely extended there. Naming mountains and recognizing them as abodes of gods is a common way of marking natural places where people haven't necessarily established their built environment but where they are nevertheless intimately connected through mythological, religious, ancestral, and psychic terms.

If a non-native person wishes to understand how a deity mountain is simultaneously a mountain and a deity as many native Tibetans do, it requires his or her inner vision or imagination to connect the presence of gods and spirits in both landscape and mindscape. Herein I restate what I wrote in my earlier work, "It [Tibet] both is an imagination and it generates imagination itself" (Smyer Yu 2011, 190). Tibet holds imaginative affordances to both natives and non-natives. It subjectively, not objectively, engages its visitors with its vibrant colors, weathered, storied landscape, and the presence of divinity in the sentient realm. All begins with the unique landscape of Tibet.

Chapter Three
Confessions of an Inner Liberation

Non-Tibetan's enchantment with Tibet has been consistent among Westerners and Chinese alike since the early twentieth century. During the Republic era, important Buddhist figures such as Dharma Masters Fazun, Taixu, and Nenghai all made their way to Tibet. Seeking philosophical and soteriological counsel from their Tibetan counterparts, they considered Tibet a fountainhead of human spiritual and moral rejuvenation (Tuttle 2005). Government officials and scholars, such Zhao Yiqing, Liu Manqing, Ren Naiqiang, and Li Anzai, all expressed their intellectual and spiritual affection toward Tibetan civilization (Pema Wangyal 2011, 1–2). In turn Tibetan Dharma masters reciprocated with Chinese Buddhist seekers by touring Chinese cities and giving teachings based on their respective lineages. Among them, the Ninth Panchen Lama and Sherab Gyatso, who taught the Dharma to Han Chinese in the Republic era, are well-remembered among Chinese Buddhists. Tibet was regarded as a Buddhist spiritual treasure-house prior to the socialist era. Those who entered Tibet often returned with enchanting messages for their compatriots. Ren Naiqiang, an ethnological historian and a Tibetologist, wrote:

> Tibetans have preserved many ancient traditions. With their Buddhist ethos they refrain from taking lives. Upon accidentally killing an insect a Tibetan would feel disturbed for a long time. In wartime they would not slaughter their captives and would instead treat them kindly. Han Chinese beggars would find food and shelter everywhere in Tibet (cited in Pema Wangyal 2011, 10).

The narratives of Ren Naiqiang and his peers, Liu Liqian and Li Anzai, are identical to their Western counterparts in which Tibet is presented as a unique civilization. However, the continuity of this transnational commonality was discontinued in the latter half of the twentieth century when Tibet entered its socialist era. There were fewer than two decades between these scholars' ethnological work and research in Tibet and the time when the People's Liberation Army marched toward Lhasa; however, the difference between these scholars' message and those of the PLA was like day and night. To the Chinese military, Tibet, which was portrayed as a hell on earth, needed a total reconstruction from the inside out. Through the troops, the Chinese state constructed a new body of knowledge which subsequently took root in the Chinese populace's collective understanding of Tibet. This body of knowledge is now an integral part of China's national archive "documenting" Tibet's oppressive past that was in need of socialist liberation and modernization. If Tibet, to the British Empire, was "a place where the order of things reasserted itself in a curious vision of hallucinatory clarity" (Richards 1996, 12), to socialist China, it was a place without civilizational magnitude beyond unimaginable human misery.

Since the 1950s the enchantment of Tibet has been suppressed in the course of socialist modernization. From the perspective of my landscape-mindscape studies I see this historical suppression as an ideological recoloring of Tibet in which Tibet's past, as found in China's political historiography, carries a tone of moral darkness rather than bearing the history of a complex civilization. In this socialist historiographical motif Tibet appears as the place of a "people without history" (Wolf 2010) outside alleged barbarism.

Ironically, the consistency of the Chinese state's grand narrative of Tibet's past is now encountering a gradual subversion from within. Since the late 1990s, numerous memoirs of former military officers and journalists have entered China's book market. These include *Diaries of Marching into Tibet* (Wei 2011), *A Witness of the Reconnaissance Division of the 18th Field Army Entering Tibet* (Wang and Huang (2001), *An Affectionate Recollection of Tibet: A PLA Soldier's Memoir* (Ling 2000). Many of these works beg the question of "who liberates whom from what?"

In these former PLA officers and aid workers' memoirs we read of their amazed discovery of the eco-aesthetic potency of the Tibetan landscape and its culturally rich social world. For instance, Kang Qing, a young female soldier sent with her peers to Tibet, and Lin Tian, a PLA journalist, respectively recollect:

> Tibet's sky is azure and without imperfection. Tibet's rivers are so crystalline and lucid that one can see to the bottom, just like us girls who are cheerful, untrammeled, wholesome, transparent, and without impurity or gloom. I like to lie under the shade of a tree and stretch my legs into the sunshine while I watch the sky. Sometimes the sun and the moon are found there together. The sky is so close to me that it feels like a comforter and I feel embraced by heaven and earth (Kang 2007, 76)

> We saw three nomad women on our way. The youngest one was helping the oldest woman walk slowly toward us. They all wore many tiny long braids that draped down their backs almost to their heels. The braids were tied together with colorful ribbons ornamented with silver coins, silver nuggets, and agates. We quickly became acquainted with each other and they allowed us to pitch our tent near theirs. By dusk, the wind calmed down. The sunset on the surface of the lake made it look like a field of pink and painted the mountains on the horizon light purple. White sheep and black goats were returning home, their wool gleaming in the sunset. What an entrancing grassland this was (Lin 1997, 374)!

These narrators were among those who participated in creating the body of knowledge motivated by their Communist spiritual commitment to saving common Tibetans from oppression. As will be shown, this fifty-year-old body of knowledge gave birth to a split image of Old Tibet and New Tibet, with Old Tibet representing moral darkness and New Tibet marking a new socialist era filled with hope for freedom from oppression. Addressing this dichotomizing legacy in my study of Tibetan landscape is critically important because China's socialist endeavor in Tibet has engendered a dominant, ideologically-sanctioned perception and a modern representation of Tibet with both political and perceptual impacts on how contemporary Tibetans view their own history and cultural practices and how their Chinese counterparts have also experienced a shift in their perceptions of Tibet. The dichotomy of Old Tibet and New Tibet continues to be found in the Chinese state's current education of its domestic public as well as in its global public diplomacy concerning Tibet's past and its current state of affairs.

In this chapter I take a historical-textual turn to address the legacy of China's Old Tibet/New Tibet as two sides of the same ideological construct created by the Chinese state in the mid-twentieth century. I also look at its subsequent cultural materiality as a collective mindscape, one that had little prior contact with geographic Tibet while still taking the moral prerogative to remap the social order of traditional Tibetan society. The dual image, that of old versus new Tibet, held in the national mindscape of China has dominated the way in which both Chinese and Tibetans within the political domain of the PRC view Tibet, and is present even in the minds of the Chinese and Tibetans with whom I have worked. It adds complication and complexity to my understanding of the intersubjective relations between landscape and mindscape involved in the series of imaginative acts native Tibetans and visitors engage in.

The specific puzzle that I wish to solve in this chapter is not why former Chinese military officers and aid workers are expressing belated affection toward Tibet, but how the potency of Tibet's physical and social landscape communicated with those visitors while they were creating the construct of Old Tibet/New Tibet under a pre-set blueprint framed in the Communist paradigm. Taking a critical reading of PLA veterans' recently available memoirs, diaries, journals, and literary works as a special type of ethnography, I see three pieces of the puzzle worth extensive discussion.

First, Old Tibet/New Tibet was materialized not merely with the PLA's physical entry into Tibet, but, more critically, out of the Chinese state's enactment of Communism as a type of de facto radical utopianism locked in a negative dependency with dystopia. As counter-intuitive as it sounds, the attempt to implement this socialist utopianism was dystopianism in practice. Striving to attain utopia is predicated on the present state being in all ways utopia's opposite. Thus, the Old and the New were (are) twins as they always appear together in the state's grand narrative about the liberation of Tibetans; however the "twins" are obviously temporally distanced. In fashioning Old Tibet as a dystopia the PLA played a significant role in the early stage of China's construction of modern Tibet.

Second, based on both current publications and archival materials it becomes possible to see that the conception and materialization of Old and New Tibets was, and is, not a one-way street. While the PLA brought socialist modernity into Tibet, marking a new era for Tibetans, many of its officers and soldiers felt a sense of "newness" from the lifeworld of Tibetans, which was manifested in Tibet's magnificent landscape, stunning architecture, and the international connectivity of Lhasa. Such "newness" was not ideologically based but was rather grounded in personal experiences of specific places, terrain, weather, people, and built environments. If the Chinese troops overpowered Tibetans with their tactical superiority, Tibetan natural and built environments profoundly overpowered many of the Chinese soldiers and officers on a different scale – an inner transformation.

Third, following the textual journey of the officers and soldiers wandering in the streets of Lhasa and on propaganda mission to villages and nomadic areas, they reveal that Lhasa and other human settlements in Tibet were not always poverty-stricken places but were hustling and bustling with merchants selling goods from abroad or with residents engaged in traditional farming and nomadic routines. A critical finding is the evidence of recurrent PLA official statistics on Lhasa's demographics mentioned in the narratives of the PLA veterans suggest a reasonable inference that the majority of the Tibetan population in Lhasa in the 1950s might not have lived in abject poverty and weren't suffering to the degree usually portrayed.

Existing scholarly works on the initial encounter of Tibetans with the PLA often focus on the similarity of human affairs more than with one group conquering another group, one civilization replacing another, or a restored empire recentralizing its politically loose geographic margins. Sino-Tibetan strategic and tactical manoeuvres in the 1950s are extensively documented in the works of such scholars as Goldstein (2007) and Grunfeld (1987). The emphasis of my "de-puzzling" the socialist construct of Old Tibet and New Tibet is not on the tactical activities of the PLA but on their ideological roles as 'uniformed missionaries' spreading the seeds of Communism among Tibetans through person-to-person contact and propaganda mediums such as pictorials and motion pictures. On the personal level they also witnessed and absorbed aspects of daily Tibetan life. My writing in this chapter is not a fact-finding mission but an interpretive device to make sense of the enmeshed socialist ideology, the religiosity of Communism, eco-aesthetics, the inconsistency of state claims and personal accounts, the paradox of modernity, and the intersubjectivity of place and people, all in a mindscape constructed to transform the landscape of Tibet into a site of China's modernization.

3.1 The second Long March

Veterans of the People's Liberation Army often regard their 1950s journey into Tibet as "the second long march" (Yin 2009), a simile evoking the image of the Chinese Red Army's Long March in the 1930s. The Long March was an epic journey of the Chinese Communist Party into a long-envisioned Red China (Snow 1994, 201). In history it was an exodus from Chiang Kai-shek's White China, war-torn and semi-colonized by Western powers. The exodus, however, turned out to be a pilgrimage to and a sacralisation of Yen'an (Shanxi Province), so that it essentially became a "sacred" site for Chinese Communists. Nicholas Clifford remarks that the Long March was "the tale of a quest, unfolding the story of a journey into the unknown" (Clifford 1997, 103) and he notes that Snow witnessed the "awakening" of a new China being born with a new kind of people (Clifford 1997, 110). As the Long March wound into the territories of numerous ethnic minorities, including Tibetans in Southwest and Northwest China, it established Mao Zedong's vision of New China. With ethnic differences united under the cause of Communism and working for a future society of absolute equality and a fair share of material abundance this was a *de facto* utopian vision traceable to Marx's envisioned Communist society but flavoured with the millenarian aspirations of Chinese peasant rebellions. In this sense, the Red Army's Long March was not merely a tactical retreat in front Chiang Kai-shek's attempt to chase Communists out of China. Mao envisioned it differently, "The Long March is a proclamation, a propaganda force; and a seeding machine" (Mao 1991, 154). The Red Army was then an army of Communist missionaries spreading the seed of their own version of utopianism in conjunction with conventional military engagements on the battlefield.

The PLA's entry into Tibet two decades later was not an exodus but a carefully planned project of the Chinese state. It was neither tailed by a hostile force nor did it encounter formidable defensive assaults from Tibetans. Rather, it was backed with supplies of superior equipment and specialists in the fields of political economy, cartography, linguistics, and Tibetology. It engaged in assignments of "mindwork" (*sixiang gongzuo* 思想工作) more than battle during its long terrestrial movement from Kham into Central Tibet. This "Second Long March" was indeed a force of propaganda and a seeding machine proclaiming the establishment of the socialist New Tibet. Engineered to serve the territorial imperative of the newly founded People's Republic of China it was propagated as a socialist liberation project.

Wei Ke, a former propagandist, photographer, Deputy Director of the Department of Youth of the PLA Tibetan Region, and the first Party Secretary of Datse County of Tibet Autonomous Region, narrated the advent of his twenty-year career in Tibet in his diaries published in the 1980s. In early 1950 his regiment received the order to liberate Tibet:

> On February 5, 1950, our regiment held the "Mobilization Meeting for Marching to Tibet, Frontier of Our Motherland." Party members above the rank of squad leader were summoned to the meeting. Major General Wu Zhong presided. Zhang Guohua, the Commander of the 18th Field Army, made a personal appearance at the meeting and delivered an important speech. With our enthusiastic applause Commander Zhang Guohua mobilized us, "… Now the Party and Chairman Mao gave us, the 18th Field Army, the glorious task to liberate Tibet and defend our nation. Our assignment is to raise the victorious flag of Mao Zedong on the soil of our motherland's Tibet! We'll raise the Five-Starred Red Flag [the Chinese national flag] on top of the Himalayas! We must drive the British and American imperialists out of Tibet! We must liberate the people of Tibet from the abyss of suffering and guard the southwestern frontiers of our motherland. This task is arduous but glorious. Tibet, since the Yuan Dynasty, has been a part of our nation, and Tibetans are members of the big family of our nation. In 1888 and 1904 British imperialists twice forcefully invaded Tibet. Tibet was gradually turned into a semi-colony. We must help our Tibetan brothers liberate themselves from the enslavement of imperialism, and return to the bosom of our motherland…" (Wei 2007, 3–4).

The territorial imperative and moral empowerment are expressed clearly in Commander Zhang's mobilizing speech. This theme has changed little in the last half century. The mission of the Second Long March was twofold: reclaiming Tibet as part of China's sovereign territory and liberating common Tibetans from alleged imperialism and domestic slavery. Wei's diaries confirm the superiority of the PLA by disclosing Chinese intelligence about the Tibetan army, "According to investigation, the Tibetan army is numbered between 6,000 and 8,000. Plus deployable militia the total number does not exceed 30,000. They have 20 outdated artillery pieces and 50 machine guns. They would be easily crushed" (Wei 2007, 5). In contrast, the PLA's movement into Tibet was supported by thirteen engineering corps and over thirty Russian-made transport planes, not to mention ground support (Wei 2007, 9). Wei's regiment alone was "equipped with 8,000 mules guaranteeing continuous supplies" (Wei 2007, 9); they had as many mules as the total number of men in the Tibetan army.

While preparing for the second long march, the soldiers were inundated with the repetitive "mobilizing" messages from their command headquarters. Most soldiers were of peasant origin and many were former soldiers of the Nationalist

Army whose motivation for joining the Communist fight against the Old Society was to rejoin their war-separated families and build their own homes. Literally in a liminal stage in their lives, they anticipated their future marriages and children. Marching forward was required so they could march backward toward their imagined happy future lives in their homeland. The Tibet mission was undoubtedly an existentially circular pilgrimage to the majority of those soldiers and they voiced concerns about their new assignment to a place that was unknown or outlandish to them.

Commander Zhang Guohua's mobilizing speech to the 18th Field Army was also meant to counter his soldiers' anxieties toward their future. After 1949 and the end of the civil war most expected to share in the rewards and bounties of the war upon their return to civilian life. The central government's directives about the Tibet mission came when many troops were entering pre-assigned defence positions outside towns, cities, and along borders. Wei Ke's regiment was about to head toward their new peacetime base in southern Sichuan; however, on January 8, 1950 the regiment received an order to stand by. According to his narrative, a rumor began to circulate among soldiers that their Commander Zhang Guohua and his high-ranking officers were summoned to Chongqing for a new assignment. Wei Ke writes in his memoir, "In terms of what the assignment is, a few junior staff officers were making wild guesses. Some said we were to be redeployed to Yunnan to clean out the remnants of Chiang Kai-shek's bandits; some said we were going to take over the base of the defected Nationalist troops stationed in western Sichuan; and some even speculated that we had been chosen by the central government as the unit to guard the city of Beijing...All of a sudden everyone was speculating" (Wei 2007, 1).

On January 22, 1950 the order for the 18th Field Army to enter Tibet was announced to the anxious soldiers. In his research, Xinhua News journalist Xiaohao, finds that many soldiers were indeed surprised by the sudden order from their headquarters. They had a preconceived image of Tibetan as "a place hung on the edge of the earth, backward, desolate, thin-aired..." and thus "a dark void" (Xiaohao 1999, 20). His other findings also conform to those of former officers like Wei Ke that many junior officers raised concerns and expressed uncertainty about their return dates, and possibly missing opportunities for marriage and the requirements for fulfilling their filial duties at home.

Commander Zhang addressed these issues in an attempt to motivate his soldiers, "Some people say Tibet is a wasteland. You look at it as such but the imperialists don't mind its desolation. For a long time they have tried to force their way in. Now the American imperialists are actively having a hand in it. How can we be less enthusiastic about our own land than the imperialists?...Some people ask if they can marry Tibetan girls? Everyone knows, over a thousand years ago, during the Tang Dynasty, Princesses Wencheng and Jincheng were married to Tibetan kings. When we arrive in Tibet you can certainly marry Tibetan girls" (Wei 2007, 22). The PLA's Tibet liberation project gave soldiers gratifying personal assurance and a universal mission posited to free common Tibetans from oppression. What is relevant to my reading of this epoch-making time of Zhang's Field Army is the dual images of Tibet in the collective mindscape of soldiers and officers: Tibet was the closest place to the sun and a crystal world full of magic; however, the sun in Tibet was "dark" because it "could not melt the shackles worn on the serfs" (Lin 1997, 28).

Sixty-seven days later, on March 29 an advance taskforce of the Field Army set out into Kham and arrived in Ganzi at 3:00pm on April 28 (Wang and Huang 2001, 25). While the current travel time from Chengdu to Ganzi by bus is approximately forty hours, it took the soldiers nearly a month, without roads, to reach this strategic location in Kham. Five months later, on September 1, 1950 the entire Field Army began to move toward Lhasa. On October 24, it overpowered the Tibetan army in Chamdu. The road into Lhasa was opened with little military effort; however it took another year for the advance troops of the Field Army to arrive in Lhasa on horseback on October 26, 1951 (Wang and Huang 2001, 139). The Army's engineering corps and many soldiers used shovels, pickaxes, rope, and dynamite to carve out what still serves as the current highway connecting Chengdu with Lhasa. On December 25, 1954 the Field Army organized a parade of over three hundred trucks to enter the ancient city in celebration of the highway's completion.

My intention in listing these dates is to highlight the long intervals of both time and space, between locations and events. Time-wise, this second Long March of the Chinese Communist Army was three times longer than its first and there were dramatic topographic differences. The historical records show that the four long years between spring of 1950 and winter of 1954 were not exhausted in the battlefield. The standard government news reports and pamphlets all make celebratory statements about the endeavour and triumph of the PLA in defeating the alleged imperialist forces harboured in Lhasa and in reconnecting Tibet with the motherland. This narrative has been broadcast for over half a century and has become the leitmotif of the Chinese state's grand narrative response to international inquiries and debates about the Tibet Question.

Concerning these temporal and spatial intervals in the early half of the 1950s, my queries are: what did individual soldiers and lower-rank officers experience in the physically and psychologically challenging topography of Tibet? What transformative changes (if any) did they experience as they moved across the Tibetan landscape from Kham to Ü-Tsang (central Tibet)? What did Tibet, in real time and lived experience, mean to them? All these questions are meant to address the soldiers' sustained indoctrination of their Tibet mission as a Communist liberation project (or perhaps utopianistic rescue fantasy) and, at the same time to bring up what has been revealed about their experience of an ecosublime state involving moments of awe, depression, and both negative and positive aesthetics toward the Tibetan landscape.

3.2 Elation and desolation in the eco-sublime Tibetan landscape

The PLA soldiers did not encounter significant defensive assaults from the Tibetans; instead they were enveloped in the undifferentiatingly hostile but eco-sublime topography and turbulent weather of Tibet. This multi-layered encounter appeared contrary to the troops' ideological indoctrination about Tibet and Tibetans as a colossal "wasteland (荒地 huangdi)" (Ling 2000, 32) and as a people who were oppressed, downtrodden, and, frankly, pitiful. New or republished memoirs of soldiers and officers show that the human cost of the PLA's Tibet mission did not so much result from battling the small Tibetan army but rather from the difficult terrain and weather conditions of the high plateau. Their recollections reveal that they recognized that the earth obviously gives and takes life but it also transmits another kind of psychic and spiritual message triggering the latent sublimity of one's mindscape.

While Wei Ke was with his regiment as a photographer and a propaganda officer, Lin Tian, a military journalist, accompanied the soldiers of the 18ᵗʰ Field Army advancing into Tibet from Kham. With the same ideological training about Tibet, he makes an exclamatory remark in the beginning of *The Diaries of My Tibet Journey*, a best seller among Chinese veterans' memoirs, "Oh...How on earth could Tibetan working people on the Kham-Tibetan Plateau live under such primitive and miserable conditions!" (Lin 1997, 1). On June 30, 1950 when the regiment he followed reached the mountains of Kangding or Dartsedor (དར་རྩེ་མདོ།), a small town marking the traditional boundary between the Han Chinese area of Sichuan Province and Kham, his first impression of common Tibetans did not indicate they were in misery but rather showed his envy and positive aesthetic appreciation of Tibetans:

> As the rays of sunlight came down from the top of the mountain, the ripples on the surface of the river bloomed profusely like transparent, magically kaleidoscopic flowers. Bird song trilled over the rushing river. In such a scene one feels that the vitality of life is so precious and time flies so swiftly. By now it was almost noon and many Tibetan porters were coming toward us. Some were rushing their mules; some trying to keep their yaks together; and some walking with empty wooden frame carriers. Men and women were all walking on

the muddy road. On a big rock by the river sat a well-built Tibetan man. His shoulders and chest were exposed in the sunlight. Two greasy-looking small pouches [amulets] hung below his neck. His face was tanned and light was radiating out from his big eyes in their deep sockets. His curly hair was dishevelled and thrown back. As he raised his head toward the sky, he put two big, dark fingers of his right hand into his mouth. In a single breath he blew a long piercing whistle. He truly looked like a legendary hero of ancient times. The sword at his waist and the big yak-leather boots on his feet made him look especially mighty. He was calling his yaks. I followed his gaze up the mountain. A herd of the colossal but domesticated longhaired animals were moving slowly downward from halfway up the mountain (Lin 1997, 6).

This type of recollected image of Tibetans is frequently expressed in the memoirs of Chinese veterans; however they are textually positioned on the margins of their narratives, recalling reflective moments when taking a break from their epic march westward into Tibet. During these moments the narrating soldier or officer stopped to regain his breath or sat on a mountain slope after a long day of road construction. At these moments it was as if they were inhaling the landscape of Tibet into their mindscape, and exhaling reflections, contemplation, and the poetic sparks of the mindscape. In recollecting his troops' movements in the mountains of Ngari, Lin reminisces:

When we were walking down from the hill the clouds in the western sky suddenly dispersed. The luminous rays of the setting sun shone like orange flames on the golden grass and the rocks on the mountain ridges in the north. They turned the snow covered peaks behind the ridges pink and the lake at the foothill purple. What mesmerizing scenery! We forgot we were in the cold wilderness and could not help but clap our hands and dance with joy...We crossed the single- log-bridge to the west side of a small river then walked north two more miles until we reached a riverbank covered by a luxuriantly green stand of poplars. Orange flowers bloomed between the trees. Small red birds chirped and a cuckoo called coo-coo-coo. Everything felt stimulating and yet peaceful. My colleagues, Ren Yongzhao and Ma Jingqiu, rhapsodized about the scenery. On the edge of the forest a few Tibetan men were building a fire to make tea. They were woodcutters hired to cut trees for our troops. I was very worried that logging would ruin this fairytale-like environment (Lin 1997, 532).

Both Wei Ke and Lin Tian were assigned to promote the goals of China's Tibet mission to soldiers as well as to Tibetans, and to record the daily movements and events of their troops with the intention that their historical records would be shared with later generations of New China and New Tibet. Not every soldier or officer had the same ecstatic state of the mind on the march toward Lhasa. Many died en route and were buried along the road they were constructing. The treacherous terrain and unpredictable weather were factors leading to the mortality of soldiers. The terrain was so high that there was often insufficient soil and not enough time to prepare graves in the thin air and driving snow. The bodies were unceremoniously "littered" in shallow pits along the road (Wang 2007, 41; Li 2010, 28).

Those who continued westward toward Lhasa advanced at a snail's pace. The average weight of the tactical gear carried by each soldier was forty kilograms. Li Chuan, another veteran, recollects:

> ...Mountains were snow covered and covered with cliffs. In the early morning the wind blew up tiny pellets of frozen snow that stung our faces. Our eyebrows and wind goggles froze. Our legs felt stiff like icicles. The higher up we went, the deeper the snow was and the thinner the air became. Our noses and mouths puffed like exhausted bellows. It took a huge effort to move one step forward. We pulled and pushed each other upward...Our regiment commander said to everyone, "We're taking the hardship to liberate Tibetan people. It's worthwhile to endure the hardship" (Li 1985, 193–94).

Additionally, there were over one thousand women soldiers and officers in the advancing Army serving as nurses, staff officers, propagandists, and performing artists. Yu Dehua, from the art troupe of the Field Army, was seventeen when she joined the long march to Tibet. In her narrative, the most dreaded time during the long, exhausting walk was when she had her period. Lacking paper and cloth she tore portions of her pant legs to make sanitary pads. Upon crossing the last of the journey's many rivers she was offered help from her male comrades, however, she was too shy to be on the back of a man. Seeing the other women wade into the waist deep river, she could not help but joined them. She recollects, "Damn, I didn't believe it would be that scary. 'Plop,' there I was in the river. The icy water immediately made my skin and muscles tighten up. It was so cold that I felt my belly, thighs, and feet were being sawed off... That day we crossed two rivers. My period stopped that night. One month, two months, and three months passed, never to return. In 1960 I was diagnosed with ovarian cysts...The rivers and mountains in Tibet are beautiful, but I hate them as long as I live. They gave me a life-long regret [infertility]" (Ji 1993, 315)

Yu Dehua was not the only female soldier to leave Tibet with painful memories. One of Commander Zhang Guohua's bodyguards witnessed a female political officer who was left behind with a Tibetan nomad family in Kham as she was about to give birth. Forty days later she rushed to catch up with her regiment leaving her infant behind with the family. They were never reunited (Li 1985, 50). When she reported back to Commander Zhang Guohua, he said to her, "You've worked hard!" Sitting up from her stretcher she replied, "It's nothing..." (Li 1985, 51).

The initial positive aesthetics and eco-sublime moments shown in the writings of Wei Ke and Lin Tian eventually shifted from their detached appreciation of the Tibetan landscape and people to their full immersion. The soldiers' bodily contact with that world often confirmed the negative aesthetic toward the magnitude of the Tibetan landscape as hostile and threatening to their physical safety. The eventually-realized state of the sublime experienced by these soldiers came at the high price of being deeply enveloped in the magnificent but life threatening conditions of the high plateau. Their moving bodies were engaged as an interface with both the earth and the sky, including being caught up in what Ingold calls "the weather-world" (Ingold 2011, 96) in which the touchscape, visionscape, soundscape, and mindscape of the person are no longer independent from the external world and eventually lose that distinction as an "exhabitant" (Ingold 2011, 96) who perceives the living world as objectively independent and thus mistakes his or her contact with it only as surficial – as if he or she were only on it, not even in it, let alone part of it.

The soldiers and officers were experiencing their eco-sublime moments that can be intellectually and spiritually rewarding but conditional in the sense that they can be accompanied by fear, oppression, depression, and even both psychological and physical injuries when the objective distance between the person and the perceived sublime landscape is dissolved or mutually immersed in the other's being. In this regard the soldiers' encounter with the Tibetan landscape was not a visual experience alone. The colorful and transcendentally inspiring appearance of the land certainly came from the reflection, deflection, and refraction of solar light and the body's physical ability to process that light's journey through the atmosphere and across the changing terrain and into the eye and brain; however this visual experience and the subsequently sublime state of the mindscape toward the Tibetan landscape is an experience of the body and mind being entered and saturated, a process that unites landscape with mindscape non-negotiably.

What exactly sustained the morale of the advancing soldiers and officers in this dualistic course of positive aesthetics and dreadful physical experiences in this epic march into Tibet? In my findings, both the morale and the moral ground of the Field Army sustained itself with a large dose of Communist "liberation theology" involved in building a new socialist Tibet. Propaganda specialists, political officers, and enlisted performing artists consistently delivered pamphlets and productions to soldiers and officers. Li Guozhu, one of the very few woman political officers in the 18th Field Army, recalls in her memoir about how the troops were inspired by the "seeds" left in Tibet by the Red Army in the 1930's:

> …several Tibetans came to our post enthusiastically helping us chop firewood, make fire, fetch water, and look after our yaks. They didn't want to leave for a long time. They

asked many questions in their broken Chinese inquiring about current happenings in China. It was so rare to meet Tibetans who could speak Chinese. They caught our attention. Who were they? What was their ethnicity? They wore Tibetan attire and had long hair. They spoke Tibetan like native Tibetans, but they turned out to be the wounded soldiers left behind by the Red Army during its Long March in 1936. In order to survive they had learned Tibetan, adapted to the life style in the highlands, married Tibetan women, and grew roots here...I was touched upon hearing their stories. I felt it was not easy for them to survive. Their resilience deserved our emulation. It was a pity that they were having much difficulty speaking their mother tongue let alone adopting the new vocabulary of the revolution. It was difficult to communicate with each other. When we were parting with them I wanted to give them gifts but could not find any. What I left with them was my sincere heart as their comrade and my deep memory of them. Chairman Mao once said, "The Red Army is the seed and the seeding machine" (Li 2010, 17).

3.3 Communist "liberation theology"

To sustain the morale of the troops, the Field Army empowered common soldiers as ideological and spiritual "liberators" by stimulating empathy from them for the allegedly suffering Tibetan people and by envisioning a liberated Tibet in the near future. With this mindset, in witnessing the death of their comrades, the meaning of death was often transcended from its medical definition to a spiritual level: the deaths were equated to martyrdom, a sacrifice for the cause of Tibet's new, Communist society free of oppression, exploitation, hunger, and other forms of suffering. The embedded logic of the Field Army's "liberation theology" was thus expressed in this melodramatic sequence: commiseration with a suffering Tibet temporally reset as "old" or "past" with values and practices contrary to its modern socialist counterpart; a long terrestrial march as a rescue mission during which soldiers' moral identity as "liberators" was reinforced as they invested their emotions, labor, physical pain, and deaths in the transcendentally magnificent but sublimely hostile landscape of Tibet; and their consistently enlivened faith in their materialization of the newness of Communism in a foreseeable future in Lhasa, the final destination of their long march.

The high morale of the Field Army could be seen as an altered state of consciousness because of its ecstatic euphoria. On his way into Tibet, Ling Xingzheng, a former PLA propaganda officer, composed this poem after viewing the advancing army column:

Oh, High Plateau...High Plateau!
Your mesmerizing landscape
Is still veiled with a thin-layered mist of wilderness!

Let me wield my paint brush
To draw a golden line of the New Epoch!

I walk to the soft, grassy hill.
The first survey pole should be erected here
To guide the iron dragon of the New Epoch,
Flying over the high mountains (Ling 2000, 31)!

According to Ling, the "golden line" and the "iron dragon" symbolized the vision of Tibet connected to the rest of China with highways and railways (Ling 2000, 31). The poem is charged with temporalized phrases with which the reader is oriented to visualize two different "time zones" with two different spatial orientations: Old Tibet ["still veiled"] is a zone of magnificence but a place of wilderness and social oppression, and New Tibet is the coming new era, waiting to be surveyed and inlaid with modern infrastructure. The embedded vision of the poet is an inevitable transformation of Tibet's "wilderness" into a place of modern order.

Obviously the soldiers and officers were infused with utopianism that can be understood as "social dreaming – the dreams and nightmares that concern the ways in which groups of people arrange their lives and envision a radically different society than the one in which the dreamers live" (Sargent 1994, 3). The Chinese Communist Revolution has been characterized as a utopian and millenarian style peasant revolt. Walter Meserve and Ruth Meserve noted, "...the Chinese utopian dream of a Communist society is expressed in an urgent desire carefully promoted by artful propaganda and the demanding attitudes of the Communist Party of China" (Meserve and Meserve 1992, 29). To trace the roots of Chinese Communist utopianism, it is not too difficult to see its theoretical and ideological ancestry from Europe. Both Marx and Engels vehemently raised their objection to the utopianism of their times; however, their objection was not against utopianism itself but rather against the methods adopted by European socialist utopians to materialize an ideal society. Ruth Levitas puts it plainly, "The difference between Marxism and utopian socialism does not...rest on the existence or otherwise of an image of a socialist society to be attained, nor even on the content of that image. It rests upon disagreements about the process of transition" (Levitas 1990, 45). Revolution geared toward the abolition of existing social classes was the prerequisite of Communist utopianism. In this sense, the present is not merely a temporal register but also a representation of an obsolete social system waiting to be replaced with a new one.

Chinese Communist utopianism consistently transposed/transposes space and time by engineering and fortifying an ideal future meant to be intensely believed. In this way it became/becomes a prominent part of individuals' mindscapes and carries the future within the lived reality of the present. This utopianism among the soldiers and officers of the Field Army was not a new development but was a replica of what had already taken place in greater China – a liberation project that replaced Old China with New China. In the same manner, the "liberation project" of the Field Army in Tibet was equally messianic with the Army positioned as the saviour and Tibetans as the recipients of their Communist salvation. In numerous veteran accounts, the troops were portrayed as "bodhisattva soldiers" (Wang and Huang 2001, 37) in creative propaganda works. This widely disseminated image of the Field Army as altruistic, self-sacrificing, and valiant eventually culminated in *The Serf* (1963). In the film, Lanka, the sister of the blacksmith, tells the protagonist, Champa, a downtrodden and hopeless serf, the news of the coming PLA: "From the east has risen the brightest sun. In this brightest sun stands the tallest bodhisattva. He sees everything. He sees that the people in the highest place in the world are living in the deepest agony! When the bodhisattva points his finger his bodhisattva soldiers cross countless mountains and rivers. They are coming to save the people from suffering. On the head of every bodhisattva soldier is a red star..."(1963). Chairman Mao, the messianic bodhisattva, leads his peasant soldiers as bodhisattva warriors to Lhasa. Negating the colorful lifeworld of Tibetans for the principal purpose of creating tension, conflict, and power in the film, it "reflect[ed] the contrasts of light and darkness, freedom and oppression," according to Wei Linyue, the cinematographer (Wei 1965, 220).

Utopianism, as a human universal, is based, according to Emanuel Berman, upon "the rescue fantasy" (Berman 1993, 45), in which the rescuer considers himself to have omnipotent power capable of saving the victim without effort. In the saving process, the rescuer idealizes himself as "an altruistic, pure-hearted gallant knight" (Berman 1993, 46). Such a rescue fantasy embedded in utopianism was evident in the early histories of the former Soviet Union and China in their "attempt to forge 'New Man' and 'New Society'" (Berman 1993, 54). The rescue fantasy is a psychological complex functioning as "a realistic frame of reference" (Berman 1993, 45) and the self-idealization of the rescuer is particularly relevant to our understanding of the ultra-high morale of the Field Army. In the psychic sense, such self-idealization is synonymous with self-enlargement: the rescuer psychically enlarges himself with a power beyond the ordinary and projects his enlarged self outwardly to the external environment. In the lifeworld that surrounded the marching troops, this psychic projection of enlarged-self yielded multiple positive effects for the Field Army. Its goal for the territorial reacquisition of Tibet stayed was the primary objective of the Army but was it psychically and spiritually transposed and elevated as a rescue mission to the extent that it carried religious overtones when the Army's creative propaganda works empowered soldiers as "bodhisattvas."

The morale of the troops increased significantly because of this. To be noted again, the Army did not encounter stiff resistance from the Tibetan army; instead the hostility it faced most during the journey was the changing topography and the unpredictable nature of the weather in the mountainous landscape. While the soldiers endured harsh weather and illnesses and witnessed the deaths of their comrades, they also experienced the eco-sublime state of the Tibetan landscape as narrated in the memoirs of Lin Tian, Wei Ke, and other veterans. However, the complex of their rescue fantasy makes them reflexively render the magnificent landscape of Tibet as less than what it presented itself as. On one side, when the landscape inspired the journal-taking soldiers, it was the place where "our soul is being elated" (Xiaohao 1999, 1) or "a state of being where life is incomparably majestic" (Xiaohao 1999, 10). Yet when the fantastically enlarged self-as-"bodhisattva soldier" is imagined, the majesty of Tibetan landscape is darkened because "to the serfs, the sun is black" (Xiaohao 1999, 28).

This shading of the initial description of the land with ideologically tinted vision is a recurrent pattern in the memoirs and journals of many of those soldiers and officers. What I have attempted to convey is that the Tibetan landscape spoke to the young Field Army personnel in eco-sublime terms. What is written in their memoirs and diaries shows the enlargement of their sense of self to match the greatness of the Tibetan landscape. This is an oversimplification of this intellectual-spiritual response to the magnificence of the Tibetan landscape because, in fact, an eco-sublime enlargement of the sense of self was quickly suppressed and swiftly replaced by the ideological enlargement of the self as Communist "bodhisattva." In this regard, it could be said that the ideologically induced sublime state of mind was consistently subverting the eco-sublime connection of the troops with the Tibetan landscape. Yet concurrently the power of the landscape subverts the artificially dark tone of Tibet, as the journalist Xiaohao says, "As our vision moves higher and higher, our soul is being elated" and "Tibet is a state of being...In such a state of being we honestly and piously believe there exists another world outside our worldly realm" (Xiaohao 1999, 10).

Again, on one hand the organically inspired "state of being" was suppressed and then reconstituted as a Communism-inspired state of mind. On the other hand it continuously overwhelmed the soldiers and officers, appearing much more transcendentally powerful than the rescue fantasy and its sustaining Communist "liberation theology" maintained throughout the mission of the Field Army. The weathered- and peopled-world of the landscape deeply entered the consciousness of soldiers and officers and changed their state of being.

3.4 Puzzling statistics and the social scene of Old Lhasa

In their research on the history of Lhasa's urban development, Zhang Yili and his colleagues find that the total population of Lhasa in the early 1950s was 30,000 (Zhang et al 2000, 396). In Xiaohao's findings, when Commander Zhang Jingwu began to work, in 1951, on the Chinese state's peace plan with the then-in-power Tibetan government, the total number of monks in Lhasa was listed as 18,000 with the following breakdown: 8,000 at Drepung Monastery, 6,000 at Sera Monastery, and 4,000 at Ganden Monastery (Xiaohao 1999, 286). This means that in the early 1950s before the Chinese state's reform over half of Lhasa's population was monastic.

In Vsevolod Vladimirovich Ovchinnikov's 1955 visit as a guest journalist from the Soviet Union he was briefed by his hosts that Lhasa had a total population of 50,000, among whom there were 20,000 monks and 15,000 merchants and craftsmen (Ovchinnikov 2009, 75). There is a discrepancy between Zhang's 30,000 and Ovchinnikov's 50,000; however each figure is proportional in relating a large population of monks relative to the general populace. These historical demographics cited in the works of Xiaohao and Ovchinnikov give reason to legitimately doubt the widely touted uneven distribution of economic resources in traditional Tibet as exemplified in Lhasa. Old Tibet, as characterized by a gross imbalance between the wealthy and the poor, is the result of a selective representation of pre-liberation Tibet. Disputing the different statistics is not my priority since they cannot be verified; however, the documented perceptions of the former PLA personnel and the state guests who toured Lhasa in the initial encounter of traditional Tibet with modern China are crucial for my interpretive understanding of how Old Tibet and New Tibet were conceived in the same temporalizing ideological framework and of how they are encountering divergent personal accounts in contemporary China.

When Commander Zhang Jingwu arrived in Lhasa in 1951, the emphasis of his immediate assignment was not to liberate the poor and the oppressed, but to "unite with" (团结 *tuanjie*) the Tibetan ruling class that included those in the monastic establishment (Xiaohao 1999, 289). Zhang's working objective shows in the distribution of silver coins as "offerings" to monks and beggars on the streets of Lhasa. Each monk received two silver coins. Khenpos and disciplinary lamas each received twenty silver coins. The young Dalai Lama then received forty silver coins (Xiaohao 1999, 286). According to Xiaohao's interview of the late Chen Jingbo, then Intelligence Chief of the 18th Field Army and Director of the Tibet United Front Department, "all old silver coins from China were spent in Lhasa, no less than several million of them...The state built several new foundries to make more silver coins" (Xiaohao 1999, 286). At the same time Zhang distributed shirts and blankets to the total of eight hundred beggars and poor people in Lhasa. Each was given a "Certificate of Offering Recipient" (Xiaohao 1999, 289). These resurfacing statistics do not support the dichotomy in reports that the majority of citizens were poor and the minority were rich as found in the Chinese state's claim; instead they suggest that the majority were at least of moderate means in Lhasa which was the religious and the political center of traditional Tibet. In other words, Zhang's initial activities, recapped in Xiaohao's work, show that the percentage of poor was low if we are to believe only 800 out of 30,000 residents of Lhasa qualified for donations; this challenges the official qualitative interpretation of these figures collected by the Chinese state. The question of who the wretched serfs were remains to be addressed.

3.5 Searching for serfs in the midst of the "black bones" and the "white bones"

Ren Huaguang, the aforementioned PLA veteran propaganda officer who served in the 18th Field Army's Engineering Corp, similarly identified blacksmiths and butchers as those at the bottom of traditional Tibetan society. Ren uses a native Tibetan phrase – "black bones" (རུས་རྒྱུད་ནག་པོ།) – to describe low social status held by "slaves" as opposed to "white bones" (རུས་རྒྱུད་དཀར་པོ།) which referred to "free men" (Ren 1959, 1–5). Both phrases appeared to be in common use among Tibetans. The term "black bones" is cited frequently in the Chinese state's official literature as an example of the alleged oppression found in Old Tibet. In the film *The Serf*, the audience finds the embodiment of "black bones" in a shackled blacksmith and his daughter. When Champa, the serf, takes a bit of food from the daughter's plate, the blacksmith stops him by saying, "Child, don't eat the food from the plate of a blacksmith. We are born with *black bones*. Whoever catches it will have the same 'black luck'" (*The Serf* 1963, emphasis added).

Currently, the most frequently referenced living example of "black bones" is a man named Laba. His short narrative is featured on the China Tibet Information Center website testifying to the dehumanizing treatment of the "black bones" under the serfdom of Old Tibet (Laba 1998). What is noteworthy is that Laba was born in 1959, the year in which the Chinese state formally dismantled the traditional Tibetan social system, yet he remembers how Old Tibet treated the "black bones" (Laba 1998). Whether or not Laba's narrative is authentic, an anthropological angle shows Ovchinnikov making a reasonable assessment that the "black bones" were a segment of the population in traditional Tibet subject to taboos based on then-common practices. His assessment corroborates the result of Chinese social scientists' fieldwork in the 1950s and the early 1960s.

In his memoir about his 1955 tour in Tibet, Ovchinnikov designates a chapter describing what he calls "People at the Bottom of Society" (Ovchinnikov 2009, 78–85). He states that they were mostly craftsmen in Lhasa. Through a blacksmith named Tsering Pentsog, he learned that the social hierarchy in Lhasa was largely determined by people's professions. Among them, thangka painters and coppersmiths who made Buddhist icons and statues held higher social status while the lowest social status ended with blacksmiths and butchers (Ovchinnikov 2009, 80). Those in the middle were jewelers, carpet weavers, carpenters, and masons. Ovchinnikov then infers from his observation that the social hierarchy in traditional Tibetan society was based on "Buddhist values," as he writes, "Blacksmiths belong to a lower caste. The professions of blacksmith and butcher are all looked upon as the despised. This type of prejudice originates from religion because Buddhism regards killing as the maximum crime. Blacksmiths are those who make the killing tools while butchers are those who use those tools" (Ovchinnikov 2009, 80).

Ovchinnikov's observation of traditional Tibet's social hierarchy matches those of PLA officers and investigative teams of Chinese social scientists. Between 1958 and 1962, the Ethnological Institute of the Chinese Academy of Science sent an investigative team to Tibet to collect field data on the economic system and social structure of traditional Tibet. Its report lists blacksmiths as "black bones" along with two other types of *dsogpa* (བཙོག་པ) or "filthy" ones, namely butchers and *nor-ro* (ནོར་རོ), the merchants selling livestock. The report states, "People are not clear why these three types are 'filthy.' They all say it has been like this since ancient times and perhaps these three types of people directly or indirectly commit killing. The prejudice against them is shown in people's not eating with them and not marrying their children" (Shu 1964, 42).

Among the three "filthy" types, the Chinese state indicates that the blacksmith is subsumed under the social class "serf." Reading Laba's short narrative closely I most certainly see the injustice experienced by his family because his father was a blacksmith, but at the same time I also see that they were not exactly "serfs:" "In Old Tibet our family roamed to different places with a tent that could not fend off rain and storms. We worked and begged. People treated us like wild dogs. I don't know where my ancestral home is. My father was a fine blacksmith, good at making locks. Noble families all liked his work, but we were mistreated and discriminated against" (Laba 1998).

It could be reasonably inferred from his narrative that his family lived a separate but unindentured life and that their suffering was caused by gross stigmatization coupled with unpredictable and poorly-paid work. According to Laba's narrative, this traditional Tibetan cultural practice continued into the socialist era. After his first marriage failed in 1977, he married again in 1984, this time to a daughter of a coppersmith. He describes this marriage as "a marriage between two families of equal status" (Laba 1998). This cultural taboo based on Buddhist belief undoubtedly contributed to the misery of Laba and his family; however it's interesting to note that it continued even after socialist liberation and well into the Cultural Revolution.

Since blacksmiths were classified as serfs, it makes every sense to reconsider who constituted the class labeled by the state as "serfs." In Goldstein's work, "serfs," strictly speaking, were not slaves completely deprived of their personal freedom; instead they had mobility as long as they fulfilled their obligations to their estate owners. Goldstein prefers to call this segment of the population the "peasantry" (Goldstein 2007, 12). Within this peasant class the economic status of individuals and their families varied. Serfdom as a social system mostly existed among the agricultural population of Tibet with serfs not always the majority population in every human settlement.

Li Wenshan, a former journalist and former deputy Party Secretary of TAR, investigated the socialist land reform in a village called Sangga in Nêdong County, Tibet Autonomous Region in 1963. In his memoir *Unforgettable Tibet* he re-emphasizes the dichotomy of the 95 % serf majority and the 5 % ruling minority, and yet his investigation of Sangga's social demographics speaks otherwise. In order to form the "Village Serf Cooperative" the village chief gathered all of the approximately two hundred households for a meeting. In Li's account villagers quickly chose their five to seven representatives to form smaller units. In truth, these families were free farmers. Those who had no-one chosen from among them were left standing in the middle of the meeting ground. They were the eleven "serf" households (Li 2001, 47), accordingly. Evidently they were the minority of their village, comprising just 5 % of the village's families. In real time, these "serfs" were those who worked as servants for wealthier families (Li 2001, 53). Li recalls the scene in the village commons:

> At first they anxiously looked around noticing the small groups of people who were drinking tea, smoking, and chatting. Nobody invited them to join their cooperative units. Finally they realized what had happened. Champa, the quiet serf, after counting the number of other serfs around him, depressingly said, "Those who can fly have organized themselves. Those who live in horse stables are all left out" (Li 2001, 47).

In Li's account of this particular case of socialist land reform the eleven serf households were the minority in their village. Li attributes the cause of this social exclusion of the serfs in Sangga to their past as servants, cooks, and maids for landowners, which meant that they had little opportunity to learn agricultural skills (Li 2001, 46). This social reality could also be read from the religious angle: social boundaries in traditional Tibet were determined not merely by economics but also by taboos sanctioned by religious practices identifying "clean ones" from "filthy ones." To be noted, Li's investigation was conducted in 1963 – another case of a Tibetan traditional custom active in the post-liberation era. Organizing the "Village Serf Cooperative" mirrored the exclusivity of the Chinese socialist revolution, too – its ideological and practical gravity was toward showcasing the marginalized population of Tibet as an act of its socialist liberation project.

The Tibetan word *serf* – *hsangbran* (ཞིང་བྲན།) is suspected to have been initially a literal translation of the Chinese phrase *nongnu* (农奴) or "farm slave" since it was absent in pre-liberation Tibet. Both the Tibetan *hsang* (ཞིང་) and the Chinese *nong* (农) mean "agriculture" or "farming." *Bran* (བྲན།) in Tibetan means servant or serf but not necessarily referring to people without any freedom. *Serf* in socialist literature refers to slave-like peasants bound to a lord. In farming areas Li and his colleagues identified the servants and maids as serfs; however, their peers working in nomadic regions did not find much of the slave-master dichotomy.

Returning to the diary of then PLA journalist, Lin Tian, who was on an investigative and propaganda mission in the grasslands of Ngari, he reveals that his assignment was to look for the oppressed population and spread Communism among the nomads. What he saw from the perspective of his Marxist political economy were three types of nomads – "A moderate nomadic household owns five or six hundred sheep. A wealthy nomadic household owns over a thousand sheep...the poor nomadic households have very few sheep; so they partially rely on hunting wild animals. Families without livestock herd sheep for the wealthy families" (Lin 1997, 378). Thus, rather than finding slaves he found tenant herders among the nomads he met. His propaganda mission to spread the seeds of Communist revolution nevertheless appeared to be successful according to his account.

The nomads in Ngari had little idea what socialist liberation was all about. Their connection with Lhasa seemed to rest upon their religious devotion to the Dalai Lama and the Panchen Lama. In Lin's recollection the highest religious leaders of traditional Tibet became the key to open a door for his propaganda team to disseminate the Chinese state's socialist message. The team's initial contact with a nomadic family in the grassland usually started with their presenting to them the posters of the Dalai Lama, the Panchen Lama, and Chairman Mao together (Lin 1997, 373, 385). This strategy gained entry into nomadic families and calmed them from the state of shock when they saw the propaganda team's military truck as a giant monster (Lin 1997, 373). All nomads receiving the three posters lifted them up above their foreheads showing their reverence. It is reasonable to assume they accepted Chairman Mao as a peer of the Dalai Lama and the Panchen Lama, not as a Communist leader. This visual strategy became the entry point of the socialist reform campaigns and modernization programs in the coming decades. It most likely was the point when the Tibetan version of "The East is Red" was conceived; thus Chairman Mao was then mystified as the "tallest bodhisattva" from the "brightest sun" as seen in the cinematic narrative of the film *The Serf.*

3.6 The clash of Marxist class struggle and Buddhist fate

In her 1959 visit to Tibet, Anna Louis Strong, a pro-Communist American journalist, was allowed entry to document how the Chinese "work teams" worked with serfs. She recalls how a serf named Lando responded to the socialist neologism "oppression" (བཙན་འཛུལ། *dsenzel*), "When the work team, in getting acquainted with serfs, asked Lando if she had been 'oppressed,' she didn't know the meaning of the word. Nobody had ever talked about 'oppression' but only about 'fate.' What happened, she thought, was her inescapable karma. So the work team made it simpler and asked: 'Did your master flog you or molest you or did he give grain for seed?'" (Strong 1959, 58).

The Tibetan word for "fate" is *li* (ལས།). It is also a key philosophical and doctrinal phrase of Buddhist teachings regarding conditions that shape one's current and future states of being. Its lexical meaning corresponds to the Sanskrit word *karma* (action) used in the Buddhist context signifying that any of one's doing leads to foreseeable effect(s). Thus *li* encompasses both acts (as causes) and the result of these acts. The current state of one's *li* is simultaneously the fruit of past acts and the cause of future outcomes. In monastic instructions as well as in popular Tibetan understanding, the word *li* has a long list of associative phrases, including *liwang* (ལས་དབང་། affinity), *ligye drebpa* (ལས་ཀྱི་སྒྲིབ་པ། karmic hindrances), and *lidri tobsa* (ལས་འབྲས་ཐོབ་ས། place where one receive ones karmic retribution). The prevalence of these terms indicates that the Buddhist worldview is deeply ingrained in Tibetan cultural consciousness among both literate and illiterate populations. Strong's encounter in the late 1950s is a telling example of the social and psychological embodiment of Buddhism among the poor, the wretched, and the illiterate, not just among the aristocratic and monastic populations; however, the native moral explanatory system concerning human sufferings had to be reordered to the socialist version.

In the colloquial sense the Chinese socialist liberation project in Tibet was intended to "overturn" (翻身 *fanshen*) the "fate" of the Tibetan peasantry with a new set of causal explanations from the perspective of Marxist political economy (Hinton 1997, vii). The *li* of the serfs then was seen as a fate laden with oppression or simply an embodiment of oppression itself in the case of Strong's witness. In working with the illiterate population, the PLA work teams, on one hand, took a gradual approach (Goldstein 2007, 37) to gain entry into the social and familial realms of the poor in Tibet by juxtaposing the Party and its leader with the religious leaders of Tibet. On the other hand they utilized visual means to convey the dichotomized meanings of oppression and liberation. In the memoirs of Li Wenshan, Lin Xingzheng, Ling Tian, and other PLA veterans and journalists, mobile film projection teams and PLA performing teams often toured towns, villages, and grasslands. Most films were produced by the PLA Film Studios, such as *The Light Shines on Tibet* (1952), *The Liberation Army Marching to Tibet* (1952), and *The Central Government Delegation in Tibet* (1956). The frequently performed stage shows include "Bitter Memories," "Champa the Serf," "Happiness of Liberated Serfs," and "Dedicate our Harvest to Chairman Mao."

As discussed previously the PLA's primary engagement in Tibet was not combat oriented but was rather what Strong calls the "social engineering" (Strong 1959, 59) of creating Old and New Tibets. As she recalls, the work teams were a "task force" of the Chinese Communist Party "to liberate and transform this Tibet at minimum human cost" (Strong 1959, 59). The task force quickly built the history of socialist modern Tibet through personal stories of suffering and fictive cinema works and stage shows. The memories of the past were limited to the bitterness and suffering of serfs, and the present was being transformed toward a Communist paradise with the arrival of the PLA as "bodhisattva soldiers." Fiction films like *The Serf* in China's Tibet liberation project have become an integral part of Tibet's modern history and a cinematically represented memory of the oppressed in Old Tibet. Traditional Tibet was transformed into New Tibet; however this New Tibet is defined by its negative dependency on the public image of Tibet's past as Old Tibet – a dystopia graphically displayed with severed body parts, shackled limbs and instruments of torture displayed on the state websites like China's Tibet Information Net or Tibet Human Rights Net.

3.7 Reminiscing about Old Tibet's enchantments

After Zhang's Field Army completed the highway from Sichuan to Lhasa, the Chinese state invited a group of foreign journalists from Italy, Poland, France, Czechoslovakia, and the Soviet Union to Tibet. Arriving between August and September of 1955, it was the first foreign delegation to visit Lhasa after the Field Army's initial entry in 1951. Ovchinnikov, as one of the delegation members, described his first impression of Tibet when he arrived:

The magnificent beauty of the Tibetan Plateau astonishes us! Nature crafts the rolling contour of the Earth's surface. All around us we see the fantastic, dream-like shapes of large and small mountains. The deafening roar of rivers and waterfalls awes us. Clouds float beneath our feet. Eagles stretch to their full six and half foot wingspan, gliding in the sky. Such majestic power is beyond the imagination of travellers. It humbles us and makes us feel insignificant and helpless. Facing the stunning power of nature the best creative works of humans lose their charm" (Ovchinnikov 2009, 1).

After arriving in Lhasa, Ovchinnikov continued:

The way all Buddhists in Asia regard Lhasa is similar to how Muslims revere Mecca or how Catholics look upon Rome. To numerous scholars of Central Asian Studies, Lhasa signifies unfulfilled aspirations and ineffable secrets! We walk through the colourful, mesmerizing, and bustling streets of Lhasa as if viewing the illustrations in a novel about the Middle Ages. Houses stand neatly like columns of fresh soldiers. The city grows freely without regimentation...We have silently walked for several hours in the streets of Lhasa. Everyone is so mesmerized by the fairytale-like scenes surrounding us that we have forgotten to take photos and jot down our impressions. We feel as if we were sent back into an ancient time. Suddenly encountering familiar things, we feel like we're on a movie set for Marco Polo's time spliced with something modern. Several PLA soldiers look curiously at a large copper teakettle in the middle of a street...(Ovchinnikov 2009, 44–45).

In 1959, first by air and then by bus, Strong with her journalist peers from eleven countries, headed to Lhasa. Her positive eco-aesthetic response to the Tibetan landscape echoes Ovchinnikov's four years earlier:

The mountains, now that we were down among them, were far more impressive than they had seemed from the plane. In the high, thin air, all nature seemed penetrated with light. Snowy peaks, rock cliffs, long sloping pastures were all more brilliant in color than any landscape I had ever seen. The sky was bluer, the grass greener, even the color of the rocks brighter and more varied in this upper sunlight than colors appear at lower elevation, blanketed by depths of air. What from the plane had appeared a monotony of gray rock and white snow broke now into a vast variety. Cliffs were red, lavender, even orange, indicating a probable presence of minerals. Pastures were dotted with yaks, sheep, and goats. Streams of clear water, blue from the melting snow, tumbled across the highway. Someday this should be one of earth's great vacationlands! (Strong 1959, 13)

Since the late 1980s when China first allowed foreigners to enter, tourists, seekers and pilgrims have flooded to Tibet proving Strong's assertion prophetic. The language of the Earth appears to transcend differences of ethnicity, nationality, and ideology. The landscape of Tibet uniformly sent an identical message to Buddhists, spiritual seekers, and Communists, that is, Tibet is a sublime place that awakens sublime responses from the human mind. The rational mindsets of soldiers, officers, propaganda specialists, and journalists all deeply entered a geopoetic trance of some sort and can be seen to have momentarily left their ideological indoctrinations aside. Like Ovchinnikov, Strong's first, raw impression of the Potala Palace was also a reflexive, place-centered appreciation. She described her first sight of it in the evening as "a red and white jewel, shining in the last gold of the setting sun…It was a new type of architecture, with the side walls sloping inward like the mountains, as if the structure were part of a living cliff. It testified to a talent for originality among Tibetans, which might again revive from the stagnation of centuries" (Strong 1959, 14).

The perceptual worlds of individual officers of the Field Army and the state-sponsored foreign journalists seem to be compatible with the initial social scene of Lhasa in the eyes of Commander Zhang Guohua and his staff – with monks as the majority residents of Lhasa and the wretched and the poor as a minority. Ling Xingzheng, one of the aforementioned former PLA propaganda officers, caught the tail end of the traditional society of Tibet when he entered Lhasa. In his account, the proportion of the magnificence of Lhasa's urban and surrounding natural landscapes, and the sight of poverty did not indicate a morally "dark" Tibet. In his memoir entitled *An Affectionate Recollection of Tibet: A PLA Soldier's Memoir*, he expresses his awe-struck moments in Lhasa. To him, as a young officer, the Potala Palace was a splendid architectural wonder that blended with the surrounding mountains; the city of Lhasa was an international city rather than a self-enclosed place; and different markets were bustling with shops, vendors, and pilgrims. Lhasa hosted the consulates of India and Nepal. Window-shopping with other PLA officers in Lhasa, Ling saw Indian and Nepali shops displaying luxury goods from Europe, e.g. Omega and Rolex watches, and German made cameras (Ling 2000, 44–60). When he and his comrades walked into Barkhor Street, he was amazed at its festivity and international connectivity, marveling in his narrative, "…Barkhor Street in Lhasa is Chongqing's Liberation Monument District, Beijing's Wangfujing and Dashilan Districts. In many ways it surpasses them. Do the shopping districts in Chongqing and Beijing have foreign shops? Do they have European goods? But Barkhor Street does…" (Ling 2000, 50).

Where are the poor and the wretched in his memory? Ling's jaw dropped when he saw Jokhang Temple. He recalls:

> What first drew our attention was not the extraordinary architecture of Jokhang Temple, but the people who were prostrating on the long slab stones in front of the Temple. They shocked us. I had never seen people prostrating like this. Facing the Temple, with their palms and knees covered with rags, three old men in their shabby clothes were prostrating – knocking their heads on the slab stones…In these bits and pieces of scenes I felt there were many mysterious, novel things hidden behind them. So I was repeating the same

question in my mind, "How on earth could China have such a magical place?" (Ling 2000, 56).

Then his superior explained to him that these prostrating, raggedly clothed Tibetans were serfs (Ling 2000, 56). Had Ling not been in uniform and in the company of his superior and comrades he would have had a different way of understanding the devotional practice of Tibetan Buddhism, which continues to be present in front of Jokhang Temple today.

Ovchinnikov's experience was similar to Ling's except that he was more open to the religious practices of Tibetans. In bustling Lhasa the Soviet journalist noticed that the presence of poverty was marginal. As a matter of fact, Ovchinnikov does not use the phrase "serf" but "beggars" and "pilgrims." He writes, "Even on an ordinary day pilgrims were everywhere in the city [Lhasa]. Pilgrims consisted of exotic magicians and other 'holy men.' They were all begging for a living" (2009, 45). In his recollection, most common Tibetans were not wretched:

> Most Tibetans' faces were handsome and healthy. Their bodies were well proportioned. They were optimistic, frank, and preferred bright-colored ornaments. Not to mention the beautiful women, but almost all men we met wore turquoise rings or necklaces strung together with colorful stones. Those respectable men of simplicity, who are accustomed to wear weapons [swords and daggers], remind us of American Indians in the novels of James Fenimore Cooper (Ovchinnikov 2009, 11).

The dualistic vision of Tibet as a dystopian world of human misery and an inspiring lifeworld in a magnificent natural landscape and with mesmerizing Buddhist society is inadvertently challenged and subverted by those who participated in the liberation project of the Chinese state. Half a century after their experience, the seed planted by the Tibetan landscape is germinating. Recollected from their memories, it reveals the land's radiant colors and spiritual brilliance, dovetailing perfectly with the expressions of Tibetophiles in contemporary China:

> Ling Xingzheng, a former PLA propaganda officer stationed in Tibet, 1959 – 61:
> *At this moment the sunrise dyes the tip of the snow mountain fiery red. Below, in the valley the morning fog has not yet dissipated, scattered here and there. They add more solitude to the surrounding mountains. Birds' chirping is coming from the dense, fog covered, forests. I only hear their singing but cannot see them...I begin to doubt my own vision as the scenery in front of me truly resembles the idyllic scenery of southern China. How on earth is this the Tibetan Plateau? How on earth is this the roof of the world? The air here is so pure and fresh, and moist. It does not lack oxygen. The colors are so rich and beautiful. This is most definitely not a dead-zone. It overflows with signs of life even in the winter* (Ling 2000, 141).

Su Yan, an aid officer currently serving in TAR:
I start falling in love with this piece of the Earth even as I am captivated by the beautiful sky above. In Tibet, we aid workers, far away from our homes and families, hold our posts and perform our duties. Moments of loneliness are unavoidable. However, every time I push open my window and breathe in fresh air, I always seize the moment to absorb this magnificent sky. She [the sky] instantly lights up the chamber of my heart. All anxiety and lonesomeness dissipate. Her immensity widens my inner world. If Tibet is the sacred space purifying my soul, its sky is the fountainhead of this purification. It is because of her that I forget worldly vanity and cast aside base hypocrisy. What it boils down to is the pure human being in the natural and existential senses (Su 1997, 70).

Xiaohao (Hao Guiyao), journalist:
The color of Tibet is most original. Some say Tibet is a world under the brush of Paul Cézanne – a world of light and transparency. One beam of light, one field of light shining from above, envelopes you. Tears quietly well up in your eyes. Your teardrops are even crystally transparent. You hear the crisp voice of your soul…Transcended from time and space the inner worlds of many people are instantly lit up. They walk toward the highest light – the spiritual lantern of the heavens (Xiaohao 1999, 82–83).

Cheng Demei, Photographer, CCTV:
I'm searching for my dream – om-mani-pedme-hum. I'm walking into my dream – freedom. This is the reason I have unceasingly walked to Tibet – the Plateau. Freedom lies in the eye-catching, gigantic but unreachable mountains; freedom lies in the footsteps of my life-journey into those immense mountains; freedom veils itself in the distant sky; and freedom resides forever in the unreachable horizons of the Earth…Tibet in my heart is not a concrete existence. Tibet is a faith, an ideal, a realm, and an affinity (Cheng 2005, 6)

Li Hong, aid officer currently serving in TAR:
Tibet's mountains are bestowed with a soul. With snow over them they look as graceful as ever. As dreamlike as it is, this ancient snow, either on the rolling horizons or hiding the sun and the moon from us, captures my soul with its entwined majesty, melody, and splendor. In the midst of this I float like a feather with the wind and recede into the pure white snow without a trace. Perhaps, this is so called "intoxication" (Li 2010, 10).

The similarities in these depictions of Tibet show that Tibet, as a concrete place, has taken root in the mindscapes of these veteran and modern socialist "thought-workers." Their positive appreciations of the Tibetan lifeworld reflect those of Lama Govinda, Alexandra David-Neal, and Ren Naiqiang all of whom entered Tibet a few decades before the PLA. While Govinda, David-Neel and Ren's positive eco-aesthetic memory of Tibet is now an integral part of the emerging Tibetophilia of a new generation of artists, administrators, and aid workers in China, the PLA veterans' writings, though coming out of the experience of being part of the "seeding machine" of China's socialist modernity, are finding a receptive audience half a century later among both Tibetans and non-Tibetans in China.

Chapter Four Memorability of place among anti-traditionalists

Half a century ago, words such as democracy, equality, and liberation, were coined in Tibetan by Chinese propaganda specialists and Tibetologists. These words were part of the political force used by the Chinese state to construct Old and New Tibet as represented by the PLA's vigorous propagation of the Communist worldview. More than fifty years later the dichotomy of the old and the new continues and has evolved to incorporate new social and personal meanings among the younger generations of Tibetans. As they struggle with notions of personal destiny and the fate of Tibet which is, foremost, the concrete place of their homeland, the meanings of modernity conveyed with these neologisms are painfully but organically manifested in the entwinement of place and memory, and in the simultaneous presence of discontent and affection toward a cultural tradition that is being renewed in the twenty-first century. This mishmash of consistencies and contradictions is a hallmark of place-based, sociopolitical discourses among contemporary Tibetans.

Shogdong (ཞོགས་དུང་), the pen name of Tagyal (བཀྲ་རྒྱལ་), a leading Tibetan cultural critic in China, describes his state of being upon visiting the Potala Palace in 2008:

> For the sake of searching for the roots of our past splendor and present decay, I set out to Lhasa…I felt elated when I saw Lhasa but I also felt saddened…and with my mind full of doubts. I felt blissful because I paid homage to Zanpo's (བཙན་པོ་ king) Palace [Potala Palace] but also felt disgusted with myself for having ditched my soul. I hurried myself, as I wanted to see more, but also slowed myself down because I was in a state of incomprehension. This mixture of anger and joy, sorrow and elation, and loss and gain was my first sensation upon arriving in Lhasa (Shogdong 2008, 7).

This conflicting state of mind is common among many of my Tibetan friends who live and work in urban China. I write this chapter as a pathology of modernity concerning the manifested *pathos* – the emotions, feelings, and pain – that arise as a consequence of China's socialist modernity. It has engendered a mindscape that is internally split into pro-tradition and anti-tradition divisions. The purpose of pathologizing such a mindscape is to discern how modern subjectivity in the case of urban Tibetans inherently hinges upon place as both geographic landscape and locus of memory. It is also my intention to juxtapose the pathology of urban Tibetans' emotional expressions toward their homeland with Chinese PLA veterans belated but positive recognition of Tibet's potency in eco-sublime and eco-aesthetic terms as discussed in the previous chapter. By focusing on Shogdong's writings in this chapter I attempt to delineate the *pathos* of modernity felt among urban Tibetans and shown in cases of self-temporalization, self-objectification, geo-psychic displacement, the inversion of forgetting and remembering, and a subaltern exercise of discursive power.

4.1 "Pulling one hair moves the entire body"

Unlike his contemporaries such as Tsering Oser, Tsering Norbu and others who express their national sentiments in the Chinese language (Smyer Yu 2011, 148–172), Shogdong's presence among Tibetans is known through his use of Tibetan language with many of his writings formally published by Tibetan language publishers affiliated with the state. Shogdong is mentioned in Lauren Hartley's "Inventing Modernity in Amdo" (Hartley 2002) and I first read his work in 2003 while I was doing fieldwork on Tibetan Buddhist revitalizations in Golok and Kham. At the time I was ethnographically situated in a Tibetan monastic environment and theoretically wrapped up in the equation that held that the revitalizations of Tibetan Buddhism were equal to the revitalizations of Tibetan culture, as was expressed in Goldstein and Kapstein's volume *Buddhism in Contemporary Tibet* (1998). I had originally trivialized Shogdong as one of the Chinese state's Tibetan functionaries who tend to debase their own traditional culture. But after teaching graduate seminars to Tibetan students and meeting Tibetan creative writers in Beijing between 2007 and 2011, my monastically-tinted view on Tibetan cultural revitalization soon encountered its own limitation: it obviously originated from my theoretical indoctrination in neoprimordialism, instrumentalism, and constructionism, all of which fundamentally rest the core of their debates on a substantive understanding of culture and identity either as a priori primordiality or as an instrument of some sort used to fulfill sociopolitical interests.

In 2010, my belated attention to Shogdong's critical standing among Tibetans literally hindered an inclusion of fresh findings in my manuscript as his arrest by the state made it impossible to meet him personally. In retrospect I see that Shogdong's public importance among Tibetans mostly lies in the "critical mass" engendered by the circulation and debate of his prolific writings. This "critical mass" does not necessarily imply uniformity among his audience; instead, it is a readership that is expressed as a unity of differences and dissent on the grounds of a collective exploration of what a modern Tibet or, more specifically, a modern Tibet imagined by Tibetans, means, in both present and future tenses. Tibet, as a physical place and an imagined future, is a highly temporalized and objectified landscape as well as a state of being with a double personality – at once an actual birthplace of Tibetans and a fragmented, polarized, and displaced mindscape. Both of these states of being are interlocked and sustain one another.

The previous passage of Shogdong's writing comes from his *Contemplation and Reflection* published in 2008 by Gansu Minzu Press. Titled "Nine Wacky Things" (ཨ་མཚར་མཚར་དགུ) and based on his trip to Lhasa, this part of his book is indicative of his cultural and placial orientation toward Lhasa in his imagination of a modern Tibet:

> It is hardly possible that a Tibetan would not want to go to Lhasa. Among them, some head to Lhasa for glamour and honor, and some for their next lifetime's ultimately ensured enlightenment. Most of them regard their homage to Potala Palace and the statue of Sakyamuni in Johkang Temple as the most grandiose quest of their lives. Lhasa in my mind is not only a Buddhist sacred place where one receives empowerment from circumambulatory pilgrimage, but, more importantly, it symbolizes an epitome of Tibetan political, economic, cultural, and historical fate. It is a point where "pulling one hair will move the entire body"[1] (Shogdong 2008, 7).

Shogdong's assessment of Lhasa as "a point where 'pulling one hair will move the entire body'" suggests the critical importance of Lhasa as the center of Tibetan national belonging. Lhasa is not only a physical location; it is also, as his writing shows, deeply rooted in his mindscape. Shogdong's physical experience in Lhasa could be a "hair pulling" moment in his personal life: his conflicting thoughts and emotions direct his body in conflicting movements between an ecstasy of homecoming and an agony of guilt. This mindscape-landscape connectivity shows what Timothy Oakes calls the "paradox of modernity" in which "Place, then, can be read as a geographical expression of modernity's paradox – that tension between progress and loss – a creative yet ambivalent space carved out somewhere between the oppressiveness of the new order and the imprisonments of tradition" (Oakes 1997, 511). In Shogdong's case, his stream of consciousness moves into the physical place of Tibet but is constantly displaced in his mindscape: he is in place but feels placeless; his elation in Lhasa confirms his sense of regaining a lost paradise but he feels simultaneously estranged from it because of its modern transfiguration and because of the self-assessed loss of his soul. The pulse of self-negation in the midst of his recollection of Tibet's past and things traditional is markedly polarized.

The *pathos* of modernity endowed to native peoples worldwide is identical: the native's reclamation of his or her past is painfully coterminous with the near-omnipresence of the psychically intrusive, bipolarizing force of modernity. What

---

[1] The original sentence is སྐྲ་སྒྲུ་གཅིག་གཞིག་ཆེན་པས་ལུས་ཡོངས་ཏེ་ཁ་གཡོས་འགུལ. It implies a domino effect.

is remembered and recollected is also fragmented, with the invoked collective past unable to stand alone but needing justification and legitimation by modern standards. The rootedness of modernity in the interior of a native turns against him every time he attempts to re-embrace his pre-modernized identity. It overwrites the re-invoked collective memories with an automatic self-correction, a return to the modern mindset, because the past is best kept at a distance, judged, exiled, or reordered and reshaped. The *pathos* of modernity does not stop here; it moves on to alter the native's sensorial experience and the very geological-cultural landscape of his birthplace.

Shogdong's pilgrimage writing bears a consistent pattern of a dual depiction-visualization of the Tibetan landscape en route to Lhasa. His native vision of the landscape is frequently juxtaposed and even overwritten with his modern geological and cartographic vision of the Earth consisting of tectonic plates and places locked into longitudes, latitudes, and altitudes. He writes:

> If you ask an Amdowa how on earth the sky-like, immense, Blue Lake [Qinghai Lake] came into being, he would ceaselessly tell you a story without an origin mixed with speculation and history. If you ask an Üpa (དབུས་པ། a person of Central Tibet) where Lake Lhamo Namtso (ལྷ་མོ་གནམ་མཚོ) came from, you'll receive a fairytale of humankind's infancy. In fact, a long, long time ago, this place [Tibet] was a vast ocean. Later different tectonic plates collided into each other. In this process, rising mountains formed a basin and retained parts of the ocean [as the current lakes]. High snow mountains have continuously fed water into these lakes until the present day. However, Tibetans haven't yet liberated themselves from their gods and demons; instead their fairytales from the Age of Ignorance continue (Shogdong 2008, 12).

In Huber and Pedersen's study of Tibetan native meteorological knowledge, they notice that contemporary Tibetans outside China are accustomed to representing their traditional knowledge system in modern scientific terms and that they claim it as a native science (Huber and Pedersen 1997, 578). What stands out in this native representation of their traditional knowledge concerning the Earth is what Huber and Pedersen call the "nature quantified" (Huber and Pedersen 1997, 580) in which both built and natural places are remapped. The qualitative distinctions found in native systems of thought recede into quantitative representations through the use of modern, technologically-advanced tools and vocabulary: thermometer, barometer, and isothermal representation (Huber and Pedersen, 580–582), etc.

It is noteworthy to point out that Tibetans outside Tibet and China positively represent their native knowledge system in modern scientific language. In contrast, many Tibetans like Shogdong, who are trained in China's modern educational system, often not only negatively represent native knowledge systems but also take them apart with the same value judgments their Chinese counterparts bear toward native belief systems and practices. Therein the story of the Earth is deprived of its mythological and spiritual contents. Creation stories are reduced as stories of humankind's infancy without historical and cultural significance, and gods and spirits are dismissed as products of human superstitions.

Shogdong and many of his peers live in a bifurcated world in which the gravitational relation of homeland and their job-based urban living environment is inversed. Their childhoods were spent in rural areas and townships of Amdo, such as Chapcha (ཆབ་ཆ), Chekha (ཁྲི་ཀ), Shamdu (ཤ་མདོ), and other places known among Tibetans for producing modern educators, cadres, writers, and filmmakers. They attended colleges in Xining, Lanzhou, Chengdu, and Beijing. Upon graduation from college, many of them found careers in these cities as school teachers, professors, government officials, Tibetan language publication editors, and media professionals. Amdo, their homeland, is for many, only two hours away by bus, private vehicle, or airplane and home has become a place of weekend and holiday visits. As they grow more rooted in their urban professional and social spheres, home appears more and more as a background rather than a foreground of their livelihood. Their urbanization and continuing systemic immersion in China's modern infrastructure and superstructure undoubtedly contribute to the solidification of the paradox of modernity in their mindscape.

The Tibetans with whom I am acquainted in urban China and who are attracted to Shogdong's writings have not lost their Amdo accent and continue to expand their repertoire of modern neologisms from Chinese, re-animating them with the meanings and contexts of existential, psychological, and spiritual agonies, dilemmas, and marginalities in their bifurcated living environment. The sense of revisiting, remembering, reconstructing or revolutionizing their collective past is resiliently present but, at the same time, their collective mindscape is clearly caught in the paradox of the old and the new, and of backwardness and progressiveness.

However, regardless of the inversed gravitational pull between homeland and urban settlement, and regardless of their positioning in the modern superstructure of China and in the intra-Tibetan discourse, many Tibetan urban dwellers whom I have met continue to be empowered by the landscape of their homeland, albeit often in their mindscapes in the forms of memories, discursive thoughts, and creative expressions. Modernity at its most pathological may have taken deep root in their mindscapes as a miasma that creeps in whenever there are openings, yet leaving the landscape of one's homeland, or keeping a geographic and an ideological distance from it, does not entail the relinquishment of its potency.

4.1 "Pulling one hair moves the entire body" — 103

Shogdong's paradoxical negation of his tradition and empowerment by the landscape of Tibet is a telling example of the potency of place. As discussed in previous chapters, such placial potency in the Tibetan context is embodied in the mindscape of Tibetans. The Tibetan landscape not only includes geological formations but is embedded with humans' ritualized and intimate relation with gods and spirits, the tracks of memories pertaining to the origin of Tibetan people, and finally the dominion of the immense landscape itself over human existential and spiritual realities. When such a potent landscape becomes an object of Shogdong's negation, rejection, and dismissal, it speaks back to him when he is physically enveloped in it:

> That morning after eating *tsamba* kneaded with plain water as my breakfast, I saw a golden ray of sunlight on the tip of the mountain behind me. I was wondering if he [the mountain] was having a luminous moment in his mind. Toward noon, the horizonless Earth kept company with an insect moving forward while admiring the eagle soaring up above. What remarks would he [the insect] utter about differences between species? That night, like a masterless dog, I took residence in a cave free of charge. Facing the endlessly flowing Milky Way, I asked myself, "Have I made a courageous vow to change Tibetans' current state of affairs?" Out of their faith Tibetans have carried countless sacks full of gold in exchange for the empowerment from countless gods and spirits. Age after age this same pilgrimage path may continue to compound the infinite number of Buddhas. In the religious eye, the Buddha and enlightened heroes manifest themselves in the magnificent mountains; the canon of the Buddha's teachings written with golden ink covers the Earth. In this infinitely expansive time and space, when all moving bodies are seen as bodies of the Buddha and all uttered speech is heard as mantras, all minds will receive enlightenment from the Buddha Dharma. When remembering the compassion of Avalokitesvara and Amitabha and when reciting the six-syllable mantra with animals and birds, one is in a delightful state of being. When imagining the homeland of King Gesar, one sees his deified thirty generals as well as Nyanchentanglha [གཉན་ཆེན་ཐང་ལྷ་] one of the nine original mountain deities of Tibet] and other gods of worldly creation (སྲིད་པ་ཆགས་པའི་ལྷ་འདི་) (Shogdong 2008, 8–9).

The natural flow of his place-induced narratives reconfirms the paradoxical manifestation of the modernity found in his other writings written in the cities of Xining and Lanzhou. These narratives, intimately enmeshed with his affection for the landscape of Tibet, are the resurfacing of his repressed native cultural upbringing as well as the voice of the landscape of his homeland itself speaking back to and through him.

Place has its own being, whether it is built or natural. Like any other species, humans are "implaced beings to begin with" (Casey 1997, x). Likewise, place is also an implaced being in human mindscape. The implacement of landscape in one's mindscape is attested to in what Casey refers to as "the memorability of place" (Casey 2000, 200). Shogdong's pilgrimage experience demonstrates that no memory is devoid of place. His memory signifies a past but this past is grounded in a particular place with all of its aspects of materiality: culture, religion, topography, and geological formation. What is remembered in time is space, not homogenous, undifferentiated space but a specific, situated lifeworld with specific mythological, historical, and spiritual markings. Such a remembered lifeworld embedded in time is the result of the implacement of landscape in mindscape from one's birth, infancy, adolescence, and adulthood. The identity of a person is inextricably tied with the topography, ecology, and social environment of the place.

The implacement of modern consciousness in Shogdong's mindscape has apparently created currents of commotions and "mind-quakes" and puts him in the paradox of modernity as he moves between urban China and the landscape of Tibet. However, when he places himself in the embrace of geographic and geological Tibet, he, admittedly or not, seems to submit himself to his native eco-sublimity in which he at once finds both the insignificance of humankind and the potential of humanity that could match the greatness of the Earth. He narrates:

> The road stretches out thousands of miles like a growing wing. Rolling mountains in the horizon are prayer beads. The Earth is like a piece of paper thrown open behind me. Looking at this land with its endless horizon makes me feel fatigued and looking at the infinitely deep sky gives me a sense of fright. The immense sky and the magnificent Earth have competed with each other's magnitude for eons in the process of human's wrestling with nature. I'm gradually realizing how insignificant humans are! In the world of unseen forces I feel human actions have little impact on nature (Shogdong 2008, 7).

These currents that express his eco-sublime feeling toward his homeland contradict his appraisal of Tibet's traditional cultural landscape as a place of "backwardness." It is not irrelevant that his appraisals have been formulated in the landscape of urban China. What he has absorbed from the urban political and cultural landscape of China is undoubtedly an integral part of his paradoxical mode of being. In the manner that the landscape of his homeland is implaced in his mindscape, the landscape of modern China is also implaced in it. It is not the landscape of Tibet in both cultural and geological terms that contradicts and transposes his place-based nativeness, but rather the modern landscape of contemporary China subjects his translocal and transnational mode of being to paradoxical conflict, commotion, emotion, and contemplation in his mindscape.

4.2 Forgetting as Remembering

Many of my Tibetan students and friends in Beijing see Shogdong as a radical modernist. In my ethnographic work with a few of Shogdong's college peers from Northwestern Minzu University who are now writers and scholars in Beijing, I find they still retain such an image of their college classmate though some of them have begun to change their viewpoints after reading his newer publications. When I proposed interview sessions with three of Shogdong's college classmates in late 2010, two of them dismissed his publications as "unworthy" because of his anti-traditional writings. I suspected that they had not yet read Shogdong's more recent writings, but one writer sat down with me for an evening meal near the university. He warned me not to look upon Shogdong as only an anti-traditionalist, emphasizing that Shogdong, unlike other urban Tibetans who are not literate in Tibetan, had his full upbringing in Amdo until he went to college in Lanzhou.

From my writer friend's view, Shogdong is an inextricable part of the contemporary Tibetan ethnic revival except that his approach is non-traditionally advocating a modern newness for Tibetans to redefine their identity, nationhood, and social presence in the boundary of China. This future-oriented ethnic revival is identical to the early period of modern China during which Chinese cultural elites were determined to construct a new China by abolishing what they perceived as "old China." In this mental and physical transition from the old to the new, native intellectuals were the vanguards of a revolution sending shockwaves to their entire nation as they smashed temples and burned books (van der Veer 2011, 272). In this regard, what is comparable between the contemporary Tibetan case and the historical Chinese case is the role of native intellectuals as "the new priesthood of the nation" (Smith 1986, 157). In my earlier work on Tibetan intellectuals situated in this modern "priesthood," I mostly emphasized their role in reorienting younger generations of Tibetans to re-embrace their Buddhist past through the traceable tracks of Tibet's Buddhist theocratic history (Smyer Yu 2006 and 2011).

Shogdong does not have the same "priesthood" status as Tsering Oser, Tsewang Norbu, and the late Yidam Tserang. He is not a charismatic leader followed by a crowd of Tibetans who share the same views; instead, his role has engendered an intra-Tibetan discourse on tradition and modernity through the circulation of his writings in books, journal articles, and online publications. He rather draws critical attention from charismatic public Tibetan figures. Tsawa Daneg, a contemporary Tibetan poet, published an essay on a Tibetan-language website in China, entitled "Eradicating Shogdong's Thought" (Tsawa Daneg 2009). This title is coined from one of Shogdong's chapters called "Eradicating the Old

Habit." As a pro-traditionalist, Tsawa Daneg cites numerous well-known lamas who are critical of Shogdong, including for instance, Dozhi Rinpoche, who remarked, "Today we have some young people who package the cruel movements of the Cultural Revolution in the clothes of science and promote them...These profligates import the garbage of Russians like treasures" (Tsawa Daneg 2009). To emphasize his critical point, Tsawa Daneg posts the rhetorical questions of Miwa Dentsen Gyaltso Rinpoche and Khenpo Tsechem Lodro from Larungar Buddhist Academy: "How could you count the elementary knowledge you copied from our little recitation book as our old habit?...Isn't it ridiculous how someone [implying Shogdong] tells us what this world is about when he has never traveled outside the Sun-Moon Mountain Pass [ཉི་ཟླ་རི་བོ། *nieda rewo*] and beyond the bounds of Silang [Xining]?" (Tsawa Daneg 2009).

Shogdong's publications draw criticism from leading figures in the current Tibetan cultural revitalizations. Many of my Tibetan students, on one hand, admire Shogdong's fearless spirit, but they also think he over-idealizes modern political practices from the West. One of the most common criticisms is that Shogdong has only lived in his home region, namely Xining and Lanzhou, and thus the geographic radius of his living environment limits his actual experience of modern politics and lifestyles elsewhere. However, this geographic limitation does not confine Shogdong's iconoclastic expressions toward his own cultural and religious heritage. Unlike his Buddhist-leaning contemporaries such as Tsering Oser, who direct their public contentions to the state, Shogdong rather makes his an anti-traditional stance, saying that it is the Tibetan traditional mode of being that has hampered Tibetans' progress toward a true, strong, modern Tibetan nation. Shogdong makes it clear that he wants his tradition to take the blame for contemporary Tibetan "backwardness" and suffering:

> We must admit the state of our decline and must search for the roots of the decline. As we know, the roots of our decline are our old habit (བག་ཆགས་རྙིང་རུལ). This old habit has begotten and nurtured a culture and its environment for thousands of years. Because of the decline of this culture, this old habit has also become aged, coarse, and petrified. The old symbolizes things of the past and the young symbolizes things new. This is the nature of existence. The old represents aging and weakening; whereas the new represents development, growth, and perfection. When new things do not replace old things, everything is stagnant and without progress. The ultimate state of Dharma holders or the state of Buddhahood, is achieved by breaking with old habits. The happiness and fulfillment of worldly life are attained by breaking with old habits, too. Therefore, we must resolutely abolish our old habits in order to build an authentic new habit (བག་ཆགས་གསར་པ) (Shogdong 2001, 2).

Begcheg (བག་ཆགས habit), initially a Buddhist term, refers to reflexive behaviors or habits that have become second nature for a person. In Tibetan Buddhist philosophical and doctrinal discussions of human social behaviors and acts of the mind, *begcheg* signifies a set of habitual behaviors which take shape with the external environment and the internal, karmic propensity of the person. When it is materialized as one's tangible personal habit, it reflexively expresses itself through one's bodily act, speech, and volition. Shogdong's use of *begcheg*, in my reading, mostly refers to the external, material culture of traditional Tibet but in a highly temporalized and objectified fashion when he adds the adjective "old" to it and juxtaposes it with the neologism "new habit" (བག་ཆགས་གསར་པ།). When it comes down to what he means by "new habit," Shogdong does not offer a clear definition or description in his texts except to connect it with "freedom" (རང་དབང་ *rang-wang*), "equality" (འདྲ་མཉམ། *dra-nyam*), "humanistic culture" (མི་ཆོས་རིག་གནས། *michu regne*), and other newly introduced terms. This is opposed to his numerous expressive critiques of the "old habit" where he gives his reader a clear delineation of what he means by the term:

> What we call the "old habit" is the primitive worldly theology (གདོད་མའི་འཇིག་རྟེན་ལྷ་ཆོས་རིག་པ།) which thinks everything in this world is governed by celestial gods (ལྷ། *lha*), waterborne spirits (ཀླུ། *gle*), and earthly deities (བཙན། *bzan*), and consists of trickeries of channeling, astrology, oracle reading, performing magic, and welcoming and sending off gods and spirits, and of the doctrine of non-self and karmic consequences. This old habit has consumed our society, life, livelihood, and state of being until today. Time and again it has thrown us into a bottomless abyss…This old habit has shackled our aspirations and memories. It has cut off our minds from all wisdom. Therefore, we are heading from decline to decline. This is how we see the current state of affairs: the primary reason of our decline is not because of warships and shackles, but is because of the soul of the old habit, which suffocates development and innovation (Shogdong 2001, 6).

In his juxtaposition and dichotomization of old versus new habit, it is discernible that Tibet, in Shogdong's mindscape, exists not in the present but in the past and the future. The present is what he perceives and experiences as "backwardness," "suffocation," and "being shackled to the past." Pathologically speaking, his way of coping with the present is clearly shown in his temporally reassigning the present difficulties of Tibetans to a past that is alleged as the fundamental cause of those difficulties. From there he goes deep into this past in an attempt to put an end to it, as a diagnostic move and a healing act. It appears that all his mental and spiritual energies converge on the "old habit" of Tibetans, a construct of his own making, as the sole target of his blame. The building blocks of such a construct are funneled through his radical modernism. His intent to erase and forget the past is a process of intensely remembering the past while inversing it by bringing it to the present for critique and public display of the wrongs of which it is accused.

As a matter of fact, the presence of the "old habit" is seen everywhere in Tibet. Shogdong's determination to make it disappear is resolute but is also unimaginable to observers. In my fieldwork in Shogdong's home area in Amdo, I see the practices of the "old habits" of common Tibetans routinely: circumambulating stupas, offering incense and butter to monasteries, and inviting monks or yogis to perform offering rituals for mountain deities. However, looking at these religious practices through the lens of his radical modernism, Shogdong refers to them as practices of what he calls "deity culture" (ལྷ་ཚོས་རིག་གནས་), a term he created in juxtaposition to "humanistic culture" (མི་ཚོས་རིག་གནས་), which he also coined. In his view, the former is "the way of gods and spirits" while the latter "the way of people" (Shodgong 2001, 10 – 11). He lumps all Tibetan religious and traditional cultural practices together as the deposit of what he perceives as "backwardness" and "decline." He narrates his experience in Lhasa among pilgrims:

> …they [pilgrims] bowed to the statues inside monasteries as well as to the columns outside them. They not only lit butter lamps but also offered money to the statues. Their faith grows even stronger when they see different colorful patterns [carved on the beams]. They touch everything that protrudes. The Three Treasures [Buddha, Dharma, Sangha] are covered by their various offerings. "Money flowers" [སྒོར་མོའི་མེ་ཏོག་ *referring to bills and coins offered to Buddha statues*] are blooming from the hands, feet, and faces of the Buddha statues. Everything feels so depressing. In order to connect themselves with Buddha Dharma they pry open or cut open precious antiques. In order to collect the soil and water (ས་སྦྱར་ཆུ་སྦྱར་) [of a sacred site] they fill their bags with water, grass, and dirt. Such an aggressive attitude of pilgrims amazes me. Such habits mixed with devotion and ignorance astonish me and make me feel they are incurable (Shogdong 2008, 23)

The alleged weakness of Tibetans, in Shogdong's eyes, inherently lies in their religious practices which are seen as acts of ignorance. In his modernist vision, he describes devotional acts such as prostrating as "trees being felled from their roots" (Shogdong 2001, 103). To continue on he then connects prostration with the servileness and submissiveness of Tibetans to hierarchy, inequality, and self-enslavement. In his book *The Call of Reason* he designates a chapter to prostration with his modernist value judgment reflected in its title – "Prostration is a Slave Mentality." Shogdong alleges the existence of this slave mentality because, according to him, Tibetans are accustomed to submitting themselves to supernatural beings and worldly powers. From his modernist view, these devotional acts become acts of ignorance and baseness. He writes, "We are slaves. We want to be slaves and we have the slave mentality inside of us. It is because for a long time we haven't had a consciousness of equality (འདྲ་མཉམ་), freedom (རང་དབང་), self-power (ཞི་དབང་), respect (རྙལ་མཐོང་), and autonomy (སེར་དབང་)…What is more important is that we have performed for generations all kinds of Dharma ceremonies that inculcated our slave mentality. We came to the world with this slave mentality" (Shogdong 2001, 101).

The pathos of Shogdong's modernism is identical to many progressive Chinese cultural critics in the late Qing and the Republic eras, such as Kang Youwei, Liang Qichao, and Lu Xun, when they encountered modern changes. The perceived "slave mentality" of the Chinese was a heated topic of their discourse on modernity. For instance, in Liang Qichao's "On the Origin of the Weaknesses of China" published in 1901, he pins down slave mentality as the basis of Chinese weaknesses, "A slave does not have the ability of self-governance, neither does he have the consciousness of independence...He takes whatever others look upon as unbearable humiliation and insult as part of his life. This is slave mentality" (Liang 1992, 73). What is also identical between Shogdong's modernism and his Chinese intellectual counterparts a century ago is that the underlying purpose of the self-debasement of calling one's people "slaves" is to build a new nation with a new people (Liang 1916, 63). It is the self-constructed old and new modes that commence a course of pathologically-discernible self-victimization, self-debasement, self-temporalization, and self-objectification for the sake of building a modern nation in an indefinite future.

Shogdong's modernist temporalizing vision of Tibet's present is so intense that he posits the possibility of a total annihilation of the old habit, as he bemoans, "When looking around and looking back, we see the roots of our decline found in our old habit. In order to let our mind and wisdom receive infinite freedom and growth, we must kill this old habit even though it is as despotic and authoritarian as our parents" (Shogdong 2001, 41). Shogdong's strident emotions coincide with the trend of ethnic revivals mimicking modern nationalism with the idea of equal rights and legitimate sociopolitical recognition. Anthony Smith notes, "To make any real headway in the modern world, ethnic movements must take their claims in political and economic terms as well as cultural ones" (Smith 1981, 20).

Clearly modern nationalism has enlivened the public visibility of ethnic revivals worldwide, including that of Tibet. Ethnic revivals frequently come into the global and local public spheres with well-defined political objectives and political platforms for self-representation based on consciously constructed ethnic histories and imagined futures. Ethnicity, in the framework of modern nationalism, is expressed publically with the narratives of its primordiality not only to its members, but to non-members as well, in a politically organized fashion. Furthermore, the primordial claim can also be replaced with the totally new, imagined future identity based on modern conceptions of freedom, equality and democracy as shown in Shogdong's case and his Chinese intellectual counterparts' discourse of nationalism a century ago. In this regard, an ethnic revival is a beginning stage for the intended establishment of modern autonomy that is not necessarily based on its past. Oftentimes, the past is looked upon as a hindrance to the intended modernity of an ethnic identity.

Obviously there are two parallel developments involved in the Tibetan ethnic revival. One is commonly recognized as the predominant trend, that is, the reclamation of Tibet's traditional, particularly Buddhist, past. Another appears on the margin of the dominant trend and rather desires to have a complete severance with the traditional past by constructing a Tibetan identity aligned with modern conceptions of nationhood. Both developments hinge their discourses and debates on how the past should be remembered. On the first side, the past is remembered as the continuation and preservation of Tibetan culture as a unique civilization. The Buddhist-oriented revival thus positively re-embraces Tibet's Buddhist history based on the Lhasa- and Dalai Lama-centered history. This trend is conspicuously shown in its uncompromising demand for the larger autonomy of Tibet in China and by claiming Tibet's primordiality. This trend is well documented in China as well as by international scholars. On the other side, the radical modernist case exemplified by Shogdong is lesser known but becoming more visible. For those who think like him, the past is remembered so as to be forgotten in order for modern empowerments to be granted to future Tibetan citizens. As Hartley notes, this radical Tibetan modernism seems to align its ideology with the Chinese experience of modernity (Hartley 2002, 1). It is true that many of Shogdong's writings were published in state-run venues such as Gansu People's Press and his anti-traditionalist view was publicly acknowledged by the state (Hartley 2002, 11). To both urban Tibetans and Chinese statesmen, Shogdong is seen as a Tibetan version of Lu Xun, a radical writer of modern China's Republic era known for his satirical depiction of traditional China as a "cannibalistic society" (Lu Xun 2009, 7–18).

I addressed the Buddhist-oriented Tibetan ethnic revival elsewhere (Smyer Yu 2006 and 2011) in terms of how memories are re-invoked toward a unified understanding of Tibetan civilizational identity. Shogdong's case also involves recalling Tibet's collective memories but with the intention to ultimately erase them because of their lack of mechanisms to address Tibetans' felt inequality in China. In this respect, ethnic solidarity can also be grounded in the common sociopolitical experience of its members in relation to their social marginality. This grounding oftentimes results from native cultural elites' discernment that their traditional cultural and governing system is absent of means for ensuring social equality and tolerance, if not appreciation, of ethnic and cultural differences. Shogdong's envisioned modern Tibet requires an invention of a new tradition or a new Tibetan ethnogenesis based on modern principles and values of equality.

Resembling his Chinese intellectual counterparts, Shogdong is initiating a collective forgetting and erasure of Tibet's past. His writings reveal a pattern of forgetting-through-recalling the past. His intentional forgetting is visibly dependent upon remembering details of Tibetan cultural practices, particularly those religious ones that he deems expressions of ignorance. Ultimately it is a reflexive remembering process but it appears as a deliberate forgetting process. Whatever is identified as ignorant and backward has to be re-surfaced in order to be the objects of his erasure. His chapter "Tossing the [Old] Habit into the Abyss" (བག་ཆགས་དོང་སྤུག Shogdong 2001, 25–41) exemplifies the linkage of his modern disembedding intent toward his own culture and his reflexive memories that are recalled merely so they can be discredited. He writes:

> In the process of cultural development, humankind had the ignorant habit of a primitive belief in gods and demons; however, those nations which became civilized earlier already tossed this old habit into the abyss. But, who on earth has numbed us until now? Among the gods and demons that we haven't been able to exorcise from the old habit, there are those who were forced out of India, exiled from the hinterland of the Han people, banished from Bhutan and Nepal, or brought in and indentured from other places. None of them found their dwelling place until they flocked together like flies at the feet of the snow mountains. And pointing at this phenomenon we rather praise it as the splendid culture of the Snowland. How ridiculous (Shogdong 2001, 29)!

The sequence of Shogdong's forgetting and remembering shows this pattern: reflexive recollecting ⇒ public discrediting/ridiculing ⇒ collective remembering. The recollecting pattern appears as what Paul Ricoeur refers to as the "habit-memory" nexus (Ricoeur 2004, 435), which is "a moving point" or a "reflexive movement" (Ricoeur 2004, 436) of memory, linking body, place, and mind. In such a nexus the past, the present, and the future are simultaneously present. The weight of this reflexive, memorial movement is the place-based habit. Habit is in this sense identical to the Tibetan lexical meaning of habit mostly as a product of one's lived environment. Like Ricoeur, I favor Bourdieu's habitus – the disposition of the individual consciousness that is inherently collective because it is environed in its native, physical but humanized place with a set of specific social and cultural meanings (Ricoeur 2004, 441). The reflexivity of habit-memory thus is trans-temporal and trans-spatial in the mindscape of the individual as a transpersonal flow of a collective memory. Because of its reflexivity and, often, unconscious state, it surfaces but is not surficial in nature as it is deeply rooted in the mindscape and like second nature for the individual. In this sense, habit-memory is synonymous with "deep memory" (Ricoeur 2004, 441) that is the perpetual ground for the individual to exercise intentional forgetting, selective remembering, and finally reordering his memory for both personal and social needs. Forgetting and remembering then do not belong to separate domains of the mindscape, but are interlocked into a dialectic relationship. Each simultaneously weakens and strengthens the other, as Ricoeur remarks, "forgetting is experienced as an attack on the reliability of memory…Memory defines itself as a struggle against forgetting" (Ricoeur 2004, 413).

In Shogdong's radical modernism, forgetting and remembering appear as both a natural temporal recalling of a past and a deliberately disembedding, temporalizing process embedded with the matrix of modern values and practices. However, on a deeper level, his recalled past is consistently lodged in specific placial terms, including "the Himalayas," "the Snowland," and "Amdo." In this regard, what is dated and temporalized is recollected reflexively as place; thus, place survives in time, but is frequently subject to displacement and replacement with fresh layers of encrustation added from the present context of the individual or the group. In spite of the commotions and violence resulting from the new encrustation, place retains itself in the midst of "dis-" and "re-" actions of the mind and body. It is simply because place is lived spatiality (Casey 1997, 5). Lived place is entrusted with memorability from the lived body/mind. Thus, habit-memory is habituated in place but moves with the moving body/mind: "Places inhabited are memorable par excellence" (Ricoeur 2004, 42) and memorable places are the inherent encrusted layers of mindscape likened to geological layers of the earth. A deep mining of it only makes it ever more present.

This is where Shogdong draws attention from his Tibetan peers and younger urban dwellers in China, especially when he discredits the social relevance of traditional Tibetan religious practices. His exclusive attribution of the alleged weaknesses and decline of Tibetan culture is popularly counterattacked by his compatriots who rather see contemporary Tibetan suffering as originating elsewhere. And yet, from the logic of Shogdong's radical modernism, Tibet is ill-prepared for the fast advancing modern political style of life in terms of the exercise of individual freedom and rights and the protection of collective wellbeing. When he discredits or ridicules Tibet's past, he mostly draws not sympathy but expressions of an array of collectively experienced pain felt over the last half a century. In this sense, his negative public testimony of Tibetans' "backwardness" and "ignorance" becomes what Ricoeur calls a "pathology of memory" (2004, 69) in which the work of remembering becomes the work of mourning and melancholia (2004, 71–72) or simply a state of desolate remembering. The wounded self "succumbs to the blows of its own devaluations, its own accusation, its own condemnation, its own abasement" (2004, 73). Such pathological pattern of memory resembles self-victimization, often a symptom of post-traumatic stress syndrome (van der Kolk 1996, 7) but absent of awareness by the suffering patient. In other words, the pathogenic background or the causal links of the illness are transferred to the patient himself: the patient finds the cause of his illness no longer elsewhere but within himself (Freud 1958, 12:152). From there the paradoxical mindscape of modernity emerges in a series of splits that are negatively interdependent: the past is temporalized for the present cause of social action; the present is spatially re-assigned back into the past which is shown to be an undesirable mode of being, and the future appears in the present in both imaginative and illusory visions of aspired-to reality. In this situation, private habit-memory or deep memory becomes a public forum in which "Memory becomes a locus of struggle over the boundary between the individual and the collective or between distinct interest groups in which power becomes the operative factor" (Antze and Lambek 1996, xx).

4.3 Subalternity of radical modernism

Like Hartley, I also think that we cannot fully understand the recent historical context of Shogdong's thoughts without bringing the late Dondrub Gyal (དོན་གྲུབ་རྒྱལ་), a widely known modern Tibetan writer, into the picture (Hartley 2002, 7). Many of my Tibetan friends in Beijing think that Shogdong's modernism is a continuation of Dondrub Gyal's vision of a modern Tibet. These two modern Tibetan thinkers are almost ten years apart in age, but both received the same state education and were influenced by the same range of Chinese modern thinkers including Lu Xun and Mao Zedong. Thus, to understand the pathological modality of contemporary Tibetan radical modernists, it is indispensable to trace the pathogenic background.

Born in Huangnan Tibetan Autonomous Prefecture of Qinghai Province in 1953, Dondrub Gyal was admitted to the Central Institute for Nationalities (Currently Minzu University of China) in Beijing in 1971. There he was fully exposed to the ideological core of Chinese modernity. After graduation, he worked for Qinghai People's Radio, at his alma mater, and at the Nationality Normal School, his last post, in Chapcha, Qinghai Province. His popularity among young Tibetans began with the 1983 publication of his poem entitled "The Waterfalls of Youth" in *Sbrang-char* (སྦྲང་ཆར་), a journal in the Tibetan language. This poem was a prophetic call for a Tibetan "new youth" movement for a modern, strong Tibet. The currents of his poeticized emotions and feelings start with the Tibetan landscape and the blue sky. These currents animate both the terrestrial and celestial realms with a gigantic, personified waterfall pouring down a cliff. The poet exclaims, "This is – the torrent of the youth of Snowland" (Dondrub Gyal 1983, 57). This personified waterfall soon commences a dialogue with "us" – Tibetan youths, in which the poet makes a collective vow through the voice of the Tibetan youths:

> The thundering voice of your torrents
> Narrates the ideals of a new generation from the Snowland.
> Conservatism, cowardice, superstition, and indolence
> have no ground to stand among us;
> Backwardness, barbarism, darkness, and reactionism
> have no residence among us.
> Oh, Waterfall,
> Our hearts and yours dance together;
> Our blood and yours seethe together.
> The path to our future will be more rugged,
> But Tibet's youths never have fear;
> We will pioneer a new path for our nationality
> ...(Dondrub Gyal 1983, 60)

Dondrub Gyal committed suicide at the age of thirty-two in 1985. Interpretations on the reason for his suicide among his friends and scholars vary but most of them commonly agree that he had lived an unhappy life after his return from Beijing to Qinghai. A few of his contemporaries whom I met in Chapcha, Chengdu, and Beijing told me that Dondrub Gyal suffered from depression during his last two years and the external social pressure to his propositions for radical changes came from pro-traditionalist Tibetans around him as well as suspicions from the Chinese state. Aside from his two unhappy marriages, he lived in isolation in Chapcha. However, his established Tibetan contemporaries in urban China, such as Gesang Yishe and the late poet Yidam Tserang, all spoke highly of his literary creativity and Tibetan national spirit. In the meantime they also witnessed the pathological mode of being toward the end of his life.

In connection with the origins of Shogdong's radical modernism, it is important to point out that Dondrub Gyal's exposure to modern thought was limited to what was sanctioned by the Chinese state. In a recent posthumous critique of his writings by a young Tibetan writer under the alias Bongtse (བོང་རྩེ) in a Tibetan language journal of Minzu University, Dondrub Gyal's modernism is discussed in conjunction with the influence of Mao Zedong's "Against the Party's Regimented Writing Style" and "The Speech on Literature and Art Symposium in Yan'an" (Bongtse 2010, 93), both of which are anti-traditional in nature calling for a socialist "new literature." In this critique, Dondrub Gyal's anti-traditionalism is likened to Mao's anti-Confucianism. He promoted the "new literature" among Tibetans though it must be recognized that the Chinese state operated all newspapers, broadcasting programs, and magazines. The condition of Dondrub Gyal's Tibetan "new youth" is to eradicate Tibetan cultural practices deemed "backward." Recalling my discussion with a Beijing-based Tibetan writer, he regards both Dondrub Gyal and Shogdong as two Tibetan Lu Xuns except that they belong to two different eras, those of Mao and Post-Mao. Both of them desired to "wake up" their compatriots' consciousness as Lu Xun and his contemporaries in the Republic era attempted, "as if waking them up from a dream-state" (Shogdong 2001, 175). Shogdong adds his own perception of why Tibetans are not "awake." He sees Tibet's development as that of a child:

> Overall the cognitive ability of this nationality is still at the stage of a child, not mature yet. This cognitive stage hasn't reached the phase of rational thinking…Tibet hasn't been a society with large human settlements, and has never gone through agricultural civilization and industrial civilization. Suddenly it emerged from a society of scattered populations that have lived among wild animals and yaks. In my view, Tibet joined modern society in the manner of what I call "the irrational leap forward." From this perspective, I have doubt about what I said before, "We need to wake people up. We need to mobilize them." We have not yet become *qualified human beings*; therefore, will the people whom we're going to wake up and mobilize be *qualified human beings*? (Shogdong 2001, 174 emphasis added).

If Shogdong's radical spirit was influenced by Lu Xun, his evolutionary view on Tibet's "immature personality" comes from his reading of Western thinkers. In terms of what he means by "qualified human beings," he admits elsewhere that he is influenced by Rousseau and Locke, both of whom are alleged to have posited the dual-idea of "natural being" and "social being." The latter has evolved from the former with complex social systems of culture, law, and governance. In a published transcription of interview notes in reference to this dichotomy, Shogdong says, "We [Tibetans] are still natural beings, not social beings" (Shogdong 2001, 176). Obviously the distance between two modes of being is not coeval but is a temporally understood, evolutionary distance between the past and the present. In the political sense, it is in fact an internalized distance of power between the dominant and the dominated in the name of modern social evolutionism.

Unlike Indian subalterns' experience of power shown in their sharply cleaved relationship with the dominant, I see Tibetan cultural elites' experience as a series of modern forces of change mixed with subalternity, empowerment, anguish, and aspirations. They are subalterns as the subjects of modern China but speak in the public sphere of the dominant; however, theirs is not free speech in its true sense but must conform to the framework and the linguistic pattern of the dominant. In this sense, they exercise their power and express their aspirations all through the state's pre-defined framework. Shogdong recently tested the consequence of crossing out of this framework and the result was imprisonment, the globally recognized response of the Chinese state to dissidence.

To answer Spivak's question, "Do subalterns speak?" (Spivak 1988) in the context of Tibetans in China, my answer is positive. Tibetan subalterns do speak in public but it is rather the voice of the dominant that speaks through them. Tibetan subalterns are at once dominated by the Chinese state and empowered with the modern universalistic discourse of rights, freedom, and democracy. The way they exercise this discourse is perceptibly oriented toward their desired vision of a modern Tibet divorced from its past. Dondrub Gyal and Shogdong both have shown their passion and have felt called to "wake up" their fellow Tibetans. In my view, there is nothing to wake up from; instead, it is rather "insurrection" that Shogdong is attempting to introduce to his compatriots, as he elaborates:

> ...what we mean by "insurrection" absolutely goes beyond the political meanings of what weapons signify. It means to look at how our seeking for saviors, depending on others, and dreaming of change – these, incumbent and narrow minded – completely destroy our personality, our social life, and our values. As we forever expect saviors, help from outside, empowerment, and nectar, we are most willing to subject ourselves to this dubious, no-eye-, no-nose-, and no-body- (ཤིག་མེད་རྣ་མེད་རྩ་མེད་ derived from *The Heart Sutra*) Old Habit. We are not debating the relevance of the word "insurrection" in our thought-world. In the way an armed struggle overthrows a reactionary government, we overthrow the rule of gods and demons, and non-self. This is how we launch a new thought-revolution (Shogdong 2001, 14).

This statement appears to mobilize a collective-consciousness change, but its directionality shows that, instead of turning to the source of inequality and oppression, it rather turns against itself by finding everything wrong with one's own state of being. Placing this statement in subaltern studies, I see Shogdong's internal displacement and temporalization of Tibet's present and past as a subaltern consciousness but it is tightly gripped or possessed by the dominant. This dynamic is also common among Indian subalterns. In Spivak's assessment, this consciousness, in fact, is not the subaltern's but rather the oppressor's (Spivak 1988, 11). It is a reproduction of the dominant consciousness in the subaltern consciousness. This was how Chinese modernity was constructed by its cultural elites: on one hand they expressed anti-Western imperialism but, on the other hand, they absorbed the power-language of the West to re-articulate and re-construct a modern Chinese identity that has little cultural association with China's past. This aspect of subalternity shows that the subaltern reproduces the social image of the dominant by critically contending with the language of the dominant while yet deeply internalizing it until it becomes unconscious. Unlike their Chinese counterparts a century ago who turned the language of Western modernity against Western imperialism, both Dondrub Gyal and Shogdong turn it against themselves. I share the same sentiment as Spivak that the subaltern consciousness is negative (Spivak 1988, 28). In the Tibetan case, it is a self-negating process.

On the ethnographic level, it is then not surprising to see that the early public presence of both Dondrub Gyal and Shogdong was positively sanctioned by the Chinese state when they launched their attacks on Tibet's past. Although both of them have deep affection for their homeland, when they negate the relevance of their culture in the modern context, their use of modern neologisms falls into the existing framework of the Chinese state: Old Tibet was full of decadence and oppression and New Tibet is a place of liberation and equality. This ideological structure was set before both writers exercised their modern agency, so the modern vocabulary used by Dondrub Gyal and Shogdong includes neologisms that were the invention of the Chinese state long before they began their invocation of a new youth movement among Tibetans in the 1980s and the late 1990s. Regardless of their insistence on a different modern Tibet with greater autonomy, the same modern translingual practice conflates their vision for self-freedom, equality, and self-governance with China's New Tibet. Both Tibetan modernists inadvertently facilitated the dominant image of the Chinese state's socialist modernity.

4.4 Pathogenic force of modernity

As I have discussed thus far, I see Shogdong's intra-Tibetan, tradition-vs.-modernity debate not as a fight between two groups of Tibetans situated in the paradox of modernity. In fact, both pro-tradition and pro-modernity groups have deep affection for their homeland. If we remove these two prefixes "traditional" and "modern" from Tibet, what is left is Tibet only. This is the actual object/subject of their collective concern and affection. Shogdong's seemingly future-oriented, anti-traditional modern Tibet, in the pathological sense, can be counted also as a return of the suppressed past inverted through his intentional forgetting: a clear symptom of the pathos of modernity and its altered state of memory. The pathogenic background of Shogdong's radical modernism is intrinsically linked with China's modernity and its grand physical modernization project that is taking place nationwide and that includes all ethnic minority regions.

In the medical sense, a pathogen, as a living agent, seeks entries to new hosts for replication and expansion, sometimes until it turns the host into its shell or until its agency replaces that of the host entirely (Pe'ery and Mathews

2007, 170). This is the pandemic pathogenicity of a pathogen. It can be likened to a xenobiotic that disrupts a biota when its accompanying toxin impairs the host; thus the xenobiotic claims the host as its own property. My metaphorical use of pathogen in the medical sense is meant to point out that our own agency is susceptible to paradigmatic changes and agentive shifts without awareness of its having harbored a foreign agent or becoming the ground for a foreign agent to nativize itself in us. This reversal or conflation of the guest and the host can also be shown in dramatic changes occurring in our mindscape due to external epoch-making events around us. Phrases like "paradigm shift," "consciousness raising," or simply "revolution" are common verbal expressions resulting from our mental commotions and transformations. Ideas and meanings embedded in these phrases often possess destabilizing, pathological, effects in psychological and psychic senses.

Modern nationalism, on one hand, bestows paradigmatic visions to ethnic revivals worldwide in terms of its universal ideas of liberty, equality, and democracy as Smith points out. On the other hand, it is also pathogenic in nature when a given ethnic group discards its "myth-symbol complex" (Smith 1986, 15–16) as the basis of its ethnie, because it is deemed irrelevant to its current collective condition and mode of being. When its cultural elites promote what I call a "foundational shift" from its mytho-historical identity claim to the set of modern values as the "operating system" or as the new basis of their collective identity, they expect empowerment from these newly embraced modern practices of politics and governance due to their experience of obvious sociopolitical marginalization. However, in the Tibetan case, this type of romantically charged modern ethnic revival does not seem to change the marginality of urban Tibetans in China. Shogdong's advocacy for a politically stronger Tibetan population in terms of autonomy and equality has obviously turned against Tibet itself rather than debating and contending directly with the Chinese state. In this regard, I see the pathogenic dimension of Enlightenment-based modern nationalism when it is nativizing itself in the collective mindscape of urban Tibetans. It is no longer a question of commonly perceived "ethnic revival" or "cultural revitalization" but is a power discourse, one taking place in a subaltern fashion.

In subaltern studies, it is commonly agreed that subalterns are those of low social classes who lack public voices and are "unfamiliar with the terms of the dominant language" (Sahoo 2006, 5). This is also affirmed by subaltern studies luminaries like Guha (1997, xiv). The Indian case of subalterns who are subjected to domination and oppression because of their involuntary exclusion from exercising the language of the powerful (Sahoo 2006, 5) is not reflected in the Tibetan case. Tibetan subalterns, in my ethnographic experience, may come from common nomadic, farming, and village backgrounds, but their later professions and permanent residence in urban China sets them apart from their familial origins in multiple ways such as geographic, cultural, linguistic, or ideological. They often sense social marginalization and cultural stigmatization when they work alongside their Han Chinese colleagues. In the meantime, they are the cultural and political elites of Tibet. They are empowered by their own people back in Tibet and by their Chinese modern education and urban professions. Their urban sojourn began with their familial investment in a hope for a better life upon their return from being educated; however, what they bring home is the *pathos* of self-temporalization, self-objectification, and even self-victimization as shown in the case of Shogdong and his predecessor Dondrub Gyal.

In my cross-regional fieldwork between Amdo and Beijing over the last five years I see university education as the primary gateway of this modernist *pathos*. Additionally, during my teaching and research at a university with the largest body of Tibetan students in Beijing, I saw how supportive their parents are to their pursuit of higher education. Many students receive a tuition waiver and living stipend from the university as a form of China's affirmative action; however, it is expensive to live in Beijing. Students' families, ranging from government officials, business owners, nomads, and farmers, give what they can to their children. Those who could not afford to buy meals at the university cafeterias brought enough *tsamba* and dried yak meat to last a semester. Both the familial and state investments in these young Tibetans are predicated on certain hopes and objectives, needless to say. While their careers may be advanced by the state's material investment in their education, their political consciousness is often gripped by the language of the dominant as found in lecture halls, reading assignments, and campus events. This ethos of the university environment marks Tibetan students as a people from a different "time zone" of the past, where the alleged existence of oppressive, barbaric "serfdom" serves as the history of Tibet. Tibetans are often reminded of being "ex-serfs" in the public space of China. The state's recent designation of March 28 as "Serf Emancipation Day" is one of many measures sustaining its modern construction of Old and New Tibet in the minds of young university students. This is the origin of the *pathos* of the subaltern power discourse among Tibetans.

Higher education is the primary pathway traveled by the ideas of a modern Tibetan nationalism and they are embodied in publicly outspoken figures like the late Yidam Tserang, Tserang Dondrub, Tsering Oser, and Tsewang Norbu, all of whom were university trained. Whether they are pro-traditionalists or anti-traditionalists, their nationalist discourses are lodged in the dichotomy of Old and New Tibet, and heritage and modern progress. In this sense, modernity is manifested as a pathogenic force engendering these multiple splits of the Tibetan modern cultural consciousness. Particularly in the case of Shogdong's radical modernism, I see this pathogenic force as a set of conflicting, contradictory, and dualistic mindsets and practices with pathological implications.

It is worth mentioning that the radical modernism of the Tibetan case bears traces of the Chinese Marxist legacy that also adds complications to scholarly interpretations of the contents of modern Tibet and Tibetan modernism. For instance, in Peter Hansen's exploration of a Tibetan subaltern study, he raises the question: "Why is there no subaltern studies for Tibet" (Hansen 2003, 8)? In his view, the primary reason for this impasse is "because Tibet is not India and Latin America" (Hansen 2003, 8), implying that the difference is that Tibet was never colonized by Europeans. The absence of European colonialism and the presence of Chinese Marxism in Tibet presents a predicament to scholarly assessments of whether or not Tibetans are in a subaltern state of being (Hansen 2003, 9). Subaltern studies across the board leans theoretically toward the deployment of Marxism as its critical basis and of Maoism as a theory of resistance in positioning the voiceless oppressed against the oppressor. Both Marxism and Maoism could be seen as a "liberation theology" of oppressed subalterns in India and Latin America. This is also how Marxism has been deployed in Tibet by the Chinese state. Perhaps, to both subaltern resistance practitioners and theorists, it is just impossible to see Marxism as an instrument of oppression. It seems, to implement subaltern studies in the case of Tibet, we have to overthrow the Marxist paradigm as the theoretical foundation.

What is clear is that the Chinese Communists introduced "a set of discourses (people, class, strata, etc.) that enabled the articulation of subaltern positions crucial to Tibetan resistance" (Hansen 2003, 17). In the history of China's socialist Tibet, Shogdong is not the only person who aspires to construct Tibetans' own modern Tibet. His parents' generation had an initial encounter with China's socialist modernity that directly contrasted with traditional Tibetan society. In his autobiography, written in collaboration with Goldstein and Siebenschuh, Tashi Tsering recalls the years from 1951 to 1957 when he was a young monk in Lhasa, "Our old, traditional, essentially static society was suddenly being bombarded with strange terms like 'socialism,' 'capitalism,' 'communism,' and 'feudalism'" (Goldstein, Siebenschuh, Tashi Tsering 1997, 41). According to him, the purpose of his life then was "...to create a new society that was both modern and just, and yet still distinctively Tibetan" (Goldstein, Siebenschuh, Tashi Tsering 1997, 5).

In Hansen's historical findings, both Chinese nationalists and Tibetan nationalists in exile share a similar political feature with modern nationalism: while the Chinese state calls its Tibetan subjects "the people," the 14th Dalai Lama addresses Tibetans as "my people" (Hansen 2003:10). Claiming and deploying "the people" or "the masses" is a common practice of both ethnic revivals and state nationalism. "The people" then often appear as a nameless mass though they are the fundamental source of empowerment of ethnic elites as well as the statesmen of an established nation-state. Hansen cites Tsering Shakya's historical finding that the Tibetan term *mimang* (མི་མང་ the people) was coined by the Chinese Communists (Hansen 2003, 17).

The Chinese Communists brought in a whole range of new vocabulary to facilitate their discourse of socialist modernity. These terms embody a set of ideas, concepts, paradigms, values, and practices that are concentrated with the "liberative" idealism embedded in Marx's proletarian vision of a new world order. From the Chinese perspective, it was this "liberative" volition of Marxism that completed the socialist revolution in Tibet. The initial "Democratic Reform" of the 1950s and the early 1960s performed in Amdo, Kham, and Ü-Tsang was most certainly a political discourse of China's Marxist modernity that originated from Europe via Russia. It was materialized in countless class struggle sessions, in the redistribution of land, and the collectivization of the means of production in towns and rural villages of Tibet. It was literally what William Hinton called "fanshen" (翻身), or an overturning of the traditional social order for the sake of constructing a new one (Hinton 1997, vii). This is indisputably part of the culture of Chinese socialist modernity.

On the practical level, the ideas of equality and liberty are universal in nature but are practiced in the framework of the nation-state known for its ideological regimentation and authoritarian governance. The particular deployment of modern universals is limited to its national sovereignty and the national agenda, and thus is not co-terminus with expressions of humanity elsewhere in the world. The Chinese use of Enlightenment-based modern universals in Tibet is intended to "make universal signs speak to particular realities" (Comaroff and Comaroff 1993, xxii). The way they were propagated to Tibetans resembled that of European missionaries as agents of modernity in Africa. The Chinese Communists aimed to (re)produce the historical consciousness of new socialist China based on a Marxist vision of a liberated proletarian society. In many ways, the reproduction of this historical consciousness has been China's "socialist civilizing project" (Harrell 1995, 3) in Tibet, which has woven the liberative context of Marxism into the local Tibetan cultural matrix by establishing the modern bureaucratic system, collectivizing land ownership, and providing young generations with modern vernacular education. Thus, the socialist utopian vision of a society with equality and human flourishing on the distant horizon has become imaginable reality in the mindscape of the Tibetan populace.

However, this future-oriented modernity has consistently put Tibetans in the position of "negation, inversion, deficiency, absence" (Comaroffs 1993, xii). In the twenty-first century, when Tibetan modernists like Shogdong linguistically continue to be confined to using the same neologisms that the Chinese state bestowed on them half a century ago, such as modernity (དེང་རབས), backward (རྗེས་ལུས), material development (དངོས་པོའི་འཕེལ་རྒྱས), and science (ཚན་རིག), the exercise of their discursive power is similarly patterned in the concepts and social realities of these neologisms. In this sense, the power of the modern Chinese state is both an individualizing and a totalizing form of power (Foucault 1982, 213). It represents itself as salvation-oriented and as knowledge of truth (Foucault 1982, 212). This intended social liberation is predicated upon "the abolition of existing networks of human relations" and "the abolition of an ancient definition of human nature" (Pickett 1996, 4). In the context of a multi-ethnic nation-state with the legacy of an imperial past, the empowerment bestowed from modernity to its subjects is not simply shown in its justification of the demolition of the old and construction of the new in the physical sense. In many ways, it is a most invasive and protective mind-work. To prove cultural and social legitimacy, the native "is willing to strip himself naked to study the history of his body, is obliged to dissect the heart of his people" (Fanon 1963, 211). This is the primary manifestation of the *pathos* of radical modernism.

"Dissecting" one's heritage is what Shogdong has done since he emerged in the public sphere of Tibetans in China in the late 1990s. He uses verbs like "dissect" (བཤའ་དཔྱད), "eradicate" (རྩ་རྫོགས), and "throw away" (ཤན་དུ་གཡུག་པ) when he recalls the collective memory of Tibet's past. The pathological modality of his radical modernism has evolved from the initial internalization of the external pathogenic force of modernity from both China and elsewhere to the current self-pathologizing state of his consciousness. In other words, the pathogenic force of modernity has taken root in his psyche and is expanding its depth and horizon in an iconoclastic fashion. Herein, I think James Hillman's delineation of pathologizing best captures the pathological consequences of radical Tibetan modernism. "Pathologizing" here means "the psyche's autonomous ability to create illness, morbidity, disorder, abnormality, and suffering in any aspect of its behavior and to experience and imagine life through this deformed and afflicted perspective" (Hillman 1976, 57). In this pathologizing state, the individual literally wants to "re-ensoul" himself as if his present psyche, as the operating system of his whole being, needs total replacement. Thus, the self-pathologizing mind is clinically identified with these characteristic symptoms: self-negation, self-antagonism, depersonalization, hyper-idealization, and confabulation (Hillman 1976, 24, 44, 56). To the pathologizing individual, Hillman points out, "It is... imperative to be as iconoclastic as possible toward vessels that no longer truly work as containers and have become instead impediments to the pathologizing process" (Hillman 1976, 97). Shogdong's self-anatomy is militantly expressed in many of his writings. He is committed to achieving the inner freedom of Tibetans by advocating "pointing the gun at oneself in order to kill off all enemies from the Old Habit" (Shogdong 2001, 253). Shogdong feels confident that he at least has inner freedom even if he does not have external freedom (Shogdong 2001, 253).

4.5 Placial antecedence of the Subaltern

When Dondrub Gyal initiates his call for a new youth of Tibet in his poem "The Waterfall of Youth," the source of the empowerment he wishes to bestow upon his peers and younger generations of Tibet comes from the animated, personified landscape of Tibet rather than the perceived political spirituality of modern universals. Scholarly readings of his literary works confirm such placed-based, poetic empowerment. In Riika Virtauen's interpretation of the imagery of water in Dondrub Gyal's literary works, the moving waters of Tibet are identified as the primary thread of his poetic expressions. This literary imagery, in Virtauen's understanding, expresses "the passage of time" and the "cultural transmission" of Tibet (Virtauen 2011, 135). This temporality of the Tibetan landscape is clearly shown in the images of rivers and lakes in Dondrub Gyal's writings.

Based on my reading of his writings and ethnographic work in the native places of contemporary Tibetan students and writers whom I know, I prefer to read the image of Tibetan landscape in Dondrub Gyal's as well as Shogdong's literary and discursive writings with a placial emphasis rather than a temporal one. My placial emphasis is premised upon the argument, initiated in the second chapter, that landscape and mindscape are mutually rooted in each other. In this inter-dwelling dynamic of landscape and mindscape, place is rooted in memory and, likewise, memory in place.

Pertinent to the increasing number of Tibetans who maintain the life style of bi-local living between urban China and native Tibetan areas, images of their homeland frequently surface when they address their modern ethnic revivals. In my earlier ethnographic work with pro-traditionalist Tibetan intellectuals, I noticed that the invocation of the Tibetan landscape was elemental in the evolutionary path of intra-Tibetan discourses of modernity in China. For instance, the imagery of mountains is the primary poetic theme of the late poet Yidam Tserang (Smyer Yu 2006, 3). Regardless of the different ideological values and sense of national belonging that he places on the same mountains in his early Communist utopian vision of the 1950s and his participation in the Post-Mao Tibetan cultural revitalizations, the mountains stand as they are (Smyer Yu 2006, 4).

Likewise, I also see the strong currents of cultural consciousness in Dondrub Gyal's writings, but I rather understand it in spatial and placial terms. Although

Dondrub Gyal chose to critique Tibetan traditional cultural practices in negative terms, his literary works often show much of his nostalgia, melancholia, sense of loss, and his emotional tie to the landscape of Amdo, his home region. Oftentimes he expresses humbleness and guilt to the landscape of Tibet and its humanized textures. In his short essay "The Narrow Path," he personifies the path of his childhood as an ancient vessel of his ancestors and Tibetan civilization. His entanglement with it is shown in his affection and blameworthiness, two opposite streams of his emotion. On one hand, he laments, "How ignorant our ancestors were! Why on earth did they choose this wretched earth to build their nests" (Dondrub Gyal 2000, 2)? On the other hand, he is soaked in deep guilt. He writes:

> When I think of it [the path], I can't help but repent. Yes, I'm a descendent of the Snowland. The blood of the high plateau flows in my veins, but I have never dug an inch of dirt and never added a shovelful of gravel to it. My legs have walked on it countless times, but I have never thought of its value and never thought of how I could add a layer of glory and a share of dignity to it. Are there any other shames and regrets that can bring me heavier pain than the one I'm having now (Dondrub Gyal 2000, 3)?

The outpouring of Dondrub Gyal's inner poesis always occurs in the moving landscape of Tibet as it is personified in the elemental components of the Earth, e.g. water, soil, stone and mountains. The elements of the Earth in Tibet move with his emotional currents and weave the literary texture of his conflicting state of mind when modernism is turned inward to look for whom to blame for the current condition of Tibetans.

Similarly, Shogdong shows his poetic appreciation of the Tibetan landscape while he negatively critiques Tibetan traditional cultural practices. The placial gravity of his voice also directs his readers toward the Tibetan landscape. In fact, Shogdong is even more specific about the cultural and religious elements embedded in the landscape of Tibet. The imagery of the Tibetan landscape in his writing animated with a range of subjects from the Tibetan earth-based pantheon, as he lists, "evil spirits (གདོན་པོ), flesh eating demons (ཤ་ཟ), hungry ghosts (ཡི་དྭགས), harmful demons (མ་མོ), walking mummies (རོ་ལངས), one-legged ghosts (རྐང་རིང) ..." (Shogdong 2001, 27). The list is long. He lumps them together as the contents of what he calls "the primitive habit of gods and demons (ཡ་ཐོག་ལྷ་འདྲེ་འབག་ཆགས). When he travels to Lhasa he animates the Tibetan landscape with these place-based beings, Buddhist monasteries, and lamas but with the intention of erasing them entirely from his homeland. However, they are so deeply rooted in the landscape as well as in his mindscape that he feels he carries them as a burden that he must bear. He writes about his thoughts moving along with the landscape on the way to Lhasa:

> I think of the shadow of a wandering monk whose heart is filled with hope. He pushes against the light of the sun and the moon, and snowstorms. He walks through no man's lands. Besides his knapsack, heavier than the magnificent mountains, what else does he possess? There are no roads and no maps to guide him. Perhaps the rolling mountains covered by clouds and the rays of sunlight, and the rivers like the veins of the mountains are his only companions (Shogdong 2008, 7).

The desolate moments of Shogdong and Dondrub Gyal are obviously expressed in placial terms as recourse to their native land. Both of these writers are agents of modernity but when they walk in their homeland, dirt, rocks, paths, rivers, and mountains start conversing with them by recalling their ancestors, childhood memories, and the gods and demons who have shared dwelling space with people since the mythological times of Tibet. One of the Tibetan students in my "Religion and Ecology" class affirmed Shogdong's passionate voice for Tibetans' own modern Tibet, but he also felt Shogdong was ignorant of the ecologically friendly gods and spirits of Tibet. This student said, "Although in the past, people performed rituals to please our earthly gods for making luck and avoiding misfortune, now these rituals have turned out to be environmentally healthy." He then pointed out that Shogdong deeply cares about the fate of Tibet but is mostly concerned with the economic and political inequality that many Tibetans experience in China. I would add that antecedent to Shogdong's political concern is the place of Tibet in both physical and symbolic senses.

In Shogdong's travel writings, he does not directly attack the Chinese state and the Han majority but his narratives make his voice irrefutably heard in terms of the fate of Tibet in his vision. He writes:

> On the way back to Xining on the train [from Lhasa], a Han woman sitting nearby was babbling loudly, "The Japanese wear masks when they visit our Potala Palace. Why do they wear masks in our holy land? You don't have to come if you think our Potala Palace is dirty! These Japanese are nothing! They have nothing to be proud of themselves!" People who say "our...ours" are perhaps those vagabonds-turned small vendors who wandered here from elsewhere, or those who have brought big businesses here, or those new masters of Potala Palace invited by Tibetans...One day, without noticing Tibetans will become slaves to the wealth of those who are saying "our...ours" (Shogdong 2008, 51).

In my pathological reading of Shogdong's writings, I see place as an inherent part of his thought-world and of the emotional currents of his affection for Tibet. Lived place is not only physical. Its physicality is embedded with history, signs, and symbols that intimately connect its residents with the land. The physical and symbolic order of place is deeply woven into people's mindscape. In other words, both landscape and mindscape are semantically synonymous as both signify the contents of one's place-based, lived experience, and memory.

The potency of place then is not limited to its material provision to its residents. Oftentimes, such potency rather originates from one's memory of it, with those memories having taken deep roots in the mindscape. In the case of Tibet, the landscape "provides an ancestral map for human activity" (Tilley 1994, 38). Both landscape and mindscape in this sense are inlaid with tracks of ancestors and spirits. Thus, place is antecedent to one's personal identity.

Shogdong's bi-local lifestyle does not change the fact that his implaced memory of his homeland does not recede into the background; instead it continues to dwell in his mindscape. It communicates with him in both conscious and unconscious fashions as I have discussed thus far. The placiality of his memory also moves with his bi-local living between his homeland and urban China. Tibet, in his memory, thus becomes "portable" or "mobile" as it moves with his body between the two places.

The notion of living/lived body in the works of Casey and Tilley best expresses how the body functions as the linkage of landscape and mindscape (Casey 2000; Tilley 2010). In the relationship between place and memory, body is the placial agent linking both together. Body, then, is an inter-being between place and memory. Implacement pertains not only to the envelopment of place around the body, but also to the moving, absorbant body/mind as it moves in place. Landscape, thus, is simultaneously implaced in the body/mind. In Casey's words, body is the "place passage" (Casey 2000, 195) between landscape and mindscape. In this sense body is a culturally constructed materiality of place. Its somatic movement in its native landscape, for example during familial chores and social events, sustains and reinforces this placial materiality rich in layers of both personal and collective memories.

Although, in the context of modern China and the current globalization of human ideas, Shogdong engages in an active imagination of a modern Tibetan nation in the sense of Anderson's "nation as imagined" (1991, 6), such a modern nation is imagined in a future tense with the set of universal ideas. What needs to be highlighted again is that Shogdong's imagined modern Tibetan nation is sustained by the landscape of Tibet implaced in his mindscape in spite of his dismissive posture toward it under the invocation of modernity. From this angle, I see the formation of a nation not simply resulting from its residents' claiming of a geographic region but also resulting from a reciprocal implacement process between the landscape of the nation and the mindscape of its residents. This mutual placing of landscape in the mindscape and the mindscape in landscape completes us as implaced beings with place-based identities existing along with our national orientation toward a place we call "nation." This simultaneously interwoven and interweaving of identity and place is what Tilley refers to as landscape as "ground" and "figure" to its residents, meaning, "It is ground in the sense that it is the geological and topographic face of the earth that they inhabit and move across. It becomes figure in a process whereby it becomes part of one's self-understanding and self-knowledge, part of the way in which one's identity is mediated and constituted" (Tilley 2010, 34). The *bio*-graphy of landscape, besides its own geologically-based subjectivity, is also a biography of the people who live in, on, and with it. Human subjectivity thus is also embedded and embodied in the landscape. The *bio* of the landscape is animated and acts reciprocally to humans. In this regard, in the reflexivity of the place-saturated mindscape, memory bonds with place and place with memory. In such a bond, the physical and the symbolic mutually saturate each other's being. In this sense, memory is place and place is memory, both of which are strikingly objectified as a sign of the paradox of modernity (Oakes 1997, 510) in the case of Tibetan radical modernism.

Chapter Five Touching the skin of modern Tibet in the New Tibetan Cinema

Beijing-based playwright Tserang Dondrub sniffled when Pema Tseden's *The Silent Holy Stone* (ཁྱིང་འཐགས་ཀྱི་མ་ཎི་རྡོ་འབུམ།) (2004) began to roll in a theater in Beijing in 2005. The tears welling up in his eyes gleamed in the flickering light as a pair of weathered hands on the screen steadily chiseled each syllable of the most recited prayer in Tibet, om-mani padme-hum (ཨོཾ་མ་ཎི་པད་མེ་ཧཱུྃ།), into the six large, separate stone tablets laid on the wintry earth. The motions of the anonymous hands, the chisel, the hammer, and the deep vocal recitation of the prayer led the anticipating eyes of a diverse audience into the landscape of Tibet as if the hammer and the chisel were carving Tibet into the mindscape of each spectator. Tserang Dondrub shed tears not only because of his native, nostalgic resonance with his people, his homeland, and his lived Buddhist spirituality but, just as importantly, because *The Silent Holy Stone* by Pema Tseden, his hometown-buddy turned famed-director, was marking the emergence of a new Tibetan cinema in the twenty-first century. In recollecting his viewing experience, Tserang Dondrub exclaimed, "This was the first film scripted and directed by a Tibetan in the one hundred year cinematic history of China. This significance, in many ways, surpasses the significance of the story in the film!" In the following six years, five more films by Pema Tseden and other Tibetan filmmakers found audience in China, Europe, and North America. Each has won awards at international film festivals in Beijing, Berlin, Busan (South Korea), Hong Kong, Shanghai, and Vancouver.

In this chapter I continue to discuss the potency of the Tibetan landscape with a focus on the pro-traditionalists' representation of Tibet. By "pro-traditionalists" I mean that this group of Tibetans regards the return of Tibetan Buddhist tradition as being the core of Tibetan cultural identity while still remaining realistic enough to recognize that the forces of change brought by modernization and globalization are destabilizing to the Buddhist values and ethos held by most Tibetans. The case in point is the cinematic Tibetan landscapes in Pema Tseden's films – a storied, weathered lifeworld – in which Buddhism is the elemental force saturating both the natural and the built environments and yet which is being destabilized, fragmented, and endangered. Set as the core of Tibetan cultural traditions, Buddhism in Pema Tseden's cinematic language is both a narrative medium and a cultural-moral agent facing new challenges. The representation of Buddhism in this case is the reverse of Shogdong's anti-traditionalist position. In Pema Tseden's filmmaking process, Buddhism is used as a haptic aesthetic

(Paterson 2007, 29) or an agent of inner touch, to connect the mindscape of the spectator with the lifeworld of Tibet.

All ethnographic and interpretive contents in this chapter are based on my collaborative work and personal friendship with Pema Tseden and his colleagues for the last five years, especially between 2007 and 2011 during which we co-taught a film course to students from North America, Europe, and different parts of China. His cinematographer Sonthar Gyal and recordist Dukar Tserang also joined my class, advising many of my students on aspects of their visual projects. In 2009, when I put together a small film co-op, our professional and personal interactions in Beijing became more frequent. Most recently, between 2010 and 2011 as I shot and edited a documentary on religion and landscape, Sonthar Gyal and Dukar Tserang lent their generous help. From Sonthar Gyal I particularly learned how Pema Tseden utilizes wide-angle shots and long takes in his cinematic narratives. Situated in this ethnographic background, this chapter is a result of my personal and professional engagement with Pema Tseden's filmmaking process and his evolving cinematic perspective which has been shared in classrooms and post-production editing rooms, on his pre-production sites in his home region, Amdo, during breaks between our mutual projects, and often at the dinner table.

5.1 Initiating cinematic landscape of a Buddhist Tibet

5.1.1 Repairing Buddhist moral fabric in *The Grassland*

This time, during the 2005 showing of *The Silent Holy Stone*, was not the first time Tserang Dondrub had shed tears when watching one of Pema Tseden's films. As a member of Pema Tseden's production crew and a screenwriter himself, he had been, in fact, deeply touched by Pema Tseden's short production, *The Grassland* (རྩྭ་ཐང་ 2003), submitted as his graduation project at Beijing Film Academy. This 20-minute short film was highly praised by luminaries of Chinese cinema. Before the script entered the pre-production stage, Xie Fei, a renowned director and the former chair of the Department of Directing at the Academy, favorably recommended it for a grant from the Academy's International Student Cinema Fund. Xie Fei himself directed *Yeshi Drolma* (2000), a love story of a Tibetan woman entangled in the overwhelming events of the mid-twentieth century, the transitional era in modern Tibetan history. His cinematic fondness for Tibet prompted his recognition of the merit of Pema Tseden's short script from among two hundred submissions for the award, and he recalled, "I noticed it [the script] was a simple story but had intricate meanings. A non-Tibetan script writer would not be able to write it as such..." (Guo 2011).

Pema Tseden names the fictitious place of the story in *The Grassland* as Melong Tang (མེ་ལོང་ཐང་). *Melong* (མེ་ལོང་) means "mirror" or indirectly "reflection," and *tang* (ཐང་) refers to "open pasture." Giving this name to the location of the story in *The Grassland* underlines his twofold cinematic intent that, on one hand, the fictive place Melong Tang is a mirror image of the social reality and communal tensions in a nomadic community in contemporary Tibet, and on the other hand, as a mirror itself, the screen physically holds the entirety of the physical-cultural landscape of Melong Tang, that is, the total lifeworld of this fictive nomadic community. In this sense, the screen is a mirror; however it is not merely a reflection of reality, but the reality of Pema Tseden's cinematic reflection of the current affairs of Tibet and his own life experience there. The fixed, flat, immobile screen is the ground of all happenings inclusive of Pema Tseden's vision of contemporary Tibet; the fictive but yet realistically narrated story of searching for a missing yak as well as for restoring a young man's conscience gone astray; and the visual connection of the motion picture itself with the inner world of the spectator.

The Grassland begins with Pema Tseden's lens following a gliding *goud* (རྒོད་), a Himalayan Griffon Vulture (*Gyps fulvus* or *Gyps himalayensis*), in the depthless blue sky. These birds are also known as *hsa-goud* (ཤ་རྒོད་) or sky burial vultures in Tibetan. Sky burial or *hsa-dor* (ཤ་གཏོར་) literally means "giving offerings to birds". The burial master is usually a lama or a layperson who is knowledgeable about both the sky burial ritual and the dismemberment of the corpse. After the corpse has been ritually prepared, the burial master calls down the flock of *hsa-goud* to "lift" the dead up into the sky. In Tibetan Buddhism, particularly in Nyingma visionary traditions, these birds are revered as *khangdrol* (མཁའ་འགྲོ་), which is often translated as "sky walkers," referring to those who are in an enlightened state but are incarnated in sentient forms (Simmer-Brown 2001, 9).

Pema Tseden's lens traces the lone vulture until it fades into the sky, then the scene tilts down to a half-frozen creek and an expansive wintry grassland scattered with woolly figures. Rolling hills on the horizon suddenly enter the audience's vision-scape. Accompanying the scene is a song from a female singer:

> Sheep are as numerous as stars,
> Herders are like the full moon,
> Yaks are like dew on blades of grass...

The song and shifting landscape scenes introduce village chief Tsezhou, who leads a yak ridden by Ama Tsomo, an elderly woman whose own yak has been stolen. They are on their way to visit the families of three young suspects. The camera follows the village chief and Ama Tsomo who is spinning a handheld prayer wheel. Her recitation of om-mani-padme-hum (ༀ་མ་ཎི་པདྨེ་ཧཱུྃ) rises into the sky and into the landscape itself as if it is a pulse of the cinematic scene. Giving viewers a sense of the passage of time, the walk continues as time moves from mid-morning sun to evening's twilight, and from expansive plains of grass to an immense frozen river and the skyline of mountains. In Pema Tseden's panoramic vision, both Tsezhou and Ama Tsomo often look like two tiny dots moving on the frozen river, across wide-open plains, and on high ridges.

In conversations about his cinematographic preferences, Pema Tseden does not hesitate to state that he prefers wide-angle lenses ranging from 16mm to 18mm and 25mm. His boom operator often complains that it's difficult to keep his boom pole from dipping into the scenes shot with 16mm or 18mm lenses that show the characters conversing in a panoramic landscape. Pema Tseden defuses the complaints by telling him with a smile, "The director's vision has to overrule technicalities." The essence of his cinematographic vision is to create a reality on the screen through which the audience is empathetically moved into the lived experience of the Tibetan characters. Landscape scenes in many cinematic productions are often displayed as background and as aesthetic enhancements that generate the ambience for characters and their stories. In Pema Tseden's films, they are "active backgrounds" (Morgan 2009, 2) or best seen as an inherent part of his cinematic foreground, which sustains and saturates characters' inner landscape and their social acts. Pema Tseden's cinematic landscapes of Tibet are metonymic in nature, and they "do not suggest their completion; rather they indicate further and larger concepts and relevance and they encapsulate rather than suggest inclusivity" (Harper and Rayner 2010, 20). The elements of a metonymic landscape function to expand the vision and image-associations of the spectator beyond the immediate screen. In other words they animate the immediate, physical, landscape encompassed by the lens, and at the same time, highlight the enacted *anima* or "soul" of the landscape through a particular personified character. In Pema Tseden's case, he clearly designates Buddhism as the *anima* of the Tibetan landscape.

Buddhism touches everywhere and everybody in Pema Tseden's films, from a flying bird, to carved rocks, the wind moving prayer flags, and the dialogues of monks and lay people. It humanizes the natural landscape of Tibet, which becomes not just any landscape but a geographically, geologically, topographically, culturally- and ethnically specific landscape. Buddhism is undoubtedly the haptic medium in Pema Tseden's film – creating, articulating, and interlacing different cinematic terrains of affect (Bruno 2002, 253) or simply giving rise to a cinematic geography of sentiments from Pema Tseden's own life experience. While his wide-angle shots portray the expansiveness of the land, the carefully chosen material expressions of Buddhism are interspersed between the natural environment and human affairs. Before the village chief and Ama Tsomo in *The Grassland* reach their destination, the gliding *hsa-goud* in the sky, the moving footsteps on the wintry brown grass, and prayer flags flapping in the wind are accompanied by the circular motion of the prayer wheel in Ama Tsomo's hand. In mid-journey they are greeted by a mani-stone carver (མ་ཎི་རྡོ་བརྐོ།| manidogou) sitting on a sheep skin and chiseling a flat rock not far from a long wall built of stacked stone tablets with Buddhist mantras and sutras carved on them. The camera moves to a close up to the stone carver's weathered hands. This close-up is not shot from a top-down angle but is on the same plane as the hands. The viewer's eyes cannot help but move toward the hands chiseling the words of a prayer into the stone tablet lying on the wintry brown grass. Approaching the hands in such a way causes the gaze to become a type of touch with its associated sensory perceptions generated by the visible. Both the tenderly wrought panoramic sweeps and close-ups in these films give a central position to Buddhism.

Giuliana Bruno's elucidation of the word "haptic" is relevant to Pema Tseden's films, "It is by way of touch that we apprehend space, turning contact into communicative interface" (Bruno 2004, 1). Regarding cinema-induced haptic dynamics Bruno treats "emotion" as the moving force indicated by its Latin etymon: "*emovere*, an active verb composed of *movere*, 'to move,' and *e*, 'out'" (Bruno 2004, 6). In this sense film is an interface, intertwinement, and bonding of motion and emotion. It is a vessel of two elemental ingredients of humanity's somatically embodied sentience, motion, and emotion.

In Pema Tseden's films, Buddhism, projected onto the land, creates the topographic symbols of the intersection of the Tibetan lifeworld and landscape embedded with specific paths, routes, and passages of motions and emotions. To reillustrate, Ama Tsomo and the village chief, Tsezhou, are the lines drawn between points that might have seemed unrelated, creating routes with Buddhist meaning, connecting through embodiment as they traverse the earth. In Pema Tseden's cinematic "mapping" process, the physical landscape and aerial sphere of Melong Tang play an antecedent role in completing the topographic map of the characters' motions and emotions, and, concurrently, actively reciprocate with the characters' somatic movements and emotive currents that arise from the Buddhist spirituality and morality in their inner worlds. The soaring *hsa-goud* (symbolizing the death-rebirth transition), the prayer flags in the wind, the old mani-stone carver in the open grassland, the singer's voice penetrating the sky and the earth, and Ama Tsomo's recitation of prayers are among the critical, externally moving points and inward leading passages of Pema Tseden's cinematic landscape of Tibet. Such cinematic topography is drawn with the characters' external paths on the natural landscape and internal passages of spirituality and conscience. Buddhism in the film is not a static doctrine confined to a monastic environment. Its agency in Melong Tang allows it to be integrated into the "geopsychic terrain" of the characters in *The Grassland*, the cinematically haptic space which is "the place where a tactile eye and a visual touch develop..." (Bruno 2002, 253).

When Tsezhou and Ama Tsomo finally find the families of the three young suspects, the elders of their community summon them to take an oath to claim their innocence. The oath itself is not lengthy when three of them utter it together:

> I hold this scripture as witness to take oath.
> Let all mountain gods be our witnesses.
> If we were the thieves,
> May we be condemned to the Eighteen Hells without escape.
> If we were not the thieves,
> Let the gods' wisdom-eye witness our innocence.

However, the audience's visual touch of this scene is not mediated only through close-ups; instead Pema Tseden's wide angle lens integrates the temporal progression of their utterance of the oath into the space of the greater physical environment of the community. Once again, landscape is antecedent to the motion of the three young Tibetans, or to the audience's sensing of their inner emotional state. The lens pans outward, following the emotional expressions of the three young men outward until it merges with the physical terrain of the very ground on which the oath is uttered, carrying the audience from the characters' inner world to the outer environment. The physical terrain, in its entirety, is imbued with the human emotional currents, becoming also geopsychic terrain. Thus, the earth animated with the smoke of incense lit by the three young men, the sound of their oaths and prayers, the wind violently blowing the prayer flags and the cairn carry the meaningfulness of the emotions. What is more haptically contagious to the audience in this dynamically-mixed state of emotions and natural scenes is when Pema Tseden's lens tilts up into the sky after the oathtaking: the intangible human voice moves upward with the incense and meets a lone *hsa-goud* soaring in the gusty firmament. The audience's visual contact with the immobile, flat screen in the theater is like a tactile eye, extending itself into Pema Tseden's cinematic landscape as if it were actually meeting the three young men, traveling up with the smoke of incense, and soaring with the *hsa-goud*. The three young men have cleared their names, and Tsezhou, the village chief and Ama Tsomo walk back home. Once again it is Buddhism that Pema Tseden deploys here to set everything in (e)motion.

The story is about to end but it surprises audience with another turn: the son of a respected elder stole Ama Tsomo's yak. The film ends with the son and his father with the stolen yak on the way to seek forgiveness from Ama Tsomo. As the silhouette of their backs blend into the vast grassland, a deep voice of a lama leads the recitation of the Four Bodhisattva Vows:

> May all beings be endowed with happiness and its causes;
> May all beings be free of suffering and its causes;
> May no being be without happiness devoid of suffering;
> May all beings dwell in a state of impartiality toward attachment and hatred.

5.1.2 Landscaping Buddhism in *The Silent Holy Stone*

Pema Tseden's *The Grassland*, was, in many ways, a preparatory work for *The Silent Holy Stone*. *The Silent Holy Stone* (hereafter referred to as *The Stone*) is a story of a young monk's life and his curiosity about the world beyond his monastery; however, Pema Tseden does not enact Buddhism in the Dharma hall of the monastery. Neither does he express it in elaborate ritual performances on the monastery grounds. The gravity of Buddhism is rather found in the vast, magnificent landscape between the monastery and the young monk's home village. In this respect, *The Stone* inherits the same cinematic narrative as *The Grassland:* the active, moving landscape is the opening scene introducing the lifeworld of Tibetans which is saturated with Buddhist signs, symbols, practices, and the affective bond between humans and the earth. Homeland (specifically in this case, Tibet) is not only a place of birth, but, more critically, it is where the earth's presence irresistibly enters and firmly dwells in the mindscape of its residents and where Buddhism is embodied in human social behaviors as well as in the built and natural environments.

The Grassland scene with Tsezhou and Ama Tsomo on the yak moving across a vast landscape is mirrored in *The Stone* except that the characters are changed to the young monk and his father. This time, the father pulls a horse on which his adult son sits as they walk back to their home village from the monastery. It is culturally appropriate that Tsezhou is supposed to walk with the yak on which Ama Tsomo, as an elder of their community, sits. However, in *The Stone*, this social order of respect for elders is fully subverted in the context of Buddhism. Now, the father leads the horse carrying his son, the monk, because what is invested in the son through his Buddhist practice grants him a higher social position than the father. In other words the social seniority of the elder is replaced by the religious and spiritual order of human relations with Buddhism resetting the usual determinants of human social positions based on age and other norms. The father comfortably leads the horse while conversing with the monk yet he still expresses his affection toward him as a father.

As they leave the monastery behind, the cinematic ambience shifts to a stunning landscape just like its counterpart in *The Grassland*. Based on my conversations with Pema Tseden concerning his use of landscape in his cinematic narratives, he considers that the ambience should not be understood as "background," "surroundings" or the "atmosphere" which envelopes a community or a human event; instead, it is better seen as a synopsis of the outer environment, the inner world, and one's bodily acts, all of which set the cinematic world in motion. In this sense the cinematic ambience generated in Pema Tseden's films consists of the earth beneath one's feet and seen at the horizon, the flux of clouds and light in the middle, the sky high above, and collective human subjectivities embedded in the landscape (Ingold 2011:115). The recurring scenes cast the physical landscape of Tibet as a critical, non-human actor whose voice is often expressed through humans. As the father and son are enveloped in the weather world of the landscape, e.g. the blue sky, the white clouds, brown grass, frosty earth, and biting wind, the father, with affection, asks the son, "Do you miss home?" and it is as if the father's voice were the voice of the very landscape that envelopes them and their horse. With the positive answer from the son, the camera continues to slowly pan the far off snow covered mountains and follow the father, the son, and the horse through the landscape. Just as in *The Grassland*, the movements of people, livestock, and the earth are coupled with a folk song. This time, it comes from a male singer:

> Tall mountains, pristine nature,
> Clear streams flow.
> Yaks, sheep, horses
> Thrive in open grassland.
> Untainted, candid people bearing a virtuous will
> And auspicious joy to set on all eternity,
> I make this wish...

The temporal progression of the song moves along with Pema Tseden's lens following the footsteps of the pair as they come upon Uncle Zoba, a mani-stone carver. Uncle Zoba, though he lives alone, is an integral part of the community. His cinematic function points to the embodiment of Buddhism in the physical landscape of Tibet. The piles of stone tablets inscribed with prayers and passages from sutras signify Pema Tseden's perspective of the full saturation of Buddhist practices in the Tibetan landscape. It is precisely such embeddedness that creates an ambience in which weather, natural objects, and Buddhist elements enter each other's modes of being: the motion of the wind is expressed in flapping prayer flags; piled rocks hold the pole for prayer flags; and each contact of the chisel and hammer with stone and rock infuses Buddhist practices into the physical landscape. The earth embraces Buddhism, making it an elemental force of the natural environment; thus Buddhism moves and is moved.

Natural and cultural elements in Pema Tseden's cinematic ambience seem to be situated outside his focal point and yet are intricately interlaced together to present the landscape of Tibet as a reflexive, Buddhist, lifeworld in which prayers travel with the wind, flow with moving water, and respire with human breath. Such a cinematic setting then is not an inanimate background but is rather an omnipresent or an all-encompassing mood pervading the inner worlds of the characters and animating the outer environment. The interlaced ambient elements in Pema Tseden's films permit the continuous movement from one state of being to another for his characters, their stories, and their dwelling places and the surrounding natural world. Everything takes place in the same enclosure – the sentient world – but with a Buddhist orientation in which the earth is shown in a transcendental light while its human counterparts cannot help but to feel nostalgic for it wherever they go.

Pema Tseden's ambient cinematography in both *The Grassland* and *The Stone*, the two productions having been made in a short span of time, show his positive aesthetics toward his Buddhist homeland. In many ways, the consistently positive appreciation of the land in these two films coincides with the global popular image of Tibet: the omnipresence of Buddhism and awe-inspiring landscapes (Bishop 1993, 40) being key. There is, however, a volitional difference between these two similar representations of Tibet according to Pema Tseden. In the Director's Statement of *The Stone* he says, "The story in the film takes place in my hometown. Mountains and rivers oftentimes enter my dream world. Truthfully narrating stories from my hometown has been my wish for many years. My mind is often full of the pulses of this wish" (Pema Tseden 2006).

From the transnational perspective, I do not see Pema Tseden's cinematic career and productions in isolation. His native upbringing speaks for itself in terms of how he has written scripts and directed his productions based on his life experience there. However it is also noteworthy that he and his productions are situated in Beijing, a transnational location where public and private, and domestic and international resources are amassed to make possible China's rapidly growing film industry. In his creative craftsmanship, Pema Tseden fully exposes himself to different cinematic genres and techniques such as those of Abbas Kiarostami, Dzongsar Jamyang Khyentse, and Eric Valli, to name a few. Many members of the production teams of *The Grassland* and *The Stone* were non-Tibetans, some of whom hold critical positions as art directors, producers, and production supervisors.

Given that Pema Tseden's productions are transnational in nature, this transnational dimension of his work in no way makes his films less Tibetan. However, his work is caught in the parallel trends of Tibetan cultural revitalization. On one hand, like many cultural critics, Pema Tseden is also committed to demystifying non-Tibetans' misconceptions about Tibetan culture and religion, as he stated during the pre-production stage of *The Stone*, "Many people tell stories about my homeland through their words or images which have, in fact, become like an immovable, mysterious veil over Tibet, creating an impression of Tibet as either a utopia or a wasteland. These people often claim their works as true representations of Tibet; however they further muddle the image of my homeland…I dislike such 'true representations'" (Pema Tseden 2006). On the other hand, his cinematic career caught the tail end of what Barnett calls "Tibetanization" in reference to the Chinese state's encouragement of the return of Tibetan traditional cultural practices the late 20th century in an effort to improve its public image (Barnett 2006). Like his native peers in different social and professional segments of contemporary China, Pema Tseden and the core members of his film crew are committed to celebrating traditional lifeways of Tibetans, especially its Buddhist civilization. Seeking authentic images of the Tibetan landscape and people is an embedded intent of *The Grassland* and *The Stone*. For Pema Tseden, like many of his contemporaries, revitalizing Tibetan Buddhist civilization is synonymous with re-embracing the traditional past. Thus, the positive aesthetics of both the Tibetan landscape and Buddhism become an inevitable necessity in his cinematography without any volition to romanticize Tibet but to "express the intersection of tradition and modernity, the piety of Tibetans' simplicity toward their religion, and the kindred spirit among the people" (Pema Tseden 2006).

5.2 Touching the Skin of the Modern Tibetan Landscape

Pema Tseden's positive cinematic aesthetics toward his homeland's physical landscape has become less prominent in his new productions in the last four years. To many of his audience members and critics this marks a sudden change in his cinematic depiction of the Tibetan landscape with monks, monasteries, prayer flags, grasslands, snow covered mountains, and eulogizing folk songs. Buddhism appears to recede from the foreground of monastic architecture and the humanized landscape with Buddhist markings to the background and margins of social and personal spaces and even further to the inner spaces of memories.

The Search (འཚོལ། Tsol) and *Old Dog* (ཁྱི་རྒན། Khyi rgan), his latest award-winning productions, mark a sudden transition from portraying the positive aesthetics of the Tibetan landscape to the crude social reality of his home region. The stories in the two films are entirely different; however, their social atmosphere is similar with both conveying the fast changing physical spaces of towns and villages as well as changing traditional values, communal ethos, and interpersonal relations. Pema Tseden's cinematic landscape no longer sends a message of "home-sweet-home;" instead his initial images of the simple but rich spirituality of traditional Tibetan people in their ancestral land are replaced with images and (e)motions of loss, nostalgia, alienation, and desolation. These are countered, however, with hope and resilience evident in his characters who are on the move to search for and regain their lost paradise and who choose to ground themselves in their ancestral memories and traditional morals.

This thematic and stylistic transition does not appear to be an indication of Pema Tseden's intent to disengage his cinematography from the Buddhist ethos and material culture among Tibetans. Instead it is apparent that he simply wants to go deeper and wider into the many social realities of his people. He desires to live up to the original cinematic goal he had when he came to Beijing – to narrate stories of common Tibetans in contemporary Tibet. *The Search* and *Old Dog* indeed live up to that promise with his own style of realism. Pema Tseden's realism is inclusive of positive cinematic aesthetics toward the Tibetan landscape but now leans toward modern elements that are destabilizing to traditional practices of Buddhism among Tibetans. He invites his audience to see and touch the landscape of his homeland as if it were a changing body: its surface is undergoing an entire transformation. Buddhism in the midst of the changes becomes an object of a human search for the lost "soul" of Tibet and is brought to Pema Tseden's cinematic foreground as a subject of moral contention on and off the screen, or between his characters and among his audience. All happenings, and the feeling tone that fully saturates the characters' inner and outer worlds, are enveloped in the forceful advancement of modern practices and values. The Tibetan landscape is no longer a composite of the Buddhist worldview and its practices. Modernization and its material consequences seep through the membrane of the Tibetan Buddhist landscape and change the spatial-psychological order that undergirds Tibetans' relationships with each other, other beings, and the land.

5.2.1 Rescuing the Buddhist "soul" of the nation in *The Search*

During the pre-production stage of *The Search* in Rigon, Qinghai Province, Pema Tseden invited my visual anthropology class of eight U.S. students to observe how *The Search* was being shot as a road movie, a cinematic genre often used to narrate stories on the move, such as a pilgrimage, a journey in search of a lost sacred object or a loved companion, or an exodus from a war torn homeland. *The Search* is about a team of filmmakers on a road trip in Amdo looking for an actor who will play Prince Drime Kunden. *Prince Drime Kunden* (དྲི་མེད་ཀུན་ལྡན་) is one of the eight national operas of Tibet. Written approximately in the thirteenth century and based on the spiritual biography of Sakyamuni Buddha, it tells the story of Drime Kunden, a compassionate Prince, who is compelled to feed the hungry, aid the weak, and eventually offer his three children, his wife, and his eyes to three Brahmins who disguise themselves as beggars to test the Prince's compassion. As soon as his compassion is proven to be genuine, the Brahmins return his children, his wife, and his vision. The opera is widely performed in villages, towns, and by nomads in contemporary Tibet. As the Buddhist spirituality in the play is articulated through the emotions of the characters rather than through Dharma talks and empowerment rituals performed by lamas, it resonates with and draws tears from the audience with the simple narrative of suffering, altruism, compassion, and spiritual liberation. The story unfolds after the king exiles his son due to misjudgment of an incident of theft in the court. The prince and his family are exiled to redeem a wrong he did not commit. They beg in villages, sleep in the open, and take residence in caves. The route of their exile eventually leads them back home into the embrace of their family. This traditional Tibetan drama can also be understood as the search for ultimate compassion and enlightenment, not in an abstract doctrinal language, but in the motions and emotions of the audience and their greater society.

When asked about his creative intent in *The Search*, Pema Tseden said he preferred his audience to choose their own interpretations of the embedded meaning of the film. One afternoon, however, he asked me to translate the title of the film into English. I proposed the translation of the literal meaning of the word "search" in Tibetan. When he and Sonthar Gyal, his cinematographer, said the word "search" alone was not "specific enough," I then insisted on his telling me what was the actual search embedded in the film crew's search for an actor. Finally I got an answer: based on an observation of the younger generations of Tibet who are losing touch with their ancient Buddhist traditions, it is a search for the essence or the soul of Tibetan civilization in the popular, contemporary realm. The opera *Prince Drime Kunden* is a signifier of Tibetan popular Buddhist spirituality, which, according to Pema Tseden, is slowly eroded by the advance of modern values. It makes perfect sense that the story of the search for an actor is embedded with the director's own search for the soul of Buddhist Tibet. In light of that, the original working title in English became "Soul Searching."

In our film class, Pema Tseden told our American students that *The Search* could be a sequel to *The Stone* because the opera *Prince Drime Kunden* is one of the most critical themes in *The Stone*. Although the storyline of *The Stone* follows a young monk, Pema Tseden's thematic emphasis on Tibetan Buddhist practices is portrayed through the lives of common people. The monks are shown going about their monastic routines; however, what connects with and emotionally touches Pema Tseden's audience is when the monk witnesses how the opera is rehearsed and performed in the village temple as part of his community's New Year celebration. In Pema Tseden's narrative to our class, he was emotionally touched the most during this part of the filming of *The Stone*. In shooting the scene of the rehearsal, the three young actors who play the children of Prince Drime Kunden all cried naturally when they sang the verses expressing their sorrow at parting with their father and being unable to say farewell to their mother. The emotional current of the film reaches another height when the opera is performed in the village temple with a crowd of mostly elderly men and women. Prince Drime Kunden cuts out his eyes and gives them away to the Brahmin. When he sings, "...May this be the last of my offerings that dispel the darkness of ignorance. Let me become a torch", Pema Tseden's lens moves from the stage to the audience. It is a moving scene: old women wipe their tears when they see the Prince painfully blinded and when the Brahmin regains his vision with the Prince's eyes. The sounds of sobbing and sniffling, and the tears rolling down the weathered cheeks of the old villagers transmit the emotion from the opera to the opera audience and then via the screen to Pema Tseden's audience. These elderly women were recruited as extras from the village where these takes were filmed. None of them were professionally trained actors – their responses were completely natural and spontaneous.

The opera scenes in *The Stone* take up approximately twenty-five minutes and all occur at the midpoint of Pema Tseden's cinematic narrative. Buddhism as a living faith among Tibetans is given center stage in the film: the center is not in the monastery but among common people. To successfully complete this long segment of *The Stone*, Pema Tseden spent many days and nights looking for the right opera actors and actresses in Amdo. It was one of Pema Tseden's own "road stories" behind the making of *The Search*. During the pre-production phase of *The Stone*, he embarked on a journey to find a village-based opera troupe that would best help him project his cinematic vision of Tibetan Buddhism being revitalized among common people. His personal encounters in this search later became the creative cornerstone of his scripting and directing *The Search*.

Unlike the uncontested cultural position of Buddhism in *The Stone*, *The Search* fully delves deeper into the social space of contemporary Tibet showing Buddhist values being challenged in modern terms. In a night club, when the team of filmmakers interviews a man in his mid-thirties for the role of Prince Drime Kunden, he tells them that he played Drime Kunden before but stopped recently because, as he says, "I dislike the role of Drime Kunden...What do you think Drime Kunden exemplifies? Drime Kunden offered his own eyes to others. That is his choice...however, why did he have to give his wife and children to others? Where did he get the right to do that? Who gave him the right?" The ambience of this scene is saturated with the overwhelming flashes of disco lights, loud music, and the noise of clinking beer bottles and wine glasses. According to Pema Tseden the history and spirituality of Buddhism is enveloped in and challenged by the modern secular, consumer world. Throughout *The Search*, Buddhism rather appears on the social margins instead of in the central position shown in *The Stone*. Buddhism as the centerpiece of traditional Tibet finds itself in a position susceptible to being marginalized, subverted, and secularized.

Although conventional markers of Tibetan Buddhism such as monks, monasteries, and prayer flags do not take center positions in *The Search*, Pema Tseden's lens does not discontinue its touch in the villages and towns where an actor is sought who will bring back the heroic, spiritual epic of Prince Drime Kunden to contemporary Tibet. It is a national treasure hunt but one in which Buddhism does not overtly enter the vision of Pema Tseden's audience in the way it did in *The Stone*; instead it comes in fragments that bear little or no traditional appearance.

The cinematic genre, cinematographic techniques, and the director's perspectives in making *The Search* as a road movie resemble those of Kiarostami in *The Wind Will Carry Us* (1999) in which an engineer attempts to document the secret funeral rituals in an Iranian Kurdish province. The engineer and his teamsters drive their jeep across the country into the Kurdish land: long, uninterrupted takes, Kiarostami's cinematographic trademark, open up landscapes of red earth, golden wheat fields, and the engineer's destination – the secluded village. Everything in the film moves and is moved. The jeep moves the landscape; the landscape moves the jeep; the conversations in the jeep draw the temporal lines of Kiarostami's cinematic narratives. Like Kiarostami, Pema Tseden's wide angle shots and long takes intimately engage the audience with the Tibetan landscape and the mindscape of the main characters – urban Tibetan filmmakers – who fill the moving jeep.

Pema Tseden's cinematic hapticity again does not rely on the conventional use of close-ups of his characters to convey tactility. Instead his wide angles and long takes in *The Search*, like those in Kiarostami's *The Wind Will Carry Us*, caress the physical landscape not only in following the footsteps of characters or tracing the paths of natural elements but also with the perspectives viewed from the moving jeep. The audience's vision reflexively assumes the location in the moving jeep either as the driver or as one of the passengers. New terrain and the ever-shifting horizon continuously enter the audience's vision. The naked eye is not merely a visual instrument, but is also a tactile extension of the skin (Pallasmaa 2005, 39). With the jeep's tires rolling down the highway, Pema Tseden's lens leads the eye of the audience to touch wherever the moving jeep goes and whatever the lens encompasses. It is a journey of touching Tibet. Pema Tseden's cinematic vision creates a haptic journey for his audience from within the narrow space of a jeep but it offers a broad vision. Through the physical touching of and being touched by the Tibetan landscape, the audience enters the current condition of the "soul" of Tibet.

In one village after another, one town after another, *Prince Drime Kunden* seems to have become past tense in present Tibet. With the drama residing only in memory the older generation of opera performers have to recall their past performances as they try to get younger actors to take an interest in modernizing the tradition. The cultural transmission between the past and the present is ruptured with the Buddhist spiritual norm being almost an anomaly in modern Tibet. The search continues with the tires of the jeep rolling across the country until the team of filmmakers finds the right actor. The search is successful but the film ends with a new predicament: the lead actress breaks up with the actor, reneging on her initial agreement to play the wife of Prince Drime Kunden if the team finds the actor who was her lost boyfriend. However, for Pema Tseden, home is home regardless of how fragmented it and its traditions appear.

To many viewers of *The Search*, Buddhism appears displaced and scattered in different locations. The mission of the team of filmmakers is to find it, whole, though by the end the mission is obviously half completed. An important component of a road film's dynamics, however, lie not in the end-result but in the journey, which is, itself, like a pilgrimage. If the sacred item or element is not acquired, the pilgrim has at least been empowered by the journey of his own spiritual emotions through the trails, paths, and passages of his pilgrimage. On their road trip the filmmakers in *The Search* find a living exemplar of Prince Drime Kunden, rich memories of older opera performers, the best actress, and the most ideal actor though they are all scattered in different villages and towns. Buddhist culture, in the film, is subject to dislocation, relocation, decay, and rebirth, and is not immune from the cycle of sentient suffering. The opera *Prince Drime Kunden* resides in every character in the film not in whole but in part, e. g. a piece of memory, a verse from the opera, or a contending expression toward the spiritual deeds of Prince Drime Kunden. The search team's hope for a holistic ending is realized in an unexpected parting scene between the actor and the actress who had once bonded in their home village when they performed *Prince Drime Kunden* together. However, the success of the search does not lie in their finally finding the actor but in the journey of the film crew in the landscape of Tibet.

5.2.2 A modern Tibet in *Old Dog*

The feeling tone in the displaced image of Buddhism continues in Pema Tseden's *Old Dog*, which, while intended to be a quick indie film with a lower budget and minimum number of characters, took nearly three years to complete. Everything in *Old Dog*, e. g. people, animals, and land, enters what Martin McLoone calls an "elemental struggle" (McLoone 2010, 135) for existential meaning. McLoone's case study of Jim Sheridan's *The Field* (1990) utilizes similar cinematic narrative styles as Pema Tseden's *Old Dog*, especially in the playing out of the kinship and moral dialectics of a son and father in the dichotomous locations of the field and the road, and the town and the country. These elemental human inscriptions and their spatiality in both Irish and Tibetan landscapes are cinematically symmetrical when they are juxtaposed or interconnected, though they differ from each other in terms of values, aspirations, and existential meanings.

The story narrated in *Old Dog* is that of a young man named Gonpo, who sells his family mastiff without consulting with his father. As soon as his father finds out, he insists on buying it back from the dog dealer in town. The multilayered tensions in the film quickly build up between Gonpo and his father. To Gonpo town is full of opportunities for material gain; whereas to his father it is a source of suffering. The pastoral ground is home to both the son and the father; however, while the father feels rooted within it, the son feels restrained by it. The road in between their pastoral ground and the town brings one overwhelming change after another. While the road leads Gonpo, on motorcycle, to the town where he sells his family dog, it moves his father, on horseback, to retrieve the sold dog from the town dog dealer. It connects the home turf with the town throughout the film by bringing in a dog thief, a new dog dealer, the police chief, and, finally a death on the roadside. Shockingly, the elemental struggle of the old man in the film ends with his killing his beloved canine companion on the side of the road.

Although the cinematic style in *Old Dog* retains some of Pema Tseden's typical depictions of the rural landscape, it moves away from a positive aesthetic style. Having received numerous awards from international film festivals in 2011, *Old Dog* has also initiated debate among Pema Tseden's audience concerning Buddhist ethics in the context of changes brought by modernization and consumerism. In addition to 2011 being a year for celebrating Pema Tseden's new productions, it also marked a new phase of his cinematic realism – a markedly documentary style incorporating factual representations of the current social conditions of Tibetans. No longer relying on the serene, idyllic scenes as the primary images of the Tibetan landscape, Pema Tseden's realism offers instead a series of overwhelmingly depressed, desolate, disorderly, infertile, and scarred scenes to facilitate the narrative. The message of the film is clear: Tibet is desperately stressed.

Old Dog is Pema Tseden's response to Chinese urban consumption of Tibetan culture, religion, and even dogs in this case. Tibetan mastiffs are an exotic commodity among urban China's wealthy class. For instance Ma Junren, a former celebrity athlete and the chairperson of the National Tibetan Mastiff Club, owns a mastiff with the highest price tag: 40 million RMB or approximately US$6.3 million (Lü 2005). Breeding, exhibiting, and trading Tibetan mastiffs have become a large part of China's consumer market. Currently among the four hundred and twenty-two officially registered Tibetan mastiff breeding sites, five are located in Tibetan regions. The rest are in non-native environments according to the National Professional Commission for Tibetan Mastiffs (NPCTM), a Chinese state organization overseen by the Ministry of Civil Affairs, the State Council, and the Ministry of Public Security (NPCTM 2008). It is in this context that Pema Tseden responds to the collective stress that contemporary Tibetans are experiencing in addition to other consequences of modernization and the proliferation of consumerism in Tibetan regions.

In *Old Dog*, Pema Tseden's cinematic hapticity almost coerces his audience into the feelings of chaos and psychological displacement. The audience is arrested with the "involuntary touches" of the lifeworld of the characters saturated with depressing moods and hopelessness over the loss of their familial and communal fabric and their traditional grounding in Buddhism. In town, wherever Gonpo goes with his motorcycle, we consistently feel a sense of irritation and repulsion from the muddy, potholed streets, piles of red bricks at construction sites, truck traffic passing through the town, the scrap metal in the backyard of the dog dealer, and a truckload of mastiffs on the roadside ready to be shipped out of their homeland. Pema Tseden further overwhelms his audience's eardrums with a cacophony of sounds and noises from all directions: semi-trucks' loud engines, air drills, broadcasting from loudspeakers, herds of yaks on the way to the slaughterhouse, and loud music blaring from shops. Pema Tseden and Dukur Tserang, his recordist and a musician, chose not to have music for the entire film. When *Old Dog* was screened at Ullens Center for Contemporary Art in Beijing in fall 2011, Dukur Tserang responded to audience's questions about why they made that choice and why the ambient sounds are annoyingly noisy, "Our intention was to weave together a symphony of bewilderment and loss. If we added music the film would not feel the breath of the earth [referring to their homeland], such as the old man's sighs and the old dog's fatigued panting." Dukur Tserang then continued to point out the emotional effect of using ambient sound instead of music, "When the protagonist [Gonpo] sees his old dog is about be locked into a cage, the sound/noise of air drills in the background shoots into his heart like a machine gun…depressing sounds of sorrow, distress, and pain are intertwined."

A cinematic landscape, like its actual physical counterpart, would not be an emotionally and aesthetically touching scene of life if its soundscape were to be muted. In a cinematic landscape, like that of *Old Dog*, people and animals move, and inanimate objects are also set in motion with the movements of metereological elements, people, and animals. Sound flows with these movements and enters people's inner world (Ingold 2011, 139). Haptic dynamics, then, also express themselves in soundscape. In this regard, the town in *Old Dog* is tiny but the commotions in it disrupt the greater whole: everything can be bought and sold, and everything can be torn down and built. The tiny town is a local hub of China's global market on the ground level and everything in it seems to be in permanent transition with many buildings half-built or half-torn-down, and with trucks moving in with merchandise and construction materials and moving out with mastiffs and yaks.

Gonpo's father returns home with his beloved old dog. Home, however, is no longer a haven. One of Gonpo's buddies visits Gonpo's father to propose a cash prize for the old dog. Gonpo's father refuses. At night the old dog barks alerting the family of an approaching thief. The attempt to steal the dog fails but Gonpo's father walks the dog to the foothill of a local sacred mountain to release it in the ruins of an old dwelling site. Herein Pema Tseden's wide angles and long takes come in again bringing the audience in touch with the landscape of Gonpo's home. The sky is blue, clouds slowly change shape in the wind high above, and the bleating of the family sheep in the valley can be heard. But, when Pema Tseden's lens follows the old man crossing the landscape, the panorama touches the audience with a Shangrila divided up with barbed wire fences. The expansive landscape is cordoned into small plots of grazing ground. After the old man leaves his dog behind, a gloomy mood fills up the panoramic vision of their homeland.

The sadness of the parting of the old man with his dog does not bring peace to either of them. Found by someone, the old dog ends up again in the hands of the dog dealer in town. Gonpo then gets into a fight with the dog dealer in an attempt to have his family dog returned only to be detained by the police chief. The police chief returns the dog to Gonpo's father and the father and son are reconciled in the police station. With the audience expecting a happy ending, Pema Tseden takes another turn: Gonpo's buddy brings in another dog dealer proposing a higher cash prize for the dog. Declining the offer, Gonpo's father sits with his dog behind the barbed wire fence. The camera's long take prepares the scene for any possibility and then, after having stared at the fence post for a long time, the old man stands up, pulls the dog over to it, wraps the chain around it, and calmly but firmly strangles the dog. The old dog painfully whines and dies against the pole.

The death at the end stirs up divergent critiques and emotional responses among Pema Tseden's audience, most of which decry the social reality of the consumer market across China as well as object to Pema Tseden's uncharacteristic portrayal of a Buddhist response. Buddhism saves neither the life of the old dog nor his master, who as a Buddhist will suffer from his intention and action of killing the dog. Superficially, the killing is recognized as the old man's act of saving his dog from being stolen, sold, or transported to urban China where the assumption is that he will have prolonged mistreatment and suffering. This "killing-for-saving" motif is common and often seen in war movies where a soldier takes the life of his mortally wounded fellow soldier so as to end his comrade's suffering. Pema Tseden's Tibetan and non-Tibetan audience seem unconvinced by this logic at the end of *Old Dog*.

To many non-Tibetan viewers it seems unrealistic that dog dealers would purchase an old dog or that a thief would risk the theft because of the fact that the old dog has little market value either as a pet or for breeding purposes. To quite a few Tibetan viewers Gonpo's father is given too much power over the life of his old dog. The scene when he releases the dog into the wilderness is plausible as a common Buddhist practice but it is illogical in the customary sense. Gonpo's father takes the collar off and unchains his dog and simply leaves him behind. Pema Tseden's gloomy long takes in this scene do not suggest the sense of freedom integral to the traditional Buddhist releasing of life; instead it appears as an act of turning a family dog into a wild dog or of a parent abandoning his child, both of which convey a sense of emotional death or the ending a kindred bond. The old man's letting the dog free to die by itself shows the dog's fundamental lack of freedom. The final act of killing the dog was particularly shocking to many of my friends from nomadic areas of Amdo. They sympathize with Gonpo's father who is disturbed, angered, and feels hopeless in the face of the overwhelmingly profit-driven behavior of people around him; however, as one audience member from a nomadic family remarked, "The life of the dog belongs to the dog and not to his master." The father is able to reconcile with his son but not only fails to protect the family dog but is the one responsible for his death.

In one of the review sessions I also raised similar questions to Pema Tseden. His creative concern is not directed to seeking cultural, religious, spiritual, and ethical consistencies. The film is meant to mirror everything inconsistent, illogical, insensitive, dislocating, and disturbing happening in his homeland. According to him and his crew members, *Old Dog* is a fiction of factual representation, not representing conventionally perceived cultural and Buddhist logic embedded in Tibetan lifeworld but rather representing the social and psychological conditions in contemporary Tibetan regions. Every act of the characters is not to be taken literally but can be seen as a signifier toward something else. For instance, when the old man remarks that Gonpo's dog dealing buddy does not look like his father, Pema Tseden's intent is rather to express the widening generational gap among Tibetans: the older generation's Buddhist-oriented ethos and the younger generation's aspiration for material wealth are disjointed. Moreover, the younger generation's desire for profit is materialized as a formidable force of negative social change resulting in stealing and selling objects and living beings that were traditionally barred from commercial exchange, such as a family dog. Therefore, the killing is not killing per se but expresses the morally suffocating social environment of Tibetans and the physically distressing transformations brought forth by modernization and consumerism.

Buddhism in this context is the crucial medium that ultimately links everything together in *Old Dog*, producing emotions not only in the cinematic story but also off-screen, among Pema Tseden's audience. It does not touch the audience with soothingly enlightening messages about life and death; instead it is shown to be vulnerable in the consciousness of the characters and their familial and social environment. When Gonpo's father wraps the chain around the fence post to put down his family dog, audience members with a Buddhist background recognize the impending death of the dog as well as the moral death of Buddhism embodied in this particular act of killing. Throughout the film, Pema Tseden's lens does not have particular foci on Buddhist scenes, such as ritual performance or devotional acts, yet he successfully emotionally and morally moves his audience along with the moving fate of the old dog in the hands of different characters: the father, the son, the dog dealers, the faceless thief, the police chief, and the barbed wire and fence post.

In linking the scenes in the film with my own ethnographic experience in Amdo, Pema Tseden's realistic reproductions of events, architectural changes, and generational displacement of people reveal the existential values and moral orientations from his home region. *Old Dog* is a distress call to Tibetans and non-Tibetans alike. He captures and integrates the real time, negative consequences of modernization into his motion picture where homeland becomes an arena of alienation, moral corruption, and struggle for both physical and cultural survival. The death of the family dog can be seen as fulfilling a sacrificial role for a fresh start of the family or as a martyrdom to pacify the mounting tensions and distresses that his master is experiencing; yet off-screen the effect is rippling through Tibetans in and outside Tibet, generating a new wave of debates and contentions on Buddhist ethics and the national integrity of Tibetans in the midst of modernization and globalization.

Buddhism, in his films, is not a moral and spiritual paragon outside the lives, the conscience, and the cultural reflexes of his characters but is an animated, immaterial component in his cinematic narratives. Herewith, the haptic effect of Buddhism could be a series of "somatic sensations" (Paterson 2007, 6), not a result of cutaneous touch or the direct skin contact but "the multiplicity and the interaction between different internally felt and outwardly oriented senses" (Paterson 2009, 768). Pema Tseden's cinematic hapticity is diffused in each of the frames of his cinematography from corner to corner, and from beginning to end, and it is not the actual, subtle emotive skin surfaces of his characters which he intends to depict but the "skin" of Tibet's landscape and its people's mindscape which is undergoing multiple transformations in terms of its environmental condition, social ethos, and people's moral and kindred ties with their land. Frame by frame Pema Tseden illustrates the changing skin of modern Tibet. The technique of his cinematic hapticity can be best described in Pallasmaa' words, "The very essence of the lived experience is moulded by hapticity and peripheral unfocused vision" (Pallasmaa 2005, 10). In many ways, the wide angles and long takes in Pema Tseden's films, especially in *Old Dog*, have an obvious preference for capturing materials and surfaces of modern Tibet with a complex language of their own. His cinematic landscape not only speaks to his audience but also enters their mindscape and emotional world nudging them to feel "ensounded," "enlightened," "enraptured," and "embodied" (Ingold 2011, 135, 138) even when the subject possesses none of those characteristics or conveys their opposite. In the world of cinema the eye and the ear are the skin: they touch and are touched.

5.3 After-effects and affordances of the New Tibetan Cinema

The landscape of home in *The Grassland* and *The Stone*, Pema Tseden's early productions, is grounded in both his cinematic panoramas and characters' inner worlds. It is immovably centered in our traditional vision of homeplace, which, as Yi-Fu Tuan points out, "nurtures biological life, commands the strongest attachment and loyalty. The word love is natural to homeplace. So many things in it give passing aesthetic pleasure...that one is hardly aware of them individually; nothing stands out in perception and as experience, but together they engender a diffuse sense of well-being" (Tuan 1993, 140). Precisely, such a positive sense of home is saturated haptically in both *The Grassland* and *The Stone*; whereas, in *The Search* and *Old Dog*, especially in the latter, the landscape of home becomes less and less protected, and its aesthetically pleasing scenes and moments are darkened by divergent values between the father and the son, and of tradition and modernity.

All four award-winning films narrate stories concerning the tensions between traditional Tibetan Buddhist values and the consequences of modernity. Three of the four films personify the tensions in a dialectical fashion utilizing the motif of the relationship between elder and youth with the appearance that the old generation upholds traditional values and practices, while the younger generation is susceptible to deviation from traditional values. Among the sons in the three films, *The Grassland*, *The Stone*, and *Old Dog*, it is only the one in *The Stone*, who, as a monk, inherits traditional values from the older generation. The other two commit stealing and lying but are eventually forgiven and reconciled with their fathers. Tradition prevails in Pema Tseden's movies but it prevails at a high price. His affection toward his homeland is obviously based on his traditionalist inclination that is diametrically opposed to that of his native peers like Shogdong, who prefer a new Tibet with modern equality, democracy, and autonomy.

In 2002 I had a conversation with one of Pema Tseden's college mates who is currently a producer in Lanzhou. His and Pema Tseden's filmmaking venture in Beijing was grounded in their clear intent for the revitalization and preservation of their native cultural heritage. They were determined to build what I call "a New Tibetan Cinema" in the Tibetan language and centered upon a visual articulation by Tibetans of Tibetan experiences. Since then, Pema Tseden has been exemplary to his Tibetan peers as he scripts his stories, casts his characters, directs his productions, and breathes life into them. This "Tibetanness" is the a priori condition of his creative premise, as he often tells his friends and the public. By no means does it suggest a self-enclosure or isolation of Tibet and Tibetans in the twenty-first century; instead he and his colleagues take a transnational approach to make their originality, creativity, and productions known in China and beyond by drawing production capital and inspiration from other regions, and by promoting themselves in the global marketplace of indie films.

Therefore filmmaking is both a means of livelihood and a method of cultural preservation. The traditions of Tibet matter and Pema Tseden and other traditionalist filmmakers' re-embrace of it is their path toward greater human flourishing in Tibet. Like Shogdong, they all grew up in Amdo and went to the same university; however, their visions of and methods of working for the well-being of Tibet appear opposite each other. In the eyes of Shogdong the "Old Habits" are annoyingly present and hinder the path to his vision of a new, modern Tibet. Pema Tseden and his pro-traditionalist artist peers see a different world for contemporary Tibetans: traditional values and practices, particularly of Buddhism, have returned after having been denigrated for decades, but they are also quickly losing ground in Tibet in the face of the forces of change brought by modernization. Shogdong recollects the past of Tibet for the purpose of judging it and then erasing it in order to make room for his envisioned new Tibet in the future tense. Pema Tseden's cinematic search and reconstruction of traditional Tibet based on Buddhist values occurs in a dichotomized fashion but obviously favors what Shogdong dismisses as "Old Habits." Pema Tseden's reconstruction of Tibet's Buddhist past in his films is related to contemporary cinematic techniques utilized in productions by filmmakers from other former Communist countries, such as Alexander Zeldovich's *Moscow* (2000). Recollections of the pre-Communist past bear the trademark of what Keith A. Livers calls "restoration nostalgia," which "simultaneously affirms the loss of collective identity, while imagining its reconstitution via images of 'homecoming' or historical continuity..." (Livers 2005, 424). Such historical continuity in Tibet was disturbed in the recent past and it is gradually returning.

Both Shogdong and Pema Tseden are two leading Tibetan cultural critics, creative writers, and artists. Both have shown tremendous affection toward their homeland. Both are recognized as belonging to the "new priesthood" of the Tibetan ethnic revitalization, and as native intellectuals they are considered to play leading roles in determining the course of their national revivals (Smith 1986, 157). Yet, their affective approaches toward their homeland are so divergent that one's past is another's present, one's future is another's present, and vice versa. In the course of Shogdong's discourse, his every step forward comes with a negation of some sort of traditional aspect of Tibet. His love of nation builds upon both what the nation should not be and should be. What should not be actually is what has been lived, broken, and returns to the present as, in his view, a hindrance; and what should be is in a not-yet state. As discussed in the previous chapter Shogdong chooses an inner revolution to wipe clean the

"Old Habit" which allegedly blocks the coming of his envisioned New Tibet. In many ways he lives in a future state; whereas, Pema Tseden's vision of a restored Tibet is not invested in a future arrival of a new modern Tibet. Instead the return of the traditional past is rather the bedrock of his creative projection of Tibet's current state of affairs. To him the modern future of Tibet has already landed in Tibet and it is not bringing true flourishing for humans or others but distress and destabilization. Therefore it is better that it be deterred or re-routed. The stolen yak in *The Grassland*, a TV set in *The Stone*, the urbanized actor of Drime Kunden in *The Search*, and the death of the family dog in *Old Dog* all point to the inauspicious presence of globalization, modernization, and consumerism. These are bad omens to be fenced off. Thus, Pema Tseden makes it clear that the fathers in all his productions are the true representations of Tibet's tradition, while the sons, with the exception of the monk in *The Stone,* are betraying the tradition, while still having the potential to be rescued.

No matter how divergent their affective approaches to Tibet might be, the works of Shogdong and Pema Tseden inevitably converge upon the same landscape and its spiritual essence – Tibet and Tibetan Buddhism – their homeland and their people's religious lifeway. From a phenomenological, not ideological, perspective, both of them are, in fact, receiving empowerment or inspiration from their common homeland for their respective creative and critical works regardless of their entanglement in the dichotomy of the old and the new, and the traditional and the modern. As discussed in the previous chapter, Shogdong, in fact, ultimately submits himself to the power embedded in the landscape of Tibet. As to Pema Tseden, he defends his native tradition relentlessly. The power of home is not necessarily exclusively embedded in kindred relations. In the worlds of both Shogdong and Pema Tseden the physical environment of home, whether consciously or unconsciously recognized, matters a great deal, conveying "insideness" (1976, 141), or the "base for departure and return in an unconscious familiarity" (Cox and Holmes 2000, 68). Fundamentally landscape-as-home entails a sense of rootedness and belonging or "a sense that contributes to feelings of self-worth" (Cox and Holmes 2000, 68). In this regard, the power that sustains Pema Tseden's cinematic restoration of traditional Tibet and Shogdong's construction of a new modern Tibet all stream in from the landscape which is the root of the total lifeworld of their common home, whether it provokes feelings of warmth and nostalgia for old tales or emotional suffering because of dishonest sons, the loss of a yak, or an involuntary killing of one's beloved dog.

The landscape of home speaks in Pema Tseden's cinematic works. He creatively transports it to Beijing, Berlin, Busan, New York, and Paris. His cinematic landscape of Tibet ties visual "knots" (Ingold 2011, 149) with his non-Tibetan audience, kindling their imagination of the Tibetan lifeworld. Revisiting Bruno's idea of cinema (*kinema*) as a medium of motion and emotion, I see Pema Tseden's cinematic landscape of Tibet has a life of its own. While it is animated with stories, events, human emotions, and scenes of the weather world of Tibet, it moves its audience members and leaves its marks, tracks, trails, and passages on their mindscape. The cinematic landscape flows with the stories in it but it is rigidly framed to mirror its real time counterpart – the physically inhabited landscape. What is included in the frame helps the audience see, through imagination, what is excluded from the frame. The actual ecological environment of a given inhabited landscape is woven together with what Gibson calls "medium, substances and surfaces" (Gibson 1986, 16), which respectively refer to the air, solid objects, and the "characteristically non-homogeneous texture" (Ingold 2011, 22) that, as it reflects and retains light, creates a unique color-saturated world distinct from other landscapes. If I see Pema Tseden's cinematic landscape from the angle of Gibson and Ingold, none of the three elemental components of landscape is physically present for the audience; however, the audience nevertheless feels connected with the cinematic mirror-images of the actual landscape. The connecting mediums are obviously not metereological elements in the physical landscape but light and sound, two essential cinematic mediums that turn the flat, white screen into a moving lifeworld, peopled, weathered, and storied.

Cinema, then, bridges the landscape with the mindscape. Ingold emphasizes that one's experience of landscape is synonymous with what he calls "an experience of light" (Ingold 2011, 96). To him landscape is never only physical and objective, outside the body and subjectivity of the human; instead it, as weather world, light world, and lifeworld, enters the human body and the mindscape. If "inhalation is wind becoming breath, exhalation is breath becoming wind" (Ingold 2011, 138) in a physical landscape. The light from the projector touching the screen and bouncing through the retinas of the audience members, enters them. The light sets the story on screen and into the mindscape of the audience, setting it all in motion.

In depicting Tibet, Pema Tseden relies on light and sound as the cinematic mediums to transport it beyond its physical bounds. Home, on the screen, is knitted together with different shades and colors of light which unfold the entangled dots and lines of human activities and trails, and the metereological fluxes on the physical terrains of homeland. Like an actual homeplace, home on the screen is also "a relational field" or "a meshwork" (Ingold 2011, 70) in which everything or everyone has his or her existential lines and paths. The places of their intersections in real life terms are houses, villages, monasteries, towns, and cities where the threads of people and events are tied together. Put simply, they are "knots" in which multiple lines touch, interconnect, and intertwine each other (Ingold 2011, 149). Such places are places of concentrated cultural and social energies resulting from exchange of goods and ideas and from trading differences on intangible collective issues. In the case of Pema Tseden's films the knots of human issues are tied on multi-dimensional transformation of the entirety of the Tibetan landscape, e.g. physical landscape, social ethics, and moral values.

As a relational field, Pema Tseden's cinematic representation of the familial, social, religious, and spiritual knots of human issues and concerns in the Tibetan landscape generates affordances to his diverse audience in Tibet, China, North America, and Europe. His motion pictures, showing human stories resulting from the tension between tradition and modernity, transmit place-based affordances to his audience. In landscape studies, as has been mentioned, affordances are seen in relational terms. A rock has no affordance to a mason until it is incorporated into his masonry; grass has no affordance to livestock until it is grazed; a cave does not become a wolf's den until the wolf dwells in it; and a tree is not lumber until the logger fells it, though prior to being felled it offered other affordances to other beings. It is only in relationship that affordance emerges. In this sense, affordances of a motion picture come alive when the film meets its audience. It affords entertainment, aesthetic engagement, or a social discourse to its viewers. For instance the affordances of James Cameron's *Avatar* (2009) are not confined to the fantastic images of Pandora but are released in a range of public discourses on indigenous land rights and ecological issues. Even catching critical attention from scholars, *The Journal of Religion, Nature and Culture* designated a special issue to the film called "Avatar and Nature Spirituality" (2010). Like the affordance of a natural object manifesting in a niche-relationship with organisms around it, the affordance of a film has its own niche. *Avatar* affords its audience a global discourse on nature spirituality, for example.

The niched affordance of Pema Tseden's films is not entertainment, as they have found almost no box office success, but shows its growing momentum in the global politics of contemporary Tibet and among Tibetans in urban China who demand more films made by Tibetans. Cinema is a powerful medium of social, political, and cultural discourse in contemporary world. The proliferation and affordability of digital video and cinema cameras and editing equipment is allowing increased visual articulation of numerous public discourses. This global phenomenon accords with one of the consequences of modernity/modernization, that is, "ocularcentrism" as "the scopic regime of modernity" as it initially appeared in Martin Jay's work (1993). It signifies a cultural and cognitive trend that our perceptions of the phenomenal world as well as our projection of future states of being are increasingly shaped by our mediated visual encounters with both local, regional, national, and global events, issues, and concerns through images transmitted through TV broadcasting, the Internet, cell phones, etc. With our increasing use of screens of all sorts, our reliance on the ocular is overcoming our experience as cutaneous beings: the eye/vision is assigned with more and more tactile tasks to sense, cognize, and interpret the fast changing world. In our ocularcentric mode of being, our worldviews are being reshaped and remolded with external visual feeds, and at the same time many articulate and defend their identities and lifeworlds with still images and motion pictures. As the idiom goes, "seeing is believing." In this background of the expanding ocular-modernity and modernization of physical dwelling spaces in China Pema Tseden's films are presenting the affordance of the ocular experience of public discourse on the fate of Tibetan traditions manifest in Buddhist social ethos and practices.

In this regard Pema Tseden's cinematic productions are not "art for art's sake" but are visionary mediums that pathologize the consequences of modernization in his homeland. Each of his film has its own centerpiece of cultural and social tension; each is thematically connected with Buddhism as the ballast of Tibetan culture and identity; and all his films are imprinted with the off-screen, economic and social changes occurring in Tibet and China, from initial Buddhist-friendly environment to the environment where Buddhist modes of being are endangered. The trend of off-screen, real-time changes parallels the thematic connection of all Pema Tseden's productions over the last half a decade in which their positive aesthetics of Tibetan landscape continue but encounter bleak, desolate, injured, hopeless scenes of characters' inner and outer worlds. In his films the sun continues to shine, the immense blue sky keeps its fantastically shaped clouds above people and their livestock and greenness returns to grassland every spring and summer, however, the traditional order of things is being rapidly reshaped. The paradisiacal feel of homeland recedes into the mindscape as a thing of nostalgia, as if it were a temporary, remembered solace or an escape from the seemingly unbeatable modern forces of change. Buddhism in the midst of these changes sinks deeper into both the landscape of Tibet and the mindscape of Pema Tseden's characters.

In this enmeshment of Buddhism and lifeworld, the storylines in Pema Tseden's latest films are more imbued with the parallel movements of the inner worlds of his characters and their outer worlds: anxieties, pains, hopes, fantasies, and searches for personal and collective destinies are personified in the movements of not only the physical landscape and meteorological mediums but also of lingering footsteps, spinning tires, and highways stretching to the horizon. Pema Tseden's cinematic touches, now more than ever, move the audience's haptic reflexes to touch, to sense, and to contemplate on his characters as real individuals with an ebb and flow to their emotional currents. Herein Buddhism retains its iconic status in the Tibetan landscape but its visuality is less objectified in physical markers such as robes, sutras, and monasteries. It is more diffused into subtle movements of facial muscles, teardrops, a reflection of the natural landscape in a character's eyes, a line of metaphoric speech, an inhalation of smoke, a dog's panting, a snow scene, a handful of dirt soaked with blood, and even an act of killing. Buddhism, thus, is Pema Tseden's haptic medium through which both his characters and the audience enter into a transnational visual touchscape: the visions and lifeworlds of the characters are empathetically transferred to their audience beyond Tibet.

This is where Pema Tseden affords his audience, whether Tibetans or non-Tibetans, to reflect and debate on the progressive but destabilizing effects of modernity in Tibet. He is inspiring other Tibetans to make films depicting the lifeworld of their communities. Sonthar Gyal, Pema Tseden's cinematographer, recently directed his own award-winning film entitled *The Sun Beaten Path* (2011). He fully inherits Pema Tseden's cinematic realism and cinematographic techniques – long takes and wide angles covering moral discourses of the old and the young generations. Additionally, a large makeup of Pema Tseden and Sonthar Gyal's audience are Tibetan students on university campuses in urban China. Pema Tseden's cinematic works are inspiring a growing number of these students to make their own productions. The department of Tibetan Studies at Minzu University in Beijing has opened credited courses and practicums for its students to make short films. Not too long from now we will witness the second and the third generations of Tibetan filmmakers emerging in China.

Chapter Six Ensouling the Mountain

The motion pictures by Pema Tseden and Sonthar Gyal are visual mediums that connect the audience with contemporary Tibet. The cinematic screen is the surface where "touching with the eyes" (Paterson 2007, 7) takes place. Touching therein is not one-way traffic: with either the audience's eyes touching the landscape of Tibet or the other way around. Instead, both at once touch the other. The filmmakers intend to touch the audience with Tibet. The audience members also have inner haptic responses to the incoming, frame by frame, touches of Tibet from the screen. The screen is the "skin" of Tibet which the eyes of the audience touch. Touch in this cinematic context is not cutaneous in nature, limited to the human skin, but rather pertains to internal empathetic tactility through which the audience members feel and which collapses emotional distance through cinematic narratives.

In my desire to learn more about the emotionality embodied in the creative works of Tibetan filmmakers and writers, I seek opportunities to work with them on film projects that allow me to search for the origin of the emotional forces and energies in their works. What I find is their homeland – the landscape – is an embodiment of their personal upbringing, their family and communal ties, and their cultural memory. Place is a critical source of the emotionality of the fictitious characters in their films and literary works and they are factual representations of the emotional states of their lives split between urban China and their homeland.

The short ethnographic vignette of the mad dash down to the glacier in the beginning of the introductory chapter came from my film log jotted down in summer 2012 when I was working with a predominantly Tibetan crew to shoot a new documentary titled "Ensouling the Mountain" at Amne Machen (ཨ་སྨྱེས་རྨ་ཆེན་) in Golok, Qinghai Province. Initially I intended to focus my documentary theme on eco-religious practices of Tibetans in Golok; however, in the actual filming during the first couple of days, I felt compelled to shift my thematic focus from the eco-religious exploration of Amne Machen (as one of the nine original mountain deities of Tibet) to the affective and emotional currents of my Tibetan crew members. Prior to the exuberantly festive expressions of the Tibetan crew members upon arrival at the glacier, emotional currents had already started building up as we moved from the foothills toward the mountain top. Except for the two lamas who were from the area, none of the Tibetan crew members had been to Golok, and yet their affection toward the mountain god and the mountain itself simply awed me. Pilgrimage, in this case, was proven to entail physical and emotional touch, with all bodily senses in touch with the physical landscape of the pilgrimage trail and site, and the pilgrims' inner world equally reaching out to touch the outer landscape and be touched by the profuse meanings embodied in it.

6.1 "Wherever I travel I can't wait to rush home!"

Hwadan Tashi (དཔའ་ལྡན་བཀྲ་ཤིས།) and Akhu Shampa (ཨ་ཁུ་བྱམས་པ།) were my initial documentary subjects. Hwadan Tashi, Akhu Shampa's nephew, is a tulku – the reincarnation of the late Siddhi Lama (སིདྷི་སྤྲུལ་སྐུ 1919–2000), a visionary master in the Nyingma order. Akhu Shampa, besides being Hwadan Tashi's uncle, is also his *yongzin* (ཡོངས་འཛིན།), or sutra reading instructor, at their monastery. In 2003 I attended the three-year-old Tulku Hwadan Tashi's enthronement. At the time I was doing fieldwork with a community of Han Chinese students of the late Siddhi Lama (Smyer Yu 2011, 38–45) and since that time I have continued to visit Hwadan Tashi's monastery. In the winter of 2011 Akhu Shampa asked me if I would join his pilgrimage with Hwadan Tashi to Amne Machen in the coming summer. The timing couldn't have been more perfect as I was planning a documentary project on the eco-religious aspect of the Tibetan landscape and I was exhilarated when Akhu Shampa agreed that the pilgrimage could feature in the documentary.

My goal was not to document our trip in a "run & gun" style, with a shoulder-mounted HD camera following the "actions" and "happenings." Besides the human activities of a pilgrimage, the landscape of Amne Machen was a critical part of my intended film. It is an epic landscape in both photogenic and folkloric senses; therefore, long takes of landscape scenes and contemplative narratives of the human subjects were planned in my primary documentary framing. There was no strict boundary between who would be before the camera and who behind it. Both Akhu Shampa and Hwadan Tashi participated in filming the landscape at Amne Machen. After our first day on the outskirts of Amne Machen, they naturally assumed themselves into the roles of both pilgrims and filmmakers. What I learned from the first three days was a technical realization and a documentary theme shift. Technically wide angle lenses ranging from 11mm to 21mm were most capable of capturing the magnificence of the mountains and human-place connectivity in which place was not "left behind" as background but was a critical participant in both pilgrimage and documentary making. Thematically during the first three days, each time we filmed or viewed footage, I saw the contemplative, awe-filled, and emotional moments of both Akhu Shampa and Hwadan Tashi. Obviously the physical place of Amne Machen touched them in the viewfinder as well as within their direct perception. I then decided to shift my thematic focus from collecting folk stories of the mountain god to the affective and emotional layers of the mountain landscape mediated through the narratives and physical movements of Akhu Shampa and Hwadan Tashi.

In the late afternoon of the third day, when we were setting up the camera for a few shots of a cave entrance at Jomo Yang-ra (ཇོ་མོ་གཡང་ར། a cave meditation site) where tantric saints such as Tangdong Gyalpo (ཐང་སྟོང་རྒྱལ་པོ།), Lhalong Paldor (ལྷ་ལུང་དཔལ་རྡོར།), and the late Siddhi Lama, undertook solitary practices, Akhu Shampa and Hwadan Tashi were fifty yards away adding rocks to the Parents' Kindness Cairn (ཕ་མའི་དྲིན་ལན་འཇལ་བའི་རྡོ།). Hwadan Tashi's giggling echoed in the narrow valley. We moved the camera to the entrance of Ani Sangmo's Meditation Cave (ཨ་ནེ་བཟང་མོའི་མཚམས་ཁང་།), another cave in which the late Siddhi Lama is said to have meditated, Akhu Shampa and Hwadan Tashi joined us. The camera began to roll when Hwadan Tashi entered the cave while Akhu Shampa stood at the entrance and encouraged him to enter slowly. Admittedly I was hoping to capture some translife connection between Hwadan Tashi and his previous incarnation, akin to how the young Dalai Lama claims the ritual paraphernalia of his predecessor affected him, as shown in the film *Kundun.*

It appeared that nothing like that happened. The cave was so narrow that I had a hard time imagining how anyone could meditate in there, and with its narrowness and inconvenient entry, I recalled local pilgrimage folklore which stated that if one enters and exits smoothly, one is karmically clean; otherwise, one is stricken with hindrances derived from past deeds of defilement. Hwadan Tashi merrily re-emerged from the exit with a huge grin on his face and we commenced to wrap up. A few minutes later when everyone was moving the gear to a different cave, he quietly stood alone in front of Ani Sangmo's Meditation Cave with tears running down his cheeks. Our log keeper quietly motioned for us to film the emotional moment. Soon Akhu Shampa came over to comfort him, "Are you all right?" Tears continued to pour out of Hwadan Tashi's eyes. Seeing it might be best to pause for Hwadan Tashi's sake, it was also noted that three of the crew members from Beijing had started feeling the effects of high altitude sickness. Feeling responsible for Hwadan Tashi's "fatigue," as well as the burden of the documentary schedule, I walked to a narrow, rapidly flowing river, relieved when my senses were enveloped in the roaring sound of the rapids that muffled the contending chatter in my head.

About thirty minutes later Akhu Shampa joined me at the riverbank and told me that Hwadan Tashi had cried not because, as we had assumed, he was fatigued, but because of the release an emotional buildup that I had not noticed for the previous three days. Toward the end of the first day after we filmed their *sangchod* (བསང་མཆོད།) or mountain god offering recitation, Hwadan Tashi had told Akhu Shampa that he was feeling sad for no reason. According to

Akhu Shampa this had happened before, when Hwadan Tashi visited the late Siddhi Lama's residence and when he contemplated the pinkish birthmark on his right palm which is identical to that of his predecessor. However, Hwadan Tashi himself did not confide in Akhu Shampa explicitly about why he had shed tears in front of Ani Sangmo's Meditation Cave. I could only think and imagine along with Akhu Shampa's assessment that Hwadan Tashi was indeed having a past-life recollection. If I were twelve-year-old Hwadan Tashi, I would feel awed but terrified to envision myself in the body of an old and spiritually fierce man who once dwelled in the darkness of the cave. This is rather a theatrical imagination of mine without confirmation from Hwadan Tashi; however, everyone witnessed his tears when he was staring at the cave. I could at least assume it was a place-induced emotional moment, meaning that the site of the cave triggered the young lama's emotional reaction.

On the same evening, before sunset, I set up a filmed interview session with Akhu Shampa in front of another cave, hoping he would share more of his thoughts and feelings originating from this pilgrimage. He began with his Buddhist vision of Amne Machen. As a monk he opposed the idea that Amne Machen should be worshipped as a worldly god (སྲིད་པ་ཆགས་པའི་ལྷ་) who is as sentient as humans are. Akhu Shampa made it clear in the beginning of the interview, "We can't invoke worldly gods to help us to become enlightened...Perhaps the gods may help you with longevity, happiness, and wealth in this lifetime, but it is futile if you entrust your future lives and your path to the Pureland to these gods." Akhu Shampa's preferred vision of Amne Machen is not a god bound by the Earth but is an enlightened being *in* but not *of* the world. To be specific, Akhu Shampa sees Amne Machen as a Bodhisattva at the Tenth-Stage or *chugye dren* (ཆོས་ཀྱི་སྤྲིན།) translated as "Dharma cloud" and referring to the highest ground of Bodhisattvahood. According to the Buddhist canonic definition, a Tenth-Stage Bodhisattva can spread Buddha Dharma like rainfall to reach every sentient being under the sky (Cleary 1993, 384). It was not surprising that Akhu Shampa, as a Bhikkhu, reinforced this vision of Amne Machen, as he stated at the outset of the interview, "As a monk, I only live in accordance with Buddha Dharma, not with our folklore." He then emphasized that the seat of Amne Machen is the Dharma Realm of Avalokiteshvara; however he did not affirm whether or not Amne Machen, the mountain god, is an incarnation of Avalokiteshvara. Among Amdowas, Amne Machen's Buddhist status is widely acknowledged; however, his most popular identities are as a wealth god, a warrior god, an ancestral god, a Dharma protector, and a soul mountain. Akhu Shampa's initial narrative of Amne Machen put a limit on his reverence for the mountain god merely as an enlightened Buddhist.

Akhu Shampa is one of many Tibetans who prefer to see Amne Machen as a transcendentally pure Bodhisattva beyond and above the worldliness of sentient beings; however, the Buddhist religiosity of Amne Machen has its own continuity inherently woven into the ecological system and the psychic domain of local people and the environment. The Buddhist identity of Amne Machen is young in comparison with its geological evolution, environmental significance, and pre-Buddhist religious meanings.

I am, as an outsider, not able to see Amne Machen as a Tenth-Stage Bodhisattva who precipitates Dharma rain; however, from an ecological perspective, I can conceive of Amne Machen as a rainmaker, a snowmaker, and an icemaker, as it is most definitely a water-gathering mountain. Water in different forms – ice, snow, clouds, fog, rain, and rivers – envelopes and saturates Amne Machen. The sound of water is omnipresent. Together with the sound of wind it travels in the air and reverberates in one's eardrums day and night. The ecological manifestations of Amne Machen's "Dharma Rain" show the fecund potency of Amne Machen. When we were at the foot of the mountain range, we frequently saw herds of wild goats and deer grazing on the mountain slopes. When we entered deeper into the mountainous landscape, we saw thick bushes, stands of forest, lone red foxes, hares, hawks, and different rodent species. What amazed our recordist and me was the "water music" generated by a few small underground rivers we accidently found, evidence that the mountainous landscape is saturated with water above and beneath the surface of the Earth. The abundance of water as a primary sustaining natural force that benefits the flora and fauna at Amne Machen compels me to recognize the mountain deity as a fertility god.

I do not intend to overlook the Buddhist significance of Amne Machen; however, from both ecological and mythological perspectives, the Amne Machen range appears to be a place full of life-sustaining elements and a supernatural being in charge of the reproduction of countless species. Ecologically Amne Machen is an important part of the Three-Rivers Source Region. The megatons of water released from the area feed into the Yellow River, the Yangtze River, and the Lanchang River (Mekong River). If Amne Machen is a Bodhisattva, he is a "Water Bodhisattva."

In Wang Wenying's geological survey, the Amne Machen area has a total of 150 square kilometers of glaciers, which is translated into a water storage capacity of approximately 14 billion cubic meters (Wang 1983, 384). The pre-Buddhist mythology of Amne Machen more realistically translates this life-sustaining power into a set of fertility-oriented eulogies emphasizing the mountain god's fecund potency bestowed to all life forms within his domain. For instance, the ritual text, titled "Manyan Bomra [another name for Amne Machen] Cleansing Prayers" (མ་ཉན་སྦོམ་བསྒྲུབ་ལས་རྒྱ་གཏན་པོའི་རི་ཡི་ཕྱག་ཁྲུས་བཤགས་སོ།།), emphasizes that human desires are endless like the sky, but among them the desire for fertility is paramount (Caibei 2012, 183). The ecosphere of Amne Machen has sustained generations of Tibetans in Golok and the surrounding watershed.

As our conversation went deeper, Akhu Shampa showed much affection to Amne Machen as the landmark of his homeland – Golok. His narrative expressed more about the ecological elements of Amne Machen than Buddhist doctrines on the mountain range. From his tone I sensed a homesickness when he talked about his travels outside Golok:

> I have been to India and Nepal from Central Tibet. When I was in Nepal I found people there planted their trees, grass and flowers. Their rivers smell polluted. We have pure clean rivers. It is so different. While in foreign lands I thought of home. I missed home very much. I have also been to Beijing, Shenzhen, Guangzhou, Tianjin and other places. When in these cities I often walked on asphalt streets and could not find grass. Wherever I went I thought of my home. When I think of the rivers, mountains, and grasslands, a happy feeling instantly arises. Such feeling is indescribable. My home is a magnificent place. No matter how far a bus might take me away from home I can't ever forget it. This is how I feel. I love my home because I love the land here and because there are clean rivers, many kinds of medicinal plants, snow covered mountains, cliffs and rocks. Because I grew up as a nomad I love everything here. Wherever I travel I can't wait to rush home!

In this narrative, home sets the precedence of Akhu Shampa's comparisons of Golok with India, Nepal, and the cities of China. It is the center of his life to which he feels he must return. In this age of globalization it is common for people to move from their homelands, with many seeming to prefer uprooting themselves from them rather than growing deeper roots. However, in the case of Akhu Shampa, home is obviously synonymous with rootedness cemented with a deep emotional attachment. As Relph puts it in his study of place, such attachment "constitutes our roots in places; and the familiarity that this involves is not just a detailed knowledge, but a sense of deep care and concern for that place" (Relph 1976, 37). Hearing Akhu Shampa's sentiments I felt that in preparing for travel he already missed home before he even left it. The emotional and psychological significance of home is of course natural and obvious, but I must emphasize that when Akhu Shampa expressed his strong feelings toward his home, he was sitting outside a cave overlooking a river and a valley covered by lush green grass. He was physically environed in Amne Machen. In this context home enters his body-consciousness as a concrete ecological environment and a pilgrimage site. At the same time I also wonder what he would say about home while standing in the middle of the township of Machen, the capital of Golok Prefecture which is being modernized and rapidly expanding with new buildings and asphalt streets. Would that be what he misses about home? I prefer to understand what he said in a pilgrimage context: the landscape of Amne Machen was drawing out his place-induced emotion.

Pilgrimage, in this case, is an activity that incorporates meaning deeper than the surface of the sacred landscape where legacies of the past saints are found and on which the abodes of gods and spirits are marked; the path of pilgrimage is not only physical. When the pilgrim walks in the landscape, it unfolds an "atlas of emotion" or an "emotional cartography" (Bruno 2002, 2) that it is not merely a two-dimensional map but which moves with the moving body and mind of the pilgrim. Emotion and motion are inherently entwined in a mutual dependency. The moving body moves the mind with all sense-scapes (Tilley 2010, 27–28) allowing the pilgrim to identify sacred sites that receive his homage. In the meantime the dyad of the moving landscape and the moving body-mind triggers emotional responses in the pilgrim to the landscape itself. From an anthropological perspective, the pilgrimage in this case is not merely the process of the emergence of what Turner calls "communitas" or the "essential-we relationship" among pilgrims (Turner 1974, 47) that is a human-oriented spiritual bonding. It also incorporates a place-human communitas. Therein, pilgrimage-inspiring places are not merely the vessel of a sacred person or a sacred event such as a chapel or temple might imply, but they have a life of their own, a combination of geological forces, ecological elements, aesthetically pleasing or inspiring ambience, and, in some places, earth-gods like Amne Machen. In this regard, the landscape of Amne Machen is seen as the organic body of a god. The pilgrim moves on the "skin" of Amne Machen. Both the pilgrim and Amne Machen touch one another with outer tactility and inner emotionality. The terrain of the pilgrimage is a geopsychic terrain – with the landscape having its own "soul" in constant conversation with that of the pilgrim.

It is clear that in the eyes of Akhu Shampa, Amne Machen is the monumental mark of Golok, his homeland. Zemgyab (འཛམ་སྐྱབས།), his cousin and a well-known folk singer in Golok, was our recordist's assistant and when we finished filming the interview with Akhu Shampa he began humming a tune before he went to sleep. Early the next morning, while waiting for the predawn light to illuminate Amne Gyag (ཨ་མྱེས་སྐྱགས།), a ridge named after King Gesar's horse whip, we heard him singing his new song in the tent. The melody cut through the thick braid of clouds floating above the valley toward Mayim Dorje Rdolgyal (མ་ཡུམ་རྡོ་རྗེའི་དྲག་རྒྱལ།) or Queen's Peak, as though his song was herding the clouds as an offering to Amne Machen's mother. After we completed our pre-dawn landscape filming, I asked him to share the lyrics of his composition:

> The tip of Amne Machen is abreast with the high clouds,
> The waves of the Blue Lake are soaring up to the sky,

The lush, emerald grassland stretches to the end of the horizon,
I'm pining for the beauty of my celestial homeland.

Fragrance fills the magic Snowland,
The wholesome landscape pervades the field of my vision,
The mountain embraces the birds of heaven and the beasts of the Earth,
I'm pining for the enchantment of my homeland.

These lyrics could be taken as yet another creative work about Tibetans' own imagining of their homeland (Brauen 2004, 132); however, understanding the words and hearing the tune in the landscape of Amne Machen required no stretch of the imagination to comprehend their connection with reality; the words and the tune were naturally part of the mountain landscape that we were physically and photographically experiencing. The morning wind was present in the thick white clouds blanketing the bodies of the mountains in the south and also calmly moving down into the valley. The landscape, just as Zemgyab sang, was the field of my vision: the seeing and the seen were inseparable from each other. Later in the day as a rainstorm approached, violent winds disrupted the calmness of the clouds resting on the mountains. The clouds swirled and danced and included us, not as bystanders, but as an integral part of the meteorological motion of wind which tore the clouds into disarray, like a spiderweb hanging in the sky awaiting its absorption into the massive, incoming, dark storm clouds. In its sublime beauty, this was more poetically potent than Zemgyab's lyrics but I understood what, in this landscape, inspired the emotions embedded in them.

6.2 "You know the origin of my ancestors"

With the exception of Akhu Shampa and Hwadan Tashi, none of our Tibetan crew had previously been to Golok; however, this did not mean that they had no knowledge of Amne Machen. Each of them, in one way or another, had connected Amne Machen with the mountain gods in his or her home village. This pilgrimage often seemed to be a homecoming to them, as though they were about to meet a relative about whom they had already heard a great deal. Jigmed, our second camera operator, was the loudest among his peers in his dash to the glacier at Queen's Peak, hollering, "Lhagyal-lo [ལྷ་རྒྱལ་ལོ།] gods win]!" He was the first to reach the glacier and roll on the ice. He was the one leading everyone else in and out of different crevices in the glacier. Seen from the ridge from which we ran to it, the glacier looked like a thin ice sheet, but as soon as we approached it, the "sheet" became an immensely mesmerizing wavy field of ice humps, walls, and hills, stretching from the foot of Queen's Peak into the valley. A glacier makes its own music when wind rushes over the surface and enters the nooks and crannies of the ice. There was also the dripping of melting ice echoing inside the ice walls that made us quiet down. Seeing the offerings left by previous pilgrims, including ritual objects and small pieces of jewelry in the crevices of the ice and on the black-graveled edges where the snowmelt sinks into the mountain and flows into the watershed caused our initial celebratory moment to evolve into a mood of outward silence and inward commemorative exchange with the meaning of the place.

After we retreated back up to the ridge from the glacier, I conversed with Jigmed while we were immersed in the breathtaking landscape:

> DSY: I watched *Herdsman*, the short film you made last year. I find your low angle shots highlight the connection of your character with many elements of the Earth, such as water, snow, grass, and rocks. Now, at the highest sacred Mountain in Amdo, how do you feel about the earth elements here?
>
> J: I grew up as a nomad. No matter where I am, at home or here with Amne Machen, and whenever I see mountains and grasslands, I feel peaceful and attentive to the sound of the land. The external vessel [the physical world] and the inner sentience all give me absolute joy.
>
> DSY: Are the mountain deities in your home area related to Amne Machen?
>
> J: When I was a boy, a *ngapa* once told me the story of Amne Machen. I can't remember everything, but the mountains back home are related to Amne Machen. For example, Dadel (དགྲ་འདུལ་), one of our mountain gods, is a younger brother of Amne Machen. Also other mountain gods like Nyangchod Shegden (ཉང་གཅོད་ཤེགས་ལྡན་), Sharzha (ཤར་ཞ་), and Lhatsan (ལྷ་བཙན་) are all relatives of Amne Machen.
>
> DSY: When I gave my talk on imagined Tibet two years ago on your campus, some scholars responded by saying: "Tibetans don't consider their homeland as beautiful as outsiders claim it is because they're used to the landscape." What do you think of this view? If you shoot a film here at Amne Machen, what kind of film would you like to make?
>
> J: I feel Amne Machen and the people [Tibetans] are fused together. People and the mountain gods are inseparable. Pilgrimage to Amne Machen is an ancient custom here. To Tibetans, pilgrimage is a kind of vitality, courage, and fondness toward the natural beauty here. Speaking of this pilgrimage, I once again feel our Snowland is so magnificently beautiful that I love it more than ever. If I shoot a film here, I want to tell a story of how Tibetans lived in the past. It would have nothing to do with modern life.

Jigmed made *Herdsman* as a graduate student. The twenty-minute production, filmed with his HD camera is about a young herdsman who loses his horse and family's sheep when he falls asleep in the tall, autumn grass. With his brother playing the protagonist, the film was shot on Jigmed's family's pastoral ground outside Chapcha, the capital city of Hainan Tibetan Autonomous Prefecture. Jigmed sets the golden landscape as center of his cinematic gravity toward which everything returns: the protagonist falls asleep on horseback and comically stays blissfully asleep even as he falls to the ground; two young thieves are attracted to the sheep grazing in the expanse of grass; and Jigmed's camera tilts from the sky to the grass on which the protagonist happily snoozes. The film depicts a nomadic life in an elemental fashion: a landscape of tall grass with snow mountains on the horizon, the blue sky, grazing sheep, and the idyllic mood of the protagonist. Everything appears paradisiacal except the theft. Viewers are shown how home is the coziest place and that one can lose everything else but the land itself.

Jigmed's Amne Machen-inspired wish to make a film of Tibet's past coincides with a cultural trend seen among Tibetan students, writers, and artists in urban China who find that seeking their ancestral roots and revisiting their birthplace are integral to their creativity. At Amne Machen, Jigmed's heightened energy was contagious to his peers. Zemgyab was not the only lyric writer among us. When we were at the Queen's Peak, Tenzin, our recordist who was a classmate of Jigmed, asked Zemgyab to compose a tune for the lyrics he had written over the last two days, titled "You Know":

> The sacred land of snow mountains
> strings together the prayer beads of my heroic ancestors.
> Brightening the footprints of the ancient Six Tribes,
> You know the origin of my ancestors.
>
> Oh, Yarlhashampo! Oh, Amne Machen!
> Among the Nine Patriarchs, you know the origin of my ancestors.
> Surrounding sacred Amne Machen,
> The gods of the royal ministers and their relatives assemble;
> Brightening up the trails that bond fathers and sons,
> You know the surnames of my ancestors.
>
> Oh, Gethung Bragdkar (དགེ་མཐུང་བྲག་དཀར)! Oh, Grongye Zhaldkar (མགྲོན་རྒྱས་ཞལ་དཀར)!
> Chosen as the minister and the chamberlain,
> You know the surnames of my ancestors.
> The interior of sacred Amne Machen is filled with treasures.
> Shining the meritorious field of the hidden treasures and armaments,
> You know the precious visions of my ancestors.
>
> Oh, Begar Dongzhong (སྦས་དཀར་སྟོང་ཞོང་)! Oh, Gotson Dorbrag (ཀོ་མཚོན་རྡོར་བྲག)!
> As heroic, peerless gems,
> You know the treasure house of our ancestors.

Unlike Jigmed, Tenzin is more introverted. At Amne Machen, he often wrote in his notebook before going to sleep. In the lyrics he shared with me, the invoked names are simultaneously the names of gods and ancient kings and ministers as well as the mountains themselves. Except for Yarlharshampo (ཡར་ལྷ་ཤམ་པོ), which is located in the Central Tibet, all the other mountains/mountain gods called upon are found in the Amne Machen range. For instance, Akhu Shampa described Gethung Bragdkar, King Gesar's minister, thusly "Longpu [minister] Gethung has a white face. His eyebrows and mustache curl upward. He raises his right hand like a treasure-flame and his left hand holds a wish-fulfilling treasure. He sits cross-legged and his Dharma body is red. On his forehead there's the Sanskrit word 'sheh'."

Coinciding with the mountain folklore in Amdo, Amne Machen, along with other mountain deities in Tenzin's lyrics, is an ancestor god and a warrior god. In these stories his Buddhist identity is not emphasized as it was in Akhu Shampa's narratives. Both Jigmed's spirited communication with Amne Machen and Tenzin's invocation of his ancient ancestors through Amne Machen are illustrative of a unique place-human relationship that is commemorative in nature. The crew members' pilgrimage experience was a remembering process but it was not a personal journey alone. It is commemorative in the sense that everyone was in a "co-remembering" (Casey 2000, xi) mode of being when walking on the same paths, touching and being touched by the same landscape, and filming and being filmed by each other at the same sacred sites of Amne Machen. What was being commemorated in the mountain was a "place memory," which refers to "the fact that concrete places retain the past in a way that can be reanimated by our remembering them" (Casey 2000, xi). In this regard, Amne Machen is both a place and a memory. In the co-remembering moments of Jigmed, Tenzin and others, the mountains were animated as mountain gods through the remembering and retelling of their stories. Memory was thus reanimated and no longer stored in the remote past or deep under the crust of the human mindscape; instead, it is and was embodied in Amne Machen. Amne Machen then is a triune whole, a god, a place, and a time (in memory). The nexus of time and place embodied in Amne Machen, in my view, can be regarded as a distinct kind of timelessness. The memory of Tibetans' ancestral past is embodied in Amne Machen in what I would call "a present past" to each generation of local people. It might also be seen as a "time gate" through which the past emerges into the present or the present returns to the past, a mountain-as-time-machine that is antecedently grounded in a place as a geological location and a cultural monument marking the place-based identity of Tibetans of the region.

Amne Machen as a monument is not a human construction but a natural geological formation that is imbued with a wealth of human cultural meanings.

This magnificent monument is exemplary of how an aspect of nature "naturalizes" a cultural memory and how this cultural memory "culturalizes" this unique natural landscape. The division between "nature" and "culture" in this case is dissolved as each converts the other into its own mode of being. The mountain is animated as a deity, as an ageless super-human being embodying human memory, while generations of its human counterparts incessantly establish their communion with it by commemorating and cherishing their ancestral past with the mountain and the mountain god. Like Ingold and Tilley, I then also say landscape is storied (Ingold 2011, 142) and thus has a biography (Tilley 1994, 33), which is inherently part of human mythical and historical memory. In many ways, such a place-biography or a biographed-place is an embodied story of how the union of gods and humans has sustained the bond between place and human.

The monumentality of Amne Machen, in this regard, affords a combined human cultural functionality of "marking," "referencing," and "temporality" (Tilley 2010, 38). Its land-marking significance does not stop in its physically awesome magnificence but continues on into the human mindscape as a reference or a temporal compass, which generates mythical, historical, existential, and affective meanings from a remote past to the present and the future. Within the human mindscape, Amne Machen then is a shapeshifter, a timeshifter, and a moodshifter but it is the human psyche bonded with the mountain in all its variety that makes the "shifts": it shapeshifts the mountain into the mountain god; it shifts the present tense of the mind to a remote past as a spatial corridor connecting the living with the dead; and it shifts the human emotionality from one touching moment to another, e.g. nostalgia, elation, melancholy, and empowerment. Such monumentality is synonymous with memorability as the potency of human memories are deeply entwined with the geological energy and embedded in the mountain. Thus, the mountain and its human counterparts commemorate and co-animate their shared memory of the past. In Hwadan Tashi's narrative of his dreams, Amne Machen is a warrior god who rides a white horse like King Gesar. He commands thousands of soldiers. In Tenzin's poetic eulogy, Amne Machen brings the ancestors of Tibet to the present. By shapeshifting the mountains into mountain gods and as storehouses of ancestral treasures and weapons, Tenzin receives the empowerment from Amne Machen. Through an I-thou invocation and imploration, Tenzin embraces the vision and gallantry of his ancestors through Amne Machen. The mode of his "you-know" speech is implicitly an affective, commemorative mode of "I-know-you."

To reemphasize, in the midst of Amne Machen's multiple identities and multidimensionality, what is critical is his assumed sentience, which permits humans to establish communication and communion with him as a sentient presence who feels, thinks, and remembers in the same way his human counterparts do except that he has lived through an ageless time in geological, cultural, and religious senses. In this regard, Amne Machen is not an object of human commemoration but is a commemorator or a co-rememberer of a place-human mytho-history. Commemoration in this context does not take place within the human realm alone. It is a collaborative, shared, and communal event of place, gods, and humans.

6.3 "*Machen Bomra* [རྨ་ཆེན་སྦོམ་ར།] is a living being"

Tserang Dondrub, Pema Tseden's hometown friend and the screenplay writer mentioned in the previous chapter, joined our filming-pilgrimage to Amne Machen. He came along with us because he had wanted to collect folk stories of Amne Machen for his own writing project. After everyone walked back from the glacier, he sat down with Akhu Shampa on the ridge overlooking the glacier and Queen's Peak. Hwadan Tashi was gathering rocks in different shapes and piling them into cairns. Tserang Dondrub asked Akhu Shampa about something he had heard, "The rumor is that Amne Machen wants to move to a different place. Is it true? Do you know where?" Akhu Shampa replied:

> Yes, this rumor has been out there for quite a few years. It is said that Amne Machen wishes to move to [Mt.] Nyanpog Yutse (གཉན་པོ་གཡུ་རྩེ). In recent years a glacier has slowly appeared on the top of Nyanpog Yutse. It had no glacier there before. So, people are saying when the ice fully covers its top, Amne Machen will move there as his new home. You see, the glacier at Amne Machen is melting away, not much is left, but the glacier at Nyanpog Yutse is growing. This talk of people is probably true.

Tserang Dondrub continued his questions, "Why does Amne Machen want to move away from here?" Akhu Shampa replied:

> About thirty kilometers from Golok Prefecture, there is a place called Dernee (སྡེར་གནས). It has had a gold mine there for the last ten years. Miners have dug deeply into Amne Machen, at least seventy kilometers from the mouth of the mine to the current depth. It is probably reaching what's beneath the glacier. If the mining continues, it will hollow out the mountain. The mountain will perish like a person with his intestines, heart, and lungs dug out. In recent years the vitality of the glacier looks feeble. Mining makes the snow mountain lose its vigor. I don't know what scientists make of this. You see, *Begar Dongzhong Chanmo* (སྒར་སྟོང་གཞོང་ཆེན་མོ Thousand Tent Glacier) is the name of the glacier because the wavy shape of the ice looks like a campsite of thousands of tents stretching out in the open. Now the ice is melting. The tents are collapsing. It is because of the mining. Amne Machen is a Tenth-Stage Bodhisattva. He doesn't have hatred for the miners but I feel it is unbearable and heart-wrenching.

According to the Qinghai Daily News, the mine at Dernee belongs to Qinghai Westwood Copper Co., Ltd., which began its mining operation in Golok in 2004. The company invested 430 million RMB (approximately US$69 million). The mining site is at the southern slope of a mountain named Dernee, which is adjacent to Amne Machen. According to the company, the mine only produces copper and the reserve is estimated at 570,000 tons (Jie 2006). The photos of the mining site on the company website indicate that it is doing strip mining. At the mining site, the skin of the Earth looks peeled off, with flesh exposed, and while I could not verify if the company has dug a seventy kilometer long tunnel that reaches under the glacier, it is certain that the landscape has been changed in the nearly ten years of operations.

In the conversation between Tserang Dondrub and Akhu Shampa, Amne Machen is naturally addressed as both a god and a person. This is more than a matter of personification in the manner of attributing human qualities to a non-human object. In their eyes, Amne Machen is simply 'one of us,' in the sentient sense, except that he possesses supernatural qualities and his body is the uniquely shaped mountainous topography. To Akhu Shampa, Amne Machen is not an ordinary, worldly, god and a person, but a Tenth-Stage Bodhisattva. To me as an empathetic listener of their conversation, I can imagine Amne Machen as an earth-god who is losing his paradisiacal home turf, a person whose body is torn and bleeding, and a bodhisattva whose silent acceptance of physical pain and emotional distress is a demonstration of the Buddhist understanding of suffering being part of the cost of sentience. Akhu Shampa prefers to take a higher ground expressing his concern about the environmentally destructive and psychically disturbing qualities of modernization across China.

From Akhu Shampa's personifying and empathetic understanding of Amne Machen as the prey of the mining company, I have learned that native Tibetans' eco-religious practices and eco-spiritual bond with the landscape of their home afford them a unique set of visions and skills to work with the land in a mutually embodied rather than a callously exploitative mode of being. By "mutually embodied" I mean landscape is not merely physically external to native Tibetans but it is rooted emotionally, mythologically, and religiously in their mindscapes. To take this line of thought further, the potency of the Tibetan landscape emanates beyond its geological domain. In my previous study of Tibetan landscape, I qualified it with the UNESCO definition of "the associative cultural landscape" as a part of the World Heritage, which possesses "the powerful religious, artistic or cultural associations of the natural element rather than material cultural evidence, which may be insignificant or even absent" (UNESCO). It could also be understood as "the ideational landscape" because its natural feature is embodied with "powerful religious, artistic or other cultural meanings" (Knapp and

Ashmore 2000, 9, 12). It is thus "both imaginative in the sense of being a mental image of something and emotional in the sense of cultivating or eliciting some spiritual value or ideal (Smyer Yu 2011, 191).

In the case of Amne Machen, the geological potency, topographical sublimity, felt presence of gods and spirits, and perceived positive aesthetics point to the natural elements of what affords native Tibetans to see and feel the landscape as an animated, supernatural but sentient being. The natural, cultural, spiritual, and psychic attributes of Amne Machen were manifest in my Tibetan colleagues' emotionality, affection, and distress. What it comes down to is that, for them, the sentience of Amne Machen *is a given* as the precondition for the information- and thought-exchange between place and people. The potency of landscape affects pilgrims' worldview and emotional states of being. Tibetans are no exceptions.

Like Akhu Shampa, Tserang Dondrub's initial vision of Amne Machen was of a Tenth-Stage Bodhisattva before we reached Queen's Peak. While Akhu Shampa emphasized the bodhisattvahood of Amne Machen from his canonical perspective that one should not worship earth gods for spiritual enlightenment, Tserang Dondrub underscored the Buddhist identity of the mountain deity more as an inherent part of Tibetan national identity. In his view, Tibetan Buddhism and culture are one and the same; thus one cannot continue without the other. His view coincides with that of many pro-traditionalist Tibetans working and living in urban China. At Jomo Yangra, I asked him what he thought of Akhu Shampa's emphatic affirmation of Amne Machen as a bodhisattva and he remarked:

> Now some Tibetans attempt to separate Tibetan Buddhism from Tibetan culture and even think each will eventually be divorced from the other. In my view, Tibetan culture is Tibetan Buddhism. No matter how we juggle the words, we cannot retain one without the other in this matter. Abandoning Tibetan Buddhism is not different from abandoning Tibetan culture. Our pilgrimage to Amne Machen is a part of Tibetan culture. We can't separate them.

Tserang Dondrub's initially strong Buddhist vision of Amne Machen seemed to have receded into the background when he sat on the ridge overlooking the glacier spreading out from the foot of Queen's Peak. As the clouds floated above and the mountain wind gusted, his commemorative mood with Amne Machen and the rest of us affirmed him as the patriarch of mountain deities in Amdo and as a warrior god and a soul mountain (བླ་རི་ *bla-ri*) more than a bodhisattva. As I noticed this perceptual change in him, I asked him, "You've lived in Beijing for many years and now you've made your first visit to Amne Machen. How do you feel?" He responded:

6.3 "Machen Bomra [རྨ་ཆེན་སྤོམ་ར།] is a living being"

Speaking of Amne Machen, there's a saying "Machen Bomra has arrived" [རྨ་ཆེན་སྤོམ་ར་ཕེབ་བྱུང་།]. He is a warrior god as a matter of fact. Amne Machen is a fierce warrior god. Now the only thing I think of is that Amne Machen is a *bla-ri* [བླ་རི། soul mountain] of the Snowland and a protector of common folks. Circumambulating the mountain benefits us. Everyone knows that. I know that, too. With my devotion I believe Amne Machen protects me and helps me fulfill my wishes.

Machen Bomra is another name of Amne Machen. The saying "Machen Bomra has arrived" is an idiomatic phrase often referring to a triumphant return and charismatic weight of a hero when winning a battle or a contest. It is an expression of the hero's absolute confidence charismatically felt by his cheering crowd. It was perceptible that Tserang Dondrub felt empowered in the presence of Amne Machen as shown in the tone of his voice and his facial expression. I continued with another question, "What does Amne Machen as a soul mountain mean to you?" He said:

Every village in Tibet has its own soul mountain. At my home village, Ama Sorge (ཨ་མ་ཟོར་དགུ།) is our soul mountain. Amne Machen is a soul mountain of all of Tibet because it is one of the original mountain deities. I cannot differentiate which place is my home, here [Amne Machen] or my birthplace. Everything is part of the whole. I feel this entire Snowland is my birthplace. My consciousness and life are all meshed in it. This is a living snow mountain. Machen Bomra [རྨ་ཆེན་སྤོམ་ར།] is a living being. Including you and everyone else, we are all enmeshed in this snow mountain. We cannot sever a single portion of us from it.

Tenzin, our recordist, interjected, "So, are we a part of Amne Machen now?" Tserang Dondrub continued:

I see Amne Machen and we belong to the same body. We cannot separate each from the other. It is just like where we are now. We blend together with Amne Machen. If we turn our back on our soul mountains, we will lose our soul. This is an inseverable relationship.

Tserang Dondrub's responses to my and Tenzin's queries coincide with the increasing national status of Amne Machen among Tibetans as shown in Katia Buffetrilles' work (2003, 12). Tserang Dondrub's talk of Amne Machen as a national soul of Tibetans is not unique to Tibet and is a concept found in modern ethnic nationalisms across the world. From the perspective of Tibetan folklore, Amne Machen is regarded as the fourth son of Ode Gungyel (ཨོ་དེ་གུང་རྒྱལ།), the patriarch of the original mountain gods of Tibet. In Amdo, Amne Machen as a mountain god, is the patriarch of all mountain gods in Amdo; therefore it is only natural that Tserang Dondrub embraces it as a soul mountain of Tibetans. What is worth mentioning is that in current scholarly research on Tibetan pilgrimage and mountain culture, *gnas-ri* (གནས་རི།) or sacred mountains, are more often discussed than *bla-ri* (བླ་རི), soul mountains. In Alex McKay's volume titled *Pilgrimage in Tibet*, Andrea Loseries-Leick offers her understanding of soul mountain, "Tibetans believe that every region has its own deity which may descend on a mountain which then becomes sacred. The mountain becomes the 'soul' of the region and thus protect and secure the wellbeing of the people around" (Loseries-Leick 1998, 158). This assessment does not quite help me comprehend Tserang Dondrub's expression of the oneness of Amne Machen and pilgrims. In my view, the sacredness of Amne Machen is a given. What needs more insightful elucidation is the deep, "soulful" emotionality that my Tibetan colleagues expressed with each other toward the mountain and the mountain deity.

I find that the works of scholars of Tibetan folklore studies, such as Danqu, Jempal Gyasto, and He Tianhui, are particularly illuminating about the psychic and emotional significance of soul mountains. Their studies present an understanding of a Tibetan archaic life science that continues to be found in contemporary rural Tibet. According to this understanding, the life-force of an organism is not confined within its body but is also present beyond the body. Danqu best explains what *bla* or soul is and how it operates. He begins with the phrase *bla-sog* (བླ་སྲོག) as the totality of a living being, which is the trinity of soul (བླ bla), life (སྲོག sog), and consciousness (རྣམ་ཤེས nam-zhes) (Danqu 2005). *Sog*, loosely translated as life, refers to the life force within the body, which sustains *nam-zhes* as the consciousness that affords the existential and psychological function of the organism. *Bla* (soul) is an inherent property of a living being; however, it freely moves in and out of the body. Furthermore, *bla* is capable of multiplying itself when necessary. Oftentimes it seeks *bla-gnas* (བླ་གནས) or soul-locations outside the body as its hiding places. What is noteworthy is that *bla-gnas* then refers not only to physical places such as mountains and lakes, but also to non-human species, such as toads, birds, and bears; thus, *bla-ri*, or soul mountain, is one of many kinds of soul-locations (Danqu 2005).

In Tibetan folklore, according to Akhu Shampa and Tserang Dondrub, Amne Machen is one of King Gesar's soul-locations; thus it is revered as his soul mountain. Besides Amne Machen, Tsongoring (མཚོ་སྔོ་རིང), Tsogyaring (མཚོ་སྐྱ་རིང), and Tsodrolring (མཚོ་སྒྲོལ་རིང) – the three largest lakes in Golok – are also his soul-locations; therefore, they are his soul lakes. Since he was the king of the Ling Kingdom, Amne Machen and the three lakes are also revered as the soul-locations of his kingdom and his people. In this regard, *bla* (soul) can be understood in both singular and plural terms as the soul of an individual or as the soul of a tribe or a nation. In the findings of Danqu and He Tianhui, *bla* becomes more powerful when it is outside one's body, for example, taking residence in a mountain, a lake, or an animal (Danqu 2005). Without bodily confinement it performs magic and miracles (He 1998, 130). The person becomes stronger and more prosperous when his *bla* is multiplied. In turn, physical places or animals in which his soul dwells become stronger. For instance, when a wild bull is chosen as the dwelling place of a human soul, it becomes more powerful than its peers; and when a tree becomes the soul-location of a tribe, it grows taller and more lush (He 1998, 131). However, in the meantime, *bla* residing in an external location are vulnerable and subject to attack from an enemy of the person or the tribe. In Jempal Gyatso's compilation of the King Gesar epic, soul-protection, soul-searching, and soul-destruction are the primary themes of the king's warfare with his enemies (Jempal Gyatso 2006). Whoever is able to destroy his opponent's soul-location, e.g. a wild bull, a spotted crow, or a fierce bear, wins the battle. In this sense, the person and his external soul-dwelling place are one and the same. Both prosper or perish together.

Tserang Dondrub's "soul talk" with Tenzin and me could be understood, from an instrumentalist perspective, as an expression of ongoing Tibetan nationalism where the stories of one's ancestral origin might be utilized as an instrument of nationalism; however, I see that Amne Machen's status as a soul mountain has deeper, more complex layers of meanings besides its potential as a nationalist instrument. Through *bla* (soul) narrated in Tserang Dondrub's conversation with us and discussed in scholarly works, I find that it is paramount that we do not reduce such "soulful talk" to talk of nationalism but recognize that the history of Tibetans needs to be seen as a history of place, gods, and humans, not just of humans.

In this regard I see the combined lifeworld of place, gods, and humans as a "rhizomic world" (Ingold 2000, 140) because their "roots," in the senses of mythology, history, and religion, are so entwined that the sphere of each intersects, overlaps, preconditions, and saturates the others; thus, this lifeworld is an embodiment of both the histories of gods and humans. Amne Machen, as a *bla-gnas* or soul-location, makes the human past present, the supernatural natural, and both realms of gods and humans sentient. Place transgresses time and sentient species with "a fundamental spiritual potency" (Ingold 2000, 54). Through the soul-locations Tserang Dondrub and his compatriots touch and are being touched by their ancestors and gods. Amne Machen, from a local perspective, is a living being who bridges the past and the present in psychic, spiritual, emotional, and haptic terms. This perspective naturally arises out of the place just as it concerns it.

6.4 "Bury them here…"

Amne Machen is ensouled with the souls of people and gods. The sense of oneness people feel with the mountain deity is sustained with rich mythological and ancestral memories in the region. While Tserang Dondrub, Tenzin and I were having the discussion of Amne Machen as a soul place, Akhu Shampa and Hwadan Tashi walked to a lone pole with a string of worn prayer flags hung on it. They beckoned to us.

We were not the only visitors to show affection to the glacier, which had offerings embedded within it. While invoking Avalokitesvara as the Bodhisattva of all Bodhisattvas and reciting OM MANI PADME HUM as the mantra of all mantras, Akhu Shampa and Hwadan Tashi buried a small collection of minerals and semi-precious stones, rare medicinal herbs, soil collected from Bodh Gaya, and pieces of cloth torn from their late masters' winter coats, all neatly enclosed in several cloth tubes, as offerings to Amne Machen.

Like the items I saw in the glacier, the offerings packed in the cloth tubes are called *ter* (གཏེར) or treasures. The lexical meaning of *ter* mostly refers to rare minerals or precious metals. Its use in Buddhism and the indigenous Tibetan Bon religion is often associated with *terma* (གཏེར་མ) and *terton* (གཏེར་སྟོན). The former means hidden religious treasures in the forms of texts, ritual objects, and intangible teachings, which are buried in the earth or stored in the "mind streams" (སེམས་རྒྱུད *sems rgyud*) of masters. The latter refers to visionaries who are able to discover the hidden treasures in the earth and the spiritual consciousness of their masters (Fremantle 2001, 17). These standard, encyclopedic explanations of *terma* and *terton* are often associated with a mystical, visionary Tibetan Buddhist discovery of spiritual treasures of the past. In the actual occurrence on Mt. Amne Machen, the hiding of a *terma* is not always an act for the preservation of a given lineage but is intended to strengthen the bond of people with their sacred places. It invests human affection and subjectivity in the land, to put it simply. Such a bond, in our pilgrimage case, monumentally reminds people of their homeland, animated with earthly gods and spirits, as a critical source of blessings and empowerments for their worldly wellbeing. In their mutual saturation, place is people, people are place, and place is the earthly gods who inextricably reside in the "mind streams" of people.

Before burying the cloth tubes Akhu Shampa said to Hwadan Tashi:

> The treasures [in the tubes] came from India, Nepal, Golok, the realm of Avalokitesvara, Mt. Wutai, Qinghai Lake, Bodhgaya in India, and other places empowered by buddhas and bodhisattvas. They hold three kinds of sand, three kinds of special offerings, offerings from over one hundred monasteries. They also contain treasures from Khenpo Jigme Phunt-

sok, the Honorable Pema Nangyal and Denpo Lama. This is a magical place to hide these Dharma treasures.

All three lamas mentioned by Akhu Shampa were renowned Dharma teachers and visionaries who played instrumental roles in Tibetan religious and cultural revitalizations in the last three decades. Regardless of the fact that they have since passed away, their legacies are remembered in the landscape of the region and in the mindscape of the people.

The body of the mountain is synonymous with the body of the mountain god. It holds the memories and mythologies of people, gods, and place. Besides being regarded as a soul-location, a Tenth-Stage Bodhisattva, and a warrior god, Amne Machen is popularly revered as a wealth god. While he continuously receives treasure-offerings from people, he displays his wealth in the form of medicinal herbs, forests, and precious minerals and metals. What is critical is that the mountain is animated with moving waters, meteorological elements, and a variety of birds and animals. The mountain is thus a life and a source of life itself, a concept that is difficult to accept for those who are trained to see the earth as inanimate material or as a depository of resources for extraction and consumption.

Taking the mining company as an example, it extracts what are deemed precious metals from the mountain without considering the mountain's ecological, cultural, religious, and emotional significances. Its relationship with it is manifested as a one-sided act of taking with the backing of a scientific reading of its geological structure and utilitarian value. The location of Dernee Mine is described plainly in the geological and meteorological survey literature of the mining company:

> The coordinates of the mine are eastern longitude 100 07′30″ and western latitude 34 23′30″. The Dernee Copper Mine is located on the southern slope of Mt. Dernee, part of Amne Machen mountain range. Its average altitude is between 3980 and 4600 meters. The relative hypsographical height is between 300 and 600 meters. The region belongs to the continental climate of the Tibetan plateau. The four seasons are not clear. The weather changes anomalously…Within the mining site animal husbandry is the primary livelihood of local people. It is an economically backward place. The mining project will bring employment and prosperity to the region (Dernee Mine Co. 2007).

Unlike the mining company, local Tibetans' reverence of Amne Machen as a wealth god rather affirms the mountain as a site of sentient flourishing and existing worldly prosperity in the sense of fertility and health as discussed earlier. Thus, Amne Machen as a wealth god in the local folkways does not imply that the mountain should be mined or plundered. The reciprocity between humans and the god is materialized through the mountain as the body of the god. The imperative embedded in such reciprocity is the felt power of the god, which compels humans to offer gifts first before they receive his blessings and empowerment. The mountain god is both a recipient and a giver. Humans and the god are interlocked in a contracted gift exchange in which, if I describe it in Marcel Mauss' words, "...this represents an intermingling. Souls are mixed with things; things with souls. Lives are mingled together, and this is how, among persons and things so intermingled, each emerges from their own sphere and mixes together. This is precisely what contract and exchange are" (Mauss 1990, 20). In the case of Amne Machen, it is both a life (a sentient god) and a thing (a mountain range). What humans give to him are things whereas what the sentient god offers back to humans is an immaterial flow of spiritual solace, commemoration of their past, and blessings for their continuity. In local folkways, what is seen as part of Amne Machen, e.g. animals and plants, is not meant to be taken for humans' excessive utilitarian purposes.

When we walked along streams and rivers in the mountain we often saw large Himalaya marmots (*Marmota himalayana*) locally known as *phyiba* (འཕྱི་བ). They are adorably chubby with golden fur and a slow gait that causes them to be the easy targets of poachers. Tenzin told us a story of how *phyiba*, known in ancient times as a fierce beast, entered a contract of peace with humans:

> This was a story my mother told me when I was a young boy. A long time ago, *phyiba* and humans started a horrifying war with each other. At that time the size of *phyiba* was quite large, like a black bear. Humans slaughtered many *phyiba*; likewise *phyiba* also killed an equal number of humans. The fight continued, it seemed, endlessly. After both sides had lost an unbearable number of lives, they decided to sit down together and negotiate. Both sides took a vow of no more killing. The proof of the vow is found in the armpits of humans and *phyiba*. Our armpits have hair while *phyiba*'s armpits do not because at the time of their taking the vow, both sides traded each other's armpits to reinforce the vow for later generations. So humans' hairless armpits went to *phyiba* while *phyiba*'s hairy armpits came to humans. *Phyiba* have kept their ancient vows and as a result of not fighting they became smaller and smaller until they reached the current size. Humans, however, have not kept their vow. We still see people kill *phyiba*. The elders in my family, though, become angry when they hear about people killing *phyiba* and they caution us that killing *phyiba* is an evil act of betrayal.

From Tenzin's family story I learned that, in the ancient past, Tibetans mostly relied on hunting for the continuity of their lives and expanding their territories. Humans were not alone in the ecosphere but one of many species. Setting environmental ethics or drawing boundaries between species has never been a one-sided decision from the ancient times of the giant *phyiba* to the present world. Because of actual or foreseeable loss, we often set limits on what we take from the earth, e.g. animals, metals, and fossil fuel. Whether manifested in an unbalanced inter-species relationship or humans' excessive extraction of resources from the Earth, it is the environment that pressures us to refrain from destructive acts because it eventually leads destruction to ourselves.

My purpose in recounting Akhu Shampa's treasure offering to Amne Machen and Tenzin's family story about *phyiba* is to reject the idea that Tibetans are "instinctual environmentalists" (Ma 2007a, 162) but to demonstrate the native environmental consciousness of Tibetans has adapted its own version of mythological and historical lessons on how to sustain an equilibrium with other species and how to humanize natural environments with minimum human intrusion. Both Buddhist ethics and pre-Buddhist honoring of one's tribal ancestors are at the root of the environmental ethics, eco-religiosity, and eco-aesthetics of native Tibetans. From both Akhu Shampa's and Tenzin's accounts I then see the interplay and inter-bonding of the earth, gods, and humans are a set of eco-religious ethics, which is not often known to non-Tibetans. Thus, it is too often that the magnificence of Tibetan landscape is only appreciated in a conventional aesthetic distance as if it were a piece of literary work or a painting. What is embedded in the landscape then remains as a blind spot.

That evening I continued my conversation with Tenzin, hoping he would shed more light on the puzzle on my mind about the currently polarized images of Tibet – the idealized versus the denigrated, the imagined versus the experienced, and the outsider's view versus the insider's view. Tenzin, first of all, expressed his viewpoint that the idea of the beautiful in both philosophical and aesthetic senses are universal but he concurred with me about the split image of Tibet among scholars and the global public:

> It is impossible that what non-Tibetans see as beautiful is not seen as beautiful among Tibetans. The main difference probably lies in the fact that having grown up here with the grass, flowers, and white clouds, we recognize everything here has soul including mountains, water, and trees. Tibet is beautiful because it has a soul inside. At my university [in Beijing] I attended many lectures about Tibet. Scholars mostly hold one of two extreme perspectives. One side stigmatizes Tibet so that traditional Tibetan society is looked upon as a kind of horrible place where Tibetans lived as slaves. The other side holds that Tibet is the last pureland on earth making it a pilgrimage destination or a dream-place. Both perspectives are not realistic; however, what the latter says about the high sky, pure water, and beautiful landscape does reflect how Tibetans preserve this piece of the earth. It is actually beneficial. Besides this point I don't know what else I can say.

I empathize with what Tenzin expresses and suggest that it is imperative to recognize that most non-Tibetans' perceptions are culturally trained and reinforced by the encounter with and internalization of images and literary portrayals of

Tibet before they even set foot there. It usually takes a literal rite of territorial passage for the non-Tibetan to recognize such trained perceptions in themselves.

6.5 "Eco-aesthetics of Touching and Being Touched"

Sitting with everyone around a fire on an early evening I jotted down a phrase in my journal, "Eco-aesthetics of touching and being touched." Now sitting in my home in Göttingen, I recall that I meant to write, "Touching and being touched as eco-aesthetics."

Whatever the word order in the two phrases, I see an eco-aesthetic act as a bodily act that environmentally and psychically involves reciprocal touches between the body and the landscape, and between the mind and the potency of the landscape manifested not only in its height, immensity, topography, and meteorological fluxes, but also in embodied religious practices, implaced cultural memories, and human emotionality entwined with them. As delineated in the introductory chapter, eco-aesthetics in this context can be understood as what Tilley calls "synaesthesia" or "the fusion of the senses" (Tilley 2004, 3) except that I do not limit the senses to the bodily senses but include one's culturally-trained internal senses and sensibility, and subsequent perceptual changes occurring along with the moving dyad of the body and the mind in the environing landscape. Aesthetics, then, does not neatly pertain to the intellectual judgments of beauty, taste, order, balance, variety, and unity that are familiar to art critics and consumers; instead, one's aesthetic judgment evolves and even undergoes sudden estrangement, breakup, or fragmentation, as the energy of the landscape invades one's body through breathing, sound, vision, and bodily contact with the surface and the atmosphere of the Earth. I could not agree more with what Mark Paterson says, "...through touch, the world is with us. It is through haptic experience that we feel engaged in the world, and through affect that the world and its objects touch us" (Paterson 2007, 101). In actually experiencing the engagement of the world and ourselves, I find that the reciprocal touches taking place between the world and humans, as in the case of Amne Machen, are not always smooth and of equal exchange between people and the landscape. The physical landscape of Amne Machen, in many ways, dictates the pilgrim's emotional state, aesthetic perception and other internal senses.

That evening I did not write beyond my first paragraph as we had to attend to Zhitan, Moshi, and Pangzi (names changed), three of our crew members from Beijing. Zhitan had worked as a cameraman on my previous projects even though his training at Beijing Film Academy was in directing. He had been to Qinghai before on a few student projects but only to low altitude areas. Zhitan recommended his classmates Moshi and Pangzi to participate as an additional cameraman and assistant. All three of them showed excitement before we set out from Beijing: Tibet sounded energizing to them.

After four days at Amne Machen, they still had not acclimated and their high altitude sickness was progressing. Our pilgrimage obviously was not an orderly traditional one conforming to local prescriptions as shown in Katie Buffetrille's circumambulation of Amne Machen some years previous (Buffetrille 1997). The filming part of our pilgrimage added more complexity to our daily routines with its physically demanding requirements for those of us handling equipment and finding ways to maximize the optimal performance of our camera. When unexpected circumstances occurred, the ideal clockwise circumambulation of the mountain or relatively uniform speed of our daily advancement was disrupted. On this particular evening Akhu Shampa phoned his friend, Gyalpe, a young doctor working at the clinic in Snow Mountain Township (གངས་ལྗོངས་ཡུལ་ཚོ། *gangjong yeltso*), to prepare for receiving the three patients the next day. This meant that we had to rush downhill and skip pre-mapped pilgrimage sites.

The newly built clinic was spacious and clean, looking more like a small hospital than a clinic with an inpatient facility and an emergency staff of three doctors and student interns from Xining available twenty-four hours a day. Zhitan, Moshi, and Pangzi were put in the same room, the clinic's first inpatients since its opening two weeks previous. The room still smelled of fresh paint. Gyalpe, Akhu Shampa's friend, came in with two student interns, looking like a character in a western movie with a shoulder holster carrying a stethoscope and other medical paraphernalia. After checking his three new patients' hearts with his stethoscope, he told me that they appeared to be suffering more from low blood sugar than altitude sickness. The interns soon started them on intravenous fluids. Meanwhile, Gyalpe asked me if I could find Chinese food for the patients, implying that they had not eaten enough because they weren't used to Tibetan food.

Snow Mountain Township has four restaurants and two convenience stores, all on the same street. The owners of three of the restaurants were out of town visiting relatives. The remaining restaurant was only serving lunch as the chef wanted to spend time with his newborn baby. By now, however, it was close to five in the afternoon. The convenience stores were our last resort. After we bought a kilo of apples, canned meat, and crackers we rushed back to the clinic. Pangzi had not improved and was still drowsy, but Zhitan and Moshi looked stable after the intravenous fluids. Pangzi ate only one bite of an apple. Zhitan and Moshi each ate an apple but did not touch the canned meat. Moshi suddenly said to Zhitan in a blaming tone, "Why didn't you buy warm food? What an awful place!" Zhitan did not know what to say but turned to me. Obviously

Moshi was upset with the food situation. I could not think of any better way to comfort them but explained to them about the restaurants we had just visited. In the meantime I surprised myself by making an unrealistic promise, "Hang in there! If no restaurants are open tomorrow morning, we'll cook for you."

By now I regretted having joked with Moshi at Jomo Yangra, the cave meditation site. At the time he seemed acclimated and standing next to me while taking a break, he asked me what altitude we were at. I teased, "It's close to the altitude of the Everest base camp." "How high is it then?" he pressed on. I replied, "Five thousand meters!" As soon as he heard this he excused himself. When he had not returned forty minutes later, I went ahead to operate the camera by myself. Then I found Zhitan and Pangzi were missing, too. That evening three of them were quiet and began to complain about having headaches and lacking strength. Pangzi looked pale and restless. Obviously altitude sickness is not contagious but it seemed that the psychological implications might have been.

As I was leaving the clinic with the Tibetan crew members, Gyalpe told us to try our luck with the kitchen in the township government building next door. The kitchen was wide open when we walked in. Two cooks had just made steamed buns and a huge pot of noodle soup but none of the food was available for us, as the supervising cook told us the kitchen was contracted out to a geological survey team. Unable to obtain warm food we at least found a room for Akhu Shampa and Hwadan Tashi who got a thermos of hot water for mixing their *tsampa*; the rest of us went to try our luck elsewhere.

Thus, our pilgrimage trip became a search for hot Chinese food. We began our door-to-door search in town. Amazingly, we got somewhat lucky. A family on a side street had recently closed a restaurant business attached to their residence. The owner was willing to loan us her kitchen and even told us to use up a sack of potatoes by the stove. The kitchen was actually a large Tibetan-style bedroom with the stove in the middle of the room surrounded by beds on three sides. The warm, cozy place was large enough to accommodate six of us, however, because it was late, the convenience stores were all closed. With no ingredients to make Chinese food Zhitan, Moshi, and Pangzi would have to wait until the next day. The rest of us were so exhausted that we went almost immediately to bed.

Based on my experience with other Han Chinese pilgrims and travelers in Tibet I figured it would take up to a week or so for the three to become acclimated. I also hoped that their being young and healthy would assist. The next morning, around seven-thirty, I went out to see if the nearest convenience store was open, but I was too early so I walked to the clinic to check how Zhitan, Moshi, and Pangzi were doing.

As soon as I walked into the clinic, Gyalpe said me, "Your *rdol* left a mess in our driveway. We just cleaned it up." When I asked the meaning of *rdol* (རྡོལ), he told me that it refers to the third generation cross between yaks and cattle, but is used as a metaphor for human weaklings. I still did not understand what Gyalpe meant so I asked an intern who told me that Gyalpe's "*rdol*" referred to Pangzi because in his weakened and confused state he had defecated in the driveway. It upset Gyalpe so much that he used the word *rdol* to indicate his assessment of Pangzi's un-fitness for travel in a high altitude area. Gyalpe overheard my conversation with his intern and said to me, "Don't mind what I said. These people always say how clean they are and how dirty we are." I felt very embarrassed and apologized on Pangzi's behalf though I also appreciated Gyalpe's honesty and straightforwardness.

Obviously the altitude sickness of Zhitan, Moshi, and Pangzi disrupted our pilgrimage and filming schedules but I had to accept it as an unexpected event just like the changing weather up in the mountains. The sublime embodied in the powerful landscape of Amne Machen is not an intellectual idea springing purely out from the human. Its greatness means not merely the size, the immensity, and the visual magnificence but also the meteorological forces and environmental conditions of Amne Machen, which equally dictate the perceptions and the physical states of the person enveloped in them. The landscape is not merely the solid ground on which we stand but also dominates us entirely with its atmospheric mediums such as air and water, the meteorological commotions and the violence that clashes with the human body through these mediums. The world thus touches us, invades us, and transforms us. In this regard, both the world and the human are carnal beings whose relation is "that of flesh to flesh" and "involves a dehiscence, an opening of my body to things, a reversible relationship between touching and being touched, myself and other, the effect of myself on things and those things on me" (Tilley 2004, 18, 30). However, as seen in this case, such relation does not always manifest itself in mutual affinity.

In the physical sense alone, besides affectionate memories and positive aesthetics, the touches of Amne Machen also produced negative physical conditions among our group, as shown in the experience of the three young filmmakers. Their physical reaction to the Amne Machen pilgrimage shows that when the world touches us, it goes deeper than the skin. Its cutaneous contact with our skin and through the pressure on our walking feet is only surficial. Layer by layer the world touches the skin, sinks into flesh, and finally invades the inner world of the body. In this process of the world's physical touch, the communication between us and Amne Machen involved what Paterson calls "fluid viscerality" (Paterson 2007, 113): plasma, lymph, mucus, pus, and other bodily fluids that define the (dys)functionality of the body and produce visceral sensations and feelings. Pangzi's discharge in the driveway of the clinic was a visceral reaction to the touches of Amne Machen. In the medical sense his body failed the environmental rite of passage of Amne Machen; however, place-human communication in this case did not stop at the physical level but evolved into a discourse of differences and identity, all in the emotionally touching manner. Gyalpe's emotional reaction to Pangzi's excruciating bodily experience went beyond his medical profession to a matter of purity and pollution or of self and other. Although Amne Machen has its own ageless geological identity, it nevertheless has a Tibetan identity.

Finally, a warm meal was cooked two hours later: fried potatoes with salt and white pepper, and scrambled eggs with tomatoes. We then rushed to the clinic with the food in pots. Moshi and Zhitan were up. Moshi still had the same temper as the day before when he spoke to us, "Where were you? We're hungry..." Pangzi was still not in good shape. Gyalpe recommended that they be sent home as soon as possible. He emphasized that the best cure for altitude sickness is to move the patient to a lower altitude location. It was indeed the best cure. Two days later, a text message came from Zhitan telling me they were enjoying noodle soup in a restaurant in Xining. Obviously their bodily comfort was found in the low altitude environment. However, I expected that they would have a delayed realization of their aesthetic and even spiritual appreciation of Tibetan landscape after resuming their routines in Beijing, as I had found in other cases of Han Chinese who felt empowerment from Tibet after returning to their home regions (Smyer Yu 2011, 81). To know for sure, I would have to wait and see.

Chapter Seven Drifting in the Mirages of the Tibetan Landscape

While completing the rough-cut of the documentary, *Ensouling the Mountain*, in early autumn 2012, I met up with Moshi and Pangzi in Beijing. Unlike when I had seen them in the mountains a few months prior, both now appeared healthy and spirited. Pangzi had recently returned from shooting a commercial for an instant noodle company in Shangrila, Yunnan, where he said he had no altitude reaction. Talking to him again, I recalled that what I enjoyed most while working with him was his enthusiastic interaction with host families at the foothills of Amne Machen. He often reciprocated with his singing of folk songs from his home province when Tibetan hosts sang. I wished he had hung on for a few more days when we were in the mountains. Moshi told me that since retreating from Amne Machen, he had been resting in Beijing. He regretted that he had been cranky about the food situation at the clinic and for the rest of the meeting Pangzi and I heard about his feelings after being in the mountains and the existential crossroad he was now facing.

Moshi confided to us that it was not the unavailability of warm Chinese food but a momentary existential breakdown that contributed to his sensitivity with the pilgrimage and the film crew. His professional direction was caught between directing and photography, yet after graduating from Beijing Film Academy with a degree in directing he had not yet laid his hands on a directing project. Thus far it was his skill in photography that had sustained his livelihood though he was really passionate about directing fiction films. In the mountains he found he was not used to taking orders and cues from me and my former Tibetan students and, in the meantime, the filming itself was physically and mentally too demanding in the midst of the unpredictably changing weather, terrain, and schedule. He admitted, "I was unable to synchronize my mood with our team as Tibet was becoming to me a harsh, unintelligible place, not romantic at all like the books I had read..." Moshi is well read in travel writings and fictions about Tibet. I recollect the book titles he mentioned having read: *The Soul is Like the Wind* (Ma 2007); *A Vagabond in Tibet* (Chai 2009a), *The Tibet Code* (He 2009), *Tibet the Dreamland* (Liu 2009), and *The Tibetan Book of Love* (Zhen Sheng 2010). These authors, after traveling or living in Tibet, tend to present Tibet as a hiding place, a far-off utopia and intimate shelter in which to narrate their life stories so the riddles, contradictions, frustrations and pains in life could naturally metamorphose into beauty, harmony, peace, and a desired romance in the immensity of the Tibetan earth and sky. Tibet was simultaneously a familiar and yet a strange place to Moshi. In my geo-anthropological terms the experienced landscape of Amne Machen shattered his preconceived mindscape of Tibet.

In this chapter, were I to follow in the footsteps of academic trends, I would be tempted to critique the "imagined Tibet" found in China that is similar to its Western counterpart in terms of self-indulgence, Orientalism, and consumption of Tibetan culture. For the time being, however, I'll refrain, finding it too easy to point a finger at the imaginer, whether individual or collective, who complicates public representations of Tibet and Tibetans, whether the imaginer is from China or other parts of the world. Critiques of imagined Tibet in both Western and Chinese scholarly discourses seem to find satisfaction by critiquing the level of representation and the dichotomized power dynamic of the dominant and the dominated, as though discerning a representation of Tibet as Orientalist, fantastic, or commercial would put a stopper on the popular imagination and fantasizing. In fact, these critiques are drowned by recurrent and growing waves of popular fascination with Tibet, within China and beyond. The critiques themselves are re-imagined and re-appropriated for social and political uses, yet Tibet stands, its uniqueness portrayed in photos, films, literary narratives, and Dharma events.

Therefore I propose a post-Orientalist reading of the changing imaginaries of Tibet in the case of contemporary China. By "post-Orientalist" I mean to bracket the mutual siege of East vs. West in general, and of Tibet vs. the West and of Tibet vs. China in particular as found in the texts of Edward Said (1979), Donald Lopez (1998), Peter Bishop (1993), Dibyesh Anand (2008), Weirong Shen (2010), Hui Wang (2011), to name a few. Orientalism, a historical consciousness concerning power and representation, also manifests a few cultural universals across different human societies: strengthening self-identity by generalizing others, in-group solidarity built upon exoticizing others, and renewal of self through the perceived empowerment from an Other in a distant land. In the twenty-first century, as these cultural universals continue to be personalized in behaviors and thought-patterns of individuals it is increasingly difficult to discern who is the Orientalist and who is Orientalized. One person could be both. Everything is going in circles: Westerners Orientalize Chinese who Orientalize Tibetans; Westerners Orientalize Indians who Orientalize Tibetans; and in turn Chinese, Indians and Tibetans Orientalize themselves, when it suits them to fit into the Orientalized images of China, India, and Tibet. This is not a chicken-and-egg puzzle but is an observable phenomenon; Tibet as a place moves in and out of the mindscapes of both the Orientalizing and the Orientalized. In this case Orientalization is then synonymous with self-affirmation, otherization, exoticization, representation, invention, imagination, fantasization, internalization of the other, and externalization of the self. As elaborated in the introductory chapter, in the case of Tibet, most of these mental activities and their social materiality are place-induced, the result of someone's travel or living in Tibet manifest in such imagination-inducing works as fictional accounts, travel writings, poetry, movies, etc.

With this said I would like to reiterate: place is antecedent to all sentient affairs on earth. It is present in memories, oral narratives, creative writings, and artworks, and on movie screens. It is also internalized in wishful thinking, dreams, hopes, and visions. The materiality and the spirituality of place are entangled and enmeshed with each other. Tibet is not an exception regarding the connectivity and entwinement of landscape and mindscape, but an example – and as such I present issues of how Tibet is simultaneously experienced as a concrete place and conceived in the mindscape of Tibetophiles in China. The social materiality of the latter in the form of literature, art, and commercials stimulates the potential for more travelers to Tibet and creates a recognizable collective desire that can be harnessed, frustrated, and then marketed in the commercial realms of tourism, entertainment, and arts, all in the name of Tibet. Tibet is a brand in China. It is both branding a particular mindscape with utopian attributes and branded as a tourist commodity.

In this chapter, I begin with my field experiences with American faculty members and students in Tibetan regions as indicators of the transnational and transpersonal nature of the commonly felt eco-aesthetic and eco-spiritual qualities of the Tibetan landscape which leaves a long-lasting mark in the mindscapes of visitors. I then engage in a critical reading of contemporary Tibetophiles' writings in China that simultaneously express the potency of Tibet in imaginative, poetic, and personalized terms, and fashion out an expanding mindscape of Tibet as a collective vessel animated with longing, desire, escape, and paradisiacal solace.

7.1 Tibet, branding a mindscape of utopia

7.1.1 An American experience

In summer 2010, I led a travel seminar for U.S. scholars to Tibet with a theme of religion, ecology, and identity. None of the participating scholars were Tibet specialists; they had backgrounds in China studies, environmental studies, religious studies, and comparative literature. The purpose of the seminar was to have contemporary Tibet as a field case for curriculum development. All thematic, academic lectures and discussions were completed in Beijing before commencing travel to Tibet Autonomous Region. Tibet, in the seminar room, was a discursive subject matter addressed in individual lectures on such topics as Bonpo, the tradition of reincarnate lamas in Tibetan Buddhist history, mountain culture and its ecological implications, Sino-Tibetan Buddhist interactions, and imagined Tibet, among others. Intellectually, Tibet appeared graspable with these informative lectures and discussions: Tibet as a Buddhist nation, a place being modernized, and a place being imagined out of proportion in geopolitical and popular religious realms. In the meantime participants were anxious to set out to Tibet. In TAR, Tibet continued to be a subject of discussion and debate during breaks and in cafes and restaurants, but the actual landscape and monumental cultural sites drew many of the seminar participants into an emotional and poetic state of mind. While marveling at the ancient architecture of Lhasa and the visually striking Tibetan Buddhist motifs, everyone spent extra time at places where the natural landscape and human cultural elements were entwined, such as Yumbu Lhakang, Samye Monastery, and Drul Yelpa Caves.

At Drul Yelpa Caves, for instance, we initially scheduled a two-hour visit. In reality, we spent over four and an half hours there. The group walked uphill, visiting individual meditation caves, shrines, and the main Dharma hall together before eventually dispersing into solo explorations and small groups with common interests. The vista points outside individual caves, the terraced shrines and the main Dharma hall were the first places to captivate participants' attention. The wide valley from which we had come was spectacularly imposing under the white clouds. The horizon was distant and yet intimately experienced by the senses from the fresh air mixed with the scent of juniper incense and the green, colorful rolling surface of the earth extending from where we stood to the edge of our vision. A comparative literature scholar remarked, "My eyes, vision, and the sight are one and the same." Standing next to her, I felt mesmerized, too. The landscape was not merely visually touching and unified with the faculty of vision but was fully enveloping and invading each of us. To me, it was an experience of turning inside out and outside in, as if my body was becoming the body of the landscape itself and vice versa.

We further delayed our schedule when a senior monk invited us into a large meditation cave. It was the place that held us the longest, with most of the group taking the opportunity to try out Tibetan Buddhist style meditation. Noticing that many of us settled in like advanced meditators sitting on our cushions, he brought wool robes to cover our backs against the cold cave air. Donning the maroon wool robes had the result of unifying the meditative mood. Besides the faint cooing of a lone wild dove outside the cave, the only sound in the silence of the cave was everyone's calm breathing. The religious backgrounds of these "advanced meditators" were agnostic, Baha'i, Buddhist, Christian, Confucianist, Muslim, and Taoist. They were not Western Dharma bums but were seriously playful when trying out a Tibetan mode of experiencing one's inner world in a cave, the ultimate inner space of the earth. Tibet was no longer a discursive topic only but personalized in each of us, just as we meditated within it.

The travel seminar program was based on a field course I had taught about religion and ecology in contemporary China with a theme of tourist consumption of native landscapes in Southwest China and Tibetan regions. The collectively euphoric moments experienced by the faculty members were akin to those experienced by my American students. In the field, whether in Yunnan or Qinghai, American students were paired up with local students. In Yunnan our field sites were Lijiang and Shangrila. Qinghai and a few tourist sites in TAR were our Tibetan sites. My American students' experiences in the townships of Suhe, a small town in Lijiang area, and Shangrila were similar in the sense that both places have almost identical urban landscape design and tourist infrastructure, e.g. cafes, bars, and teahouses with ethnic motifs. Their resemblance is expressed in the discernible architectural flavors and interior decorations, all of which are geared toward showcasing local authentic traditional cultures in fine masonry, carpentry, craftsmanship, and folk arts. Both places are compact and tourist-friendly, and yet send out a potent visual and haptic sense of time lag to visitors, as if they have traveled back in time to discover a place of a distant past undisturbed by the intrusions of the modern world.

In modern China tradition is often perceived in the past tense regardless of its coevalness with the contemporary world. In the tourism industry human talents are mobilized to utilize visual and haptic effects to temporalize a life style or a cultural motif as something from the past but they are spatialized in a well-crafted place that stimulates the senses and imaginative faculty of the visitor.

In Shangrila, paired up with local students, my American students explored the small but enchanting cityscape which receives over six million tourists annually (Li and Guo 2011). What they soon found out about this bustling township is that most houses along the streets are not residential quarters but shops, cafes, teahouses, restaurants, and art galleries, most of which are decorated with Tibetan prayer flags or other cultural symbols. The names of these businesses often contain words like "Tara," "Tantra," "Khampa," "Makyi Ama," "King Gesar," and "Snowland." Their owners vary from Khampas and Amdowas and Naxi to Han Chinese, Nepali, Indians, and Europeans. Interspersed among the Tibetan-looking businesses, one can find Western restaurants like Helen's Pizza Ristorante and Socialist Bar. The cityscape of Shangrila is undoubtedly a recent creation for tourist consumption, a reconstructed "tradition" with a sense of adventure contained within an aesthetically pleasing and physically comfortable place. In comparison, those students who went to Qinghai yielded a different experience of Tibet. We mostly stayed in the homes of Tibetans in villages where there were no bars and teahouses. The absence of city lights and a bustling consumer environment presented us no other choice but to interact with our Tibetan host families. Our daily activities included herding goats up to the mountains in early mornings, helping village doctors dry and grind medicinal herbs, stacking up hay for winter's fuel, soaking ourselves in hot springs with local Tibetans, taking lessons from elders about the geomancy of their villages and local sacred sites, hiking on goat trails up to surrounding mountains, and sitting around the kitchen fire at night. Culture shock and physical discomfort also accompanied many of my students who experienced gendered divisions of labor and differing social spaces for women and men, absence of shower facilities, and repetitive foods and drinks, e.g. noodle soups, salted black tea, and sheep meat. Taking a drive to a hotel in the nearest town for showers and laundry was often considered a "luxury trip" for those who needed a break from the lifestyle of their host families. The most memorable parts of my students' experiences in Qinghai were their felt intimacy with local people, livestock, and landscape. One of my students wrote in her ethnographic assignment:

> Milking yaks is women's work, while slaughtering the yaks is the job of men. The yaks did not take kindly to the group of gawking Americans, and were skittish as we approached them. As the one female of the group, I was the one expected to do the milking. I crouched down and watched as a woman milked, though the yak's long tangled hair obscured her hands, so I couldn't see how she was actually milking. When she pulled the bucket out from below the yak I was expecting there to be much more milk than what I saw. I was impressed by how much effort it took for her to produce such a small quantity of milk. Suddenly the bounty of yak dairy products displayed on our table came to represent a lot of time and effort spent…After dinner it continued to snow, so Akhu Nima performed a ritual to ask the local deities for good weather. I had never witnessed any kind of Buddhist ritual or heard chanting before, so the experience was very new to me. In the middle of the night I woke up to go outside, and was astonished by what I saw. Since we'd arrived it had been snowing, so I was unaware of our surroundings, but now the snowstorm had passed, the moon had already set, and the stars were so bright that I could see in extraordinary detail the bent, snow-laden grass within the courtyard, and the illuminated hills beyond the village. The stars themselves were unbelievably bright, and more numerous than I had ever imagined. The beauty of the night sky left me speechless. The scene was so gorgeous it felt surreal, particularly with the haunting howls of faraway dogs… (Stone 2008).

My recollection of my students' field experiences in Qinghai is not meant to make an arbitrary statement that Tibetan villages in Qinghai present a more organic Tibet than their counterpart in Yunnan. I admit that a part of my subjective engagement with Tibet is concerned with the idea of authenticity of what I experience, therefore I could imaginatively entertain the idea of an authentic Tibet; however, as a social scientist, it just does not work with the plain facts of the recent history of Tibet which has and continues to undergo China's modernization in both ideological and physical senses. Tibetan society no longer adheres to the past pattern prior to the introduction of China's socialist system in the middle of the last century. My students' experiences in Yunnan and Qinghai are both authentic in their own ways.

On the Qinghai side, the authentic experience refers to the students' direct living experiences with their host families, gender dynamics, culture shock, and communal intimacy. On the Yunnan side, it means the tourism-mediated experience of Tibet. In the township of Shangrila this "mediated Tibet" entered the minds of my students when they were sipping hot tea, drinking noodle soup, or walking on streets adorned with signs and symbols of traditional Tibet comprised of mostly Buddhist elements and motifs. Comparatively speaking, natural landscapes, especially those considered as scenic sites, are being fenced in as geological parks or natural reserves more rapidly in Shangrila than in Qinghai. However, regardless of these two differing authenticities, both the images and physical presence of Tibet impresses and even brands itself indelibly on the minds of its visitors as a stunning, luminous place of simplicity. I re-emphasize such an appearance of Tibet as the optical, environmental, and eco-spiritual phenomenon I attempt to articulate thus far by evoking my students' experiences. It is not exclusively a Western experience shown in my American students' experiences, but is transnationally and transpersonally found also in experiences of Chinese travelers.

7.1.2 A Chinese experience

It is worthwhile to dwell on the case of Shangrila a bit more in terms of how Chinese Tibetophiliac scholars' experiences promote Tibet as a paradise on earth in China. The success story of the tourist development in Yunnan's Shangrila could be equated with the success of marketing Zhongdian as Shangrila, the name invented by James Hilton in his bestseller fiction *Lost Horizon* (1933). The name change process began with the tourist industry and soon involved Zhongdian County and Yunnan provincial governments. Finally the State Council officially approved the new metamorphosis of Zhongdian into Shangrila (Luo 2002, 19) and since that time tourism has changed all aspects of this small township. In this process it seems indisputable that human imagination is materialized in a concrete place.

It could be well said that Hilton posthumously brings economic prosperity to Shangrila, his imaginative creation now part of the local economic miracle. Naturally, his *Lost Horizon* is once again a popular read among Tibetophiles in China. My American students purchased the book as a reference for their writing projects and it is readily found in bookstores and souvenir shops in Shangrila. The English version is reprinted and distributed by Yunnan People's Publishing House. Next to the English version, I noticed four Chinese versions translated by Luo Cheng (1999), Hu Rui and Zhang Ying (2006), Bai Yixin and Zhao Jinqiu (2007), and Zhang Tao (2011). Bai Yixin and Zhao Jinqiu's version published by Yunnan University Press interested me the most, with its pictorial additions of local scenery, architecture, and art. Landscape photos, portraits of unknown Tibetans, and travel route illustrations are inlaid together with the text of the translation, combining Hilton's fiction with a pictorial guide book, giving the impression that the translators or the publisher intentionally conflate the fictionality of Hilton's Shangrila with the reality of the local geography. In 2011, when I was flipping through the colorful pages at the bookstore, I asked the young salesperson, "Among the four Chinese versions which one is sold most?" The answer was, "This one!" – she pointed at the version in my hands. On the way back to Beijing that summer, I saw this translation again displayed visibly in the bookstores at the airports of Shangrila and Kunming.

What interests me about this Chinese version of Hilton's fiction is not its pretentiously colorful page layout that has no direct correlation with the fiction's storyline, but its introduction by Li Xu, a senior researcher at Yunnan Provincial Academy of Social Sciences and the author of *Portraying Tibet: the Distant Horizon* (1999) and *Guests of Tibet* (2000). Li titles his introduction as "The Not-Yet Disappeared Horizon," an obvious reference to Hilton's "Lost Horizon" in which the fictitious Shangrila is a lost but rediscovered paradise on earth. While he reminds readers that Hilton's Shangrila is a fiction, Li establishes a common ground with Hilton by narrating his own story of the past eighteen years of wandering through the mountains, forests, and human communities in Shangrila as a concrete place. He writes:

> This is where the difference lies between the British writer James Hilton and me. Hilton relied only on the experiences of a few explorers and missionaries to build up "Shangrila" in his fiction. This world-famous writer had never set foot on this magic piece of the earth. After careful reading of his famous fiction, I have finally found the fundamental common ground between us. We are both idealists seeking perfection. Both of us love and celebrate peace in life. The difference between us is: Hilton deposits his life and social ideals into his fictitiously constructed Shangrila whereas I set my soul and ideals, my feet and eyes concretely on the immense land of this region (Li 2007, 3).

Shangrila is apparently Li's home away from home. He describes it to his readers with a flood of poetic phrases eulogizing the unique landscape of the Shangrila region – "exceptionally charismatic," "soulful intoxication," "supernatural tranquility," "hearty delights," "profoundly affecting," and "wildly peaceful" (Li

2007, 3–5). His succumbing to the enchantment of Shangrila is visibly topophilic; he finds its landscape animated with supernatural powers of nature and thus it speaks to him with an irresistible sense of religiosity. Li narrates such a state of his mind in other passages:

> That is a place that suddenly kindles one's religious feelings and floods one's mind with all kinds of wonder and imagination. In that place one is immersed in a kind of supernatural calm in which one hears one's heartbeat, breath, and warm blood rushing inside the body…Boundless plains sit between snow mountains. As they open up to my eyes, their horizons expand further and further. The end of my vision is still filled with snow mountains. Above the mountains is the blue sky. The waist of the blue sky is wrapped with white clouds. Streams flowing over the plains carve out lines of the landscape moving with the waves of the wind. On a mid-summer day when yellow, purple, white, and all other colorful flowers bloom, a carpet of flowers adorns the earth as if all gems were inlaid in it. The fragrance of the flowers intoxicates one's senses. Walking through the plains is like walking into the dreamworlds of little girls in fairytales (Li 2007, 4–5).

Reading between the lines I see how the physical landscape of the mountains and the plains conjoins Li's mindscape and engages it in a poetic style. In the midst of clouds, wind, water, earth, flowers, and colors, the landscape's horizon and his mindscape seem to move in unison. They are woven together with Li's sense-scapes. Thus landscape enters mindscape, and vice versa. Shangrila brands Li's mindscape of Tibet as "a utopia" (2007, 2) causing him to profess the same sentiment as other Chinese Tibetophiles.

In such writings, linear logic – that Tibet is imagined, marketed, and consumed – does not fully explain the heightened fascination of tourists, backpackers, artists, and writers toward Tibet. To reiterate what I have attempted to establish thus far, Tibet is, to start with, a power place. Commercial manipulations and fantastical projections of Tibet are preconditioned upon its geological, environmental, cultural, and eco-spiritual potency.

7.2 Tibet, branded as a dreamworld

In contemporary Tibetan studies in the West, Åshild Kolås' *Tourism and Tibetan Culture in Transition* (2008) is the most comprehensive case study of Shangrila concerning how economic development weaves together sacred landscape and human imagination and that development's subsequent impact on cultural identity. The chapters are interspersed with numerous critical phrases – "power place," "imagination," "authenticity," "cultural commodification," and "dreamscapes." Kolås' concern with native Tibetans' wellbeing is the critical thread of her work. One of her keen observations is that Shangrila is a product of "cultural commodification" (Kolås 2008, 8) in China's tourism industry, in which Tibetan culture has "become objects of preservation efforts, as well as products to be bought and sold in the global tourism market" (Kolås 2008, 25). In this dual course of human moral concern and commercial interest, Tibet is an object seized and branded simultaneously as a cultural heritage and a commodity to be exchanged for profit.

I also see Shangrila as an object of acquisition, manipulation, and consumption. In the meantime, in my fieldwork and in reading the literary narratives of Chinese Tibetophiles I regard it as the materiality of a utopian geography localized in Shangrila. Shangrila in this sense is interchangeably understood as an actual geographic location in Deqin Tibetan Autonomous Prefecture and Hilton's fictional fantasy world built upon the Tibetan landscape. In many ways Shangrila is synonymous with Tibet except that it is localized in a smaller geographic place. It speaks for Tibet in both eco-religious and fantastical terms.

I find Kolås' discussions on power place and dreamscape particularly revealing about the inherent correlation of the geographic Shangrila as a power place and Shangrila as "a space of dreams" (Kolås 2008, 104). This is clearly a set of landscape-mindscape relationships at work. In her study it is natural that she evokes Mt. Khawa Karpo as a *gnas chen* (གནས་ཆེན་) or a great sacred site, which indicates the power of Shangrila originating from its eco-religious reality. As discussed particularly in Chapter Two and Six the power is the perceived sacredness embedded in a landscape of religious significance. In the works of scholars such as Huber (1999) and Michaels (2003), the power of landscape is not merely the physical place of nature and human dwelling but is also a realm of gods, demons, and spirits – a range of sentient beings who are invisible but have felt presence in the human psyche. This knowledge of the Tibetan landscape is commonplace among native Tibetans and scholars of Tibetan landscape studies; however, in the case of how Shangrila has become a desirable tourist destination and a place of dreams, this eco-religious dimension of the Tibetan landscape is not frequently referenced in the marketing of Shangrila's fantastical qualities to potential tourists across China and beyond. Instead, a set of positive aesthetics and earth-inspired spiritual terms in travel writings, literary works, and commercial advertisings build Shangrila as a mindscape of its own.

When I was in Shangrila with my students for our 2008 field course, it was already a well-established tourist town. Like my students, I heard the story that everything began with Sun Jiong, a young tour guide in the late 1990s. The story related that when he was taking a national standards test for tour guides in Beijing a question caught his fascination: "Which part of Yunnan does 'Shangrila' refer to?" His answer was Deqin Tibet Autonomous Prefecture. Another version of the story also began with Sun Jiong but the difference is in the test question he encountered: "Which language does the word 'Shangrila' come from in the Himalaya regions?" His answer was Tibetan but as soon as he came back from Beijing he began to study Hilton's fiction and felt his imagined Shangrila had to be in Deqin.

In 2011 when I returned to Shangrila in spring and summer for the field course and a faculty workshop on landscape and ecology, I brought up the story of Sun Jiong to a staff member of an environmental NGO, our collaborating institution based in Shangrila. She responded, "Sun Jiong isn't just a tour guide. The whole Shangrila came out of his design. He now works in the central government in Beijing." She then recommended Tang Shijie's writings. According to her, Tang has been a close friend of Sun's since the late 1990s. Becoming a prolific writer since that time, his fiction and investigative journalism works include *The Plateau's Sun* (1985), *The Magic Cave* (1989), *Soul Sways in the Wind: Shangrila from Fantasy to Reality* (1999), and *Musing Yunnan* (2001). Based on his interview with Sun Jiong, Tang tells his readers:

> In February 1991 a Chinese translation of *Lost Horizon* was published by Guangdong Tourism Press but the title of the book was changed to *Shangrila*. Surprisingly, a few years later feverish search for Shangrila began in Kunming, the spring city of Southwest China. A graduate of Yunnan University in economics, the then twenty-seven year old Sun Jiong was the marketing manager of an international tour company in Yunnan. In 1995 Sun Jiong participated in the National Best Tour Guide Test in Beijing. One of the test questions was about the geographic origin of the English word "Shangrila." The explanatory part of the question said the word first came from a British fiction called *Lost Horizon* about a story taking place in a Tibetan area in Southwest China. The sharp-minded Sun Jiong immediately thought of his home province Yunnan, "Would Shangrila be in the Tibetan region of Yunnan?" Upon returning to Kunming he found the book *Shangrila*. Pondering over James Hilton's question at the end of the story – "Do you think he [the protagonist Conway] will ever find it [Shangrila]?" Sun Jiong said to himself, "I must find it. I will find it!" (Tang 2006).

The rest of the story is that Sun had an exploratory trip to Deqin Tibet Autonomous Prefecture in 1996. While there, he met with Gasang Dondrub, then the Party Secretary of the Prefecture. They hit it off on the idea of renaming Zhongdian as Shangrila. Later that year the Prefecture started its tourism development initiative in the region with the approval from Yunnan provincial government and the following year the provincial government made a public statement that Shangrila was located in the Prefecture. The rest of the storyline is identical to that of Kolås' findings. What is critical to me is Tang's emphatic point: "Shangrila began as a dream. When people search for it in this real world, they enter a new dreamworld. The discovery and confirmation of Shangrila in Deqin Prefecture is not the end of the dream but is a renewal and re-blossoming of the dream" (Tang 2006).

To be noted, Sun Jiong joined the governing body of Shangrila County in 1997. He started out as an assistant county governor, became a deputy governor, and then a secretariat of Deqin Prefecture (Tang 2006). He was an integral part of engineering Shangrila as "a dream project."

This project is the result of the state-corporate alliance but it rested upon the existing popular enchantment of Tibet in China. It involves not only China's tourism industry but also its entertainment world and publishing business. Tang's ten-year screenwriting project – *Shangrila* – co-authored with Liu Jinyuan and Wang Zifu, was finally premiered at CCTV on May 6, 2011 as a thirty-six episode TV show. Tang initiated this grandiose project with Deqin Prefecture at the turn of the century and it was later financed by the Propaganda Department of Yunnan Province and commercial film conglomerates like Beijing Yangguang Shengtong Media Art, Zhejiang Huace Film and TV, and Yunan Yunding Film and TV (Zheng 2011). This multi-episode TV show tells a love story of a Tibetan tribal chief's daughter in 1936. One of the critical characters in the story is an American pilot who falls in love with the chief's daughter. This character seems to have been developed as a conflation of Hilton's protagonist Conway and Colonel Claire Lee Chennault, a retired U.S. air force officer serving as Chiang Kai-shek's chief air adviser in the 1930s. Chennault, in China, is better known for his leading the "Flying Tigers," a group of American volunteer pilots fighting the Japanese in Southwest China. Interestingly, the American character in the TV show is also named Conway. The teaser before each episode begins with an aerial shot of mountains with the view moving down to the grassland territory of nomads on horseback, coupled with a song:

> In the distant horizon
> There lie beautiful sacred mountains.
> That place is called Shangrila –
> The home of our heart and dream!
> Shangrila –
> You are a colorful dream...(Jiang 2011)

The teaser bears the creative signature of Tang and his co-authors.

"Dreaming Shangrila is a complex, networked project," said one Tibetan scholar at a university in Kunming in a lecture to my students about the recent economic history of Shangrila. As a native of Shangrila he advocated the state and commercial promotion of his hometown; however, I noticed that his intent was not set on the dreaming part of this grand tourism project but rather on raising the standard of living among the local population, an aspect I will return to shortly. By "networked" he meant that Shangrila instantly became a meeting ground of multiple mutual interests that intersected at the tail end of the last century from both local and provincial governments and a range of venturesome companies. Both Deqin Prefecture and Yunnan provincial government made off-the-book promises to those companies that offered finances to their feasibility study of future investment and tourist resource evaluations. Hong Thai Travel Services of Singapore, Chongqing Textile Holding Group, Ningbo Firskids Holding Group, Chongqing Beer Holding Group, and China Everbright Group were among the companies promised with favorable terms for their investments in Shangrila. The appraisal of the tourist value of Shangrila was published: 50 billion RMB (Luo 2002, 19; He 2010, 82). This is the monetary value of Shangrila as a commercial brand.

A little over a decade later this state-sanctioned dream project is reaping abundant profits from the expanding tourism in Shangrila. In 1996 the tourist revenue of Shangrila (then called Zhongdian) was 80 million RMB from 174,200 tourists. In 1997 the revenue jumped to 150 million, nearly double from the previous year with 540,000 tourists contributing to the increase. Two years later the revenue reached 540 million RMB as Shangrila received 1.1 million tourists. In 2001 the revenue was 900 million RMB (Tang 2006). In 2008, 4.3 million tourists poured into Shangrila. The revenue that year was 1.8 billion RMB. The annual growth rate of Shangrila's tourism was approximately 30 % (He 2010, 82) between 2000 and 2010. If this growth rate is maintained, it will take less than five years for Yunnan Province and its investors to cash in the initially estimated total value of Shangrila.

The commercial branding of Shangrila has been obviously successful. Besides the "masterminds" like Sun Jiong, Gasang Dondrub, and Tang Shijie, Yunnan Provincial Shangrila Project Research Team also deserves credit for this success. In 1997 the specialists of the Team from Renmin University, Yunnan Center for Economic Studies, and Yunnan Social Sciences Academy concluded in their report that the spirit of Shangrila is reflected in "both the Oriental utopia depicted in *Lost Horizon* and the theme of the eternal peace and simplicity, and harmonious relationships between people and nature [in Shangrila]" (Luo 2002, 20). On September 9, 2010, the front page of Yunnan Daily featured a brief article on the success of Shangrila's tourism. The reporters characterized the brand of Shangrila as "the most ideal home of humankind" (Yang and Li 2010).

7.3 Seeking material empowerments in the dreamworld

Shangrila, branded as a dreamworld, is an economic miracle for Deqin Prefecture and Yunnan Province. The local economic development has obviously entered the phase of continuing growth. But the question remains: while many tourists, lone travelers, writers, and artists feel a sense of homecoming when they arrive in the township of Shangrila or walk into the awe-inspiring landscape of the surrounding mountains, do local residents also feel empowered by the perceived fantastical quality of their homeland?

In Kolås' study, Shangrila's economic leap-forward activates the agency of local Tibetans in the arena of identity reclamation. Because this unique brand of tourism is dependent upon anything Tibetan, it then inadvertently supports the public presence of Tibetan identity, as Kolås writes, "Tibetans can be seen as 'winners' of this 'representational game,' because Shangrila is reaffirmed, with the help of tourism, as a 'Tibetan' place" (Kolås 2008, 120). Her focus is on the authenticity of Tibetan culture sought by both local Tibetans and tourists. Reading through her last chapter "Tourism, Place-making and Tibetan Identity" I am not able to piece together an authentic Tibet either from the tourist angle or from the eyes of local Tibetans; however I understand her critical question – "Authentic for whom?" (Kolås 2008, 124) based on my work and living experience in Beijing, Qinghai, southern Gansu, and western Sichuan. To me, the question of authenticity is synonymous with the question of primordiality in the search for "authentic" Tibetan culture in contemporary China. Like other subjects of different ethnic origins, Tibetans have gone through a series of socialist reforms and modernization programs. In the twenty-first century Tibetans are becoming more mobile, too. They travel or relocate themselves to other parts of Tibet or to urban China. In the meantime their local Tibetan identity is increasingly becoming a Pan-Tibetan identity in the midst of China's expanding market economy into Tibetan regions.

The case of Shangrila, then, is not an exception but another instance of how the market economy generates political currency for Tibetans to reclaim their cultural identity. In comparison with Tibetan counties in Qinghai and southern Gansu, Tibetans in Shangrila appear to be the winners of this political currency when considering their relatively lower demographic percentage in the county. My question is – "In what ways do they authentically represent their native culture?" I raise this question out of my observation of the generically "Tibetanized" township of Shangrila. This Tibetan appearance is easily found in Lhasa, Labrung, Langmusi, or Kangding. Kolås' question of "Authentic for whom?" raises another question, "Who is authenticating local Tibetan culture?"

Without more sustained fieldwork and access to other statistics, I cannot answer these questions or solve these macro-assessment puzzles. What I can share with my readers are my ethnographic encounters in Shangrila, which I hope are informative of how the dialectics of outsiders' Tibetanization and local Tibetans' de-Tibetanization are manifested in the materiality of this spectacular dream project. Shangrila, as a dream project, was initiated mostly by outsiders, and most businesses in town are owned by outsiders. The complex consequences of Shangrila as an unprecedented tourist development are a puzzle, but it is likely that mostly outsiders are "Tibetanizing" Shangrila as their commercial interests depend on such an image. In my field experience I find local Tibetans are caught in a neither-nor state of being: while their "Tibetanization" in appearance reinforces their ethnic image, it is, in practice, rather de-Tibetanizing them especially concerning the use of Tibetan language, as the entanglement of their livelihood with the tourist economy obliges them to speak Mandarin and/or English.

Norbu, in his mid-thirties, was a driver for my field class in Shangrila. Self-employed, his 2007 Land Cruiser was his primary means of livelihood. On the third day of our trip, on the way to a nature reserve park in the mountains, I sat next to him. Finding that it would be a four hour drive, I pulled out my Tibetan grammar book from my backpack. He asked me what I was reading and when I showed him the cover of the book he chuckled, "You're supposed to recite it loudly!" "Where are you at now?" he continued. I replied, "I'm at the comparative forms." Norbu started reciting, "*nas-las-vbyung-khungs-dgar-sdud-de, vbyung-khungs-dngos-la-gang-sbyar-vthus*...I'm helping you memorize it..." I went along with him reciting the "grammar formulas" in the book multiple times. He was like a school teacher when he explained the formulas. He then said, "You don't really need Tibetan to do your research here. Many of us [Tibetans] don't speak it much now. English and Mandarin are most useful here in Shangrila." Impressed with his knowledge of the text, I asked, "Were you a teacher before?" "I was a monk at Songtsenling Monastery for fourteen years. I memorized the grammar book when I was fifteen," he replied.

In retrospect I think it is not Norbu and his companions who do not want to speak their native tongue on a daily basis, but rather the sphere of their livelihood in Shangrila's tourist industry that presents little opportunity for them to speak it. Instead, as he said, Mandarin and English are favored in Shangrila, being the lingua francas for domestic tourists of China and international visitors from other countries. I felt for Norbu, living in a town that is Tibetan in appearance but that has been "Tibetanized" merely for the commercial consumption of Tibetan culture. Based on my reading of the writings of Tang Shijie, Li Xun, Liu Jinyuan and others, the physical transformation of Shangrila township was a purely imaginative engineering. The purpose, as Tang Shijie's co-author Liu Jinyuan says, was "to translate popularity into productivity" (Liu 2009), justifying Tibet's magnificence being turned into a range of consumer products. Liu recollects his walk in the township in 1999 with Chelhata, then governor of Deqin Prefecture and now Party Secretary of Lhasa Municipality:

> On an early evening of spring 1999 Chelhata brought me to a dilapidated residential area on the edge of the county seat [new town]. Broken walls lay scattered in the twilight. Birds were flying over our heads back to their nests. Chelhata said to me, "This is Dukezong, a thousand-year-old ancient town. We must restore it and show its new vitality!" When we walked back to the new town, we saw the street full of pale tiled buildings. He remarked, "Don't we often say the more ethnic we are the more international we will be? We must tear off these tiles and replace them with a Tibetan look (Liu 2009).

In the next few years the old town was restored and the generic modern look of the new town began to change to a Tibetan appearance. Chelhata "shapeshifted" both the old and new towns, and made both look "traditional" and thus tourist-ready.

The course of Norbu's life was also undergoing transformations at the turn of the century. Norbu left Songtsenling Monastery in 2003 at the age of twenty-nine. In the early 1990s he already worked on the side as a tour guide for individual travelers, most of whom were nature photographers, writers, and university professors from big cities in China. He made friends with them and often when they came back to Shangrila they would look for him again. In 1998 he bought a used Beijing Jeep, expanding his livelihood as both a driver and a guide but finding it impossible to continue as a monk given his frequent absence from the monastery and the questionable ethics of making money. Since then he had changed his vehicle three times, paying nearly half a million RMB for the Land Cruiser out of his savings and earnings from selling some of his family yaks and free range pigs. He felt lucky because he was self-employed while many from his village made 60 to 100 RMB a day if they and their horses were hired by tour companies for tourists' horse rides. He made 600–1000 RMB a day depending on how he negotiated with his clients. Norbu looks like a winner, benefitting from Shangrila's tourism but from a cultural preservation perspective his economic transformation is a loss to Tibetan culture in both religious/cultural and linguistic senses.

Two days after returning from the mountains the class visited Eco-Village, a community center two miles outside Shangrila Township that had been built by an environmental NGO. Riding in Norbu's Land Cruiser again, he told me his home village was not too far from the community center. When we arrived three staff members greeted us. One was a temporary worker from a local village and the other two, a thangka artist and a literacy teacher, were Tibetans from Qinghai. My students, who were anticipating interactions with local Tibetans were divided into three smaller groups for thangka painting, embroidery, and circle dance. Not having a lot of enthusiasm for such programmed activities, they slowly slipped out of the center and found themselves sitting on the pasture outside enjoying the late morning sun. I took the opportunity to find out more about how Eco-Village operated in Shangrila.

Norbu and the thangka artist showed me around the center and from them I learned that it was initially built as a showcase of sustainable living and a learning center for promoting Tibetan literacy, gender equality, and environmental awareness to local Tibetans. However, these ideas were not fully materialized. For various reasons villagers rarely showed up at the community center so Eco-Village began to use the space to receive visitors, host conferences, and as rental space for university field projects. I circled the center built on the edge of a village opening to a large pasture connected with the foothills of a few high mountains. Its architecture is similar to the houses in the neighboring village but larger in scale. The interior is designed with Tibetan motifs but with a hybridized urban flavor, e.g. spot lights, mini-bar, multimedia equipment, and built-in speakers. The thangka artist quipped that what was "eco-" about this community center was its "eco-restroom" with composting toilets which used sawdust. Eco-Village positioned itself to teach and transfer ecological know-how from elsewhere to local Tibetans without consideration of the fact that Tibetans have their own knowledge about the human-earth relationship. In this case I wondered how much time a family would spend on making saw dust for the toilet and why Eco-Village did not initiate a project to systematically collect local knowledge about sustainable living.

Scholars and journalists in China also conduct serious studies of the materiality of Shangrila as a world of dreamers. Like Kolås, they recognize the rapid economic growth. When it comes down to cultural aspects of Shangrila, many of them use the phrase *zengquan* (增权) or "empowerment" in their discussion of the current state of local Tibetans. Most of them acknowledge the economic empowerment of Shangrila to Tibetans (Guo 2010, 76) but in the cultural arena some of them point out that the illiteracy rate of Tibetans is still at 59.34 % (Luo 2002, 23) and that "As Mandarin is widely promoted, many Tibetans no longer speak their native tongue, especially young people" (He 2010, 83). In relation to the identity issue of local Tibetans, some Chinese scholars argue that local Tibetans have more pride in their culture (Guo 2010, 81), while others say this identity empowerment is a matter of "pure commercial performance" (He 2010, 83). With all things considered in the making of Shangrila, this "pure performance" is undoubtedly catering to non-Tibetans' consumption of Tibetan culture and landscape.

7.4 Drifting in the Mirages of the Tibetan Landscape

7.4.1 Geo-poetic affordance

Tibet is simultaneously branded as a commodity and branding a mindscape of dreams and fantasies in China (Kolås 2008). Meanwhile, I argue that Tibet as an actual geographic-cultural place plays the antecedent role in expressing itself as a power place and generating an earth-inspired spirituality in China and elsewhere. As Sun Jiong and his subsequent government supporters "authenticated" at the outset, Shangrila stands as a replica of Hilton's fictive Shangrila: "a silent serenity," "concentrated loveliness," "a deep unrippled pool," and "a living essence, distilled from the magic of the ages and miraculously preserved against time and death" (Hilton 2006, 242, 261). The geo-poetic nature of Hilton's fiction is reproduced in contemporary Shangrila, but at the outset, it is the place itself that inspired imagination and was then the setting for making imagination present.

Reading through *Lost Horizon*, I find that Hilton's Shangrila is not entirely his own creation. He references and fictionalizes personal accounts of Antonio de Andrada, Athanasius Kircher, Jean de Thévenot, and Cassiano Beligatti, who traveled to Tibet as missionaries and explorers in the seventeenth and eighteenth centuries (Hilton 2006, 144–145). Hilton's cultural portrayal of Shangrila is a mini-Tibet to which was ascribed a "lamasery," "theocracy," and "the heathen Tibetan" (Hilton 2006, 144, 154, 189). These terms reflect the cultural conception of Tibet in the West in his time. Tibet was not absent in Western cultural consciousness in the 1930s; thus his fictional writing possesses a detectable amount of factual representation of Tibet from credible sources. Tibet as an actual place spoke to him indirectly through the writings of missionaries and explorers. Thus, Hilton embeds his findings from secondary sources into his characters. For example, in one scene, Conway, the protagonist in *Lost Horizon*, walks into the night under the silver moon:

> Suddenly, on a flutter of air, came sounds from far below. Listening intently, he could hear *gongs* and *trumpets* and also the massed *wail of voices*. The sounds faded on a veer of the wind, then returned to fade again. But the hint of life and liveliness in those veiled depths served only emphasize the austere serenity of Shangrila. Its forsaken courts and pale pavilions shimmered in repose from which all the fret of existence had ebbed away, leaving a hush as if moments hardly dared to pass. Then, from a window high above the terrace, he caught the *rose-gold of lantern light*; was it there that the lamas devoted themselves to *contemplation* and the pursuit of *wisdom*...(Hilton 2006, 154–155).

I add the italics to indicate that his poetic and theatrical prose is sustained by his knowledge of Tibetan Buddhism enacted in a monastery: monks' chanting in unison, the golden light from the butter lamps, and their devotion to meditation and enlightenment. In fact this monastic scene under the moonlight could be found in many places in contemporary Tibet. Hilton did not go to Tibet but Tibet entered his mindscape through the travel writings of missionaries and explorers he read before writing his fiction.

This is what I refer to as "the mirage effect" of place, which bounces from landscape into mindscape, and can eventually become a creative motor in the human mind. In the literal sense a superior mirage is an illusory image of an actual place projected in the sky by the atmospheric refraction of light; thus it is both illusory and real. Its visual effect often sparks awe, marvel, and imagination. In the context of contemporary Tibet, the mirage effect refers to a range of images, publicly shared imaginations, literary works, and creative arts, which portray Tibetan landscape, people, culture, and religious practices based on personal accounts of travel and work experiences in Tibet. Unlike Hilton's Shangrila or Tibet drawn from secondary sources, the "mirages" of Tibet in the mindscape of writers like Li Xun or Tang Shijie are often a combination of their own travel experience, culturally-conditioned perceptions and images, and inner responses to all external inputs in imaginative, poetic, or intellectual terms. These "mirages" do not stop or fade into the horizon of the individual mindscape but become present in the social realm through the person's creative activities. In the context of Tibet, the mirage becomes a shared mindscape with a life of its own, generative and contagious in nature.

The Chinese mirage-makers of Tibet are a special group of Tibetophiles. Most of the authors and artists I have mentioned so far belong to this unique class of people whose literary works and creative arts based on their personal experiences in Tibet are widely published in China. In their careers they have been *zangpiao* (藏漂) or "Tibet drifters," meaning that they have lived or traveled in a Tibetan region for at least a year or longer. The phrase "Tibet drifter" is an established term in contemporary China, indicating Tibet-inspired New Age spirituality among Chinese. Mainstream media, such as Xinhua Net and Baidu, also recognize this Tibet-based popular trend. Xinhua News featured an article in 2009 titled "Tibet Drifters in Lhasa: In Search of a Spiritual Home." The reporters wrote, "Tibet drifters are a part of the special cultural landscape of Lhasa. These drifters from outside Tibet reflect the unique spiritual charm of Lhasa" (Liu and Cao 2009). These two sentences are identical to what is written in Baidu Encyclopedia about Tibet drifters. It is not clear who cites whom; however, both sources highlight the spiritual aspect of the "drifting." Baidu Encyclopedia says, "Tibet drifters are those who work, live or travel in Tibetan regions of China but are not residents of Tibet...They roam between the sky and the earth of Tibet, and on the streets of Lhasa searching for 'Shangrila' in their ideals and for what was once lost in their souls" (Baidu). A very popular recent writing of a Tibet drifter is titled *Tibet Drifting* published by Oriental Publishing Center based in Beijing (Mu 2012). The author Mu Ge, a scholar specializing in Western philosophy, lived in Tibet for four years as an aid worker. He wrote the book, a fictional story, in which the breathtaking Tibetan landscape is a space where his characters express the sense of spiritual homelessness and existential meaninglessness all too common in modern urban China.

In discussing Tibetophiles and their mirages of Tibet, I wish to re-emphasize Gibson's idea of affordance concerning place-organism relationship, which is generally understood as how a given environment provides organisms with that which fulfills its utilitarian needs. In relation to humans, an affordance of place often goes beyond the utilitarian dimension, as Gibson writes, "The perceiving of an affordance is not a process of perceiving a value-free physical object to which meaning is somehow added in a way that no one has been able to agree upon; it is a process of perceiving a value-rich ecological object" (Gibson 1986, 140). Among the elements the Tibetan landscape affords the mirage-makers in China are light, color, mountainous topography, space, and water in the forms of glaciers, ice, lakes, rainfall, rivers, and snow, with all of these elements becoming mediums of their thoughts, imaginations, fantasies, and soulful narratives. Mirage in the mindscape is thus also an optical phenomenon manifested as visions, dreams, and imaginations transmitting the real and the illusory simultaneously. When place-rooted ecological and cultural elements enter the mindscape of the Tibetophile, they become a unique type of affordance allowing the mirage-maker to transform the Tibetan landscape into a geo-psychic terrain of his own making imbued with emotions, sentiments, existential conditions, and spiritual states, all unique to himself and his own social environment. This mirage of Tibet emerges as a poeticized, romanticized, reshaped, or re-appropriated Tibet; a special domain in which the self of the mirage-maker is environed and finds its lost soul restored in the land as a spiritual Other. I call this particular type of affordance "the geopoetic affordances" signifying the value-rich and value-added Tibetan landscape with all things included: the geological, the geographic, the meteorological, cultural, social, psychological, religious, spiritual, the medical... you name it.

The mirage effect from the writings and artworks of many influential Tibetophiles in China has a clear pattern of simultaneous transposition, transference, entwinement, division, and polarization between the mirage-maker as Self and the perceived/experienced Tibet as the Other. On one hand the Tibetan landscape as an Other overpowers the consciousness of the mirage-maker and subjects it to a confessional mode of being. On the other hand the mirage-maker remaps and re-projects the Tibetan landscape as an archetypal spiritual destiny or an ever-expanding horizon of a heroic journey. This dialectical *poeisis* of Tibetan landscape and the Tibetophile's mindscape expresses itself in the dualities of escape and reunion, ailment and healing, failure and triumph, doubt and confidence, reverence and condescendence, and frontier and centrality.

7.4.2 Utopian attributes of Tibet

The materialization of Hilton's Shangrila in Yunnan over the last decade has been premised on the existing popular fascination of Tibet in China known as *xizangre* (西藏热) or "Tibet fever." This popular fascination has been reshaped, redirected, and refunneled into the tourism industry as a consumer desire for a paradisiacal place of beauty, magnificence, and peace – or simply as what Chinese travel writers often refer to as "the last pureland on earth." This advertising motif parallels the publication of creative works by Tibet drifters, or rather Tibet mirage-makers in this case. Herein I draw a fine line between the mirages of Tibet floating in commercial images and literary works, arts, and motion pictures, and the Tibetan landscape itself. With persistence I emphasize that it is the landscape that empowers the mirage-makers with its visually-stunning and spiritually awe-inspiring qualities. Non-Tibetans' narratives about Tibet have never been absent of these qualities since the Jesuit missionaries of the seventeenth century and later explorers and seekers set eyes on it. In actuality many parts of Tibet could be named after Hilton's Shangrila.

Prior to the formal state recognition of Zhongdian as Shangrila, there already existed the talk of a Greater Shangrila in the neighboring territories of Sichuan, TAR, and Yunnan (Hu 2010, 1), not to mention other Tibetan regions whose astonishing landscapes resemble or even surpass Hilton's Shangrila. These breathtaking places were (are) just inaccessible for tourists because of natural barriers of waters and high mountains and the absence of infrastructural support to accommodate the massive number of tourists locations such as Shangrila and Lhasa now absorb annually. For instance, in the eye-witness accounts of individual travelers and exploratory writers, the pre-1997 Shangrila was "very primitive, very poor, very cold and lacking oxygen, but had immense mountains, large rivers, expansive grasslands, and big forests" (Zhang 2007, 48). It was a place that had a "stunningly beautiful landscape but was extremely poor, and was socially harmonious but behind the times" (Liu 2009).

What I am arguing here is: Tibet was (is) a utopia in the topographical sense. Its utopian attributes continue to stream into the public sphere of China through the works of mirage-makers like Tang Shijie and Li Xun. I see the conflation of their personal fantasies and dreams with Tibet, but it is absolutely critical to me that I illustrate how the mirage-makers re-possess Tibet as the space of their own nostalgia, dreams, and visions – the illusory components reflective of their personal and social conditions. For the following paragraphs I make a legitimate supposition that Tibet, as a utopia, was not as a fictitiously perfect human society as the word "utopia" often signifies but a place with natural barriers limiting access to outsiders in the past and so it was able to retain a cultural uniqueness in addition to some degree of protection from environmental degradation. Thus, utopia in this part of the chapter is a toponym that has a corresponding topography of horizons, frontiers, edges, gaps, and in-betweens (Marvin 1993, 407– 408) that constitute its inaccessibility but which possess potentially contagious *poeisis* and sublime inspiration that provokes psychic and spiritual responses from those who come into contact with it. This is the moment when the self of the mirage-maker recreates itself in the otherness of Tibet. In this process a topographical utopia is turned into a fantastical utopia of the mindscape.

7.4.3 Escape, self-exile and metamorphosis in "magical Tibet"

Chai Chunya, the writer I reference in the introductory chapter, is now a celebrated author and a documentary filmmaker. His popular recognition rests upon his lived experience in Tibet from which he has drawn his creative inspiration. His works are going beyond Mainland China and are distributed in Taiwan and Europe. "Tibet fever" is spreading widely in China; however, the number of the mirage-makers of Tibet is only a handful. The "chic" group in Beijing are not found in academia but comprise a small number of creative writers, artists, and filmmakers, such as Tsewang Norbu, Dai Wei, Xie Fei, and Ma Lihua; however their publications and artworks reach a wide audience in China. Through Pema Tseden and Tsewang Norbu I met Chai in 2009. Subsequently he visited my class at Minzu University. In 2010 he gave me his *A Vagabond in Tibet* (2009a) and *Red Sheepskin Book of Tibet* (2009b), both of which were published in Taiwan. Expecting more robustly forthcoming accounts of his experience in Tibet regardless of his fictional rendition of it, I was nevertheless impressed with his narrative skill and creative talents that brought me into the world of his Tibet – a "magical Tibet" as he calls it (Chai 2009b, 9). In this magical Tibet, the grass is green, the snow is white, and the sky is blue; however, it is revealed more as the psychic field of the author than the actual ecological and cultural world of Tibet. Its imagery is woven together with the author's felt sense of loneliness, wilderness, harshness, barrenness, primitiveness, nakedness, uncertainty, poverty, exile, silence, and spiritual rebirth. Chai's *Vagabond* is particularly telling of his Tibet journey as a journey of being saved and reborn as a new person. Chai writes:

> At a snail's pace you enter the grassland like a water droplet rejoining a ripple on a lake or like a cloud merging into the sky. In the abstract sense your entry into the grassland is an entry into quietude as a hermit who voluntarily leaves behind the city noises or as a misanthropist. You are indulging in self-exile. In your vagrant journey you find art and in your own flesh you see a new will to survive. In the eyes of bystanders this journey is perhaps a flight, an escape, and a betrayal to the city, or a graceful gaze before diving into nature where you find refuge and homecoming (Chai 2009a, 38).

The affordance of the Tibetan landscape to his poetic prose is self-evident, but when he enters Tibet, or "nature" in this case, it is not all home-like. It rather becomes a place "totally separated from the world," as he continues his narrative:

> This place has no electricity, no telecommunication, and is absent of everything modern civilization has. This is an exile in a distant land, a Dostoyevsky-like exile as if you were in Siberia – a place where prisoners lose their freedom, except without high walls, torture, shackles, soldiers, and a sadistic warden. Neither are you surrounded by thieves, murderers, snitches, and professional revolutionaries here...This is a self-exile, an escape from the modern city. It gives you complete loneliness, imprisons you where you stand, and separates you from modernization. This is a self-internment for refusing conformity and pollution. This is liberation of the soul in the company of Kerouac on Desolation Peak. With poet Gary Snyder's arrangement Kerouac spent half a year as a fire lookout on top of Desolation Peak in the Cascade Mountains. Snyder gave him an opportunity to experience Zen mind, Zen flesh, and Zen bones in loneliness; to be in the company of 180,000 Buddhas scattered out in the universe; and to take residence in a mandala, in Buddha Nature and Emptiness, and in eternity in a flash (Chai 2009a, 112–113).

In this narrative Tibet becomes a time lag, a marginal space, a harsh, desolate passage for a neophyte to complete a rite. What is obvious is that Tibet is not at all as animated as the "nature" he dived into earlier; instead it is metaphorized as a self-built prison for a spiritual breakout or break-through. I wonder if Tibetans are permanent prisoners in "Dostoyevsky-like exile." In any case, this Tibet is the ground on which the author edifies himself to a spiritual peak experience with Jack Kerouac. Chai shapeshifts Tibet into Kerouac's Desolation Peak – a passage to the universe of enlightened beings. In truth Kerouac spent a summer not half a year on Desolation Peak. In the end the solitude on the Peak was too much to bear and he "wrote to Snyder that his Buddhism was dead" (Tonkinson 1995, 27). Kerouac's writings are spiritually inspiring but his Buddhist destiny still remains unclear, posthumously. After descending from

Desolation Peak, depression, alcoholism, and a split spiritual state between basic Buddhist morality and his perceived omnipresence of Zen mind in alcohol and sex accompanied him as he expressed in *The Dharma Bums* (Kerouac 1986).

Chai's *Vagabond* is a fiction; thus, historical, cultural, and ecological inaccuracy are acceptably secondary to its storyline; however, he makes it known to his readers that this fiction is fully based on his lived experience in Gama Village of Dege County in Ganzi Tibetan Autonomous Prefecture, Sichuan Province and that the protagonist is himself (Chai 2009c, 132). As Chai also publicly admits that he is a Nyingmapa practitioner, it is natural that his readers wish that he could have given credits to his Tibetan teachers for his felt spiritual euphoria in Tibet rather than to Kerouac.

On April 4, 2011, Chai gave a talk at Renmin University titled "My Incurable Loneliness," in which he narrated his literary success story to a large audience. A Tibetan participant commented that many Tibet-related literary works were written as outsiders looking in. Chai responded, "This is the issue that I must confront. I must prevent Said's style [referring to Orientalism as critiqued by Said] and avoid looking at Tibetans and Tibetan culture with our Han worldview. I must place myself in the position of Tibetans." Chai had received similar comments from his Tibetan readers in the past. In 2009 shortly after the publication of *Vagabond*, *Unitas*, a monthly magazine in Taiwan, featured Chai's article "Magical Journey to Tibet in Troubled Times," as a self-introduction of the newly famous author. Chai reminisced about an encounter with a comment from a Tibetan friend of his: "It is impossible for me to connect your work with the Tibet where I have lived. The names of people and places, and past and present events in your book all appear very Tibetan but, honestly, there is a thick wall separating my Tibet from yours" (Chai 2009c, 131). Chai lashed out with criticism of his friend:

> As individuals, who can say we own the entire Tibet? This friend of mine, born in a military officer's family, received all her education in the Chinese language. She went to Lhasa after graduating from college. Her life has been completely cut off from farming and herding. She has been to agricultural and nomadic areas of Tibet, but what is the difference between her trips and those of superficial Han Chinese tourists? How would she understand the harsh work for sowing and harvesting? How would she understand the inner world of poor people?…Based on my childhood in an agricultural village and my herding experience with nomads at Gama Village at the age of thirty, I have more qualification to write about agricultural and nomadic societies; I am more gifted to enter the inner world of farmers and nomads. I can even shamelessly say: my skill in agricultural and nomadic work is as fluent as my writing skill (Chai 2009c, 131).

I know this Tibetan friend of his. She is a globally acclaimed author based in Beijing and Lhasa, and a critic of China's policy implementation in Tibetan regions.

It was she who lifted Chai out of his existential and spiritual breakdown in 2005 by introducing him to Gama Village as a schoolteacher. Chai seemed to have a momentary discrediting reaction to his friend's comment and, at the same time, a solidly self-edifying affirmation. Earlier I called this the post-Orientalist phenomenon and the heart of the issue is the question of authenticity and representation on the personal level and its accompanying social impact.

It is not unusual that Chai evoked Edward Said in his success story. Said's *Orientalism* is a widely read text among contemporary scholars, writers, and cultural critics in China, especially in relation to the topic of Tibet. The first Chinese translation available in the PRC came out seven years ago (Wang 2005) and it is commonly read along with Foucault's works on power. In many ways, the availability of Said's *Orientalism* in Chinese has energized China's version of post-colonial studies in which Said's critical perspective is mostly utilized for analyzing the Orientalized image of Chinese in the West (Ma 2006, 26). Among scholars of contemporary Tibetan studies in China, Wang Hui and Shen Weirong are the most active ones who allege that Westerners Orientalize Tibet, along with using Lopez's *Prisoners of Shangri-La* (1998) as their primary theoretical ballast. However, in the midst of critical backlash at the Orientalism of the West, both Wang and Shen are also facing the growing awareness of the Orientalization of Tibet among Han Chinese. In reference to how Yunnan's Shangrila is commodified, Shen remarked, "Politically speaking this is incorrect...It cheapens our cultural tradition. This is an internal Orientalism that ingratiates the West" (Shen 2010, 109). In the same vein, Wang stated, "Orientalism is not merely a phantom of the West. It is now becoming a creation of our own" (Wang 2011, 37).

To be noted, the way in which Wang, Shen and other scholars in China employ Said's perspective is caught in the dichotomy of China and the West, the East and the West, or Tibet and the West as if the two sides were uncompromisingly polarized and mutually unintelligible because of the one-sidedness of the extreme idealization and demonization of the non-Western native. In this regard, Wang and Shen and their adherents could be reasonably alleged to be exercising their nationalism against the West in their critiques.

Chai's literary creativity, built upon Tibet, is a complex case of realism and fantasy. Before I allege the existence of Orientalist sentiments and expressions in his writings, I make a disclaimer that my post-Orientalist reading of his works is only intended to highlight the internalized, personalized, and individualized but-once-collective perceptions, imaginations, and fantasies of an Other; thus it is not intended to discredit his hard-earned literary achievement. As I elaborated earlier, my post-Orientalist approach acknowledges the historical consciousness of Orientalism as an inherent part of the Western imperial perception of non-Western others; however, this rigid historical dichotomy of "the West and the

Rest" disintegrates as the questions of self and the other and of power and representation are found universally across human societies especially in an era of heightened globalization. Thus, I re-emphasize that one could be both the Orientalizing and the Orientalized. In the case of the mirage-makers of Tibet in China, the post-Orientalized Tibet is foremost a geographic place of unfamiliarity and yet it is a field of spiritual enchantment and a state of trance from which one returns home with a series of revelations and self-claimed magic and miracles. What is critical is that the post-Orientalist consciousness transmutes the actually awe-inspiring earth, sky, and water of Tibet into a mirage real in image but illusory in nature when the mirage-maker fills it up with a sequence of his or her soulful realization or spiritual liberation; thus Tibet is displaced and re-placed as a ground of the mirage-maker's pilgrimage and subsequently felt transcendence.

In the case of Chai, his literary re-creation of himself in Tibet is sequenced from being an escapist from urban China to a schoolteacher, a pilgrim, a spiritually renewed person, an embodiment of Tibet, and an acclaimed fiction writer. It is a story of a hero's return. Tibet has nurtured him. It is natural that he addresses Tibet as "magical Tibet." He writes:

> Tibet is magic ... Instead of saying Tibet is a magical land, it is rather better to say Tibetans are a magical people. These people [Han Chinese], too mediocre and too worldly, live a materialistic life in cities. They need Tibet – a high, distant, inaccessible place – to anchor their yearning for a spiritual life. Because of this I believe no matter how deeply people degenerate, the yearning for divinity runs like an underground river deeply hidden inside the Earth. Tibet as magic is a reality. To Han Chinese, facing this reality only requires honesty, humiliation, and courage. Seen from the philosophical perspective, Tibet's magic is an ancient wisdom manifesting itself in the metaphysical and idealized manner. It is a life-principle that transcends worldliness and arrives in the realm of divinity. As such, Tibet's magic extricates humanity from bestiality (Chai 2009c, 121).

This was written during his post-Tibet phase after his books were successfully published in Taiwan and mainland China. Reading through *Vagabond* and *Red Sheepskin Book of Tibet*, one cannot help but single out the words and phrases that indicate Chai's Orientalist sentiments: "natural," "naked," "primordial," "mysterious," "phantasmic," "magic," "wilderness," "pure soul," "perfect highland," and the list goes on. In his narrative the Tibetans around him are not the "magical people" he claims them to be and as a narcissistic protagonist, he is more often the magic-in-the-making. He depicts himself as "a great soul who is being nurtured by the grassland and is suckling from the illumination of the Earth" (2009a, 186), and as "a lone wolf in the grassland who stands on the crest of a hill silently looking over everything" (2009a, 189). Following along with his "magical" perspective and poetic prose the reader can imagine him as "a handsome vagabond" undergoing a spiritual transformation in Tibet that is metaphorized as "the silent Earth in its primordial state...peaceful, mysterious, and phantasmic" (2009a, 252).

While he recognizes the primordiality of the Tibetan landscape, it is worthy of critique to notice that he visualizes the bodies of Tibetans in the same fashion. A simple scene of a teen boy taking a bath in a hot spring reveals a temporal-spatial displacement of Tibetans who are relegated to a primordial time, as Chai writes,

> Off the road we saw two hot springs breathing out steamy vapors. Jamyang Tsering took off his clothes. His skin was pale. The foreskin of his penis was still intact. This innocent virgin boy jumped into one of the hot springs and happily started bathing himself...This is the Indian country in the writing of Thoreau. This is the purely Tibetan country where human nature is awakened, restored, and liberated, and where the soul sets itself free in the ways of the Indians, the Tibetans, the plants, and nature (Chai 2009a, 74).

If there were an undercurrent in this passage, it would be the author's fantastical vision in which his spiritual virginity is restored while considering himself as an equal of Thoreau. From the perspective of post-colonial studies, Chai has revealed his perspective that Tibetans exist outside of time, eternally archetypal, eternally "natural" and "innocent" or conversely, "primitive" and "bestial."

Continuing to journey with Chai in his writings we find that unlike the virgin boy keeping him company at the hot springs, Tibetans around Chai include a masturbating man, a "slut," a nomad woman outcast, a wealth-obsessed lama, a drunkard, a mentally-ill man, and a bandit. As hardships of native Tibetans are diluted by his poeticization as though they are the natural course of being since primordial time, his own urban existential disorientation, narcissistic lonesomeness, and felt spiritual euphoria take precedence. What is Tibet in Chai's recollection then? It is the beautiful but outcast woman Yangchanma who gives birth to a son for him [the author has made no public admittance about having a child with a Tibetan woman; so take it figuratively] (2009a, 255), it is Cosmos flowers blooming on the grassland which make him think of his loved ones, and it is a thing that he loves but cannot touch. So, he leaves Tibet with his conflicting geo-phantasmic psychic terrain:

> I'm leaving, Ah, Jomolungma [ཇོ་མོ་གླང་མ Mt. Everest]!...I'm gazing up into the distant, immense firmament filled with rivers of stars. I'm mesmerized by the silent vultures like dots of black ink in the snow. I'm refusing to communicate with anyone. My loneliness is incurable. Such loneliness – an ailment hidden in my body – is suddenly erupting like a volcano. I have held the thought too long: death is a kind of alien landscape. It is neither sad nor dark. Please allow me to leap into this alien landscape because it is so enthralling. You bless

me with love almost in a sacred fashion. I am so deeply touched by your pure soul that I have learned to love this world, but this also makes me move farther away from you. The absolute beauty is untouchable like the dead bodies of mountaineers frozen in the glacier of the mountain. They preserve youthful, deliciously fresh smiles; however if they ever break the ice, the smile will instantly vanish, decay, decompose into the soil, and become unbearable to look at. Our affection is a light of fantasy, beautiful but unrealistic. I restrain myself from touching the real you. In such a state of soul-trance I'm returning to Beijing (2009a, 256–57).

Chai tells his readers that he adopts the literary genre known as "magical realism" akin to Gabriel Garcia Marquez's *One Hundred Years of Solitude* (2009c, 129). His repeated invocation of the Beat Generation at his magical turning points gives readers an impression that it is not Tibetan saints but the Buddhism-inspired writers and poets like Kerouac and Snyder who transcend his existential disorientation and spiritual confusion. The landscape of Tibet often appears as the externality of his "incurable loneliness," a simultaneously real and figurative world of desolation from which he re-emerges as a new, whole person.

Chai's soulful narratives, utilizing the genre of magical realism, resemble the style of the nineteenth century Orientalist writers, as Said characterizes them, "Every one of them kept intact the separateness of the Orient, its eccentricity, its backwardness, its silent indifference, its feminine penetrability, its supine malleability..." (Said 1979, 206). Tibet is Chai's "Orient" in which he caresses the grassland like a goddess' soft, aromatic shoulder (2009a, 2), relates to the nameless horses, yaks, and wolves (2009a, 119), hears the love-making sounds of his neighbor's wife (2009a, 113), peeks at a young man's pubic hair glistening in dim firelight through his unzipped fly (2009a, 157), watches a mentally disabled person streaking through the village (2009b, 270), walks away from the outcast woman when she hollers, "Hurry, I bore you a son" (2009a, 255), and imagines himself as a dead body feasted on by vultures (2009b, 315). This primitive, civilizationless and yet pristinely magnificent place gives him a total rebirth. Chai's narrative could be read as personally experienced spiritual magic and miracles in Tibet but it also appears remarkably Orientalist.

On the other hand, it would be a mis-accusation to regard Chai only as an Orientalist. In the public arena, with his "conscience as a Han Chinese writer," he makes atonement for the wrongs of "the Communist imperialist invasion" and "the state chauvinism" (2009c, 123). He points out his peer writers who "do not expose Tibetans' sufferings, humiliation from being colonized...instead with their false romanticism and layers of lies they fictionalize a Tibet as an idyllic place of snow mountains, grasslands, monasteries, lamas, beautiful women, steeds, yaks and sheep" (2009c, 123). Chai lumps together this type of Han Chinese writer, characterizing their Tibet-related literary works as "a mirage of their adolescent wet dreams" (2009c, 127).

In the post-Orientalist era, Orientalist sentiments stream through one's mindscape not necessarily as one side of a dichotomy to be noticed, highlighted, defended or tackled. They equally flow in the cultural consciousness of the anti-Orientalist, the justice-worker, the defender of the indigenous modes of being, and the member of an Orientalized culture. In Chai's creative narratives, public statements, and expressions of his conscience, he carries a complex of a Tibetophile, a Dharma bum, a seeker, a dreamer of the impossible, a creative consumer of Tibet's landscape and culture, a mirage-maker, an anti-colonialist, anti-Orientalist, and an Orientalist. Post-Orientalism is a latent Orientalism as Said predicted (Said 1979, 206), coming, when it does, in the entwinement of negated forms and affirmed expressions. In spite of Chai's critical spirit, he is, himself, a mirage maker, relying on the power of the Tibetan landscape.

Chapter Eight
Conclusion – Mindscaping Tibetophilia

A week before Chai Chunya's talk at Renmin University, Pema Tseden sent me a text-message inviting me to the premiere of Dai Wei's *Once Upon a Time in Tibet* (2011) with Sonthar Gyal, Dukar Tserang, Tserang Dondrub, and other core members of his filmmaking. Prior to *Once Upon a Time in Tibet*, Dai Wei was already widely known among artists and filmmakers in Beijing for her fiction film *Ganglamedo* (2006). As friends of Pema Tseden, Dai Wei gave us VIP seats. The theater was festively packed. In the hallway I saw familiar faces of Tibet fans from Beijing Film Academy, CCTV, the Central Academy of Drama, singers, actors, writers, and a few PR directors of film gear rental companies. In many ways, the premiere was a congregation of Tibetans and Tibetophiles in Beijing. Jinwei, the anchor hostess of China Movie Report, CCTV-6, commenced the premiere.

Once Upon a Time in Tibet, set in 1942 in Western Yunnan, tells the parallel love stories of a U.S. Air Force pilot Robert (Joshua Hannum) with Yangtso, an outcast woman (Song Jia), and Gyatso (Peter Ho) with Yangchan (Zhu Ziyan), a slave couple whose lives are owned by their lord. After surviving his plane crash, Robert, snow-blind, collapses in a small nomadic community. The elders assign Yangtso to be the caretaker of "the red haired devil." The love story of this outcast pair begins when Robert's sight recovers. Meanwhile, the slave owner orders Gyatso to capture a foreigner (European) who has murdered a Tibetan woman. Robert is mistaken as the murderer. The drama enters multiple complications. The story ends tragically with the deaths of Yangtso and Gyatso, in the arms of their lovers.

The audience applauded Dai Wei and her crew when the film ended and Jinwei invited them onto the stage. The curiosity of the audience was evident in their questions about how the production team survived the harsh high altitude environment of Tibet and what personal reflections Dai Wei and the actors had. The primary location of their shoot was at Lake Namtso with an altitude nearly 5,000 meters. Peter Ho elaborated on his effort to assume himself into the role of the heroic but shabby looking slave by not taking showers. Song Jia told the audience how her high altitude sickness worsened after shooting scenes in which she had to run. No single audience member asked a question about the portrayal of Tibetan culture in the film. Pema Tseden was quiet during the Q & A in spite of the fact that Dai Wei gave him the opportunity to speak up when she mentioned to the audience the presence of "her distinguished friend, Pema Tseden" in their midst.

Chapter Eight Conclusion – Mindscaping Tibetophilia — 213

The next day, taking a lunch break during our collaborative project, I sat down with Tserang Dondrub, the screenwriter and hometown buddy of Pema Tseden and we traded our impressions and thoughts on Dai Wei's film. His critique was leveled at quite a few of the scenes he thought were culturally unrealistic, for instance, the film's emphasis on the small nomadic community's social system being serfdom. His argument was that the social system of nomads in eastern Kham was tribal based and without slavery. The last scene showing the deaths of Yangtso and Gyatso upset him most; a crowd of prostrating pilgrims was totally indifferent to the shooting deaths of the people in their midst. Tserang Dondrub was also a little disappointed with Dolma Gyab's playing the role of the slave owner. His feelings were spurred for two reasons, first because he felt that, as an actor, Dolma Gyab was better suited in the kinds of roles he had played in Pema Tseden's films: the son who sells his father's mastiff in *Old Dog* (2010), the drunkard who objects to Buddhist altruism in *The Search* (2009), and the son who steals the neighbor's yak and lies to his parents in *Grassland* (2004), and because it had the sting of betrayal to have Dolma Gyab join Dai Wei's project that catered to a particular image of Tibetans.

As for myself, I told him I had watched Dai Wei's film as an intertextual reading of an invented theme saturating many creative productions about Tibet, whether films, TV shows or novels, and especially state-sanctioned works. This "pan-artistic theme" is Tibet being reinvented as Hilton's Shangrila but with additions that have unique "Chinese characteristics." For instance, the imaginative storylines of Dai Wei's *Once Upon a Time in Tibet* and Tang Shijie's TV show *Shangrila* are both drawn from Hilton's *Lost Horizon*. Both productions have the identical American pilot set in the same historical background and geographic location – Western Yunnan during World War II. In these two different productions, local Tibetans nurture the same injured American hero back to life, portray common Tibetans as a people of innocence and simplicity but as drastically unfree, and they roll out spectacular landscape scenes of snow mountains and grasslands. The main characters in these two productions as well as others are often those on social margins: outcasts, marginalized victims of religion and society, and comically foolish individuals. The protagonists' stories nearly all end tragically and male characters are commonly found psychologically defeated, physically maimed or castrated.

In Dai Wei's *Once Upon a Time in Tibet*, Robert and Yangtso, both outcasts, fall in love with each other but Yangtso tragically dies in the end. In Chai Chunya's *Vagabond*, the protagonist Yaga is infatuated with Yangchanma but turns his back on her when she gives birth to their son. Champa, the slave, in Li Jun's *The Serf* (1962) takes a vow of silence in resistance to the inhumanity of serfdom; Luobu in Tian Zhuangzhuang's *Horse Thief* (1988) loses his heroic vitality to his religion and the "old social order;" In Joan Chen's *Xiu Xiu: the Sent-Down Girl* (1998), the Tibetan protagonist Lao Jin (Losang Chöphel) is a handsome man capable of love and affection but castrated in an inter-tribal feud. In *Once Upon a Time in Tibet* an idiotically cheerful Losang (Sanmuke) proposes a polyandrous marriage of Robert, Yangtso and himself. Dai Wei or her screenwriter overlooked the cultural fact that polyandry only takes place among brothers who marry the same woman. A similarly simple-minded character appears in Chai's *Red Sheepskin Book of Tibet,* not as a self-nominated polyandrous candidate but as developmentally childlike Nyingma Tsering getting drunk or running naked through the village. These characters are unintelligible but funny and, therefore, entertaining. They are cinematic lubricant, moving the main storylines forward with comic scenes. In each of these productions everything happens below the snow covered mountains under the sublime blue sky; in the mindscape of Shangrila as materialized in mediums of all sort, e.g. motion pictures, literary works, travel writings, and tourist commercials. Tibet continues to see its multifarious mirages in contemporary China.

* * *

8.1 The missing Orient in Post-Orientalism

To end this book I start with rethinking of Orientalism in post-Orientalist terms. Throughout the book I express my reluctance to have a uniform characterization of the works of Chinese writers and artists as Orientalist productions regardless of the fact that Wang Hui and Shen Weirong recognize Orientalist sentiments in the state-corporate engineering of the commercial image of Shangrila in Yunnan and popular writings on Tibet in general. From a post-Orientalist perspective, Orientalism is no longer merely "a Western style for dominating, restructuring, and having authority over the Orient," "a willed human work," "the stage on which the whole East is confined," "an imperial institution," "a system of representations framed by a whole set of forces," and "the distillation of essential ideas about the Orient" (Said 1978, 2, 15, 63, 95, 205, 202). This dichotomy of the Orient and the Occident does not help me articulate how similar Orientalist sentiments find their way into the literary and cinematic portraits of Tibet by Chinese and Tibetan writers and artists. The "Orient," seen in the case of Tibet in the twenty-first century, is often a personalized, individualized "Other" – a subject – which is not confined in its geography but moves and is moved by those in contact with it. It touches the body and the mind of the visitor and moves him or her aesthetically, intellectually, and even emotionally. In turn the visitor moves it out of its geographic location via his or her remembered perception. Tibet as this "Other" becomes a part of the life experience of the visitor. And yet subsequent complications occur when the "remembered perception" is creatively and critically rendered into productions about Tibet for public consumption.

Throughout this book it is recognizable that I have minimized the presence of the Orientalist discourses of Said and Lopez except for keeping the critical discourse on the dichotomization, dialectics, and entwinement of self and other as a human universal in both intellectual and existential senses. However, the objective field of contemporary Tibetan studies in China and the West points to a sustained body of literature dedicated to critiquing the presence of Orientalism in non-Tibetans' perception of Tibet. The works of Wang Hui and Shen Weirong are exemplary of this ongoing critical effort among scholars in China. Lopez, Brauen, and their peers in the West probably never expected that such scholars as Wang and Shen would extensively reference their works to build a case of Orientalism in China. The difference between the Western scholars and their Chinese peers is that Lopez's writings, for instance, represent his own scholarly views, interpretations, and arguments; whereas the works of Wang and Shen reflect their personal views and experiences on one hand, and express their patriotism and "national defense" for the sovereignty of China on the other hand. In some ways, the tones and concerns in their works resemble those of imperial scholars of China's long dynastic era during which successive emperors gave royal recognition of scholarly achievements but also commissioned scholars to be advisors and counsel on imperial matters.

Take Wang's *The Tibet Question between the East and the West* for example. In it Wang affirms the commonly accepted view among Western scholars that Orientalized Tibet is rooted in the West's mysticism toward the Orient (Wang 2011, 25) and one version is constructed as Shangrila – a fantasy world – "a world that is mystical, spiritual, full of revelations, non-technological, peace-loving, moral, and miraculous" (Wang 2011, 29). Wang continues, "Western society has never been able to leave behind such Orientalist episteme. Those, who feel hopeless about their own society and the modern world, quickly find soulful consolation in their imagined Tibet" (Wang 2011, 37). Tibet then stands as an Oriental Other in Wang's critique of the imagined Tibet in the West. This critical trajectory is an extension of the original perspectives of his Western contemporaries; however, Wang tends to re-emphasize the scandalous nature of Westerners' mystical approach to Tibet as a contribution to the Nazi search for their racially pure ancestors. Wang writes, "Tibet is the mystical and wisdom-filled homeland of Aryan ancestors" (Wang 2011, 25). Tibet is thus associatively hinted at for the Chinese readership as a fantasy world of Hitler thanks to Wang's meticulous paraphrasing of Brauen's findings (Wang 2011, 23). As the title of his book suggests, the Tibet Question is the foreground of his addressing the West's Orientalized Tibet. In this context Wang reminds his readers of the record of British imperial expansion in India, Nepal, Burma, and briefly Tibet, and of the U.S. involvement in Tibet issues during the Cold War era (Wang 2011, 38–71). Thus the historically inherent association of Orientalism with Colonialism is re-emphasized for Wang's readership.

In comparison, Shen's critique of Orientalism begins with his long years of lived experience in Europe and North America as narrated in his *In Search of Shangrila: Essays on China Studies, Philology and Virtual Tibet*. When he laid his hands on Said's *Orientalism* in Europe in the 1990s, he was immediately "drawn to and touched by critical theories of colonial and post-colonial studies represented by Said" (Shen 2010, 55). From then on he began to reflect on his personal experience with Western scholars and Tibetan studies. To him, Said's work is "a goblin-revealing mirror for deconstructing the Western authority over Oriental studies and dispelling cultural imperialism" (Shen 2010, 55). Shen's critical remark is not only directed toward the past generations of Western Tibetologists like Giuseppe Tucci and Herbert Frank, but also toward those who began their careers in the 1970's. Shen lumps together this new generation of Tibetologists as "a group of snotty Orientalists" (Shen 2010, 66).

Like Wang, Shen also re-emphasizes scandals that have occurred among Western Tibetan Buddhists. He dwells on sex scandals, citing June Campbell's allegation of a senior lama who "sexually exploited a young woman disciple in her twenties" (Shen 2010, 97). He gives an account of Gendün Chöphel (Shen 2010, 98–99) as an alcoholic, an opium addict, and a sex maniac who, when thrown into prison, "dared to demand the authorities give him a blow-up doll to satisfy his sexual lust" (Shen 2010, 99). Shen's repeated critical target is the late Chögyam Trungpa Rinpoche. Apparently based on his reading of Jeffery Paine's *Re-Enchantment: Tibetan Buddhism comes to the West* (2004), Shen reconstructed the image of this controversial but legendary tantric master as a drunkard, a drug user, and an orgy master behind whom was "a long line of female disciples waiting to practice tantrism in bed with him" (2010, 80–81;119–120). This allegation is made, noticeably, without remarking on the wider literature on the positive impact of Chögym Trungpa Rinpoche's teachings on Western Buddhists.

To both Wang and Shen, Orientalism is not merely a state of mind exerting representational power over the Oriental. It is more about the materialization of Westerners' fantasies about a superior race and a type of spiritually-elating but scandalous sexual practice. Having carefully revisited their critiques a few more times, I have a hard time seeing much of an essentialized Orient or Oriental other than the stereotype of Tibet as the dreamworld of the West and Tibetans as a peace-loving people. What stands out in their critiques is rather the Westerners' self-indulgence in their utopian dreams and sacralized sex.

To me, the works of Wang and Shen are rather reorienting me to see fresh dynamics in the critique of Orientalism they inherit from Lopez and like-minded Western scholars. The critique, in fact, essentializes Westerners as dreamers, fantasizers, utopians, and even victims of their own obsession with Tibetan Tantrism. Thus, the Westerners are as much "Orientalized" as Tibetans in the critical process when they are shown to be fools of their own fantasy, materializing the Orient in both their psyche and social acts. In this regard, the critical narratives of Wang and Shen yield a double re-essentialization, re-affirming the Western stereotype of Tibet as a Shangrila by re-typecasting Westerners as a collective personality obsessed with a non-existent Tibet as their "inalienable Other" (Shen 2010, 109).

Both the Orient and the Oriental do not exist. This is an age of Orientalism without the Orient (Chiou 2010, 73). If there is the Orient or the Oriental, it is simply called "the Other" which is an inalienable part of Self. Truly, Self is found in the Other and the Other in Self. This is an ontological universal. However the Orient is being projected, it is "Orienting" us to see who is projecting what and on whom. The projected Tibets in the works of Lopez, Brauen, Wang, and Shen all point fingers at the West. The missing Orient is rather found in the critic and the maker of the Orient. Does our chase end here? If we end here, what is all the fuss we make about Tibet? Is Tibet, as an enchanting Orient, solely our making? Is geographic and cultural Tibet also molding us – artists, critics, scholars, and writers – shaping the ways we respond to each other and how we tell the public about Tibet?

I propose that Tibet is a post-Oriental Other in global, local, institutional, and personal terms. Its Otherness is not locked in its geographic, cultural, and political boundaries. Neither does it belong to the exclusive privilege of Western Tibetophiles. It is rather diffused in geopolitical debates, public discourses, and personal humanitarian or spiritual aspirations. The examples of the Tibet-related scholarships of Wang Hui and Shen Weirong are indicative of how personal research, patriotism, and national interests are inextricably entwined. In this complex fusion of the personal, the national, and the public, Tibet's Otherness is subject to ideological, conceptual, and physical transformations from its allegedly oppressive past to the present socialist status. It is relentlessly defended from Western Tibetophiles' idealization of its past as a sacred Other which is subversive to China's Old Tibet as a hell on earth. This contested Otherness of Tibet continuously undergoes "shapeshifting" as an illusory Other, a fantasized Other, and a liberated Other in different domestic and geopolitical arenas. However, as discussed in the individual cases of this book, this scholar-state process of

"Othering" Tibet in China is encountering the global popular appreciation of Tibet as a spiritual source of sentient flourishing and as a positive reference for the environmental sustainability of the Earth.

The popular realm of contemporary China is enthusiastically receptive to this global consciousness of Tibet as a sacred Other, with its transpersonal qualities complicating the dualistic Orientalist critique of imagined Tibet. In many instances, as I demonstrate in different parts of this book, that the classic Orientalist divisions of Orient and Occident no longer have analytical efficacy for our understanding of the popularly-accepted transpersonal recognition of Tibet's own humanistic traditions, awe-inspiring landscape, and spiritual methods for sentient and ecological health. I also recognize the simultaneity of the splits and the transnational acceptance of Tibet as a sacred Other in the cultural consciousness of the individual artists, filmmakers, writers, scholars, and students about whom I write in this book. Among this diverse group of individuals, Tibet's Otherness is not merely external Other in geographic, cultural, and linguistic terms, but is an Other most present in the mindscapes of these individuals who have lived in, traveled to, or worked in Tibetan regions. In this regard, I insist again that contemporary Tibetan studies have to take a post-Oriental turn for the sake of allowing more insights into the growing multi-disciplinary inquiries about the emotionality, religiosity, spirituality, and aesthetics of Tibet's global presence. This book does not cover everything Tibetan but its effort to work on small pieces of the puzzle, e.g. landscape, mindscape, affect, and eco-religiosity, is undoubtedly attempted as a contribution to our understanding of bigger issues of both scholarly and public concerns about how Tibet is experienced and conceptualized in China.

8.2 Tibet as a geopsychic terrain

Tibet – as an Orient, an imagination, a dreamworld, a fiction, a cinema, or a mirage – is indisputably an Other in the context of contemporary China. As I discuss throughout the book, the making of this Other is a project of both Tibetans and non-Tibetans. The Tibets re-created by the traditionalist and the modernist Tibetans in the cases of Shogdong, Pema Tseden, and others characteristically embody their respectively believed ideologies, perceived realities, practiced worldviews, and the envisioned futures of their homeland; however, I cannot emphasize enough the rhyzomic lifeworld that encompassed both the landscape of Tibet and the mindscape of their place-based memories, nostalgia, and emotions, and how the landscape and the mindscape both take roots in each other.

In the case of the reconstruction of Tibet as an Other in the popular realm of China, the potency of the Tibetan landscape shows itself in myriad expressions in the creative mindscape of an increasing number of Han Chinese writers and artists. Their re-created Tibets are equally place-based embodiments of their social conditions, ideological orientations, and traveling, working and living experiences in Tibet. However, the mirage effects from their re-creations are obviously not identical to their Tibetan counterparts in terms of a range of divergent volitions, meanings, genres, and envisioned public responses. The religiosity and the psychological impacts of the Tibetan landscape on native Tibetans have been widely researched and documented in the works of Rene de Nebesky-Wojkowitz (1975), Alfred Rolf Stein (1972), Toni Huber (1999), and Mona Schrempf (2002). In comparison, the different set of dynamics in the Chinese re-creations of Tibet as an Other is under-studied and therefore it might be a topic for further research.

Tibet, in the creative works by Chinese writers and artists is affirmatively an Other, but like all works of art, the subject is repossessed and remolded as a vessel of the Self of the artist. It is often a personal complex of the artist expressed through imagery and reflection of the Tibetan landscape. In this regard, this re-created Tibet is both an Other and a Self or an Other repossessed and re-ensouled by the Self.

Take Ma Lihua, the renowned travel writer and the former Editor in Chief of China Tibetology Press for example. In Shen's accolade, she is iconically considered "a legend" and "a literary genius" whose scholarly contribution to Tibetan studies can humble "a hundred Tibetologists" (Shen 2010, 181). The literary mirage of Tibet that Ma has crafted is based on her work, living, and travel experience in Tibet since 1976. She missed the "rescue fantasy" of the military officers like Lin Tian and Ling Xingzheng in the 1950s but caught the inauguration of China's full-scale infrastructural modernization of Tibet as well as the accompanying popular rediscovery of Tibet as a pureland on earth. To me, Ma's contribution to China's Tibetan studies and the popular fascination of Tibet is a prototype of the creative repossession of Tibet replenished by the complex of one's own psyche and social conditions. On the one hand, she opens her mindscape to the overwhelmingly sublime energy of Tibetan landscape:

> Mountains are colossal and waters are massive. These immense mountain ranges and rivers have shaped this desolate and cold plateau. I think inwardly: Where else in this world will I find higher mountains and loftier hills? The horizon, upon which I stand, is several thousand meters above the sea level and thus is the tip of the world. I love it when my vision is filled with mountains. I find delight in seeing them from all possible angles: eye level, overlooking, from below, and at a distance; I am fond of looking at them in the different shades and shadows of the dawn, the dusk, and the mid-day sun; and I trek through them as much

as I can with different means: vehicle, horse ride, and walking. Mountains have been my companions in Tibet for the last eighteen years (Ma 2007a, 1).

Outside the window the red rolling mountains are still the same but the flora blanketing them is rather becoming ever more colorful. How on earth can such brilliant blue and purple flowers exist? Each field of the blue or the purple emits sparks of luminescence as mesmerizing as polished sand grains. The flowers embraced by the green leaves adorn the mountain slopes like a vibrant tapestry. I have never seen such scenery. Unexpectedly, I realize beauty takes different forms to express itself. So does affection (Ma 2007b, 256).

At the same time, that affection floods her mindscape of Tibet with her own innermost, value-rich expressions:

This nation of souls owns the infinite time and space, and has dissolved finite boundaries of individual consciousness. Group dance and chorus are their distinguished features. One has no need for a last name. Neither does one care for the continuation of his bloodline, the accumulation of wealth, striving or competition. Hence, one has no subsequent upsets, anxiety, depression, fear, worries, crisis, and hopelessness, and is so carefree about misfortune and fortune, and agony and pleasure that one enters the world again and again with humble origin. Worshipping nature and the equality of all lives, one is indifferent to impoverishment. Treating everyone under heaven with compassion regardless of how those people show off their material superiority, this is a classic goodhearted personality. It is possible to be an instinctual ecological preservationist, a philosopher who has transcended time and space, and a minstrel who foresees the fate of the heaven and the earth (Ma 2007a, 161).

Shen, as "a fan of hers," regards Ma's relationship with Tibet and Tibetans as that of milk and water, inseparable from each other (Shen 2010, 180–181); however, Ma makes rhetorical questions and frank remarks indicating otherwise: "You can appreciate a beautiful and comforting idyllic poem [Tibet] to your heart's content from a distance, but do you identify with it" (Ma 2007a, 161)? "It is neither possible to invite them [Tibetans] into my car, offering them shelter from the rainstorm nor is it possible for me to get out of my car and walk together with them in the storm" (2007a, 162).

The dichotomy of self and other is poetically and critically articulated throughout Ma's travel writings. Her trilogy (2007a, 2007b, and 2007c) reads like a three-staged pilgrimage in her mindscape of Tibet. It leads from positive aesthetics of Tibet's landscape to her own split view on the "this worldliness" of Han people and "the other worldliness" of Tibetans and finally to her realization of Tibet as the place of her inspiration best seen from a distance that allows her to see "eternity in a flash" (2007a, 135). Like other Tibet drifters, Ma drifts in both the physical landscape and her creative mindscape of Tibet.

8.2 Tibet as a geopsychic terrain — 221

Looking again at the works of the writers and artists I have cited in this book, I see a pattern: their publicly shared memoirs, travel anecdotes, and fictionalized autobiographies all signify that the contents of their mindscapes eventually merge with, re-color, metaphorize, or flood their perceived landscapes of Tibet and thus speak the voices of their own minds through the metaphor of Tibet. Each writer or artist orients the audience toward individual and distinct versions of Tibet:

> Lama Anagarika Govinda appeared to be more enchanted by the sublime, luminous mountains of Tibet than Tibetan Buddhism when he was in Tibet;
> PLA officers like Huang Zongjiang, Lin Tian, Ling Xingzheng, and Wei Ke in the 1950s were indoctrinated to see Tibet as an oppressive society but are now belatedly revealing to the Chinese public the heavenly earth of Tibet they witnessed as young soldiers and officers;
> Shogdong dreams for a new modern Tibet but it is hindered by the presence of what he sees as Tibet's backward past: the embodiment of Buddhism, gods, demons, and spirits in the land of Tibet and in the minds of his compatriots;
> Akhu Shampa misses home before he even leaves. Jigmed visualizes Amne Machen as a treasure house and Tserang Dondrub reveres the living mountain. Meanwhile Moshi and Pangzi can hardly deal with the environmental potency of Golok;
> Pema Tseden cinematically searches for a Buddhist Tibet that is being eroded by advancing modernization;
> The masterminds of Yunnan's tourist development – Sun Jiong, Tang Shijie, and Chelhata – have miniaturized Tibet in Shangrila as a paradise on earth;
> Chai Chunya magicalizes Tibet as a desolate encampment of his self-exile for his subsequent spiritual rebirth and literary rejuvenation;
> Dai Wei cinematically recreates a pre-socialist Tibet – a fusion of Hilton's Shangrila, a Sino-U.S. alliance against the Japanese, positive Buddhist images, the oppressive slavery system, and innocence and compassion of nomads;
> Ma Lihua, while absorbing the magnificent beauty of the Tibetan landscape, realizes the spiritually overwhelming simplicity of a Tibetan lifestyle as admirable but not meant for her own life;
> Wang Hui and Shen Weirong represent the Western imagination of Tibet as a dreamworld and an Orientalized fantasy but have not yet demonstrated what they mean by "the real Tibet" (Shen 2010, 123).

Among them, there is no single uniformly recognized Tibet, all are bits and pieces from the experiential perceptions of these writers and artists; however, a common theme interlacing together their texts and artworks is Tibet's extraordinary landscape.

8.3 Tibetophilia, topophilia, and eco-aesthetics revisited

After serving as a Xinhua News journalist in Tibet for a decade, Hao Guiyao, pen-named Xiaohao, and mentioned in chapter three, returned to Shandong, his home province, in 1993 in a state of disorientation. He confides his existential difficulties to his readers:

> After ending my living in Tibet for over ten years I returned to Shandong. I suddenly felt my spirit had lost its direction. I felt like a cloud of Tibet floating rootlessly over the earth of Shandong. Tibet is a Buddhist world where people's inner worlds find satisfaction because they have answers about where their souls reside. I was once immersed in and intoxicated by such peace and content of that world. After returning to Shandong and seeing the sudden change of my living environment I panicked as I realized that the soul must have its own decent residence (Hao 2008, 1).

In my reading of the works of Hao and his contemporaries, Tibetophilia is a type of topophilia, an affective bond between landscape and mindscape. The fusion of landscape and mindscape then becomes a geopsychic terrain (Bruno 2002, 253) in which the Tibetophile traverses the physical landscape of Tibet and, at the same time, finds new openings, frontiers, and horizons in his or her mindscape. In this encounter, merger, and communion of landscape and mindscape, the personhood of the Tibetophile undergoes challenges, shocks, ecstasy, realization, self-reassurance, renewal, restoration, or regression, among other responses. This affective bond is not one-sided. As shown in different chapters, the landscape of Tibet also "talks back" and "loves back" to the Tibetophile. It often kicks off the electrifying currents of awed moments, reflections, and imaginative thoughts in the participant's mindscape. The Tibetophiliac geopsychic affect is charged with a range of feeling- and emotion-induced nostalgia, wishful thinking, dreams, hope, and visions.

If I use the phrases from Ivakhiv's study of power places, Tibet, as a geopsychic terrain of both landscape and mindscape, is a certain vibration, a moment of attunement, an energy body, a spectrum of higher frequencies, a numinous Other, and a point of dynamic transference (Ivakhiv 2001, 8, 52, 190, 192, 223). It is thus *enlightening* in the sense that the mindscape environed and affected by the Tibetan landscape illuminates itself within. What has not been felt is felt; what has not been touched is touched; what has not been seen is seen; what has receded into the past is being recalled into the present; what has been present is being pushed back into the past; what has not been contended with is contended with; what has been destroyed is being repaired and restored, and what has not existed is being added.

Since the early 1990s, China has begun to see its own version of popular Tibetophilia. Throughout this book, I attempt to recapture the geopsychic theme among the works of Chinese and Tibetan writers and artists and have found that it resembles a road movie or the moving landscape of a drifter with a clear kinetic pattern of meaning-seeking during the drifting and dreamed destiny. By "meaning-seeking" I mean that the inner world of the drifter, as shown in the works of Shogdong, Pema Tseden, Chai Chunya, and Ma Lihua, often relies on the outer world or the landscape of Tibet for the literary or cinematically articulated existential or spiritual meanings felt by the drifter. In other words, the drifter turns inward while his or her body moves outward in the landscape of Tibet. Tibet illuminates the mindscape of the drifter as if it compelling him or her to an inner journey.

In his introduction to Ma Lihua's trilogy, Li Jingze, a renowned literary critic and Editor in Chief of the People's Literature Magazine, hails Ma as a pioneer of the "new discovery" of Tibet which "transcends our experience and has become a dream, a foresight, a place for discovery…and a spiritual Other" (Li 2007, 11). Meanwhile Li points out that Tibet seen as a "spiritual park" originates from "our modern anxieties" (Li 2007, 12). As shown in Shogdong's pathogenic modernity, Pema Tseden's endangered tradition, and Chai Chunya's "incurable loneliness," it is precisely the disorienting modernity that causes the artist or the writer to blend and re-animate his or her autobiography in the landscape of Tibet. This is eco-aesthetics at work as I have discussed thus far.

Landscape and mindscape are never two separate domains. The human body-mind is antecedently enveloped in landscape. If there is total separation, it is merely one-sidedly perceived by the human mind. In the case of the writers and artists considered in this book, their *self-revealing* narratives are all grounded in their in-it-experiences in Tibet. This is eco-aesthetics at work. As delineated in the opening chapter, eco-aesthetics is understood in the original sense as "perception by the senses" (Berleant 2010, 20). The vital agentive act of the eco-aesthetic nature of a person is to touch and to be touched or, more accurately, to be in a state of simultaneously touching and being touched. In the anthropology of landscape, eco-aesthetics is "a synaesthesia – the fusion of the senses" in which "Sensation is a communion, or coexistence, between body and thing" (Tilley 2004, 14). To add, sensing and sense-generated sensations are not merely the surficial contacts between the walking soles of the feet and the earth, or between facial skin and the vapors of foggy weather. They are both physical and psychic. By "psychic" I mean the touched/touching mindscape or the inner being of the person releases light from within and thus produces imagination, dreams, creativity, and visions.

Eco-aesthetics thus signifies sense-generated perception, which, as Tilley describes, "is a mode of action in relation to life activities, providing knowledge of what the environment affords, and such knowledge is potentially inexhaustible because of the possibilities for sensitizing the perceptual system and attuning it to phenomenal diversity of the environment: its textures, colours, surfaces, smells, sound, tastes, and sights" (Tilley 2004, 23). In this regard, landscape or, more accurately, our perception of landscape is not external to us but enters our mindscape through our bodily immersion in it. Besides air and water, the colors and the geological forces of it equally enter our body-mind. "Places nest in landscapes" (Tilley 2004, 25). So too do they nest in mindscapes.

With this said, most of the writers and artists referenced in this book revere Tibet as a sacred, or at least special and inspiring, place. Their geopoetic expressions prompt me to say that to both the native Tibetan artists and this group of Han Chinese Tibetophiles, Tibet is an entheogen, which literally means "in touch with the divine within" (Shanon 2008, 52). Tibet, in this sense, could be seen as a psychoactive sacramental or a sacred medium transmitting the contents of their land inspired mindscapes in poeisis or in the language of the transcendental. As shown in their cinematic and literary works, Tibet, as a psychoactive sacramental, enables the mindscape of the artist or the writer to engender "unitive consciousness," "feelings of positive affect," or "a sense of immediacy and temporality" (Hruby 2001, 59). These entheogenic characteristics of a psychoactive sacramental coincide with the felt magic of Chai Chunya, Ma Lihua's visions of the soul (Ma 2007c, 36), Tang Shijie's "colorful dream" (Tang 2011), to name a few. The landscape of Tibet has entered the mindscapes of a group of creative individuals in China who are the mirage-makers of Tibet influencing aesthetics and value-judgments of countless potential visitors to Tibet.

Eco-aesthetics in these individual mirage-makers' cases is "a haptic aesthetics" (Paterson 2007, 11) involving both tactile and psychic touches between the world and the body-mind. Through such outer and inner touches, "the world is with us" (Paterson 2007, 101) and we are with the world; and the world speaks to us and we speak through the world. The eco-aesthetic reciprocity between landscape and mindscape is thus a process of sentient sensing of the world and oneself. To re-emphasize the entwinement of landscape and mindscape in my Tibet case, I say: mindscape is equally weathered and full of narratives yielded from the body-mind's sensing, touching, remembering, and re-envisioning of landscape. This leads to the primary point of this book: Tibet does not prioritize how we imagine, fantasize, or recreate it; instead it is, in fact, the other way around: the lifeworld of Tibet touches us before the outpouring of our sentiments, emotions, perceived realities, moralizing critiques, and reflexive Orientalism disguised as a pilgrim's revelation, humanitarian concerns, or euphoric expressions of felt self-realization.

8.4 An anthropological mindscape of Tibet

Approaching the end of this book, I would like to reflect on my anthropological subjectivity with Tibet as a field of my ethnographic work, an arena where I share my viewpoints with my scholarly peers, the homeland of many of my friends, a terrain in which I sense the ancient vision of *anima mundi* (regardless of what current social science consensus would suggest), and a piece of the Earth which gives me countless vistas, panoramas, horizons, starry nights, moments of feeling minute and insignificant, and sublime states of being when it overpowers self-centric and ethnocentric pulses in my cultural consciousness.

While critiquing the creative works of filmmakers, artists, and writers in China, I have often wondered how I would write about Tibet if my livelihood depended upon creatively representing Tibet's people and land; if I were a native county cadre in Shangrila caught between modernization and cultural preservation; if I were a fundraiser for an NGO specializing in nature conservation; and if I were a fiction filmmaker who has to balance his creative aspiration and perceived consumer demand for specific cinematic contents. I have also questioned the perspective of my reviews of other representations of Tibet. I can see the roots of my intellectual judgmentalism as originating from my acquired Western social scientific perspectives, my lived experience in Northern California, and the memory of my childhood in a once-less-populated urban place in southern China that was rich in the idyllic landscape of parks, forested hills, lakes, rivers, and rice fields. I am most certain that these contents of my subjectivity influence the way I have written this book with a high possibility of transferable and transposable nostalgia, ideals, moral grounds, hopes, and visions for a world that can support the flourishing of all sentient beings.

An anthropologist is never only a social scientist. My own affective bond with Tibet and my Tibetan friends reveals itself in my nocturnal dreams of friends and their home villages and pastoral grounds, in the solar-powered classrooms and libraries I built together with Tibetan school teachers, and in my ongoing research and film projects, and in a flux of text-messages, the short greetings and updates from my Tibetan friends and students that arrive regularly into my China cell phone left roaming in the U.S. and Europe:

"Akha I miss you!"
"I bought a motorcycle!"

"Help me recharge my simcard!"
"I'm on the way to Golok digging caterpillar fungus..."
"Hey, I heard you're in New York."
"I wrote a new script!"
"Where are you?"
"I found a job in Lhasa."
"When are you coming back?"

This cell number is a "tele-path" between Tibet and me.

The field of anthropological research in this era of globalization is never "out there" but extends itself into the personal and institutional worlds of the anthropologist. If I have a fantasy about Tibet, this "tele-path" would be a passage leading me to write a screenplay based on the life stories of my Tibetan friends, and stories of their animated home environment. If I ever shoot a film like this, I would use anamorphic lenses to squeeze in the scenes of the expansive landscape as much as possible as an integral part of human storylines with the intention to restore their sublime originality on a wide screen. It would be a cinematic experiment to put into practice my theoretical claim that humans can experience the earth's own subjectivity.

It is therefore inevitable that "Landscape," "place," "mindscape," "potency," and "eco-aesthetics" are the mantras of this book. If I take "mantra" literally as "instrument of thought" (MacDonell 1927, 162), these words and their associated phrases are indeed instruments or vessels of my anthropological thought woven together with my cross-regional fieldwork in Beijing, Amdo (Qinghai and southern Gansu), TAR, and Yunnan; parallel immersion in the theoretical literature of place and landscape studies; and harnessing support from or advancing arguments similar to such brilliant thinkers as Bruno, Casey, Gibson, Ingold, Paterson, and Tilley in anthropology of landscape and its neighboring disciplines. My choice for the instrument of my thought was made after returning from China. Especially after re-reading my fieldnotes, I found that the most ideal theoretical language for this book would come from Bruno's "geopsychic terrain;" Ingold's "sentient ecology," "storied landscape," and "rhyzomic world;" Tilley's "sensescapes," "the body-subject," and "synaesthesia;" and Casey's "memorability," "emplacement," and "body as inter-place."

With this said I am prompted to explain why I draw very few theoretical perspectives from existing literature in modern/contemporary Tibetan studies, which I have faithfully referenced in most of my writings. If I could externalize my anthropological mindscape of Tibet it would consist of two domains that border each other but do not quite speak to each other regardless of the fact both sides concern themselves with Tibet. One side speaks the language of the "mantras" evoked above, while the other side expresses itself in an anthropocentric way concerning mostly human politics and not opening itself up to the presence of place, landscape, and earth-based deities as human companions in Tibet. This part of my mindscape has been the dominant part of my focus since early in my graduate and professional career. For my first monograph I extensively drew perspectives, arguments, and reasoned debates from anthropology to articulate my understanding of the current conditions and the interactive modes of being of Tibetan Buddhist communities with their Chinese counterparts.

The way I reference the works of many anthropology-based authors has been characteristically manifested in the tensioned, contested relationship between the Chinese state's policy implementation, Tibetans' negotiation and resistance to it, and Chinese Buddhists' frustrated aspirations for new forms of Dharma practices and their maneuvering in the regulatory interstices of the Chinese state's restrictively sanctioned social space of religion. *The Spread of Tibetan Buddhism in China* (2011) is thus imprinted with a set of dichotomies and their dialectic relationships thematically stringing together ethnographic data, policy interpretations, and anthropological analyses of social conditions and behaviors of Tibetans and Chinese Buddhists. My findings, like those of other scholars, reveal which human social tensions, inter-ethnic conflicts, and state interventions dominate scholarly interpretations, debates, and discourses on Tibet related issues. This is what I mean by "anthropocentric." The thematic line of Tibetan cultural and religious revitalizations since the 1980s has been sustained as such.

Goldstein begins his introduction of his widely read *Buddhism in Contemporary Tibet*, co-edited with Kapstein, by setting the tone of the Chinese state's taking a "reversed course" (Goldstein 1998, 1) away from its past iconoclastic approach toward religion. In the same manner Kapstein presents his ethnographic account of the revival of the Drigung Powa Chenmo in the northeast of Lhasa (Kapstein 1998, 95–119). In these texts, the 1990s are presented as a period of the Chinese state's policy relaxation, a dynamic that permitted the return of Buddhist practices in Tibetan regions.

Since the turn of the century, more publications have emerged bringing forth fresh findings and theoretical perspectives. Barnett's idea of "Tibetanization" (Barnett 2006, 39) is a frequently referenced point among his peers for the purpose of highlighting the context of Tibetan cultural and religious revitalizations in the last two decades of the twentieth century. At the same time, the complexity of Tibetan cultural revitalizations continues to undergo changes and reveal fresh dynamics. Tibetan Buddhism is ever more entangled in China's market economy as shown its presence in tourism and ethnic consumer products (Kolås 2008; Hillman 2009) as well as an increase in practitioners. In this context Tibetans are being drawn deeper into China's rapidly expanding modernization program in Tibet. The theoretical paths of many Tibet scholars have inevitably crossed those of the pan-disciplinary studies of modernity in non-Western contexts.

The conceptualization of modernity among Tibet scholars is then increasingly contextualized with that of China. As Ronald Schwartz phrases it, "the gift of modernity" (Schwartz 2008, 4) to Tibetans from the Chinese state is a focal point in the current studies of Tibet. Thus, the modern transition of Tibet and Tibetans is ever being underlined and conjoined with modernity studies in Chinese contexts. The current scholarly findings of Tibet's modernity can be seen as an Other modernity or as "a powerful imaginary," as Schwartz resituates Lisa Rofel's model of China's modernity in Tibetan context (Schwartz 2008, 3). This "otherness" of Tibetan modernity is then connected with the social and economic marginality of Tibetans (Fischer 2005), their suppressed political expressions (Robin 2012, 123), and environmental deterioration (Bauer and Childs 2008, 5–7).

I see this scholarly trend of contemporary Tibetan studies as a process of "authenticating Tibet" (Blondeau and Buffetrille 2008) combing through and combing out different versions of modern Tibet: the injured, the socialist, the Chinese popular, the globally influenced, and the traditionally-grounded but threatened. In the midst of this, native Tibetan scholars raise the issues of power and representation in the West: "Tibetans are seen merely as victims who are unable to speak for themselves...the Tibetan issue is treated as an inevitable question of a 'backward nation resisting the march of modernity'" (Tsering Shakya 1991, 23). Thus, Tibet and Tibetans appear to be drawn as subjects into our thick discourses of human politics without much credit given to their own voices. It is indeed the voices of the modernites, whether statesmen, public intellectuals or scholars, who frequently speak for Tibetans. As a social scientist, I see identifying patterns, articulating observations, and drawing generalities as part and parcel of my workflow; thus representation in deliberation or by accident is inevitable. However, I have sensed that there must be other ways for us to see and understand how we perceive Tibet antecedently as a place with power of its own.

In my eyes the power of Tibet shows its forces in myriad ways. The geological force, first of all, incarnates Tibet as the highest place on earth. The pedospheric skin of Tibet is not a flat, smooth surface but a diverse mountainous topography dynamically interfacing with its surrounding atmosphere, hydrosphere, and biosphere. The mountainous solid skin of Tibet is fully enveloped and saturated by a powerful hydrosphere to the extent that it can be said that Tibet is an ocean on land. Its water sustains a dozen nations and several billions of people in Asia as highlighted in the introductory chapter. In my fieldwork in rural Tibet the sound of a mountain is often synonymous with the sounds of water. Water is omnipresent in the mountains as snow, ice, and glaciers, and as starting points of rivers, streams, and creeks. It makes deafening noise as well as melodic sounds as it flows around a bend or wraps around a boulder in a stream, or when it drips beneath an ice sheet or flows in a subterranean river. This geo-ecological force of Tibet is a critical source of life to the billions of people and countless non-human species within its reach. It amazes, tips, and reshapes the environmental consciousness of those who have had physical immersion in it. Their awed, on-site moments are often later translated into potent language for social engagements and political changes.

Buddhism, the dominant fiber of Tibetan civilization, is another form of Tibet's power, and it is growing roots outside Tibet among Australians, Chinese, Europeans, North Americans, South Americans, and South Africans. While Tibetan civilization has long been discerned as "a most backward, feudalistic serfdom" (Li 1965, 133) and, seen from outside China, as a victim of a humanitarian crisis since the middle of the last century, the presence of Tibet in the global arena of religion and spirituality has a different storyline: Tibet is enchanting and intriguing spiritually-inclined people around the world with its form of Buddhism. Tibetan lamas are the emerging "masters of divinity" on the landscape of world religions. Their disciples are found among politicians, celebrities, corporate executives, scholars, students, small business owners, and office clerks. Their outreach is not limited to the spiritual realm of the individual disciple but is also found in the application of tantric teachings in hospice care, prison chaplaincy, therapeutic practices, and conflict resolution and peace-building.

Chinese Buddhists in China are not left out of the reach of Tibetan Dharma masters. In less than two decades, Tibetan Buddhism has become a formidable "competitor" to Chinese Buddhism. It enters private homes and businesses, and university campuses and NGO offices. If the Chinese state truly implements its constitutionally sanctioned religious freedom, a few high lamas and their lay sanghas would not hesitate to build Tibetan monasteries in urban centers or increase the scope of educational and public outreach. The force of Tibetan Buddhist spirituality draws its adherents to Tibet.

As more and more people travel to Tibet and return with their stories narrated in eco-spiritual and eco-aesthetical terms, it is too limiting to perceive their experiences of their body-minds only as a "New Age Orientalism" (Lopez 1994), or as an ethnographic account of Chinese or American Buddhist "occupation" of Tibet (Mullen 2001, 91–119). This is where it is important to begin to rethink how the power of Tibet is articulated. This is also where I begin to see more of my own mindscape of Tibet originating from fieldwork assignments and personal living experiences there.

My mindscape of Tibet is of a placial complex in which my perceived landscape or the lifeworld of Tibet is nested. It is a transport of a living environment as an optical phenomenon with sounds, scents, and metereological fluxes transformed into internally heard, colorful, remembered motions and images. The ecological and cultural potency of the landscape is thus metamorphosed into a visually affective potency that retains the power of the landscape but, at the same time, kicks off a series of intellectual, reflective, emotional, creative, and imaginative motions responding to the powerful presence of Tibet as both a geographic place and a placeless place in my mindscape. Tibet, either in its landscape or in my mindscape, gives an affordance or a medium of all sorts to my anthropological writing, ecological perception, humanitarian emotion, filmmaking, and an empathetic understanding of Tibet-stimulated imaginations, creative imagery, and self-realizations from both Tibetans and non-Tibetans.

My mindscape is capable of producing its own mirage of Tibet, resembling a moving cinematic terrain expressing a perceptual unity of how I assess other people's mirages of Tibet. In this regard, this book is a mirage of Tibet. I have perused a range of creative writings and cinematic productions not only from an anthropological angle but also from other perspectives and motives, e.g. literary, creative, imaginative, and critical. My mirage of Tibet in this book is woven together with what Hayden White would call "the fictions of factual representation" (White 1978, 121) – combinations and fusions of my trained critical skills, and fictionalized biographies, poetically rendered travel writings, and cinematic narratives of Tibetans and non-Tibetans. What is factual in this midst is each subject's bodily presence in Tibet and his or her subsequent re-coloring, re-imagining, and re-constructing of Tibet with unique combinations of autobiographical issues, values, and worldviews. This fiction of factual Tibet resembles a "landscaping" in the sense of a gardening or urban landscape design. While the earth itself does not change, its image is being altered and re-ornamented with added elements and aesthetic intentions. Similarly, whether intended for creative consumers of entertainment or for raising critical awareness from the public, many of the reconstructed Tibets offered in this book are amalgamations of perceived geographic Tibet and cultural and ideological ornaments that are not native to Tibet. This makes the work of "authenticating Tibet" ever more challenging and yet stimulating as each case presents itself like cinematic terrain on which both the elemental components of Tibet and personal emotions and imaginations move together to complete their stories. Tibet is then a medium linking, transmitting, and conjoining landscape with mindscape.

References

Books, Articles and Papers

Anand, Dibyesh. 2008. *Geopolitical Exotica: Tibet in Western Imagination*. Minneapolis: University of Minneapolis Press.

Anderson, Benedict. 1991. *Imagined Communities: Reflections on the Origins and Spread of Nationalism*. New York: Verso.

Antze, Paul and Michael Lambek. 1996. "Introduction: Forecasting Memory." In *Tense Past: Cultural Essays in Trauma and Memory*, edited by Paul Antze and Michael Lambek, xi-xxxxiii. New York: Routledge.

Baidu Encyclopedia (百度百科) "Tibet Drifters" (藏漂). http://baike.baidu.com/view/3346676.htm. Accessed December 12, 2012.

Baker, Ian. 2004. *The Heart of the World: A Journey to the Last Secret Place*. New York: Penguin Books.

Barnett, Robert. 2006. "Beyond the Collaborator-Martyr Model: Strategies of Compliance, Opportunism, and Opposition within Tibet." In *Contemporary Tibet: Politics, Development, and Society in a Disputed Region*, edited by Barry Sautman and June Teufel Dreyer. 25–66. Armonk, NY: M.E. Sharpe.

Barnett, Robert and Ronald Schwartz, eds. 2008. *Tibetan Modernities: Notes from the Field on Cultural and Social Change*. Leiden: Brill.

Bauer, Kenneth and Geoff Childs. 2008. "Demographics, Development, and the Environment in Tibetan Areas." *Journal of the International Association of Tibetan Studies* 4:1–8.

Bellezza, John Vincent. 2005. *Spirit-Mediums, Sacred Mountains and Related Bon Textual Traditions in Upper Tibet: Calling down the Gods*. Leiden: Brill.

Bender, Barbara. 2001. "Introduction." In *Contested Landscapes: Movement, Exile and Place*, edited by Barbara Bender and Margot Winer. 1–20. Oxford: Berg.

Bender, Barbara. 2002. "Time and Landscape." *Current Anthropology* 43:S103-S112.

Bender, Barbara, Sue Hamilton and Christopher Tilley. 2007. *Stone Worlds: Narrative and Reflexivity in Landscape Archaeology*. Walnut Creek, CA: Left Coast Press.

Berleant, Arnold. 2010. *Sensibility and Sense: The Aesthetic Transformation of the Human World*. Exeter, UK: Imprint Academic.

Berman, Emanuel. 1993. "Psychoanalysis, Rescue and Utopia." *Utopian Studies* 4(2): 44–56.

Bishop, Peter. 1993. *Dreams of Power: Tibetan Buddhism and the Western Imagination*. London: The Athlone Press.

Blondeau, Anne-Marie and Katia Buffetrille, eds. 2008. *Authenticating Tibet: Answers to China's 100 Questions*. Berkeley: University of California Press.

Bongtse (རོང་རྩེ). 2010. "A Discourse on Tibetan Modern Literaure in Relation to the Cultural Revolution" (རིག་གསར་དང་འབྲེལ་ནས་དེང་རབས་བོད་ཀྱི་རྩོམ་རིག་ལ་དཔྱད་པ་རོག་རོ་རྐྱག་གི་བཤད་བཅོས), *Voice* (ང་རོ) – *A Tibetan Journal of Minzu University of China* 5:83–94.

Brauen, Martin. 2004. *Dreamworld Tibet: Western Illusions*, Trumbull, CT: Weatherhill.

Bruno, Giuliana. 2002. *Atlas of Emotion: Journeys in Art, Architecture and Film*. New York: Verso.

Bruno, Giuliana. 2004. "Cities, Cinema: Image of Flows, Flows of Images" [lecture notes], in the Lecture Series *Making the City with Flows? Managing Places of Interchange and Architecture of Mobility*. Paris, France. Institut pour la Ville en mouvement, http://www.ville-en-mouvement.com/. Accessed July 05, 2013.

Budd, Malcolm. 1996. "The Aesthetic Appreciation of Nature." *British Journal of Aesthetics*, 36(3):207–222.

Budd, Malcolm. 2000. "The Aesthetics of Nature." *Proceedings of the Aristotelian Society*, New Series. 100:137–157.

Buffetrille, Katia. 1997. "The Great Pilgrimage of A-mye rma-chen: Written Tradition, Living Realities." In *Mandala and Landscape*, edited by Alexander W. MacDonald, 75–132. New Delhi: D.K. Printworld.

Buffetrille, Katia. 2003. "The Evolution of a Tibetan Pilgrimage: The Pilgrimage to A myes rMa chen Mountain in the 21st Century." In *21st Century Tibet Issue, Symposium on Contemporary Tibetan Studies*, 325–363. Taipei Taiwan: Mongolia-Tibet Commission.

Bunkse, Edmunds V. 2007. "Feeling is Believing, or Landscape as a Way of Being in the World." *Geografiska Annaler*, 89B(3):219–231.

Caibei, 2012. *Research on Mountain Deities at Mt. Amne Machen* 《阿尼玛卿山神研究》. Beijing: Minzu Press.

Campbell, Joseph. 1968. *The Hero with a Thousand Faces.* Princeton: Princeton University Press.

Carlson, Allen. 1984. "Nature and Positive Aesthetics." *Environmental Ethics* 6:5–35.

Carrington, Michael. 2003. "Gentlemen and Thieves: The Looting of Monasteries during the 1903/4 Younghusband Mission to Tibet." *Modern Asian Studies* 37(1):81–109.

Casey, Edward. 1997. *The Fate of Place: A Philosophical History.* Berkeley: University of California Press.

Casey, Edward 2000. *Remembering: A Phenomenological Study.* Bloomington: Indiana University Press.

Casey, Edward. 2005.
Earth-Mapping: Artists Reshaping Landscape Minneapolis: University of Minnesota Press.

Chai, Chunya (柴春芽). 2009a. *A Vagabond in Tibet* 《西藏流浪记》. Taipei, Taiwan: Unitas Udngroup.

Chai, Chunya (柴春芽). 2009b. *Red Sheepskin Book of Tibet* 《西藏红羊皮书》. Taipei, Taiwan: Unitas Udngroup.

Chai, Chunya (柴春芽). 2009c. "Magical Journey to Tibet in Troubled Times" 《騷亂時期的西藏魔幻之旅》. *Unitas* (聯合文學) 299:120–135

Chai, Chunya (柴春芽). 2010. *The Seventh Treasure Book of Grandma Ayima.* Taipei: Unitas Udngroup.

Chai, Chunya (柴春芽). 2011. *The Silent Mani-Song* 《寂静玛尼歌》. Shanghai: Shanghai People's Press.

Chen, Xiaodong (陈晓东). 2002. *The Red Radiance of Nyingmapa: A Vajrayana Pureland in Today's Larungar Valley* 《宁玛的红辉-今日喇荣山中的一块密乘净》. Nonsellable edition. Wuhan, China: Shenweide Investment, Inc.

Chen, Xujing. 1934. *The Way Out for Chinese Culture*《中国文化的出路》, Shanghai: Commercial Press.

Chen, Yalian (陈亚莲). 2005. *My Ten Years in Tibet* 《我的西藏十年》. Changchun, Jilin: Jilin Art Press.

Cheng, Demei. 2005. *High Altitude Effects: The Love Knot of Cheng Family of Four with Tibet* 《高山反应 – 程氏一家四代的西藏情结》 Beijing: China Tibetology Press.

Chiou, Der-Liang. 2010. "Orientalism without Orient(ation), or the Other Orient." *Cultural Studies* 10:69–102.

Chögyam Trungpa. 1995. *Born In Tibet*. Boston: Shambhala Publications.
Cleary, Thomas. 1993. *The Flower Ornament Scripture: A Translation of the Avatamsaka Sutra*. Boston: Shambhala Publications.
Clifford, James. 1988. "On Orientalism," in *The Predicament of Culture: Twentieth-Century Ethnography, Literature, and Art* by James Clifford, 255–276. Cambridge: Harvard University Press.
Clifford, Nicholas R. 1997. "White China, Red China: Lighting out for the Territory with Edgar Snow." *New England Review* 18(2):103–111.
Comaroff, John.L. 1996. "Ethnicity, Nationalism, and the Politics of Difference in an Age of Revolution." In *The Politics of Difference: Ethnic Premises in a World of Power*, edited by Edwin. N. Wilmsen and Patrick. McAllister.162–184. Chicago: The University of Chicago Press.
Comaroff, Jean. and John. Comaroff. 1993. "Introduction," in *Modernity and Its Malcontents: Ritual and Power in Postcolonial Africa*, edited by Jean Comaroff and John Comaroff, xi-xxxi. Chicago: The University of Chicago Press.
Cosgrove, Denis and Veronica Della Dora. 2009. *High Places: Cultural Geographies of Mountains, Ice and Science*. New York: I.B. Tauris.
Cox, Helen M. and Colin A. Holmes. 2000. "Loss, Healing, and the Power of Place." *Human Studies* 23(1):63–78.
Dalai Lama. 1997. *My Land, My People: the Memoirs of His Holiness, the Dalai Lama of Tibet*. New Delhi: Srishti Publishers and Distributors.
Daniels, Stephen and Denis Cosgrove.1988. "Introduction: Iconography and Landscape." In *Iconography and Landscape: The Iconography of Landscape*, edited by Denis Cosgrove and Stephen Daniels, 1–10. Cambridge: Cambridge University Press.
Danqu. 2005. "The Idea of Soul Storage in Tibetan Epics" 《试论灵魂寄存观念在藏族史诗创作中的作用》. CASS Institute for the Study of Ethnic Minority Literature. Accessed February 12, 2013. http://iel.cass.cn/news_show.asp?newsid=4011&pagecount=3.
de Nebesky-Wojkowitz, René. 1975. *Oracles and Demons of Tibet: the Cult and Iconography of the Tibetan Protective Deities*. Graz: Akademische Druck-u. Verlagsanstalt.
Dawa Norbu. 2001. *China's Tibet Policy*. Richmond, Surrey: Curzon.
de Nebesky-Wojkowitz, René. 1998. *Oracles and Demons of Tibet: The Cult and Iconography of the Tibetan Protective Deities*. New Delhi: Paljor Publications.
Dernee Mining Co. 2007. "Environmental Report of Dernee Mining Project in Golok, Qinghai Province" 《青海省果洛州德尔尼铜矿工程2007年水土保持监测报告》. Accessed November 10, 2012. http://www.handlers.cn/mydown/15822.htm.
Desert Bell (沙漠驼铃) 2008 "Entering Magic Tibet and Feel the embrace of the Blue Sky" 《走人神秘的西藏 感受蓝天的拥抱》, http://hi.baidu.com/egzctjfaopkpvwe/item/ad824c159a44fbfc9c778a10. Accessed December 20, 2008.
Dondrub Gyal (དོན་གྲུབ་རྒྱལ).1983. "The Waterfalls of Youth" (ལང་ཚོའི་རྦབ་ཆུ), *Sbrang-char* (སྦྲང་ཆར), 2:56–62.
Dondrub Gyal. 2000. "The Narrow Path" (小路), in *Singers without Regret: A Commentary on the Works of Contemporary Tibetan Writers* 《歌者无悔—当代藏族作家作品选评》, edited by Degyid Tso, 22–24. Beijing: Minzu Press.
Diki Tsering. 2000. *Dalai Lama, My Son: Mother's Story*. New York: Penguin.
Dreyfus, Georges. 2005. "Are We Prisoners of Shangrila?: Orientalism, Nationalism, and the Study of Tibet." *Journal of the International Association of Tibetan Studies*, 2005, (1):1–21.

eBeijing.gov.cn "Shangri-La County," http://www.ebeijing.gov.cn/Elementals/eBeijing_Neighbourhood/t962578.htm. Accessed October 21, 2012.

Fabian, Johannes. 1983. *Time and the Other: How Anthropology Makes Its Object.* New York: Columbia University Press.

Fischer, Andrew.M. 2005. *State Growth and Social Exclusion in Tibet: Challenges of Recent Economic Growth.* Copenhagen: Nordic Institute of Asian Studies Press.

Fisher, John A. 2003. "Environmental Aesthetics." In *Oxford Handbook of Aesthetics*, edited by Jerrold Levinson, 667–678. Oxford: Oxford University Press.

Fanon, Frantz. 1963. *The Wretched of the Earth.* Translated by Constance Farrington. New York: Grove.

Foucault, Michel. 1980. "Two Lectures." In *Power / Knowledge: Selected Interviews and Other Writings, 1972–1977*, edited by Colin Gordon, 78–108. Brighton: Harvester.

Foucault, Michel. 1982. *Beyond Structuralism and Hermeneutics*, Chicago: University of Chicago Press.

French, Patrick. 2004. *Tibet, Tibet: A Personal History of Lost Land.* London: Vintage.

Freud, Sigmund. 1958. "Remembering, Repeating, and Working Through," in *Standard Edition, vol. 12*, translated and edited by James Strackey, 147–56. London: Hogarth Press.

Geertz, Clifford. 1973. *The Interpretation of Culture.* New York: Basic Books.

Gibson, James. 1986. *The Ecological Approach to Visual Perception.* New York: Psychology Press.

Goldstein, Melvyn C. and Kapstein, Matthew T., eds. 1998. *Buddhism in Contemporary Tibet: Religious Revival and Cultural Identity*, Berkeley: University of California Press.

Goldstein, Melvyn C. 1998. "Introduction." In *Buddhism in Contemporary Tibet: Religious Revival and Cultural Identity*, edited by Melvyn Goldstein and Matthew Kapstein, 1–14. Berkeley: University of California Press.

Goldstein, Melvyn C. 1999. *The Snow Lion and the Dragon: China, Tibet, and the Dalai Lama.* Berkley: University of California Press.

Goldstein, Melvyn C. 2007. *A History of Modern Tibet, Volume 2: The Calm before the Storm: 1951–1955.* Berkeley: University of California Press.

Goldstein, Melvyn C., William R. Siebenschuh and Tashi Tsering. 1997. *The Struggle for Modern Tibet: The Autobiography of Tashi Tsering.* Amonk, New York: M.E. Sharpe.

Guo, Wen (郭文). 2010. "Effects of Rotating Model and Community Empowerment in Rural Residents' Participation to Tourist Development: A Case Study of Yubeng Village" 《乡村居民参与旅游开发的轮流制模式及社区增权效能研究 —— 云南香格里拉雨崩社区个案》. *Tourism Tribune* 3(25):76–83.

Grapard, Allan. 1982. "Flying Mountains and Walkers of Emptiness: Toward a Definition of Sacred Space in Japanese." *History of Religions* 21(3):195–221.

Grapard, Allan. 1989. "The Textualized Mountain – Enmountained Text: the Lotus Sutra in Kunisaki." In *The Lotus Sutra in Japanese Culture*, edited by George Tanabe and Willa Jane Tanabe, 159–190. Honolulu: University of Hawaii Press.

Greider, Thomas and Lorraine Garkovich. 1994. "Landscape: the Social Construction of Nature and the Envornment." *Rural Sociology* 59(1):1–20.

Grunfeld, A. Tom. 1987. *The Making of Modern Tibet.* London: Zed Books Ltd.

Gruschke, Andreas. 2008. "Nomads without Pastures?: Globalization, Regionalization, and Livelihood Security of Nomads and Former Nomads in Northern Khams." *Journal of the International Association of Tibetan Studies* 4:1–40.

Guha, Ranajit. 1997. "Introduction." In *A Subaltern Studies Reader, 1986–1995*, edited by Ranajit Guha, ix-xxii. Minneapolis: University of Minnesota Press.

Hansen, Peter H. 2003. "Why is There No Subaltern Studies for Tibet?" *The Tibet Journal* 4:7–22.

Hao, Guiyao (郝桂尧). 2008. *I'm a Shandong-nese* 《俺是山东人》. Beijing: Xinhua Publishing House.

Harper, Graeme and Jonathan Rayner. 2010. "Introduction – Cinema and Landscape." In *Cinema and Landscape*, edited by Graeme Harper and Jonathan Rayner, 13–29. Chicago: The University of Chicago Press.

Harrell, Stevan. 1995. "Introduction: Civilizing Projects and the Reaction to Them," in *Cultural Encounters on China's Ethnic Frontiers*, edited by Stevan Harrell, 3–36. Seattle: University of Washington Press.

Hartley, Lauran. 2002. "'Inventing Modernity' in Amdo: Views on the Role of Traditional Tibetan Culture in a Developing Society." in *Amdo Tibetans in Transition: Society and Culture in the Post-Mao Era*, edited by Toni Huber, 1–26. Leiden: Brill.

He, Ma (何马) 2009 *The Tibet Code* 《藏地密码》. Chongqing, Sichuan: Chongqing Publishing House.

He, Tianhui (何天慧). 1998. "Tibetan Yak Culture in King Gesar Epic" 《论格萨尔所反映的藏族牛文化》. *China Tibetology* 1:130–35.

He, Xinghua (和兴华). 2010. "An Assessment and Strategic Discussion of the Current State of Tourism in Shangrila, Yunnan" 《云南香格里拉旅游现状的评价及对策探讨》. *Yunnan Science and Technology Management* (云南科技管理) 3:82–84.

Hillman, Ben. 2009. "Ethnic Tourism and Ethnic Politics in Tibetan China." *Harvard Asia Pacific Review* Spring:1–6.

Hillman, James. 1976. *Re-Visioning Psychology*. New York: Harper Perennial.

Hilton, James. 1933. *Lost Horizon*. New York: William Morrow and Company.

Hilton, James. 1999. *Lost Horizon* 《消失的地平线》. Translated by Cheng Luo (罗成). Shanxi Normal University Press.

Hilton, James. 2006. *Lost Horizon*. Kunming, Yunnan: Yunnan People's Publishing House.

Hilton, James. 2006. *Lost Horizon* 《消失的地平线》. Translated by Rui Hu (胡蕊) and Ying Zhang (张颖). Kunming: Yunnan People's Publishing House.

Hilton, James. 2007. *Lost Horizon* 《消失的地平线》. Translated by Jinqiu Zhao (赵净秋) and Yixin Bai (白逸欣). Kunming: Yunnan University Press.

Hilton, James. 2011. *Lost Horizon* 《消失的地平线》. Translated by Tao Zhang (张涛). Chongqing, Sichuan: Chongqing Publishing House.

Hinton, William. 1997. *Fanshen: A Documentary of Revolution in a Chinese Village*, Berkeley: University of California Press.

Hruby, Paula Jo. 2001. "Unitive Consciousness and Pahnke's Good Friday Experiment." In *Psychoactive Sacramentals: Essays onEntheogens and Religion*, edited by Thomas B. Roberts, 59–70. San Francisco: Council on Spiritual Practices.

Hu, Hongjiang (胡洪江). 2010. "Co-Constructing the Eco-Tourist Zone of Shangrila" (共建香格里拉生态旅游区). *The People's Daily* (Overseas Edition). September 30, 2010.

Hu, Shi. 1936. "Full Internationalization and Wholesale Westernization" (充分世界化与全盘西化).In *Speeches on Westernization, Vol.III* (全盘西化言论三集) by Hu Shi, 80. Hong Kong: Student Council of Lingnan University.

Huber, Toni 1999a *The Cult of Pure Crystal Mountain: Popular Pilgrimage and Visionary Landscape in Southeast Tibet*. Oxford: Oxford University Press.

Huber, Toni, ed. 1999b. *Sacred Spaces and Powerful Places in Tibetan Culture: A Collection of Essays*. Dharamsala, India: The Library of Tibetan Works and Archives.

Huber, Toni. 2002. *Amdo Tibetans in Transition: Society and Culture in the Post-Mao Era*. Leiden: Brill.

Huber, Toni and Poul Pedersen. 1997. "Meteorological Knowledge and Environmental Ideas in Traditional and Modern Societies: The Case of Tibet." *The Journal of the Royal Anthropological Institute* 3(3):577–597.

Hughes, J. Donald and Jim Swan. 1986. "How Much of the Earth is Sacred Space?" *Environmental Review* 10(4): 247–259.

Husserl, Edmund. 1970. *The Crisis of European Sciences and Transcendental Phenomenology: An Introduction to Phenomenological Philosophy*. Translated by David Carr. Evanston: Northwestern University Press.

Husserl, Edmund. 1982. *Ideas Pertaining to a Pure Phenomenology and to a Phenomenological Philosophy*. Translated by F. Kersten. The Hague/Boston/London: Martinus Nijhof Publishers.

Ingold, Tim. 1993. "The Temporality of the Landscape." *World Archaeology* 25(2):152–174.

Ingold, Tim. 2000. *The Perception of the Environment: Essays on Livelihood, Dwelling and Skill*. London: Routledge.

Ingold, Tim. 2011. *Being Alive: Essays on movement, knowledge and description*. London: Routledge.

International Campaign for Tibet (ICT) 2012 "Self-Immolations in Tibet," http://www.savetibet.org/resource-center/maps-data-fact-sheets/self-immolation-fact-sheet. Accessed October 21, 2012.

International Campaign for Tibet (ICT) "Tibetan Environment," http://www.savetibet.org/resource-center/all-about-tibet/tibetan-environment. Accessed June 08, 2013.

Ivakhiv, Adrian J. (2001). *Claiming Pilgrims and Politics at Sacred Glastonbury and Sedona Ground*. Bloomington: Indian University Press.

Jay, Martin. 1993. "Scopic regimes of modernity." In *Force Fields: Between Intellectual history and Cultural Critique*, edited by Martin Jay, 114–33. London: Routledge.

Jempal Gyatso. 2006. A Complete Collection of the King Gesar Epic《格萨尔王全传》. Beijing: Wuhai Media Press.

Ji, Youquan (吉柚权) 1993. *White Snow: Liberating Tibet*《白雪－解放西藏纪实》. Beijing: Zhongguo Wuzi Press.

Jie, Lina, 2006. "Dernee Copper Mining Project Began Its Production"《德尔尼铜矿开发项目建成试投产》, *The Xinhua News*, December 2. Accessed March 3, 2013. http://www.qh.xinhuanet.com/2006–12/02/content_8675703.htm.

Johnson, Russell and Kerry Moran. 1999. *Tibet's Sacred Mountain: the Extraordinary Pilgrimage to Mount Kailas*. South Paris, ME: Park Street Press.

Kapstein, Matthew. 1998. "A Pilgrimage of Rebirth Reborn: The 1992 Celebration of the Drigung Powa Chenmo." In *Buddhism in Contemporary Tibet: Religious Revival and Cultural Identity*, edited by Melvyn Goldstein and Matthew Kapstein, 95–119. Berkeley: University of California Press.

Kang, Qing (康清). 2007. "Growing up in Tibet"(在西藏长大). In *We Grew up in Tibet*《我们在西藏长大》, edited by Li Qing(李青), 74–81. Beijing: China Youth Press.

Kerouac, Jack. 1986. *The Dharma Bums*. New York: Penguin Books.

Knapp, A. Bernard and Ashmore, Wendy. 2000. "Archaeological Landscapes: Constructed, Conceptualized, Ideational." In *Archaeologies of Landscape: Contemporary Perspectives*, edited by W. Ashmore and A.B. Knapp, 1–33. Malden, Massachusetts: Blackwell Publishers, Inc.

Kolås, Åshild. 2008. *Tourism and Tibetan Culture in Transiation: A Place Called Shangrila*. London: Routledge.

Kohn, Hans. 1944. *The Idea of Nationalism: A Study in Its Origins and Background*. London: Transaction Publishers.

Laba (拉巴). 1998. "I am a Blacksmith" (我是铁匠). *Chinese Tibet Information Center*, http://zt.tibet.cn/tibetzt/tibet50/htxz/doc/105.htm. Accessed December 01, 2012.

Lee, Feigon. 1996. *Demystifying Tibet: Unlocking the Secrets of the Land of the Snows*. Chicago: Ivan R. Dee.

Levitas, Ruth. 1990. *The Concept of Utopia*. Syracuse: Syracuse University Press.

Lama Anagarika Govinda. 2005. *The Way of the White Clouds*. New York: The Overlook Press.

Li, Guozhu (李国柱). 2010. *The Life of a Woman Soldier in Tibet* 《一个女兵的西藏人生》. Beijing: China Tibetology Press.

Li, Hong (黎宏). 2010. *Reminiscing Tibet*《感念西藏》. Beijing: Party School of the CPC Central Committee.

Li, Jingze (李敬泽). 2007. "Preface to the Trilogy: How the Silent Snow on the Mountains Keeps Me Spellbound" (山上宁静的积雪，多么令我神往). In *Trilogy of Ma Lihua's Tibet Journey: The Soul is like the Wind, Red Mountains of Eastern Tibet*, and *Traversing Northern Tibet*, by Ma Lihua, 1–13. Beijing: China Tibetology Press.

Li, Jun (李俊). 1965. "Discovery and Practice: A Summary of the Assignment Directing The Serf "(探索与实践 — 影片《农奴》导演工作小结. In: 《农奴：从剧本到影片》(The Serf: From Screenplay to Film), 133–150. Beijing: Chinese Cinema Press.

Li Wenshan (李文珊). (2001). 《难忘西藏》(*Unforgettable Tibet*). Lhasa: Tibet People's Press (西藏人民出版社).

Li, Xu (李旭). 1999. *Portraying Tibet: the Distant Horizon*《遥远的地平线》. Kunming, Yunnan: Yunnan People's Publishing House.

Li, Xu (李旭). 2000. *Guests of Tibet* 《藏客》. Kunming, Yunnan: Yunnan People's Publishing House.

Li, Xu (李旭). 2007. "Preface: The Not-Yet Disappeared Horizon." In *Lost Horizon*, by James Hilton《消失的地平线》, translated by Jinqiu Zhao (赵净秋) and Yixin Bai (白逸欣). Kunming: Yunnan University Press.

Li, Yingqing (李映青) and Guo Anfei (郭安菲). 2011. "Tourism in Shangrila Brings Wealth to Tibetan Farmers and Nomads" (香格里拉旅游致富藏族农牧民). *China Daily*,《中国日报》.

Liang, Qichao (梁启超) 1916 "An Account of the Future of New China Xin-zhong-guo wei-lai ji" (新中国未来记) in *A Collection of Fictions* 《小说零界》. 23–24. Beijing: Peking University Press.

Liang, Qichao. 1992 "Zhong-guo ji-ruo su-yuan lun" (On the Origin of the Weaknesses of China) in Xia Xiaohong (ed.), *The Collection of Liang Qichao's Works*, 73. Beijing: China Broadcasting Press.

Lin, Tian (林田) 1997 *The Diaries of My Tibet Journey* 《藏行记实》, Beijing: Chinese Tibetology Press.

Ling, Xingzheng (凌行正) 2000 *An Affectionate Recollection of Tibet: A PLA Soldier's Memoir* 《感念西藏：一个金珠玛米的回忆》, Beijing: The PLA Art Press.

Liu, Jiang (刘江) and Kai Cao (曹凯) 2009 "Tibet Drifters in Lhasa: In Search for a Spiritual Home" （拉萨"藏漂"：寻找心灵安放之地）. http://news.xinhuanet.com/newscenter/2009-03/28/content_11087017.htm. Accessed, November 10, 2012.

Liu, Jinyuan (刘进元). 2009. "Shangrila and Human Imagination" (香格里拉和人的想象力). http://www.chinawriter.com.cn. Accessed May 30, 2011.

Liu, Sha (刘沙). 2009. *Tibet the Dreamland* 《西藏梦想地》. Shanghai: Shanghai Literature and Art Publishing House.

Livers, Keith A. 2005. "Empty is My Native Land: the Problem of the Absent Center in Alexander Zeldovich's *Moscow.*" The Russian Review 64:422–39.

Lopez, Jr., Donald S. 1994. "New Age Orientalism: The Case of Tibet." *Tricycle: The Buddhist Review* 3:3.

Lopez, Jr., Donald S. 1998 *Prisoners of Shangri-La: Tibetan Buddhism and the West.* Chicago: University of Chicago Press.

Lopez, Jr., Donald S. 2001. "The Image of Tibet of the Great Mystifiers." In *Imagining Tibet: Perceptions, Projections, and Fantasies*, edited by Thierry Dodin and Heinz Rather, 183–200. Boston: Wisdom Publication.

Loseries-Leick, Andrea. 1998. "On the Sacredness of Mount Kailasa in the Indian and Tietan Sources." In *Pilgrimage in Tibet*, edited by Alex McKay, 143–164. Richmond, Surrey: Curzon Press.

Lü, Wei (吕威). 2005. "Ma Junren's Most Expensive Tibetan Mastiff is Worth 40 Million: Raising the World Champion Dog" (马俊仁最贵藏獒值四千万 要把狗培养成世界冠军2005年03月01日), http://news.xinhuanet.com/sports/2005-03/01/content_2631778.htm. Accessed July 07, 2013.

Lu Xun (鲁迅) .2009. "Diary of a Madman" (狂人日记) In *Outcry* 《呐喊》 by Lu Xun, 7–18. Modern Chinese Literature Digital Library.

Luo, Changping (罗昌平). 2002. "Decoding Shangrila" (破译香格里拉)，*China Commerce* 《中国商界》. 5:19–23.

Ma, Jiangao (马建高). 2006. "Post-Saids' Orientalism: Outline of Postcolonial Theory Studies of 1990s in China" (萨义德的《东方主义》之后——20 世纪90 年代国内后殖民理论研究综述). *Journal of Yancheng Teachers College* 《盐城师范学院学报》，Vol. 26 No. 26 (1):26–32.

Ma, Lihua (马丽华). 2007a. *The Soul is Like Wind* 《灵魂像风》. Beijing: China Tibetology Press.

Ma, Lihua (马丽华). 2007b. *Red Mountains of Eastern Tibet* 《藏东红山脉》. Beijing: China Tibetology Press.

Ma, Lihua (马丽华). 2007c. *Traversing Northern Tibet* 《藏北游历》. Beijing: China Tibetology Press.

MacDonell, Arthur A. 1927. *A Sanskrit Grammar for Students.* Oxford: Oxford University Press.

Machik "Our Work," http://www.machik.org/index.php?option=com_content&task=view&id=22&Itemid=48. Accessed June 08, 2013.

Makley, Charlene. E. (2007). The Violence of Liberation: Gender and Tibetan Buddhist Revival in Post-Mao China. Berkeley: the University of California Press.

Mao, Zedong (毛泽东) 1991. "论反对日本帝国主义的策略" (On the Strategies Fighting Japanese Imperialism). In 《毛泽东选集》 (Collection of Mao Zedong's Works), Vol. 1. Beijing: The People's Press (人民出版社).

Marcus, George. 1994. "After the Critique of Ethnography: Faith, Hope, and Charity, But the Greatest of These Is Charity." In *Assessing Cultural Anthropology*, edited by Robert Borofsky, 40–54. New York: McGraw-Hill, Inc.
Mathiessen, Peter. 1987. *The Snow Leopard*. New York: Penguin.
Matless, David. 1991. "Nature, the Modern and the Mystic: Tales from Early Twentieth Century Geography." *Transactions of the Institute of British Geographers* 16:272–86.
Mauss, Marcel, 1990. *The Gift: the Form and Reason for Exchange in Archaic Societies*, New York: W.W. Norton.
McGranahan, Carole and Ralph Litzinger, eds. "2012 Self-Immolation as Protest in Tibet." *Hot Spot Forum, Cultural Anthropology Online*. April 11, 2012. http://culanth.org/?q=node/526. Accessed October 21, 2012.
McGranahan, Carole and Ralph Litzinger. 2012. "Introduction," *Hot Spot Forum, Cultural Anthropology Online*. April 11, 2012. http://culanth.org/?q=node/526. Accessed October 21, 2012.
McLoone, Martin. 2010. "Landscape and Irish Cinema." In *Cinema and Landscape*, edited by Graeme Harper and Jonathan Rayner, 131–146. Chicago: The University of Chicago Press.
Meserve, Walter J. and Ruth I. Meserve. 1992. "Revolutionary Realism: China's Path to the Future." *Journal of South Asian Literature* 27(2):29–39.
Miao, Supei (苗素培). 2007. "Fifteen Years in the Wind and Snow of the Plateau" (风雪高原15年), In *We Grew up in Tibet* 《我们在西藏长大》, edited by Li Qing (李青), 19–33. Beijing: China Youth Press.
Michaels, Axel. 2003. "The Sacredness of (Himalayan) Landscapes." In *Sacred Landscape of the Himalaya*, edited by Niels Gutschow, Axel Michaels, Charles. Ramble, and Ernst Steinkellner, 13–18. Vienna: Austrian Academy of Sciences Press.
Miller, Robert. "'The Supine Demoness' (Srin mo) and the Consolidation of Empire." *Tibet Journal* 23(3):3–22.
Mollison, Bill. 2002. *Permaculture: A Designers' Manual*. Tyalgum, Australia: Tagari Publications.
Morgan, Daniel. 2009. "The Place of Nature in Godard's Late Films," *Critical Quarterly*, Vol. 51, No.3, (Fall 2009): 1–24.
Morphy, Howard. 1995. "Landscape and the Reproduction of the Ancestral Past." In *The Anthropology of Landscape*, edited by Eric Hirsch and Michael O'Hanlon, 184–209. Oxford: Clarendon Press.
Mu, Ge (穆戈). 2012 *Tibet Drifting* 《藏漂》. Beijing: Oriental Publishing Center (东方出版社).
Müllen, Eve. 2011. *The American Occupation of Tibetan Buddhism: Tibetans and Their American Hosts in New York City*. Münster, Germany: Waxmann Publishing Co.
National Professional Commission for Tibetan Mastiffs (NPCTM) [中国藏獒专业委员会] 2008 "中国藏獒协会介绍,"http://www.aoere.org/introduce.asp. Accessed May 20, 2012.
Oakes, T. 1997. "Place and the Paradox of Modernity." *Annals of the Association of American Geographers* 87(3):509–531.
O'Connell, W.J. 2003. *A Plumber's Progress: Pilgrimage to the Heart of Tibet*. Dunedin: Longacre Press.
Ovchinnikov, Vsevolod Vladimirovich. 2009. 《1955年西藏纪行》 (*1955 Tibet Travel Log*), translated by Zhang Xiaomei. Beijing: Chinese Tibetology Press.
Paci, Enzo. 1972. *The Function of the Science and the Meaning of Man*. Translated by Paul Piccone. Evanston: Northwestern University Press.

Paine, Jeffery. 2004. *Re-Enchantment: Tibetan Buddhism Comes to the West.* New York: W.W. Norton & Company.

Pallasmaa, Juhani. 2000. 'Hapticity and Time: Notes on Fragile Architecture.' *The Architectural Review* May:78–84.

Pallasmaa, Juhani. 2005 *The Eyes of the Skin: Architecture and the Senses*, Hoboken, NJ.: Academy Press.

Paterson, Mark. 2007. *The Senses of Touch: Affects and Technologies.* Oxford: Berg.

Paterson, Mark. 2009. "Haptic geographies: ethnography, haptic knowledges and sensuous dispositions." *Progress in Human Geography* 33(6):766–788.

Pe'ery, Tsaft and Michael B. Mathews. 2007. "Viral Conquest of the Host Cell." In *Fields' Virology* Vol.I, edited by David M. Knipe and Peter M. Howledy, 168–208. Philadelphia: Lippincott Williams & Wilkins.

Pema Tseden. 2006. "Director's Statement," http://www.tibetmovie.com/, Beijing, China. Accessed March 2012.

Pema Wangyal. "Tibet in the Eye of Han Chinese in the Republic Era." *Tibet Watch*, spring 2011, special issue.

People's Daily (人民日报). 2012. "The Volume of Passenger Traffic of Qinghai-Tibet Railway Exceeds One Billion" (青藏铁路客运量首超千万), http://finance.people.com.cn/money/GB/17312687.html, Accessed March 9, 2012.

Pickett, Tery H. 1996. *Inventing Nations: Justifications of Authority in the Modern World*, Westport, Connecticut: Greenwood Press.

Pickowicz, Paul and Jinying Zhang. 2006. *From Underground to Independent: Alternative Film Culture in Contemporary China.* Lanham, Maryland: Rowman & Littlefield Publishers.

Quan, Xiaoshu (全晓书) and Wang Pan (王攀). 2007. "The 17th People's Congress Representative says – 'Tibet is not having too many tourists but too few'" (十七大代表：到西藏旅游的人不是太多，而是太少了"), http://news.xinhuanet.com/newscenter/2007-10/17/content_6893863.htm. Accessed November 7, 2010.

Rabinow, Paul and William M. Sullivan. 1987. "The Interpretive Turn: A Second Look." In *Interpretive Social Science: A Second Look* edited by Paul Rabinow and William M. Sullivan, 1–30. Berkeley: University of California Press.

Reinhard, Johan. 1985. "Sacred Mountains: An Ethno-Archaeological Study of High Andean Ruins." *Mountain Research and Development* 5(4):299–317.

Relph, Edward 1976 *Place and Placelessness.* London: Pion Limited.

Relph, Edward. 1981. *Rational Landscapes and Humanistic Geography.* London: Groom Helm.

Ren, Huaguang (任华光). (1959). 《西藏记事》 (*A Recollection of Events in Tibet*), Zhengzhou: Henan People's Press (河南人民出版社).

Richards, Thomas. 1996. *Imperial Archive: Knowledge and the Fantasy of Empire*, London: Verso.

Ricoeur, Paul. 2004. *Memory, History, Forgetting.* Chicago: University of Chicago Press.

Robin, Françoise. 2012. "Fire, Flames and Ashes. How Tibetan Poets Talk about Self-Immolations without Talking about Them." *Revue d'Etudes Tibétaines* 25:123–131.

Sahoo, Sarbeswar. 2006. "Civil Society, Citizenship and Subaltern Counterpublics in Post-colonial India." In *Sociological Perspectives on Globalization*, edited by Ajaya K. Sahoo 57–88. Delhi: Kalpaz Publication.

Said, Edward. 1979. *Orientalism.* New York: Random House.

Said, Edward. 2007. 《东方学》 (Orientalism). Translated by Wang, Yugen (王宇根). Beijing: SDX Joint Publishing Co.

Sardar, Ziauddin. 1999. *Orientalism: Concepts in the Social Sciences*. Philadelphia: Open University Press.
Sargent, Lyman Tower. 1994. "The Three Faces of Utopianism Revisited." *Utopian Studies* 5 (1):1–37.
Sautman, Bary and June Teufel Dreyer, eds. 2006. *Contemporary Tibet: Politics, Development, and Society in a Disputed Region*. New York: M.E. Sharpe.
Schrempf, Mona. 2002. "The Earth-Ox and the Snowlion." In *Amdo Tibetans in Transition: Society and Culture in the Post-Mao Era*, edited by Toni Huber, 147–172. Leiden: Brill.
Schuyler, Kathryn Goldman. 2012. *Inner Peace – Global Impact: Tibetan Buddhism, Leadership, and Work*. Charlotte, North Carolina: Information Age Publishing.
Schwartz, Ronald. 2008. "Introduction: Tibet and Modernity." In *Tibetan Modernities: Notes from the Field on Cultural and Social Change*, edited by Robert Barnett and Ronald Schwartz, 1–34. Leiden: Brill.
Shanon, Benny. 2008. "Biblical Entheogens: a Speculative Hypothesis." *Time and Mind*, 1 (1):51–74.
Shen, Weirong (沈卫荣). 2010. *In Search of Shangri-la: Essays on China Studies, Philogophy and Virtual Tibet* 《寻找香格里拉》. Beijing: Remin University Press.
Shen, Xiaomeng, Thomas E. Downing and Mohamed Hamza, eds. 2010. *Tipping Points in Humanitarian Crisis: From Hot Spots to Hot Systems*. New York: Publication Series of UNU-EHS.
Shogdong (ཤོག་དུང་). 2001. *The Call of Reason* (རྟོགས་པའི་རྔ་འབོད་), Lanzhou: Gansu People's Press.
Shogdong (ཤོག་དུང་). 2008. *Contemplation and Reflection* (རིགས་ཤེས་ཀུན་གྲོལ་), Lanzhou: Gansu Nationality Publishing House.
Shu, Jiexun (舒介勋). 1964. 《囊色林谷卡调查资料》(*Research Materials concerning Nang-she-ling Area*). Beijing: Institute of Ethnological Research, Chinese Science Academy (中国科学院民族研究所).
Simmer-Brown, Judith. 2002. *Dakini's Warm Breath: the Feminine Principle in Tibetan Buddhism*. Boston: Shambhala.
Smart, Ninian. 2009. "Religious Studies and Comparative Perspective." In *Ninian Smart on World Religions: Selected Works, Volume I* edited by John Shepherd, 5–12. Burlington, VT.: Ashgate Publishing Company.
Smith, Anthony. D. 1981. *The Ethnic Revival*, Cambridge: Cambridge University Press.
Smith, Anthony. D. 1986 *The Ethnic Origins of Nations*, New York: Basil Blackwell.
Smyer Yu, Dan. 2006. "Emotions under Local Nationalism: The Primordial Turn of Tibetan Intellectuals in China." *Pacific Rim Report* No. 42. USF Center for the Pacific Rim.
Smyer Yu, Dan. 2011. *The Spread of Tibetan Buddhism in China: Charisma, Money, Enlightenment*. London: Routledge.
Snow, Edgar. 1994. *Red Star over China: The Classic Account of the Birth of Chinese Communism*, revised version. New York: Grove Press.
Spivak, Gayatri Chakravorty. 1988. "Can the Subaltern Speak?" In *Marxism and the Interpretation of Culture*, edited by Cary Nelson and Lawrence Grossberg, 271–313. Urbana: University of Illinois.
Stein, Rolf Alfred. 1972. *Tibetan Civilization*, translated by J.E. Stapleton Driver. Stanford: Stanford University Press.
Stone, Emily. 2008. "Fieldnotes from Qinghai." Unpublished paper.
Strong, Anna Louise. 1959. *When Serfs Stood up in Tibet*. Beijing: New World Press.

Su, Yan. 1997. "西藏的天空" (Tibet's Sky). In *Entering Tibet: Interviews with Aid Workers to Tibet*《走进西藏 — 援藏札记援藏干部访谈录》, edited by Xie Tiequn (谢铁群), 69–72. Lhasa: Tibet People's Press.

Tambiah, Stanley.J. 1970. *Buddhism and the Spirit Cults in North-east Thailand*. Cambridge, Cambridge University Press.

Tang, Shijie (汤世杰). 1985. *The Plateau's Sun*《高原的太阳》. Beijing: October Literature and Art Press.

Tang, Shijie (汤世杰).1989. *The Magic Cave*《魔洞》. Kunming: Yunnan People's Publishing House.

Tang, Shijie (汤世杰). 1999. *Soul Sways in the Wind: Shangrila from Fantasy to Reality*《灵息吹拂 – 香格里拉从虚拟到现实》. Beijing: China Writers Publishing House.

Tang, Shijie (汤世杰). 2001. *Musing Yunnan*《冥想云南》.Tianjin: Baihua Literature and Art Publishing House.

Tang, Shijie (汤世杰). 2006. "Shangrila: the Modern Legend of a Cultural Brand" (香格里拉：一个文化品牌的现代传奇). http://bj.sina.com.cn/t/2006–11–08/1501110023.shtml . Accessed on May 10, 2013.

Taylor, Bron. 2010. "Avatar as Rorschach." *Journal of Religion, Nature and Culture*, 4 (4):381–383.

Thubron, Colin. 2011. *To a Mountain in Tibet*. London: Chatto & Windus.

Tilley, Christopher. 1994. *A Phenomenology of Landscape: Places, Paths and Monuments*. Oxford: Berg.

Tilley, Christopher. 2004. *The Materiality of Stone: Explorations in Landscape Phenomenology*. New York: Berg.

Tilley, Christopher. 2010. *Interpreting Landscapes: Geologies, Topographies, Identities*. Walnut Creek, CA: Left Coast Press.

Tonkinson, Carole, ed. 1995. *Big Sky Mind: Buddhism and the Beat* Generation. New York: RIverhead Books.

Trace Foundation "Our Work," http://www.trace.org/our-work. Accessed June 10, 2013.

Tsawa Daneg (ཚ་བ་ཀུན་སྒྲོག). 2009. "Eradicating Shogdong like Dissipating Smoke and Ashes" (ཤོགས་དུང་དོར་སྒྲོགས་སྤ་བའི་རྣམ་དཔྱད་བཞག་པ།), http://www.tibetcm.com/html/list_03/5ea9aaa4cf2d8d48066c5571af6cb821/. Accessed January 11, 2013.

Tsering Shakya. 1991. "The Myth of Shangri-la: Tibet and the Occident." *Lungta* (Journal of Tibetan History and Culture), *Special Issue Tibetan Authors*, 20–23.

Tuan, Yifu. 1993. 'Desert and Ice: Ambivalent Aesthetics.' In *Landscape, Natural Beauty and the Arts*, edited by Salim Kemal and Ivan Gaskell, 139–157. Cambridge: Cambridge University Press.

Tuan, Yifu. 1998. *Escapism*. Baltimore: The John Hopkins University Press.

Tukeba (途客吧). 2012. "Reflections on Tibet" (西藏感想).   http://www.tukeba.com/share/f8d8f2f93720b5e7.html. Accessed on August 10, 2012.

Turner, Victor. 1967. *The Forest of Symbols: Aspects of Ndembu Ritual*. Ithaca: Cornell University.

Turner, Victor, 1974. *Dramas, Fields, and Metaphors: Symbolic Action in Human Society*, Ithaca: Cornell University Press.

Tuttle, Gray. 2005. *Tibetan Buddhists in the Making of Modern China*. New York: Columbia University Press.

UNESCO. "Cultural Landscape." http://whc.unesco.org/en/culturallandscape/. Accessed June 03, 2013.

van der Kolk, Bessell. A. 1996. "The Black Hole of Trauma." In *Traumatic Stress: the Effects of Overwhelming Experience on Body, Mind, and Society*, edited by B. A. van der Kolk, A. C. McFarlane, and L. Weisaeth, 3–23. New York: The Guilford Press.

van der Veer, Peter. 2012. "Smash Temples, Burn Books." *The World Religious Cultures* 73:17–26.

van Gennep, Arnold. 1960. *The Rites of Passage*. Translated by Monika B. Vizedm and Gabrielle L. Caffee. Chicago: The University of Chicago Press.

Vertovec, Steven. 2007. "New complexities of cohesion in Britain: Super-diversity, transnationalism and civil-integration." West Yorkshire, UK: Communities and Local Government Publications.

Virtanen, Riika J. 2011, *Tibetan Written Images: A Study of Imagery in the Writings of Dhondup Gyal*. Publications of the Institute for Asian and African Studies 13, Helsinki, Denmark: the University of Helsinki.

Vukovich, Daniel. 2011. *China and Orientalism: Western Knowledge Production of the PRC*. London: Routledge.

Wang, Gui and Huang Daoqun (王贵、黄道群). (2001). 《十八军先遣侦察科进藏纪实》(*A Witness of the Reconnaissance Division of the 18th Field Army Entering Tibet*). Beijing: Chinese Tibetology Press (中国藏学出版社).

Wang, Hui (汪晖). 2011. *Tibet Question" between the East and the West* (东西之间的"西藏问题"). Beijing: SDX Joint Publishing Company.

Wang, Jianhua (王建华). 2007. "Our Work and Life" (我们的劳动生活). In *We Grew up in Tibet* 《我们在藏长大》, edited by Li Qing (李青), 34–49. Beijing: China Youth Press.

Wang, Wenying. 1983. "Glaciers in the North-Eastern Part of the Ch'ing-Hai-Hsi-Tsang (Qinghai-Xizang) Plateau (Tibet) and Their Variations." *Journal of Glaciology* Vol.29, No.103, 384–391.

Wang, Yuechuan. 2010. "From 'walking out of the Orient' to 'discovering the Orient'." (从"走出东方"到"发现东方"), http://blog.sina.com.cn/s/blog_5a963ebc0100huxi.html, accessed on 11/29/2013.

Wei, Ke (魏克). 2007. 《留在雪域高原的脚印》(*Footsteps Left on the High Snowlands*). Beijing: Minzu Press (民族出版社).

Wei, Ke (魏克). 2011.《进军西藏日记》(*Diaries of Marching into Tibet*). Beijing: China Tibetology Press.

Wei, Linyue (韦林嶽). 1965. "谈谈《农奴》的摄影" (A Chat on the Cinematography of The Serf). In: 《农奴：从剧本到影片》(*The Serf: From Screenplay to Film*), 218–229. Beijing: Chinese Cinema Press (中国电影出版社).

Werblowsky, Raphael Jehudah Zwi. 1998. "Introduction: Mindscape and Landscape," In *Sacred Space: Shrine, City, Land*, edited by Kedar, Benjamin Z. and Raphael Jehudah Zwi Werblowsky, 9–17. London: Macmillan Press.

White, Hayden. 1978. *Tropics of Discourse: Essays in Cultural Criticism*. Baltimore: Johns Hopkins University Press.

Wilby, Sorrel. 1988. *Journey across Tibet*. Chicago: Contemporary Books.

Winkler, Daniel. 2008. "The Mushrooming Fungi Market in Tibet Exemplified by Cordyceps sinensis and Tricholoma matsutake." *Journal of the International Association of Tibetan Studies* 4:1–47.

Wolf, Eric R. 2010. *Europe and the People without History*. Berkeley: University of California Press.

Yang, Junlei. 2010. "The Orientalist Discourse in the Research on Chinese Films outside China" (海外中国电影研究的东方主义话语方式), *The Journal of Shanghai University*, Vol.17, No.5, pp.61–69.

Xiaohao (晓浩). 1999. 《西藏1951年》(*Tibet in 1951*). Beijing: Minzu Press (民族出版社).

Xinhua News (新华社). 2010. "The Number of Tourists to Tibet Breaks Records" (西藏旅游接待人数创历史新高), http://www.gov.cn/jrzg/2010-12/24/content_1772272.htm, Accessed on April 7, 2011.

Yang, Meng (杨猛) and Yinfa Li (李银发). 2010. "Constructing Shangrila as An International Tourist Destination" (香格里拉全力打造世界旅游胜地). *Yunnan Daily*, September 9. http://news.yunnan.cn/html/2010-09/09/content_1337686.htm. Accessed July 20, 2011.

Yeh, Emily. 2004. "Property Relations in Tibet Since Decollectivisation and the Question of 'Fuzziness'." *Conservation & Society*, 2(1):163–187.

Yeh, Emily 2005 "Green Governmentality in Western China: 'Converting Pastures to Grasslands'." *Nomadic Peoples*, Vol.9, Issues 1 & 2, 9–29.

Yeh, Emily and Mark Henderson. 2008. "Interpreting Urbanization in Tibet: Administrative Scales and Discourses of Modernization." *Journal of the International Association of Tibetan Studies* 4:1–44.

Yin, Fatang (阴法唐). 2009. Interview transcription from 《急速出征——十八军进藏纪实》(*Rapid Expedition – the 18th Field Army Entering Tibet*), Documentary film, CCTV production, 2009.

Zhang, Huijun (张慧君). 2007. "Zhongdian – the Memory of Shangrila" (中甸——香格里拉的记忆). *Ethnic Today* 《今日民族》, 8:49.

Zhang, Tianpan. 2013. "Another Kind of Orientalism: the Behind Scene of China Elements in Hollywood." (另一种"东方主义"——好莱坞的中国元素背后), South Review, No.12, http://www.nfcmag.com/article/4112.html, accessed on 12/02/2013.

Zhang, Yili (张镱锂), Li Xiubin (李秀彬), Fu Xiaofeng (傅小峰), Xie Gaodi (谢高地) and Zheng Du (郑度). 2000. "An Analysis of Changes in the Land Use in Lhasa" (拉萨城市用地变化分析), in: *ACTA Geographica Sinica* 《中国地理学报》 55(4):395–406.

Zhen, Sheng (榛生). 2010. *The Tibetan Book of Love* 《藏地情书》. Changchun, Jilin: Jinlin Publishing Co.

Zheng, Qianshan (郑千山). 2011. "Author Tang Shijie Recounts his Creation of *Shangrila*" (作家汤世杰回顾《香格里拉》创作). http://blog.sina.com.cn/s/blog_4e6209390100rmiz.html. Accessed on May 15, 2013.

Zhong, Xiuping. 2013. "Either ignorant or bluffing – I tell you how the West produces 'China'," the Renren Network, http://blog.renren.com/share/1170177525/15309472828, accessed on 11/30/2013.

Zhou, Ning. 2005. "Barbarism of Civilization: the Image of China in the Creed of Orientalism" (文明之野蛮:东方主义信条中的中国形象), *Journal of Humanities*, No.6, 86–96.

Films

Avatar. 2009. Directed by James Cameron. Twentieth Century Fox Film Production.

The Central Government Delegation in Tibet 《中央代表团在西藏》. 1956. The Central Documentary Film Studio.

Embrace. 2011. Directed by Dan Smyer Yu and Pema Tashi. Dongyang Mirage CineMedia Co.

Ensouling the Mountain. 2012. Directed by Dan Smyer Yu. Dongyang Mirage CineMedia Co. (rough cut).

The Field. 1990. Directed by Jim Sheridan, Noel Pearson for Granada Film Released by Avenue Pictures.
Ganglamedo 《刚啦梅朵》. 2006. Directed by Dai Wei (戴玮). an independent production.
Film Personage: Pema Tseden. 2011. Directed by Guo Kuiyong. CCTV-6.
The Grassland (རྩྭ་ཐང་ *tzangtang*). 2003. Directed by Pema Tseden. Beijing Himalaya Audio & Visual Culture Communication Co, Ltd.
The Horse Thief 《盗马贼》.1986. Directed by Tian, Zhuangzhuang (田壮壮). Xi'an Film Studio.
The Light Shines on Tibet 《光明照耀着西藏》. 1952. The People's Liberation Army August First Film Studio (中国人民解放军八一电影制片厂).
The Liberation Army Marching to Tibet 《解放西藏大军行》. 1952. The People's Liberation Army August First Film Studio (中国人民解放军八一电影制片厂).
Milarepa. 2006. Directed by Neten Chokling. Shining Moon Productions.
Moscow. 2000. Directed by Alexander Zeldovich. Studio Telekino.
Old Dog (ཁྱི་རྒན་ Khyi rgan2008 .(. Directed by Pema Tseden. Beijing Himalaya Audio & Visual Culture Communication Co, Ltd.
Once upon A Time in Tibet (西藏往事). 2010. Directed by Dai Wei (戴玮). China Cinema Corp.
The Past of Tibet (西藏往事). 2009. CCTV.
The Search (འཚོལ་ Tsol). 2008. Directed by Pema Tseden. Beijing Himalaya Audio & Visual Culture Communication Co, Ltd.
The Serf (农奴). 1963. Directed by Li Jun (李俊). The People's Liberation Army August First Film Studio (中国人民解放军八一电影制片厂).
Shangrila 《香格里拉》. 2011. TV Show. Directed by Jiang Jiajun (蒋家骏), Beijing: Beijing Yangguang Shengtong Media Art, 2011.
The Silent Holy Stone (ལྷིང་འཇགས་ཀྱི་མ་ཎི་རྡོ་འབུམ་ *lang-jeg-je-mani-dobem*). 2004. Directed by Pema Tseden. Beijing Himalaya Audio & Visual Culture Communication Co, Ltd.
The Sun Beaten Path (དབུས་ལམ་གྱི་ཉི་མ་). 2010. Directed by Sonthar Gyal. Fang Jin Film and TV Culture Communication (Beijing).
Travelers and Magicians. 2003. Directed by Khyentse Norbu. Prayer Flag Pictures.
The Wind Will Carry Us. 1999. Directed by Abbas Kiarostami. Mark II Production.
Xiu Xiu: the Sent-Down Girl. 1998. Directed by Joan Chen. Good Machine and Whispering Steppes L.P.
Yeshi Drolma. 2000. Directed by Xie Fei. Beijing Film Studio.

Index

absorptive mode, 46
actors, searching for, 140–141
aesthetics
– eco-, 25–26, 43–47, 178, 223–224
– environmental, 69
affection
– for landscape, 80, 124
– for Old Tibet, 93–97
– for Shangrila landscape, 191
– for Tibet, 5, 12–15, 47–51, 71, 219–220
affordances
– of film, 153
– geopoetic, 202
– Gibson on, 26–27, 49–50
– of place, 69
Akhu Norbu, 32–33, 34, 58–59
Akhu Shampa, 157–159, 161, 168, 169, 174–175
altitude sickness, 179–182
ambient light, 51
Amdo region, 34–35
– see also Amne Machen (mountain); Sambha Village
Amdo Tibetans, 32
American scholars, travel seminars for, 36, 185–187
American students, field courses for, 36, 187–188, 189
Ami Megbon (mountain god), 59–60
Ami-chiri (mountain), 66
Amne Machen (mountain)
– abundance of water at, 160–161
– Akhu Shampa on, 168, 169
– communication with, 167–168
– as cultural memory, 167
– in mindscape, 167
– mining at, 168–169, 175
– mountain god, 159, 164, 166, 169, 170–171, 175–176
– as place-memory, 166
– as soul mountain, 171, 173
– treatment of topic, 41
– Tserang Dondrub on, 170–171

Amne Machen pilgrimage
– emotions, 1, 156–157, 157–159
– glacier, 1, 163–164, 174–175
– Han Chinese crew members, 178–184
– landscape filming, 1, 2, 157
– songs, 162–163, 165
– treatment of topic, 41
– Tserang Dondrub, 168, 170
– weather, 163
Ani Sangmo's Meditation Cave, 158, 159
anthropological mindscape, of author, 226–227
anthropology, reflexive, 6
anti-traditionalists, Tibetan
– vs. pro-traditionalists, 150–151
– see also Dondrub Gyal; Shogdong
army see People's Liberation Army
authentic Tibet, 188–189, 196
Avatar (film), 153

"backwardness," of Tibet, 106
Baidu Encyclopedia, 201–202
Baker, Ian, 48–49
begcheg (habit), 106–107
Beijing
– fieldwork in, 29–32
– Tibetan students, 119
– travel seminar for American scholars, 185–186
– urban landscape, 44
"Beijing-drifters" (*beipiao*), Tibetan, 14–15, 29–30
Berman, Emanuel, 85
birds see vulture
bla (soul), 172–173
"black bones," 88
blacksmiths, 89
bla-gnas (soul-locations), 172, 173
bla-ri (soul mountain), 171, 172, 173
bloggers, 12–13
body
– and landscape, 21–22
– and memory, 126
– and place, 67–68, 126

Bongtse, 114
books
- memoirs of PLA veterans, 72, 79–80, 81
- Tibetan grammar book, 197
- travel writings on Tibet, 5, 183
- *see also* fictional books; *individual titles*
Bruno, Giuliana, 132
Budd, Malcolm, 44
Buddhism
- conversion of Tibet, 55
- mandalas, 54
- *see also* Tibetan Buddhism
Buddhist-oriented revival, 110
bus ride, to Sambha, 43
businesses, in Shangrila, 187

Cameron, James, 153
case study, of Shangrila, 191–192, 196
Casey, Edward, 22–23, 45, 67–68
caves *see* meditation caves
Chai Chunya, 11–12, 204–205, 206–207, 208–211
characters, tragically ending, 213–214
Chelhata, 197–198
Chen Xiaodong, 48
Chen Yalian, 12
Cheng Demei, 97
China (PRC)
- Cultural Revolution, 105
- market economy, 36
- oppression of Tibet, 9
- Orientalism of, 207
- perception of Tibet, 4, 11, 14, 31, 71–72
- representation in films, 16–17
- "Tibet fever," 203
- Tibetan Buddhism in, 227
- *see also* Chinese Communists; People's Liberation Army; urban China
Chinese
- attracted to Tibetan Buddhism, 32
- and Otherness of Tibet, 218–219, 220
- slave mentality, 109
- *see also* Han Chinese
Chinese Communists
- discourses introduced by, 120–121
- "liberation theology," 83–86
- socialist land reform in Sangga, 90–91
- socialist modernity, 121–122
- utopianism, 84–85
Chinese Communists' propaganda
- mission in Ngari grasslands, 91
- PLA triumph in Tibet, 78
- *The Serf* (film), 85, 88
- by "work teams," 92, 93
Chinese media
- on Tibet as hot spot, 9–10
- *see also* Xinhua News
Chinese scholars
- field courses for, 36
- influence of Lopez and Said on, 16
- and Western perception of Tibet, 3
Chinese students, field courses for, 36
Chinese Tibetophiles, 11–15, 201–203, 204, 222, 223
- *see also* Chai Chunya; Chen Yalian; Hao Guiyao; "Tibet-drifters"
Chinese translations, of *Lost Horizon*, 190, 193
Chögyam Trungpa, 66–67, 216
cinematic ambience, of Pema Tseden's, 136
cinematic hapticity, of Pema Tseden, 142, 144, 148
cinematic landscape
- in *The Grassland* (film), 130
- in *Old Dog* (film), 145
- in Pema Tseden's films, 131–132, 132–133, 149, 151–152
- in *The Silent Holy Stone* (film), 134, 135–136
civilization, soul of Tibetan, 139–140
coins *see* silver coins
commercial branding, of Shangrila, 195
communication, with Amne Machen, 167–168
Communists *see* Chinese Communists
companies, investments in Shangrila, 195
consciousness
- environmental, 177
- subaltern, 116–117
- of Tibetan students in Beijing, 119
Cosgrove, Denis, 28
costs, of housing in Beijing, 29
craftsmen, in Lhasa, 89
crying, 128, 158, 159
cultural memory, 167

Cultural Revolution, 105
culture
– "power," 9
– Tibetan, 170, 196, 227

Dai Wei, 31, 212–213
Dalai Lama (14th), 66, 67
damo langren see Chai Chunya
Danqu, 172
death, of PLA soldiers, 80–81
deities *see* gods and deities
Della Dora, Veronica, 28
demographics
– Lhasa, 87–88, 96
– Sambha, 52
demons, 55, 111, 124
denbe dgra-lha festival, 60
Deqin Prefecture *see* Shangrila
Dernee Copper Mine, 169, 175
Desert Bell (blogger), 12–13
Desolation Peak, 205–206
de-symbolizing approach (*qufuhaohua*), 31–32
de-Tibetanization, 197
"Dharma vagabond" *see* Chai Chunya
diaspora *see* exile
dichotomies
– imagined vs. real Tibet, 24
– natural vs. social beings, 115
– Old vs. New Tibet, 73–75
– of the West, 18
disorientation, of Hao Guiyao, 222
documentary, "Ensouling the Mountain," 156
dogs *see* mastiffs
Dolma Gyab, 213
Dondrub Gyal, 113–115, 117, 123–124
dream project, Shangrila as, 192–195
Drul Yelpa Caves, 186
Dukur Tserang, 145

earth (*sa*), 59
earthly deities, 55
earthwork, 39, 45, 46
eco-aesthetics, 25–26, 43–47, 178, 223–224
ecological know-how, 199
ecological value, of Tibet, 8–9
eco-spiritual dimension, of landscape, 35

eco-sublime experience, 24
Eco-Village, 198–199
emotions
– at Amne Machen pilgrimage, 1, 156–157, 157–159
– crying, 128, 158, 159
– homesickness, 161–162
– and landscape, 36
– and motions, 132, 162
– in *Prince Drime Kunden* (opera), 140
– in Tibetan films, 146, 156
– *see also* affection
empowerment
– by landscape, 25
– of local Tibetans, 199
enchantment *see* affection
"Ensouling the Mountain" (documentary), 156
environment, and organism, 27, 49–50
environmental aesthetics, 69
environmental consciousness, 177
environmental value, of Tibet, 8–9
"epic landscape scenes," 2
"escapism," 38
ethnic revival, 109–110, 118, 120–121
exile, Tibetans in
– "memorial place," 67
– native knowledge, 101–102

fantasy, 20
– *see also* rescue fantasy
fate, of Tibet, 125
"fate" (*li*), 92
female soldiers, 81
festival, denbe dgra-lha, 60
fictional books
– *Lost Horizon*, 37, 189–190, 193, 200–201, 213
– on Tibet, 183
– *Vagabond in Tibet*, 11–12, 205, 206
Field, The (film), 143
field courses
– for American students, 36, 187–188, 189
– for Chinese scholars and students, 36
– *see also* travel seminars
fieldwork (of author)
– about, 29

– in Beijing, 29–32
– in Lhasa, 35, 36
– in Qinghai, 32–35
– in Shangrila, 35
film co-op, in Beijing, 30
filming *see* landscape filming
filmmaking process, by Pema Tseden, 129, 131, 132, 142
films
– actors, searching for, 140–141
– affordances of, 153
– *Avatar*, 153
– emotions in Tibetan, 146, 156
– *The Field*, 143
– *The Grassland*, 129–131, 132–134, 136
– *Herdsman*, 164–165
– landscape-mindscape relationship by watching, 152
– *Old Dog*, 138, 143–148
– *Once upon a Time in Tibet*, 31, 212–213
– production in high altitude environment, 212
– representation of China in, 16–17
– *The Search*, 138, 139–140, 141, 142–143
– *The Serf*, 85, 88
– *The Silent Holy Stone*, 128, 134–136, 137, 140
– Tibetan Buddhism in Pema Tseden's, 128–129, 131–132, 132–133, 138, 148, 154–155
– traditional values vs. modernity in Pema Tseden's, 149
– transnational production, 136–137
– *The Wind Will Carry Us*, 141
– *see also* cinematic …; "New Tibetan Cinema"
"filthy" class, 89
fog, manipulating, 34
food, for Han Chinese pilgrimage crew members, 179–180
forgetting, and remembering, 111–112
friends, author's bond with Tibetan, 225–226

generational gap, 147
geopoetic affordance, 202
geopoetics, 47–49, 51
geopsychic affect, 222
Gibson, James, 26–27, 49–50, 50–51, 202

glacier, at Amne Machen, 1, 163–164, 174–175
gods and deities
– earthly, 55
– inter-dwelling with, 61, 69
– *klu*, 60
– offerings to, 59, 60
– of *sa*, 59
– Shogdong on, 111
– significance of, 62
– *see also* mountain gods and deities
Goldstein, Melvyn C., 120
Golok *see* Amne Machen (mountain)
grammar book, Tibetan, 197
Grapard, Allan, 54
Grassland, The (film), 129–131, 132–134, 136
grasslands *see* Ngari grasslands
"great mystifiers," 3–4
Gyaltang *see* Shangrila

habit (*begcheg*), 106–107
– *see also* "old habit"
habit-memory, 111
hail clouds, shooting into, 63
Han Chinese
– Amne Machen pilgrimage crew members, 178–184
– and magical Tibet, 208
– perception of Tibet, 30
Hansen, Peter, 120–121
Hao Guiyao, 222
– *see also* Xiaohao
Hao Peng, 10
He Tianhui, 172–173
Herdsman (film), 164–165
hidden religious treasures (*terma*), 1–2, 174
high altitude environment, film production in, 212
high places, 28
Hillman, James, 122
Hilton, James, 3–4, 37, 189–190, 193, 200–201, 213
Himalaya marmots (*phyiba*), 176
Hoffmann, Ernst Lothar *see* Lama Anagarika Govinda
home, and place, 66
homesickness, 161–162

horn, yak, 60
host families, American students' stay at Tibetan, 188
hot spot, Tibet as, 9–10, 15
housing, costs in Beijing, 29
hsa-goud (vulture), 130
Huber, Toni, 101
Hughes, J. Donald, 57
human weaklings (*rdol*), 181
humanization, of place, 22
Hwadan Tashi, 157–159

"I," narrating, 6–7
identity, Tibetan, 196
imagination, 20, 70
imagined Tibet
– complexity of, 4
– modern nation, 126
– and post-Orientalist approach, 19
– vs. real Tibet, 24
– of the West, 3
immaturity, of Tibet, 115
indigenous people, and place, 61–62
Ingold, Tim, 64, 68, 152
"insurrection," 116
intersubjectivity, 7, 8, 64
invasion of Tibet *see* second Long March
investments, in Shangrila, 195
invocations, by Akhu Norbu, 58–59

Jigmed, 164–165
Jokhang Temple, 95–96

Kerouac, Jack, 205–206
Kiarostami, Abbas, 141
killing, 146–147
klu (waterborne deity), 60
knowledge, native Tibetan, 101–102, 199
Kolås, Åshild, 37, 191–192, 196

Laba ("black bones" man), 88, 89–90
Lake Yamdrok Yumtso, 13
Lama Anagarika Govinda
– on landscape, 47–48
– on mountains, 22
lamas, 174–175, 229
land reform, socialist, 90–91

Lando (serf), 92
landscape
– absorptive mode, 46
– affection for, 80, 124
– bodily experiences of, 21–22
– Chai Chunya on, 205
– connection with, 36, 69–70
– at Drul Yelpa Caves, 186
– eco-aesthetics, 25
– eco-spiritual dimension, 35
– emotional connection with, 36
– emphasis of Dondrub Gyal, 123–124
– geopoetics, 47–49, 51
– and home, 66
– hostile, 82
– luminosity, 50–51
– Ma Lihua on, 219–220
– meaning of, 21
– mirage effect, 202–203
– moving, 43, 46
– as multidimensional world with other beings, 33
– Ovchinnikov on, 94
– passage of time-space, 65
– and perception of Tibet, 30
– and pilgrimage, 162
– potency of, 103
– *sa*, 59
– of Sambha, 44–45, 46
– and second Long March, 86
– of Shangrila region, 190–191
– Shogdong on, 101, 103, 104, 124–125
– and song of Zemgyab, 163
– Strong on, 94
– subjectivity of, 63–64, 68
– Tibetan Buddhism in, 134–135, 135–136, 137
– Tibetans' bond with, 169–170
– tipping points, 27–28
– touching of, 156, 178
– treatment of topic, 39
– *see also* cinematic landscape; mountains; urban landscape
landscape filming, 1, 2, 31, 34, 157
– *see also* cinematic landscape
landscape-mindscape relationship
– of Chinese Tibetophiles, 222

Index — 251

- of cited writers and artists, 221
- as combined placiality, 68
- eco-aesthetic reciprocity, 224
- eco-sublime experience, 24
- geopsychic affect, 222
- Li Xu's affection for Shangrila, 191
- nodes of, 57
- in Sambha, 58
- semantically synonymous, 125–126
- by watching films, 152

landscape photography, 44
language, Tibetan, 23, 197
legend, of Yutog Yontan Gonpo, 63
Lhasa
- fieldwork in, 35, 36
- Jokhang Temple, 95–96
- Ling on, 95
- low class, 89
- Ovchinnikov on, 94, 96
- Potala Palace, 12–13, 95, 98
- Shogdong on, 100
- social situation (1950s), 87–88
- tourism, 10, 35–36

li ("fate"), 92
Li Chuan, 81
Li Guozhu, 82–83
Li Hong, 97
Li Jingze, 223
Li Wenshan, 90
Li Xu, 190–191
Liang Qichao, 109
"liberation theology," Communist, 83–86
light, 50–51
Lin Tian, 72, 79–80, 91
Ling Xingzheng, 83–84, 95–96
Little Lhasa *see* Shangrila
Liu Jinyuan, 197–198
Long March, 75
- *see also* second Long March
Lopez, Donald S.
- distinction of Tibetology, 5
- Orientalism discourse, 3, 4, 16, 17–18
Lost Horizon (novel), 37, 189–190, 193, 200–201, 213
low class, 88–90
luminosity, 50–51

Ma Lihua, 219–220
Machen Bomra (mountain) *see* Amne Machen
Machu (river), 43, 60–61
magical realism, 210
magical Tibet, 204, 208
mandalas, 54–55
mandalization, of Sambha, 56–57
market economy, in China, 36
marmots, Himalaya, 176
mastiffs, 143, 144, 145–147
Matless, David, 48
media *see* Chinese media
meditation
- of Akhu Norbu, 58–59
- of American scholars, 186–187
meditation caves
- Ani Sangmo's Meditation Cave, 158, 159
- Drul Yelpa Caves, 186
- on Sambhadrubgne, 56, 58–59
meditation retreat house, planning, 32–33
Melong Tang (fictitious place), 130
memoirs, of PLA veterans, 72, 79–80, 81–82, 82–83
memorability, of place, 58, 103–104
"memorial place," 67
memory
- and body, 126
- cultural, 167
- and forgetting, 111–112
- habit-memory, 111
- pathology of, 112–113
- and place, 65, 67, 112, 127, 166
military *see* People's Liberation Army
milking, of yaks, 188
mindscape
- Amne Machen, 167
- anthropological, 226–227
- meaning of, 20
- mirage effect, 201
- Old Town Shangrila, 37
- place-memory, 65, 67, 166
- temporality of, 20–21
- of Tibet, 229–230
- *see also* landscape-mindscape relationship
Mindscaping the Landscape of Tibet (book)
- goals and approaches, 6–8
- mantras and language, 226

– treatment of topics, 38–42, 185
mining, at Amne Machen, 168–169, 175
mirage, of Tibet, 230
mirage effect, 41–42, 201, 202–203, 208
missing Orient, 217
mobilization, for second Long March, 76
modernism *see* anti-traditionalists; radical modernism
modernity
– "ocularcentrism," 153–154
– paradox of, 100, 102, 104
– pathos of, 98–99, 100–101
– socialist, 121–122
– Tibetan, 228
– vs. traditional values, 149
– treatment of topic, 40
modernization
– consequences of, 148, 154
– of Sambha, 52
– as threat, 31
– and Tibetan Buddhism, 138
monks, in Lhasa, 87
monument, and place, 56
morale, of PLA soldiers, 82, 83
motion pictures *see* films
motions, and emotions, 132, 162
motivation, of PLA soldiers, 77–78
mountain gods and deities
– Ami Megbon, 59–60
– Amne Machen, 159, 164, 166, 169, 170–171, 175–176
– nine original, 64–65
– reciprocity between humans and, 175–176
mountains
– Ami-chiri, 66
– Lama Govinda on, 22
– Ma Lihua on, 219–220
– Nyanpog Yutse, 168
– Pagö-pünsum, 66–67
– Sambhadrubgne, 54, 56–57, 58–59
– as theme of Yidam Tserang, 123
– *see also* Amne Machen
movies *see* films
moving landscape, 43, 46
Mu Ge, 202
My Ten Years in Tibet (book), 12

narratives
– self-referential, 6–7
– of travelers, 22, 47–49
nation, 65–66, 126
nationalism, 118, 120–121
natural beings, vs. social beings, 115
nature, 46, 69
Nêdong County *see* Sangga Village
"neo-Orientalism," 17
New Age Orientalism, 17
New Tibet, vs. Old Tibet, 73–75
"New Tibetan Cinema," 40–41, 128, 149–150, 155
– *see also* Pema Tseden
ngapa *see* yogis
Ngari grasslands, propaganda mission in, 91
noises, in *Old Dog* (film), 144–145
nomads, social hierarchy, 91
Norbu, 197, 198
novel, *Lost Horizon*, 37, 189–190, 193, 200–201, 213
Nyanpog Yutse (mountain), 168

Oakes, Timothy, 100
oath, in *The Grassland* (film), 133
"ocularcentrism," 153–154
offerings
– to deities, 59, 60
– to glacier, 1, 174–175
Old Dog (film), 138, 143–148
"old habit," 107–108, 109, 111
Old Tibet
– affection for, 93–97
– vs. New Tibet, 73–75
– oppression in, 92, 93
Old Town Shangrila, 37
Once upon a Time in Tibet (film), 31, 212–213
opera, *Prince Drime Kunden*, 139, 140, 141, 142–143
oppression (of freedom of expression), sub-alternity of radical modernism, 115–116
oppression (of serfs), 92, 93
oppression (of Tibet)
– self-immolation of Tibetans, 9
– *see also* second Long March
organism, and environment, 27, 49–50

Index — 253

Orientalism
- about, 184
- Chai's sentiments, 208, 210
- of China, 207
- Lopez's discourse, 3, 4, 16, 17–18
- missing Orient, 217
- "neo-Orientalism," 17
- New Age Orientalism, 17
- from post-Orientalist perspective, 214–215
- Said's discourse, 16, 207, 216
- of the West, 207, 215–217
- see also post-Orientalist approach
Otherness, of Tibet, 217–219, 220
outlaws, in Sambha, 57
Ovchinnikov, Vsevolod Vladimirovich, 87, 88–89, 93–94, 96

Pagö-pünsum (mountain), 66–67
Palace, Potala, 12–13, 95, 98
paradox, of modernity, 100, 102, 104
pathogen, 117–118
pathogenic force, of radical modernism, 119–120, 122–123
pathology, of memory, 112–113
pathos, of modernity, 98–99, 100–101
Pedersen, Poul, 101
Pema Tseden
- cinematic ambience, 136
- cinematic hapticity, 142, 144, 148
- cinematic transition, 137–138
- filmmaking process, 129, 131, 132, 142
- *The Grassland* (film), 129–131, 132–134, 136
- *Old Dog* (film), 138, 143–148
- *The Search* (film), 138, 139–140, 141, 142–143
- vs. Shogdong's views, 150–151
- *The Silent Holy Stone* (film), 128, 134–136, 137, 140
- traditional values vs. modernity in films of, 149
- transnational film production, 136–137
people
- claiming, 120–121
- and place, 2, 8, 33, 64
- treatment of topic, 38
- see also indigenous people

People's Liberation Army (PLA)
- affection of soldiers for Tibet, 14
- Long March, 75
- treatment of topic, 39–40
- see also second Long March
People's Republic of China see China
photography, landscape, 44
phyiba (Himalaya marmots), 176
pilgrimage
- dynamics of, 24
- and landscape, 162
- see also Amne Machen pilgrimage
pilgrims, 25, 108
PLA see People's Liberation Army
place
- affordances of, 69
- as antecedent to all affairs, 185
- and body, 67–68, 126
- high places, 28
- and home, 66
- humanization of, 22
- and indigenous people, 61–62
- meaning of, 22
- memorability of, 58, 103–104
- and memory, 65, 67, 112, 127, 166
- mirage effect, 201
- and monument, 56
- paradox of modernity, 100, 102, 104
- pathos of modernity, 98–99
- and people, 2, 8, 33, 64
- power, 192
- rootedness to, 68, 161
- significance of, 7
- soul-locations, 172, 173
- subjectivity of, 68
- of Tibet, 5
- in time, 20–21
- see also landscape
place-human bonding, 19, 32, 34
place-memory, 65, 67, 166
placiality
- combined, 68
- meaning of, 23
- of Shogdong's memory, 126
poems
- by Dondrub Gyal, 113–114
- by Ling Xingzheng, 83–84

polarization, images of Tibet, 177–178
population
– of Lhasa, 87–88, 96
– of Sambha, 52
posters, propaganda, 91
post-Orientalist approach, 18–19, 207–208, 214–215, 218
Potala Palace, 12–13, 95, 98
potency, of landscape, 103
power, of Tibet, 228–229
"power culture," 9
power place, Shangrila as, 192
prayer, most recited, 128
PRC see China
Prince Drime Kunden (opera), 139, 140, 141, 142–143
profits
– opportunities for, 36
– from Shangrila tourism, 195
propaganda see Chinese Communists' propaganda
prostration, 108
pro-traditionalists, Tibetan
– about, 128
– vs. anti-traditionalists, 150–151
– see also Pema Tseden
psychoactive sacramental, Tibet as, 224

Qinghai Province
– field course for American students, 187–188
– fieldwork in, 32–35
– Lhasa railway, 35
– see also Amdo region
qufuhaohua (de-symbolizing approach), 31–32

radical modernism
– pathogenic force of, 119–120, 122–123
– subalternity of, 115–116
– see also Dondrub Gyal; Shogdong
railway, Qinghai-Lhasa, 35
rapids, of Machu, 61
rdol (human weaklings), 181
real Tibet, vs. imagined Tibet, 24
realism, 144, 210
reflexive anthropology, 6

religion see Buddhism
remembering, and forgetting, 111–112
Ren Huaguang, 88
Ren Naiqiang, 71
rescue fantasy, 85–86
revitalization, of Tibetan culture, 227
Ricoeur, Paul, 111, 112
ritual techniques, for weather control, 62–63
rivers
– crossing of PLA soldiers, 81
– Machu, 43, 60–61
– see also rapids
rootedness
– to place, 68, 161
– as place-memory, 65
roots, of Sambha, 64

sa (earth/landscape), 59
sacred sites see temples
Said, Edward, Orientalism discourse, 16, 207, 216
Sambha Village
– demographics, 52
– eco-aesthetics of, 43–47
– history, 54, 57, 61, 69
– landscape-mindscape relationship, 58
– Machu river in, 60–61
– mandalization, 56–57
– modernization, 52
– origin of name, 53–54
– roots, 64
– sanctity, 58
– springs, 60, 61
– weather control, 62–63
Sambhadrubgne (mountain), 54, 56–57, 58–59
sanctity, of Sambha, 58
Sangga Village, socialist land reform, 90–91
scandals, of Western Tibetan Buddhists, 216
scholars see American scholars; Chinese scholars
Search, The (film), 138, 139–140, 141, 142–143
searching, for actors, 140–141
second Long March
– Communist "liberation theology," 83–86
– death of PLA soldiers, 80–81

– and landscape, 80, 86
– memoirs of veterans, 72, 79–80, 81–82, 82–83
– mobilization for, 76–77
– morale of PLA soldiers, 82, 83
– motivation of PLA soldiers, 77–78
– "newness" felt by PLA soldiers in Tibet, 74
– planning, 75–76
– superiority of PLA, 76
– time span, 78
– triumph of PLA, 78
– women soldiers, 81
self-immolation, of Tibetans, 9
self-referential narratives, 6–7
seniority, 134–135
sentient ecology, 26
Serf, The (film), 85, 88
serfs, 90, 91, 92, 93
Shangrila
– commercial branding, 195
– as dream project, 192–195
– Eco-Village, 198–199
– field course for American students, 187
– fieldwork, 35
– Kolås' case study, 191–192, 196
– landscape of region, 190–191
– local Tibetans, 196–197, 198, 199
– name change to, 189
– origin of name, 37
– other locations resembling novel, 203
– as power place, 192
– Tibetanization of, 197–198
– transformation into tourist commodity, 37, 189, 192
"Shangrila" (imagined Tibet), and post-Orientalist approach, 19
Shangrila (TV show), 194
Shen Weirong, 3, 4, 207, 215, 216–217
Sheridan, Jim, 143
Shogdong
– about, 105
– author's view on, 99
– on "backwardness" of Tibet, 106
– critics of, 105–106
– on fate of Tibet, 125
– imagined modern Tibetan nation, 126
– on immaturity of Tibet, 115

– on "insurrection," 116
– on landscape, 101, 103, 104, 124–125
– on Lhasa, 100
– and neologisms of Chinese state, 117
– on "old habit," 107, 109, 111
– vs. Pema Tseden's views, 150–151
– on pilgrims, 108
– placiality of his memory, 126
– on Potala Palace, 98
– radical modernism of, 110, 112, 117, 122–123
shooting, into hail clouds, 63
sickness, altitude, 179–182
Siebenschuh, William R., 120
Silent Holy Stone, The (film), 128, 134–136, 137, 140
Silent Mani-Song, The (fiction), 12
silver coins, distribution of in Lhasa, 87
slave mentality, 108, 109
Smithson, Robert, 45
Snow Mountain Township, 179–181
social beings, vs. natural beings, 115
social hierarchy, 88–89, 91
– *see also* low class
social situation, in Lhasa (1950s), 87–88
socialist land reform, in Sangga, 90–91
socialist modernity, 121–122
soldiers *see* People's Liberation Army
songs
– at Amne Machen pilgrimage, 162–163, 165
– in *Shangrila* (TV show), 194
Sonthar Gyal, 155
soul, of Tibetan civilization, 139–140
soul (*bla*), 172–173
soul mountain (*bla-ri*), 171, 172, 173
soul-locations (*bla-gnas*), 172, 173
sounds, in *Old Dog* (film), 144–145
Spiral Jetty (earthwork), 45
spirits *see* gods and deities
spiritual experience, 48, 49
– *see also* eco-spiritual dimension
springs, in Sambha, 60, 61
Stone, The (film) *see Silent Holy Stone*
Strong, Anna Louis, 92, 94, 95
students
– field courses for American, 36, 187–188, 189

– field courses for Chinese, 36
– Tibetan in Beijing, 119
Su Yan, 97
subaltern consciousness, 116–117
subaltern studies, for Tibet, 120
subalternity
– of radical modernism, 115–116
– slave mentality, 108, 109
subalterns, 118–119
– see also serfs
subjectivity
– of author, 7, 225
– of landscape, 63–64, 68
Suhe (town), 187
Sun Jiong, 192–194
Swan, Jim, 57

Tagyal see Shogdong
Tang Shijie, 193, 194
Tashi Tsering, 120
temples
– Hughes and Swan on, 57
– Jokhang Temple, 95–96
– on Sambhadrubgne, 56
temporality, of mindscape, 20–21
Tenzin, 165–166, 167, 177
terma (hidden religious treasures), 1–2, 174
"third pole," Tibet as, 8
"Tibet fever" (*xizangre*), 203
Tibetan Buddhism
– in China, 227
– Chinese attracted to, 32
– Dalai Lama (14th), 66, 67
– hidden religious treasures, 1–2, 174
– lamas, 174–175, 229
– in landscape, 134–135, 135–136, 137
– *li* ("fate"), 92
– mandalas, 54–55
– and modernization, 138
– in *Old Dog* (film), 147
– in Pema Tseden's films, 128–129, 131–132, 132–133, 138, 148, 154–155
– power of, 229
– religious practices, 108
– in *The Search* (film), 141, 142–143
– and Tibetan culture, 170
– in the West, 4–5, 19, 216

– see also yogis
Tibetan language, 23, 197
Tibetan studies, cross-regional, 28–29
Tibetanization, of Shangrila, 197–198
"Tibet-drifters" (*zangpiao*), 14, 201–202
– see also Ma Lihua
Tibetology, 5
Tibetophiles see Chinese Tibetophiles
Tilley, Christopher, 25–26, 56, 126–127, 224
time, place in, 20–21
time-space, passage of, 65
tipping points, 27–28
touching
– of landscape, 156, 178
– by world, 181–182
tour guide, Norbu, 198
tourism
– growth, 10
– Lhasa, 10, 35–36
– reasons for, 10–11
– Shangrila as dream project, 192–195
– tour guide, 198
tourist commodity, transformation of Shangrila into, 37, 189, 192
traditional values
– vs. modernity, 149
– see also anti-traditionalists; pro-traditionalists
train, Qinghai–Lhasa, 35
translations see Chinese translations
travel seminars
– for American scholars, 36, 185–187
– see also field courses
travel writings, on Tibet, 5, 183
travelers
– empowerment by landscape, 25
– expectations of, 35–36
– narratives of, 22, 47–49
– see also pilgrims
treasures see terma
triumph, of PLA in Tibet, 78
Tsawa Daneg, 105–106
Tserang Dondrub, 128, 168, 170–171, 213
Tukeba (blogger), 13
TV show, *Shangrila*, 194

urban China, Tibetans in
– and ethnic revival, 118
– paradox of modernity, 102
– pathos of modernity, 98
– students in Beijing, 119
– see also "Beijing-drifters"; Shogdong
urban landscape, of Beijing, 44
U.S. see American ...
utopia, Tibet as, 203–204
utopianism, 84–85
Ü-Tsang region see Lhasa; Ngari grasslands

Vagabond in Tibet (fiction), 11–12, 205, 206
"Village Serf Cooperative," 90–91
villages see Sambha; Sangga
visual articulation, of public discourses, 153–154
vulture (*hsa-goud*), 130

Wang Hui, 3, 4, 207, 215–216, 216–217
water, abundance of, 160–161, 228–229
waterborne deity (*klu*), 60
"Waterfalls of Youth, The" (poem), 113–114
weather
– at Amne Machen pilgrimage, 163
– control by yogis, 62–63
– see also fog; hail clouds
Wei Ke, 76, 77–78
West
– captivating power of Tibet, 5
– dichotomies of the, 18
– Orientalism of, 207, 215–217

– perception of Tibet, 3, 4, 16, 200
– Tibetan Buddhism in, 4–5, 19, 216
– see also American ...
Wind Will Carry Us, The (film), 141
women soldiers, 81
"work teams," propaganda, 92, 93

Xiaohao, 86, 87, 97
– see also Hao Guiyao
Xie Fei, 129–130
Xinhua News, 10, 201
xizangre ("Tibet fever"), 203

yak horn, 60
yaks, 134, 188
Yamdrok Yumtso (lake), 13
Yidam Tserang, 123
yogis (*ngapa*)
– in Sambha area, 53–54
– weather control by, 62–63
– see also Akhu Norbu
"You Know" (song), 165
Younghusband, Francis, 48
Yu Dehua, 81
Yunnan Province see Shangrila; Suhe
Yutog Yontan Gonpo, legend of, 63

zangpiao see "Tibet-drifters"
Zemgyab, 162–163
Zhang Guohua, 76, 77–78
Zhang Tianpan, 16–17
Zhongdian see Shangrila

www.ingramcontent.com/pod-product-compliance
Lightning Source LLC
Chambersburg PA
CBHW052015290426
44112CB00014B/2252